V. S. NAIPAUL

The Loss of El Dorado

V. S. Naipaul was born in Trinidad in 1932. He went to England on a scholarship in 1950. After four years at Oxford he began to write, and since then he has followed no other profession. He is the author of more than twenty books of fiction and nonfiction and the recipient of numerous honors, including the Nobel Prize in 2001, the Booker Prize in 1971, and a knighthood for services to literature in 1990. He lives in Wiltshire, England.

ALSO BY V. S. NAIPAUL

NONFICTION

The Writer and the World
Between Father and Son: Family Letters
Beyond Belief: Islamic Excursions Among the Converted Peoples
India: A Million Mutinies Now
A Turn in the South
Finding the Center
Among the Believers
The Return of Eva Perón (with *The Killings in Trinidad*)
India: A Wounded Civilization
The Overcrowded Barracoon
An Area of Darkness
The Middle Passage

FICTION

Half a Life
A Way in the World
The Enigma of Arrival
A Bend in the River
Guerrillas
In a Free State
*A Flag on the Island**
The Mimic Men
*Mr. Stone and the Knights Companion**
A House for Mr. Biswas
*The Suffrage of Elvira**
Miguel Street
The Mystic Masseur

*Published in an omnibus edition entitled
The Nightwatchman's Occurrence Book

The Loss of El Dorado

The Loss of El Dorado

A Colonial History

V. S. NAIPAUL

Vintage Books
A Division of Random House, Inc.
New York

VINTAGE BOOKS EDITION, APRIL 2003

 Published in the United States by Vintage Books, a division of Random House, Inc., New York. Originally published in Great Britain by André Deutsch, in London, 1969, and subsequently published in the United States by Alfred A. Knopf, a division of Random House, Inc., New York, in 1970. First published by Vintage Books in 1984.

Library of Congress Cataloging-in-Publication Data
Naipaul, V. S. (Vidiadhar Surajprasad)
The loss of El Dorado
p. cm.
ISBN 1-4000-3076-5
1. Trinidad—History. 2. El Dorado. I. Title.
F2120.N3 2002
972.983—dc21
200266182
CIP

www.vintagebooks.com

Printed in the United States of America
10 9 8 7 6 5 4 3 2 1

Contents

PART THREE: THE TORTURE OF LUISA CALDERON (1797–1813)

Maps

Venezuela, Trinidad and the Eastern Caribbean

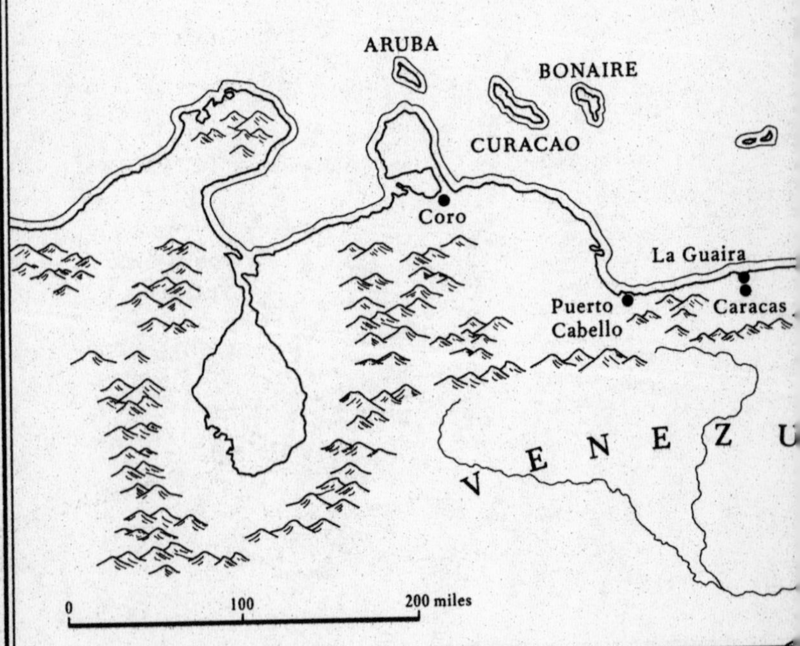

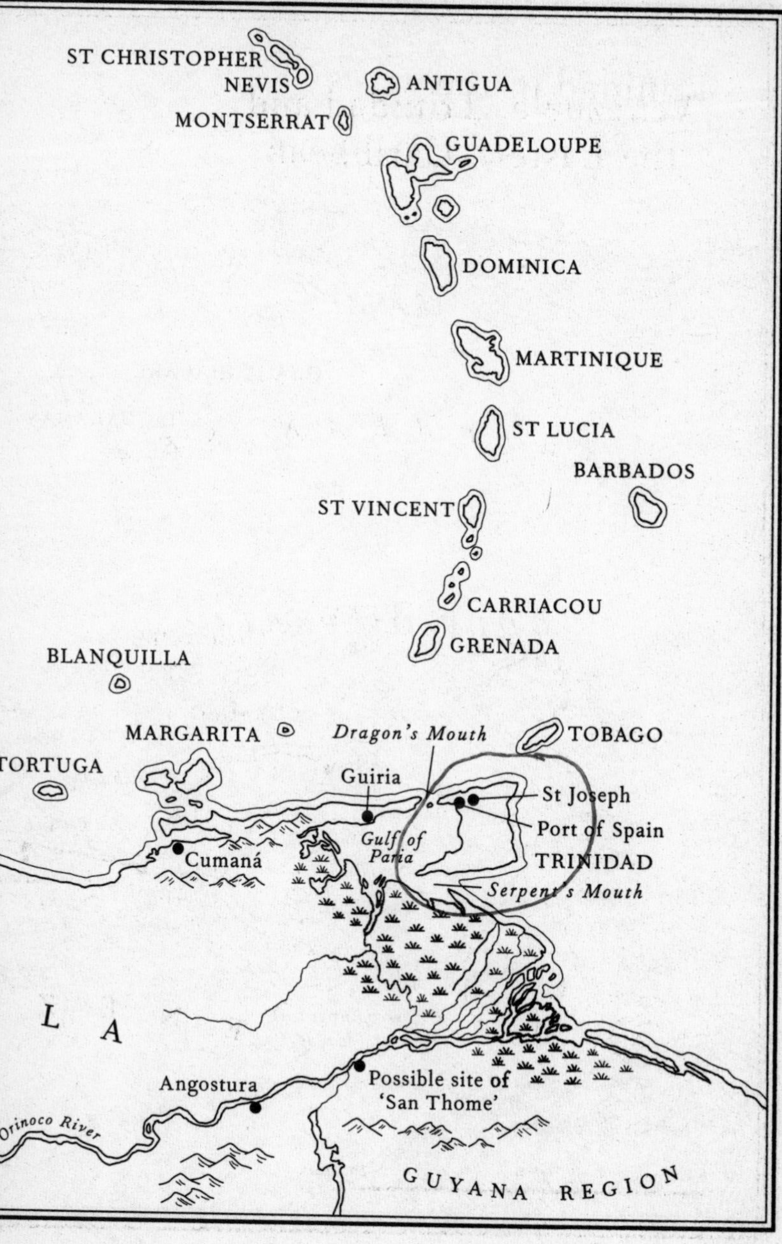
ST CHRISTOPHER
NEVIS
ANTIGUA
MONTSERRAT
GUADELOUPE
DOMINICA
MARTINIQUE
ST LUCIA
BARBADOS
ST VINCENT
CARRIACOU
GRENADA
BLANQUILLA
MARGARITA
Dragon's Mouth
TOBAGO
TORTUGA
Guiria
St Joseph
Port of Spain
Gulf of Paria
Cumaná
TRINIDAD
Serpent's Mouth
E L A
Angostura
Possible site of 'San Thome'
Orinoco River
GUYANA REGION

Trinidad in 1797

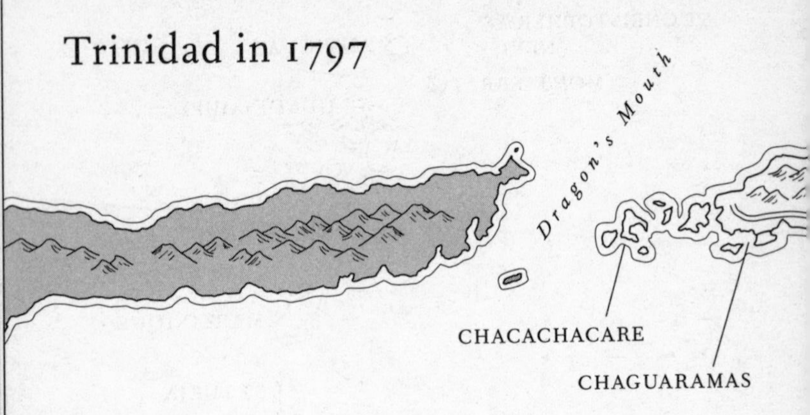

GULF OF PARIA

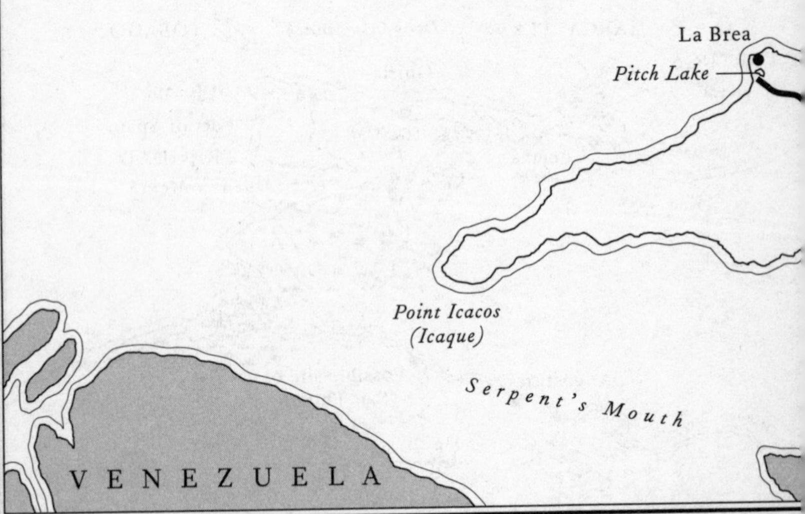

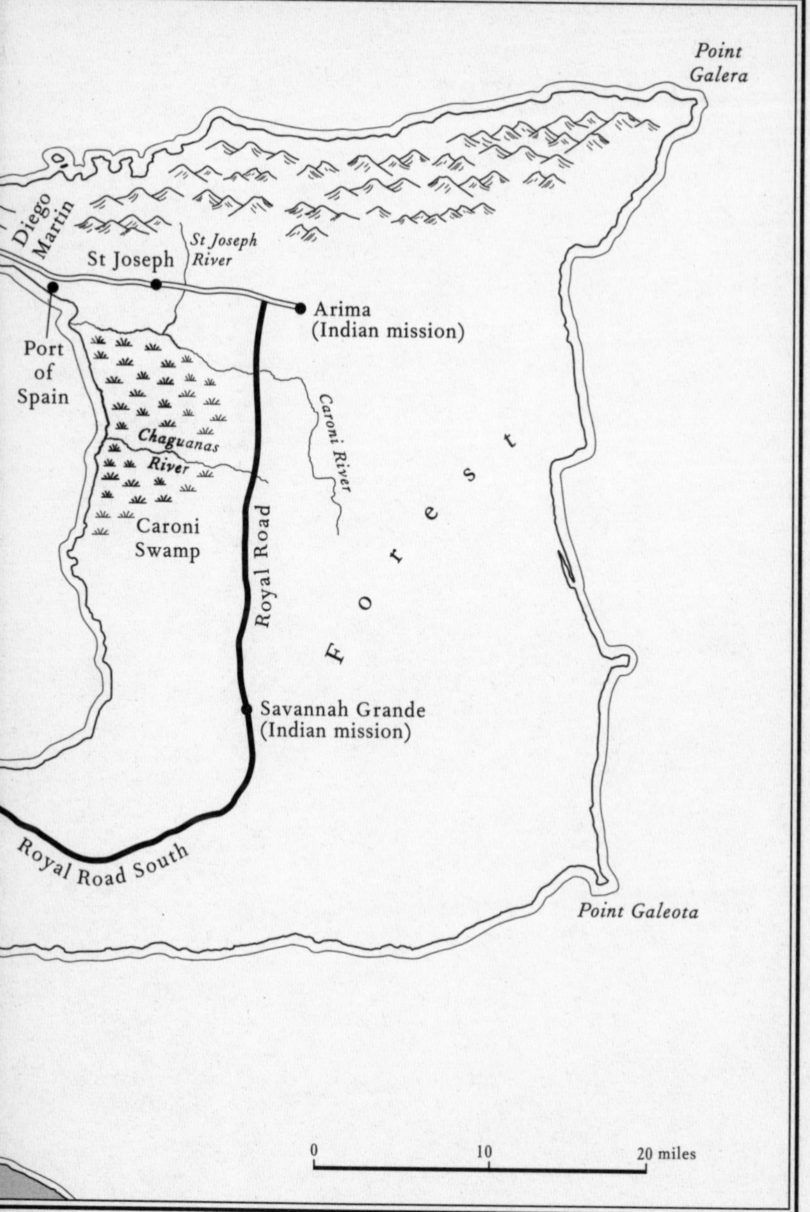
Point Galera
Diego Martin
St Joseph
St Joseph River
Arima
(Indian mission)
Port of Spain
Caroni River
Chaguanas River
Caroni Swamp
Royal Road
Forest
Savannah Grande
(Indian mission)
Royal Road South
Point Galeota
0
10
20 miles

Foreword

MY ANCESTORS began to go from India to Trinidad about a hundred years ago. I was born in 1932 in a small country town called Chaguanas, a mile or two inland from the Gulf of Paria, in the house my grandfather had built in 1920. This house, with its balustraded roof-terrace and Hindu sculptures, would not have been out of place in an Indian town. Today in Trinidad it is an architectural oddity; but then it fitted. Chaguanas was a mainly Indian settlement. Hindu and Muslim festivals were celebrated; Hindi (or its Bhojpuri variant) was the first language I heard.

All this seemed so settled and complete it was hard to think of Chaguanas being otherwise. It was hard to feel any wonder at the fact that, more than four hundred years after Columbus, there were Indians in a part of the world he had called the Indies; and that the people he had called Indians had vanished. They had left no monuments; they were not missed. Chaguanas was a place-name, no more; many Indians turned it into 'Chauhaan', a Hindu caste-name.

Wonder came later, with my own sense of being cut off from a past; and wonder grew during the writing of this book. One day in the British Museum I learned about the name of my birthplace. Spanish imperial correspondence was slow; it could take two years for a letter from Trinidad to be read in Madrid. In 1625, eight years after Ralegh's attempt on the 'gold-mines' of Guiana, the Spaniards were still exchanging letters about the consequences. 'I asked you', the King of Spain wrote to the Governor of Trinidad on 12 October 1625, 'to give me some information about a certain nation of Indians called Chaguanes, who you say are above one thousand, and of such bad disposition that it was they who led the English when they captured the town. Their crime hasn't been punished because forces were not available for this purpose and because the Indians acknowledge no master save their own will. You have decided to give them a punishment. Follow the rules I have given you; and let me know how you get on.'

What was done isn't known; but soon, in the place called Chaguanas, no one would know that there was once a people called Chaguanes. The fact of their existence is recorded, so far as I know, only in this document; and this document was disinterred from the Spanish archives only in 1897.

People who write about Ralegh usually have to hurry back with him to the Tower of London; they pay as little attention as Ralegh himself to what was left behind. An obscure part of the New World is momentarily touched by history; the darkness closes up again; the Chaguanes disappear in silence. The disappearance is unimportant; it is part of nobody's story. But this was how a colony was created in the New World. There were two moments when Trinidad was touched by 'history'. This book attempts to record those two moments. The story ends in 1813. Indians from India began to arrive in 1845; but the colony was created long before that.

The Loss of El Dorado

PROLOGUE

The Dispossessed Conquistador

THIS BOOK is made up of two forgotten stories. The first is the story of the end of the search for El Dorado. The story is usually told in Sir Walter Ralegh's words and as part of his experience alone. It begins with his raid on Trinidad and South America in 1595 and ends with his inexplicable return in 1617, a prisoner paroled from the Tower of London. El Dorado, though, is essentially a Spanish delusion. The inland town of St Joseph in Trinidad with its port, 'which they call of Spain' – the settlement Ralegh raided – had been founded as the base for El Dorado. It was the total achievement of a seventy-five-year-old conquistador; it came at the end of one of the great Spanish journeys across South America. For the conquistador the El Dorado adventure ended in kidnap, solitude and lunacy. His province – the dream of the third Spanish marquisate in the New World, after Mexico and Peru – became the ghost province of the Spanish Empire.

The second story occurs nearly two hundred years later. It is the story of the British-sponsored attempt, from the newly captured island of Trinidad, to set going a revolution of high principles in the Spanish Empire. There was a complication. Trinidad, the base for revolution, was at the same time being established as a British slave colony. The complication was expressed in a scandal. On the two days before Christmas Day 1801 Luisa Calderon, a Spanish mulatto girl of fourteen or fifteen, was taken up to the garret of the Port of Spain jail, which had become a centre for Negro discipline, and tortured. The subsequent trial of the British governor – later one of Wellington's generals in the Peninsular War and one of the heroes of Waterloo – was a London sensation.

The history of Port of Spain, a special New World adventure, is contained in these stories. A place like Port of Spain, in the uncluttered New World, has no independent life; it alters with the people who come to it. Sir Walter Ralegh had also dreamed of a South American revolution: the people of the Inca or Inga liberated from Spain by the people of Ingla-tierra (in fulfilment of an Indian prophecy) and incorporated into a British empire of equity, beauty, wealth and mingled wisdom (Indian youths were to be educated in England and married to English-women). The South American revolution, when it came, had English support. But the English aim was trade; and the British Empire, when it came to Trinidad, once a part of 'these provinces of El Dorado', came as an empire of plantations and Negroes, the whip, the branding-iron, the knife (for cutting off Negro ears), the stake and the torture cells of the Port of Spain jail.

It was a failure. The South American revolution took on a life of its own; Port of Spain didn't become the great British trading port of an independent South America. And even at the time of the torture of Luisa Calderon the British Empire was shifting east, to Asia. The slave islands in the west were soon to be run down, and Port of Spain was once again a remote municipality. It was the end of the adventure.

THERE HAD BEEN a golden man, *el dorado*, the gilded one, in what is now Colombia: a chief who once a year rolled in turpentine, was covered with gold dust and then dived into a lake. But the tribe of the golden man had been conquered a generation before Columbus came to the New World. It was an Indian memory that the Spaniards pursued; and the memory was confused with the legend, among jungle Indians, of the Peru the Spaniards had already conquered.

Always the Indians told of a rich and civilized people just a few days' march away. Sometimes there were pieces of gold, finely worked; once a temple of the sun was found in the jungle; once a crazed explorer returned with a tale of an enormous city of long straight streets, its temples full of golden idols. After Mexico, Peru and New Granada anything was possible; after fifty years and a score of disasters rival conquistadores could still race one another to Spain to ask for permission to explore some new region of promise. The search that had begun in the west of the continent moved east. In 1569 three men claimed Trinidad for the highest reasons. The man who was chosen to reduce the Indians to Christianity landed with twelve priests; a fortnight later he reported complete evangelical success; then he disappeared.

Of all these journeys little remains. The conquistador who found nothing had nothing to report. Believing in wonders, he had no gift of wonder. Columbus, coming to Trinidad, thought he had come to the outer approaches of the Garden of Eden. He asked the natives for pearls: pearls were created from drops of dew falling into open oysters. The natives were pale: a disappointment: the greatest riches of the world were to be found in the lands of the blackest Negroes. On the Atlantic, the Ocean Sea, flying fish had just been fish that flew into Columbus's ship: another confirmed item in the created world's finite catalogue. It is an English soldier who, crossing to Trinidad a hundred years later, will write like a discoverer: 'Oftentimes we might see a great multitude of thease flying fishes flie togeather, beinge pursued by some other fishes, as if thease had bin some flocke of larkes dared by the hobbie [a falcon].'

To the conquistador where there were no wonders there was nothing. A place was then its name alone, and landscape was land, difficult or easy. Valleys, mountain ranges, peaks, woods, meadows, rivers, plains and springs, with naked, noble natives: this inaccurate catalogue is a Spanish priest's description of Trinidad in 1570. The spareness of much Spanish narrative is a Spanish deficiency. Untouched by imagination or intellect, great actions become mere activity; it is part of the Spanish waste. El Dorado becomes an abstraction; deaths become numbers.

And then, unexpectedly, there is a human voice, confirming that landing on Trinidad, that island of formally imagined valleys, rivers, plains and springs. 'Your Majesty will be quite right to marvel at getting a letter from someone as humble as myself but . . .' It is a letter of complaint to King Philip II; it is from a survivor of that landing of 1570, the year of four El Dorado disasters. Trinidad had been 'dispeopled', the writer said: the Spaniards had died or left. The writer, Francisco Vazques de Bravo, had gone on to Margarita, the pearl-island, and there for twenty-five years he had served the King. He had been, that is, a loyal subject; and he had been doing well until the last two years. Then corsairs, French and English, began to come to Margarita. Spanish officials traded with them. Trade with foreigners was illegal; and Bravo, a loyal subject, protested.

All the officials took against him. The governor threatened him in public, 'saying that the houses I have – which are the best in this place – he is going to leave outside that town wall he is building – and that isn't going to do much good and is costing a lot of money – and that since these houses are going to be outside the wall they will have to be pulled down and he says he is going to harm me in other ways as well and this is because he says I give my mouth too much liberty and all this is because of the aforesaid hatred and enmity he bears me because I speak the truth openly and because I am a man of sixty-six and have very many small children and I am not exactly the least propertied man in this island and he can therefore do me a lot of harm.'

The egoism is another side of the Spanish simplicity. Bravo didn't say, but the Margarita town wall was necessary. Some months before, Captain Amyas Preston had raided; and Ralegh, after his sacking of Port of Spain and St Joseph in Trinidad and his exploration on the Orinoco river, had also tried to raid Margarita.

Bravo wrote to the King in October 1595. Sixty or seventy

years earlier, letters from Puerto Rico were read in Spain within three months. But the Empire and the paperwork had grown; it was fourteen months before Bravo's letter reached the King. It was personally minuted and passed on to the Judge of All Irregularities. The region was of importance. The largest El Dorado expedition (the money for the ships borrowed from Flemish merchants) had recently left Spain for Trinidad. Ralegh's raid had been like another proof of the existence of El Dorado. And in the previous month the King of Spain had declared his second bankruptcy.

The man on whom the quest depended was the seventy-five-year-old conquistador Ralegh had dispossessed. All the knowledge of El Dorado he had acquired over fifteen years and three journeys, at the cost of a fortune, had been plundered by Ralegh and set out in Ralegh's new book, *The Discovery of the Large, Rich and Beautiful Empire of Guiana*. That book, published months after the event, had also told of the conquistador's capture and disgrace: his soldiers massacred, his Trinidad settlements sacked, handed over to the exultant Indians and burnt, after the jail had been opened and the Indian chiefs unchained.

Now, when help was coming, when the King himself was interested, the old conquistador was beyond help. He was in the wilderness, on an island in the Orinoco river with less than a dozen followers. He was hiding from his Spanish enemies, to whom Ralegh had delivered him. He was almost certainly lunatic now; he would never see a town again.

PART ONE

The Third Marquisate

1. The Mountain of Crystal

1592–1595

THE DISPOSSESSED conquistador was Antonio de Berrio. He had come out to the Indies for the first time sixteen years before as a retired soldier of sixty. Born in 1520, the year of Cortés's march on Mexico, Berrio had fought in many of the wars that proved and at the same time wasted the Spanish glory. He had fought at Siena; against the Barbary pirates; in Germany; in the Netherlands under the Duke of Alba; in Granada against the rebellious converted Muslims. He had seen two of his brothers die in battle; a third brother had died at Lepanto, the famous Spanish naval victory over the Turks that yet settled nothing.

Berrio married late, at fifty-three or fifty-four. His wife was the niece of the conquistador, Quesada, who had captured the treasure of the Chibchas and had founded, in what is roughly Colombia, the Spanish kingdom of New Granada. Quesada was rich; his estates were worth 14,000 ducats a year; he had the title of Adelantado. But Quesada wanted to be the third marquis of the New World, after Cortés and Pizarro. El Dorado, if he discovered it, was to be this third marquisate: this was the bargain he had made as an old man with the King of Spain. His expedition lasted three years; twenty-five people survived out of 2,000. Quesada himself died some years later, disfigured by leprosy. His estates in New Granada passed to his niece and through her to Antonio de Berrio. This was the inheritance that Berrio, when he had retired from the wars in Europe, came to the Indies to claim in 1580. He was sixty, but his family was young. His eldest daughter was five, his son two.

When Berrio got to New Granada he found that a clause in Quesada's will required him 'most insistently' to continue the search for El Dorado. 'I judged,' he wrote five years later, 'that it was no time to rest.' And thirteen years later, when the search had become a way of life, he could give no other explanation. 'The circumstances and my own inclination were sufficient of themselves to persuade me to it; and so I decided to make ready and set forth in quest thereof. I collected a large force of men and a great quantity of horses, cattle, munitions and other necessary stores; and with this equipment, which cost me a great deal of gold, I started.' But those preparations, set out in one sentence, had taken three years.

Berrio made three journeys. The first lasted seventeen months; men died. The second ended after twenty-eight months. 'While I was having canoes made to travel down this river, a captain mutinied and fled with the majority of his men, so that I was obliged to start after him.' Time vanishes in Berrio's narrative, like effort, like the landscape itself; and Berrio is ready to start on his third journey. Ten years have passed. He is seventy; he has six daughters; his son is now twelve and will explore with his father.

This was the great journey; it was the journey Berrio referred to again and again, not because of the wonders he had seen or because he had crossed a new continent, but because half-way across he had performed a deed which linked him in his own mind with the heroes of antiquity.

The plan was to drop down the Orinoco to the highlands of El Dorado and from the river to search out a pass in the mountain range that was thought to guard the fabulous city. It was a small expedition, less than a hundred and twenty men, with few porters or Negroes. Half the men were on the river in twenty canoes, under Berrio's command; half were with the two hundred horses on the river bank, under the command of an old soldier who had served Quesada.

In this way they travelled for a year. No pass through the mountains offered itself. Then it was the rainy season. On the flooded banks of the Orinoco they camped; and the trouble started. 'The canoes had been lost, and three troops of Spaniards, thirty-four men in all, deserted, taking many horses with them. A disease almost like the plague killed all my porters and more than thirty Spaniards.' To prevent further desertions and to destroy thoughts of return to New Granada, Berrio ordered all the remaining horses to be killed. It was the heroic action at which, when the journey was over, he never ceased to marvel.

They ate the horses. They hollowed out four canoes from tree-trunks and dropped down the river until they came to Carib country. The Caribs ate men. Twice a year Carib fleets of up to thirty canoes went up the river, hunting; for three hundred and fifty leagues the river banks had been depopulated, eaten out. But the hunting party Berrio met was friendly. They offered food. They also offered to guide Berrio part of the way to El Dorado. They took him to the mouth of the Caroni river, to the territory of a chief called Moriquito.

Moriquito was sullen; he was in touch with the Spaniards on the north-eastern coast. Berrio was almost back in civilization. Moriquito said it was only a four-day march to El Dorado, but Berrio didn't like having Moriquito at his back. 'I had only fifty soldiers, and only fifteen of these were in good health. I couldn't leave the canoes either, because if these were lost all was lost.' Five more of his men fell ill; and when there was a quarrel with Moriquito about food Berrio decided to move on.

His care now was to survive, to get out of the Orinoco and to reach a Spanish settlement. Some way down river he found a Spanish anchor: an El Dorado disaster of fifty years before: a famous conquistador had died, a companion of Cortés. But the chief to whose territory Berrio next came was friendly. He was eighty years old and friendly with everybody, even with Caribs.

He knew Trinidad well. He had spent his boyhood there to be out of the way of some tribal war at home, and he said he had met a lot of foreigners. The Orinoco estuary wasn't easy; he thought he should provide Berrio with a pilot.

'I went down the Orinoco to the sea. This river goes out by so many arms and narrow channels that it inundates a two-hundred-league stretch of coast for more than forty leagues inland. The arm by which I came out faces the island of Trinidad, which is four leagues from the mainland. I was determined to remain there and to settle the island, and to reassemble my men in order to enter Guiana again. But God and my fortune willed it that as soon as we were in the sea we were separated. The vessels were small and the soldiers ill and inexperienced and unable to row. I arrived in Trinidad with twenty men and stayed there for eight days, although all my men were ill.'

He chose the sites for the settlements he had in mind: the port, the inland town on the river. There were traces of gold in the ravines; and the river, as if in mimicry of Guiana, had the name of Caroni. 'I found the island very thickly populated by natives of a very domesticated race; and the land was very fertile.' Then he got his sick men into the canoes for the last, dangerous stretch of the journey through the currents of the Dragon's Mouth to the pearl-island of Margarita.

The journey had taken eighteen months. It had broken Berrio. The eight-day survey of Trinidad had been his last lucid effort, just above the level of a permanent fatigue. The first thing he heard in Margarita was that his wife had died at the other end of the continent, in New Granada. 'It happened,' he wrote the King, 'that she left in your Indies two sons and seven daughters' – a daughter had been born after he had left – 'to serve Your Majesty. I have spent the dowry of the girls.'

His request wasn't for money. He wanted his son, now fourteen, to inherit the quest and its certain reward. But the journey had also marked Berrio's son. He was sent by his father to Caracas and New Granada to get more men and supplies. He was expected to return; but he stayed home in New Granada.

Berrio's journey forms no part of the El Dorado legend. The Spanish Empire was vast. Berrio's reports of a failure were soon lost among the unsifted, accumulating imperial records at Simancas in Spain. All that was known of Berrio was what Ralegh had written. When Berrio's papers were recovered, three hundred years later, the Spanish Empire was over and the El Dorado legend was fixed: it was Ralegh's.

THE GOVERNOR OF Margarita was a very young man harassed by a large family. But he was welcoming. He lodged Berrio in his house, lent him money and promised him men. He said he had heard about Berrio's difficulties on the Orinoco and had sent out a relief party just the week before. Berrio didn't expect such concern. He had decided long ago that 'men born in the Indies' were 'constant only for three days'. He wrote to the King of Spain about the good governor. At the same time the governor wrote to the King and offered to find El Dorado himself. Berrio, the governor said, was an old fool; he had taken the wrong route, destroyed half his force and had missed the relief party out of stupidity.

Some months later the relief party returned to Margarita with three hundred Indian slaves from Moriquito's territory. Slaves were always needed in Margarita for the pearl-fisheries; they were used up rapidly with the diving. Slaves were obtained from the mainland and from Trinidad, sometimes by capture, but also by fair barter with chiefs or the heads of families. For three or four hatchets a Carib would sell a nephew or a niece; he asked a little more for his daughter. A girl of twelve or thirteen could change hands in Margarita for 150 pesos, at a time when a peso was worth an English crown.

But the slave-trade in Indians was illegal; and Berrio thought that Moriquito, already sullen, would never now allow Spaniards to go through his territory to El Dorado. Berrio complained to the governor and wrote to the King. Indians couldn't be 'sold like Negroes'. Indians were the King's subjects. Negroes were not; they were natural slaves. The governor arrested the leader of the relief party and released him two days later. It was the way of the Indies: *se obedece, pero no se cumple*: the law was to be obeyed but not followed. Then Berrio saw that the governor, the leader of the relief party and Moriquito were all friends and slavers together. He had misread Moriquito's sullenness; he had made three enemies.

Berrio was ill, subject to intermittent fevers. He asked the governor to speak out, to say whether he and his friends wanted to go looking for El Dorado themselves. The governor said no. Berrio didn't believe him. 'He denied it because I was his guest.' Berrio's code, by which he also interpreted the actions of others, was still Spanish, of Spain. He offered half his marquisate to the governor in return for his help. Together they would settle Trinidad; together they would go through Moriquito's territory to El Dorado. The governor refused: Berrio had nothing to offer.

BERRIO HAD MADE his offer because there was a new El Dorado excitement. A man called Albujar had reappeared after sixteen years in the jungle, the only survivor of an almost forgotten El Dorado expedition; and versions of his story were going round the Indies. Albujar, it was said, had been in charge of the expedition's munitions. The munitions had blown up and Albujar had been sentenced to death in a special form: he was set adrift on the Orinoco in a canoe. The expedition was wiped out by Indians. But Albujar was rescued and nursed. For a fortnight he was led blindfolded from settlement to Indian settlement and displayed. At noon one day he came to another settlement. The blindfold was taken off, and Albujar found himself in the Great Manoa, the city of the golden man.

'He travelled all that day through the city, and the next day from sun rising to sun setting ere he came to the palace of Inca.'

Albujar was given a room in the palace and well entertained. He learned the language; in some versions of the story he married an Indian woman. One day the Inca asked Albujar whether he wanted to stay or to go back to his own people. Albujar said he wanted to go back. The Inca gave farewell gifts of gold and had Albujar led to the borders of his territory. It was dangerous then for Albujar; all his gold was stolen by primitive Indians. He managed to keep only some gold beads in a calabash; the Indians thought the calabash contained food.

Albujar may never have existed. No one saw him, and the story was that he didn't live long after his return. He died at Puerto Rico, waiting for a ship to Spain. No one saw the gold beads; they were left with Albujar's confessor to pay for masses. El Dorado, which had begun as a search for gold, was becoming something more. It was becoming a New World romance, a dream of Shangri-la, the complete, unviolated world. Such a world had existed and the Spaniards had violated it. Now, with a sense of loss that quickened their imagination, the Spaniards wished to have the adventure again. The story grew subtler with Spanish failure. It took the Spaniards beyond the realities of their life in the bush; it teased every deprived sense.

The city of Manoa was in the jungle, but it was in a cold high region. The food was good. 'The people eat maize, which does not distend them, instead of roots and other foods which produce effeminate races.' They were not naked bow-and-arrow Indians; they were clothed. They used coined gold, but their banquets were also drunken and spectacular. Yet they fought only with javelins, so that it was possible for an ordinary man from the outside world to be unique. The golden man, far from being the mystery, was the explanation: he was a descendant of the Inca who had escaped from Peru.

But the Indianized Spaniard was an old story; and the story of Albujar's return to the world, down the Orinoco to Trinidad and Margarita, which completed the El Dorado romance and excited

Berrio and excited Ralegh, might even have been an echo of Berrio's own journey.

In Caracas there was a Spaniard of some education, Domingo de Vera. He heard of Berrio's journey and of the slaughter of the horses in the middle of the unknown. He thought it a 'deed worthy of being set beside those feats of antiquity that made the doers great, famous, immortal'; and it angered him that Berrio should be in distress. 'There is this about the great actions of living men: they are calumnied by many, praised by few and rewarded by no one.' Vera had money. At least – it is all that is known about him – he owned Negroes and his wife had jewels and personal Negro attendants; in Caracas in 1592 Negroes were rare and valuable. Vera recruited twenty-eight soldiers in Caracas and went to Margarita and offered his services to Berrio.

Vera was not of the Indies. Berrio told him of the third journey and of the humiliations of the past year as a guest and dependent in the house of his enemy. It was worse, Berrio said, than anything he had known in more than ten years of wandering. Vera pledged his loyalty to the hero and his quest, and Berrio named Vera 'campmaster for El Dorado' in place of his absent son.

The first duty of the campmaster, and it was urgent after the Albujar excitement, was to settle and pacify Trinidad. Berrio had chosen the site and he had a plan for rearranging the Indian tribes on both sides of the Gulf of Paria. Vera acted with dispatch. On 18 April 1592 Berrio gave Vera his letters of commission. Four weeks later Vera landed in Trinidad with his soldiers, a friar and a notary.

At 'the port of Cumucurape', which is today part of Port of Spain, formal possession was taken of the island, 'frontier and point of entry for the river Orinoco of the very rich provinces of Guiana, Dorado and Manoa'. Vera cut down a forty-foot tree and fashioned a cross. Then, 'taking off his hat and making due reverence' to the cross, he called on the friar to help him raise it. Vera marked out a small square beside the raised cross, calling on the notary to observe and bear witness. Then he drew his sword and said: 'I take possession by turf and twig! *Yo corto esta yerba.*' He slashed at the branches of the surrounding trees and at the grass, and held up his sword in one hand and cut twigs and grass in the other.

The notary said he had witnessed the act of possession. With his sword still raised, Vera said: 'Caballeros, this possession I take in the name of the King our master and his governor Antonio de Berrio. If among your worships there is someone who in the name of some foreign prince or any other person wishes to make some question with me of this possession I have taken, then let him step forward, and I as the faithful vassal of the King our master and campmaster-general of his general Antonio de Berrio will undertake to answer him, whether I am armed or not.'

Vera spoke loudly and clearly so that no one could mistake what he said. Again and again he called: 'Is there anyone here who gainsays me?' The ensign stood with his flag unfurled and the soldiers shouted, 'Long live the King and his governor! This possession has been well taken and we all stand here to defend it against anyone who says otherwise.'

Then – 'after the aforesaid on the aforesaid day and month of the aforesaid year in the aforesaid port', according to the notary – it was time to take possession of the native Indians. Vera, speaking through an interpreter, told two chiefs, who had been looking on, that he had taken over the island and intended to build on it 'a city or two or more' of Spaniards. The chiefs were now vassals of the King of Spain; they would be instructed by Spaniards in 'all that appertained to our holy Catholic faith'; they would also be protected against Carib raids. The notary thought that the chiefs were agreeable and Vera made them touch a book in token of their vassalage.

Vera and his men returned to their boats and rowed past the Indian village of Conquerabia to the Caroni river. They went up the river, between populous villages and fields of maize, sugarcane, potatoes and cotton, until they came to the village of the chief called Guanaguanare. Here, four days after he had taken possession of the island, Vera was ready to found the city of St Joseph of Oruña, Oruña after the family of Berrio's dead wife.

Vera called Guanaguanare and his Indians together and told them he had taken them over in the name of the King of Spain and was going to instruct them in the Catholic faith. The notary thought the Indians 'rejoiced'. Vera read out Berrio's letter of commission. In this letter Berrio spoke of his journeys and sufferings, of the 100,000 dollars of fine gold he had spent, the six hundred leagues of the Orinoco he had travelled. The settlement of Trinidad, he said, was a great service for God and the King, and important for the discovery of El Dorado.

Vera paced out the plaza of the new city and said: 'City of St Joseph de Oruña, I found thee in the name of the King our lord and his governor Antonio de Berrio. If there is anyone here who disapproves or has thoughts of hindrance, let him go out to the field now with me.' All the Spaniards said that the city was fairly founded and stoutly maintained and they would assist in its defence. Vera called on the notary to bear witness to the event and the site. The possession by turf and twig was repeated, and the challenge, that no one took up.

Vera addressed the Indians. For fifty leagues around they and their land were to be shared out among Spanish settlers. The faith was to be exalted, crimes punished, justice established. No more Indians would be taken away as slaves to Margarita. There would be protection against raids by Caribs, French and English. (At that moment Captain Benjamin Wood was entering the Gulf of Paria with four ships.) The plaza of the city would be where he, Vera, now stood. He marked out the plots for Spanish dwelling-houses at the sides of the plaza. He marked out the site of the church and named it Nuestra Santa de la Concepción. And just as Cortés, founding Vera Cruz, even on the march to Mexico, had first of all put up a gallows and a pillory, so now Vera, proclaiming the new law in Guanaguanare's village, had a tall thick pole driven into the ground, to serve, he said, as gallows and pillory for delinquents and evil-doers.

He ordered the friar to offer a mass to St Joseph, of good fortune, so that the saint might intercede with God for the protection, peace and growth of the city. The mass was said, a complete cabildo or city council was appointed; and everything that had been done that day was cried round the new city by Hernando, Vera's own Negro.

THERE WERE between thirty-five to forty thousand Indians on the island and they were not all, in the approving Spanish phrase, 'Indians of peace'. Vera with his twenty-eight soldiers couldn't begin to pacify them. But Berrio in Margarita at last got some money from New Granada and was able to get fifty recruits; he said they cost their weight in gold. They went over to Trinidad and Vera began to act.

The plan was to make allies of a wandering tribe, the Arwacas, and to settle them on evacuated lands on both sides of the Gulf of Paria. The area around the new town was the first to be pacified and resettled. Vera thought it went well; it hadn't been necessary 'to inflict punishments or death, as the natives of their own free will had proffered peace and service'. Vera said nothing about Guanaguanare. Four years later a visiting official, summarizing the history of the settlement, wrote: 'Guanaguanare withdrew elsewhere.'

But the act of possession was illegal. Trinidad had not been granted to Berrio by the King of Spain. It had been granted to the governor of Cumaná, and he presently appeared and began to make trouble. The governor of Cumaná was as old as Berrio; he was a seasoned Indies hand, a trader in Indian slaves, a friend of Moriquito's. He was a law-breaker claiming legality. He could be handled only in the way of the Indies, where the law was to be obeyed but not always followed. This was possible because each official had a separate contract with the King; legality could be measured by achievement and every man was therefore as strong as he made himself.

Berrio didn't reject the claims of the governor of Cumaná. He only said that Trinidad was pacified and settled already. All the island needed to become 'the richest commercial centre of the Indies' were merchants of probity and some tax-free Negroes, perhaps five hundred pieces. He didn't feel he could hand over such a place without direct instructions from the King. This was what he also wrote to the King. Then, with fifteen new recruits, he went to Trinidad. He had more men than the governor of Cumaná; he couldn't be evicted. It would be three years before he heard from the King: three years to find El Dorado: legality, the third marquisate and 'the greatest grandeur and wealth that the world holds'.

He found the island far from calm. The pacification hadn't gone as well as Vera had said. English traders were making mischief among the Indians, and there were reports that Indians were being taken back to England to be trained as interpreters. The man-eating Caribs, moving down from the northern islands to the empty island of Tobago, were a threat to everyone.

Berrio had only a hundred men; he couldn't wait too long. He sent Vera with thirty-five men across the Gulf to take possession of the lands on the Orinoco and to look around. He himself stayed behind in St Joseph, 'old and useless and not wishing to be a burden on them'.

Four weeks later Vera returned. He had lost ten men. But he brought gold: seventeen golden eagles and jackals, finely worked. And he brought more than gold: he said he had found El Dorado. He spoke of the cold, high city with its temples full of gold. He spoke of a clothed, civilized, artistic people who had an especial skill in making straw animals, 'so lifelike it is something to see'. They had come from the west; just twenty years before, they had conquered the jungle Indians. It was the new empire of the Inca who had escaped, 'where there are so many Indians as would shadowe the sunne, and so much golde as all yonder plaine will not conteine it'.

The story was broadcast round the Indies. The seventeen golden eagles and jackals became 'forty of the most pure plates of golde curiously wrought, and swords of Guiana decked and inlayed with golde, feathers garnished with golde, and divers rarities': Captain Amyas Preston heard this from a Spaniard who said he had spoken to Vera. At Cartagena the story was that El Dorado had been conquered and the golden man had sent in tribute to the King of Spain 'the portraiture of a giant all of gold, of weight forty-seven kintals, which the Indians there hold for their idoll'. A Frenchman who knew Trinidad turned the golden eagles and jackals into 'two millions of gold'.

The legality or illegality of his presence in Trinidad was no longer important. Berrio wrote to King Philip II announcing the discovery of El Dorado. He asked for no reward for himself. He had the third marquisate; that had been agreed long ago; and soon he would be able to reward all his followers. But he wanted more than money for the twenty men who had stood by him through the thirteen years of the quest, the three journeys and the humiliations. He wanted these men to be 'distinguished and honoured'; he wanted twelve of them to be made Knights of Santiago. For men soon to be rich beyond ambition, a request for honour, from the bush of St Joseph: Berrio was of Old Spain still.

And there was nothing there. Vera had explored little Berrio hadn't explored, had heard nothing Berrio hadn't heard. There was gold in Guiana, in small quantities. The artefacts of Peru had spread through South America; Moriquito had for some time been bartering gold 'plates' with Spanish officials on the coast. The Indians were in touch. The joke was on Vera when, being offered some gold for a hatchet, he 'shewed it to the souldiers and then threw it from him, making shewe not to regarde it'. Vera, discovering the details of the legend for himself, thought he was confirming their truth. He had heard of the golden man and the ceremony of gilding. Now from Indians in the jungle he heard of the orgies of El Dorado, when 'they take of the said golde in dust and anoynt themselves all over therewith to make the braver shew; and to the end the golde may cover them, they anoynt their bodies with stamped herbes of a glewy substance'.

El Dorado was only a day away, the Indians told Vera. 'Wee sayde wee would goe thither; they tolde us they were now in their *borracheras* or drunken feasts, and would kill us.' It was like proof. The legend of El Dorado, narrative within narrative, witness within witness, had become like the finest fiction, indistinguishable from truth.

THE INDIANS had told Vera that a thousand men would be needed to capture El Dorado. Such a force was beyond Berrio's resources, and it was decided that Vera should go to Spain with the evidence of the golden eagles and jackals and get the help of the King.

But first the entry to El Dorado through Moriquito's territory had to be secured. Vera had lost ten men there in an ambush, and Moriquito had to be punished. Moriquito ran to his Spanish friends on the coast, the slave-traders, and asked to be hidden; he offered gold, but he was handed over to Berrio's men and executed. Moriquito's uncle was put in chains and for seventeen days led 'like a dog from place to place, until he had payde an hundreth plates of golde and divers chaines of spleen-stones for his ransome'.

After the severity there was an attempt at conciliation. Moriquito's son was baptized, called Don by Berrio's men and treated with much respect. But the Indians, who were 'of war', remembered the severity alone; the Berrio faction that was created within the tribe wasn't important. The area had to be garrisoned. Berrio's small force was now split between the mainland and St Joseph in Trinidad, and he was like a man besieged in both places. The devil, Berrio used to say, was the patron of this quest.

The governor of Cumaná continued to claim Trinidad. He sent

to tell Berrio he was going to kill him. The governor of Caracas refused to allow Berrio to recruit any more men in Caracas and sent out an expedition of his own. Sudden fire on the brown grasslands encircled and consumed all the hundred and seventy men. Two years later the local Indians, exaggerating, told Ralegh they had killed three hundred. The young governor of Margarita continued to be obstructive. It was, again, an equivocal comfort when, defending Margarita against an English privateer, he was killed. Indian hate, an attack by cannibals from the north, a raid by a privateer: they were all among Berrio's anxieties. A hundred men had wrecked Margarita; Berrio in Trinidad had less than fifty.

Vera had left to raise men in Spain. But Vera was delayed for many months in Caracas. He was full of his news; it went ahead of him. Captain Amyas Preston heard. Captain George Popham 'surprised' a Spanish ship going home to Spain and found copies of Vera's documents about Trinidad and the lands of the Orinoco: the various acts of possession, the founding of the Trinidad city, the discovery of 'all the riches' of El Dorado ('If it should heere bee set downe, foure leaves of paper would not containe it'). Even before Vera had got to Spain his news had got to London, to Sir Walter Ralegh at Durham House on the Thames.

Ralegh was forty; he had not long finished his first spell of imprisonment in the Tower of London. Berrio was seventy-four; after fourteen years he had found El Dorado. And he could do nothing but wait; he had never been more vulnerable. In his settlement of St Joseph, a few thatched huts on the narrow muddy river with the golden name of Caroni, he was like a prisoner already.

DURING THESE waiting months another drama touched Berrio, and he never knew. In June 1593 the English ship *Edward Bonaventure* came into the Gulf of Paria, 'hoping there to find refreshing'. For six months the crew had been living on rice alone; now they were starving. The captain saw Berrio's men in the port of St

Joseph, on the site of the Indian village of Conquerabia, and didn't land a party: Spain still had a reputation. The *Edward Bonaventure* had been at sea for more than two years. It had made a famous journey, from England to the East Indies, back across the Indian Ocean, around the Cape of Good Hope and up and across the Atlantic. The last stop, for water, had been at the island of St Helena two months before.

Ten men had gone ashore in the ship's boat. St Helena was 'not an earthly paradise, as it is reported'. The island was deserted, hot and hilly. The Portuguese had planted some lemon trees and fig trees for the benefit of sailors. There was only one building, a 'chapell'; and in this building, when the men from the *Edward Bonaventure* landed, someone was singing. They pushed the door open and saw a naked man. He was very frightened. He thought they were Portuguese and were going to kill him.

He was an English tailor who had gone to sea and had fallen ill. He had been set down on St Helena and had lived there alone for fourteen months. He spent his days in the chapel, hiding from the sun. When he understood that the newcomers were his countrymen, 'what betweene excessive sudden feare and joy, he became distracted of his wits, to our great sorrowes'. Forty goat-skins were drying in the sun. 'For wante of apparell' they made him 'two sutes of goats skinnes with the hairy side outwards, like unto the savages of Canada'.

He was still alive when the *Edward Bonaventure* came into the Gulf of Paria, but perhaps dead when after eight days the ship with the starving crew went out again through the Dragon's Mouth: a ghost ship already, its journey soon to end in mutiny, derangement, mystery.

This is the story in Hakluyt's *Voyages*. A hundred years later it went to the making of *Robinson Crusoe*.* The shipwreck, in the same narrative in Hakluyt, occurred to another mariner on an

* See note, p. 358.

island in the Bermudas; but Defoe placed it on an empty island visited by man-eating Caribs like those Berrio feared. To the west was the river Orinoco with 'the great island Trinidad, on the north point of the mouth of the river'. Crusoe's island existed: it was Tobago. The Spanish soldiers, so vulnerable and so menacing in Defoe's story, existed: they came from Berrio's city of St Joseph.

Fact and fiction meet: Berrio links the two fantasies of the New World. To be the first man on the earth, to see the first shoots of the first crop, to let off 'the first gun that had been fired there since the creation of the world': it is an aspect of what the El Dorado quest had become. And *Robinson Crusoe* in its essential middle part is a monologue; it is all in the mind. Men are nearly always far away, active but silent, privately engaged, as though seen through a telescope.

Those starving soldiers of Berrio's: they must be rescued, because men feel for men. But how will they obey, when (as Crusoe has reasoned it out) the only good is survival? They must sign a contract: the message is sent. But then Crusoe remembers there is no pen and no paper in this world. With this difficulty, irrational and concrete as in nightmare, the dream of innocence, resource and power ends. Crusoe is rescued.

FROM WITHIN it was all anxiety, but Spain still had a reputation and it continued to serve Berrio in Trinidad. Foreign ships that came were as circumspect as the *Edward Bonaventure*. When in the new year a few more soldiers arrived from New Granada, Berrio preferred to send them to join the garrison in Moriquito's territory. In Trinidad, in St Joseph and the Port of the Spaniards, as Conquerabia began to be called, the Spaniards waited and watched. Sometimes they smelted trial quantities of local ore; Berrio's friar was the 'refiner'. Sometimes they had to fight off Guanaguanare's dispossessed Indians. The Arwacas Indians did their job and warned of foreign ships entering the Gulf of Paria from the south. Berrio didn't look for trouble then. He didn't try to stop Indians being taken back to England to learn English. He allowed ships to take on provisions and water and sometimes, though it was illegal, to trade. No Spanish ships came that way. Berrio and his Spaniards, like shipwrecked men, lived off the land.

Captain Jacob Whiddon was allowed to land and take on water and wood. But he asked too many questions; he prowled about the Gulf; and his story, that he had come out to look for the *Edward Bonaventure*, was absurd. Some Arwacas Indians went out in a canoe one day to Whiddon's pinnace. There were dogs in the canoe, the native Caribbean dog which some early travellers said didn't bark. The Indians said they were going to hunt deer in the woods; they invited the sailors to go hunting with them. The sailors agreed, 'but were no sooner one harquebuze shot from the shore, but Berrio's souldiers lying in ambush had them al'.

The incident is obscure – the story is Whiddon's – but deaths occurred, and Captain Whiddon hurried away to England to report to his master. Sir Walter Ralegh was among other things a professional privateer. Jacob Whiddon was his chief captain. He had been sent to look around.

Ralegh was planning a big attack. He wanted to outnumber and overwhelm. He was planning more than the plunder of St Joseph and the El Dorado quest. He was planning an empire of Guiana in which Indian numbers and English skill would destroy the power of Spain at its source, in the Indies. The quest he could share with Berrio; but he went beyond Berrio. Berrio, if at this stage he could have explained his purpose, might have said that he wanted gold and the third marquisate; and he might have represented this as a service to his King, who alone could confirm a subject in the enjoyment of wealth and honour. It would have stopped there, a personal achievement, in a void like the South American jungle itself, linking to nothing. Ralegh could merge personal ambition into a greater cause. He had an idea of society and association which Berrio, for all his old soldier's diplomacy with disaffected natives (in the Netherlands, Granada or South America), didn't begin to have.

The lucid, three-dimensional view of the world and its possibilities wasn't Ralegh's alone. Laurence Keymis, fellow of Balliol College, Oxford, who was Ralegh's associate, wrote this about the Spanish weakness: 'These huge countreys of the Indies, having no common linke of affinitie, lawe, language, or religion, and being of themselves able to maintaine themselves without forreine commerce, are not so simple, as not to knowe their owne strength, and to finde, that they doe rather possesse Spaniardes, than that they are possessed by them.'

Beside this, Berrio is made to look like a man from another age. The Spaniards, paying for their history, the centuries of Muslim rule and the slow cleansing of their land, remained individuals, committed to a holy war and an outdated code of chivalry, the cynical underside of which in the New World left each man isolated and committed in the end only to personal survival.

Waiting for the Queen's commission, Ralegh in London became as possessive about El Dorado as Berrio in Trinidad. Both men had their anxieties. The governor of Cumaná, pressing his claim to Trinidad, turned up at the Port of the Spaniards one day with some soldiers and asked Berrio to leave. He went away when Berrio refused. But Berrio was agitated; he asked his men – the *Robinson Crusoe* nightmare: fact again answering Defoe's imagination – to make a written declaration of their loyalty.

About the same time Ralegh heard that a young English courtier was about to make an expedition to Trinidad and El Dorado. It wasn't serious; it was just for the experience, 'as tendering the ripeness of his yeares', and was partly the Queen's idea. The young man had wanted to go to the South Seas. The Queen said no; that journey was too dangerous for someone only twenty. Ralegh raged; but he was made to wait until the end of the year for his own commission. If any harm came to the Indian kings, he wrote later, 'farewell all good from thence, for, although myself, like a cockscomb, did rather prefer the future in respect of others, and sought to win the kings to her Majesty's service than to sack them, I know what others will do'.

THE YOUNG MAN was Sir Robert Dudley, the illegitimate son of the Earl of Leicester. Sir Philip Sidney was his first cousin; his mother was first cousin once removed to Queen Elizabeth. To the compiler of a dictionary of biography in the next century the young Dudley was 'a compleat gentleman' in the Elizabethan way: 'an exact seaman, a good navigator, an excellent architect, mathematician, physician, chymist and what not'. He was tall in the saddle, noted for his tilting and noted too 'for being the first of all that taught a dog to sit in order to catch partridges'.

The life that began so well was soon to go sour. When, some time after his return from Trinidad, his claim for legitimacy was rejected, he left his second wife and their children and exiled himself to Italy. There he used the titles denied him in England. He became a Catholic and a persecutor of such English heretics as were available. In the beginning he kept in touch with England, sending back designs for new ships and, once, a 'Proposition for bridling the impertinency of Parliament'; but over the years he became an Italian nobleman, his loyalties to Florence alone.

His works on navigation, published in Italian when he was seventy-two, were dedicated to the Grand Duke of Tuscany; a dedication repeated on the map of Trinidad and Guiana, embellished with ships and naked Indians, with place-names in Italian (S. Gioseppe for St Joseph): the knowledge preserved, the nature of the venture fifty years before abolished, when the beach of an island in the New World was his stage and to his English followers he had been 'the onlie mirrour of knighthoode', and when he had sent to Berrio (or had pretended to send) a message of disdain on behalf of 'our most gratious Queene, who in dewtifull allegance wee are bounde to defende'.

More than allegiance had changed. That time in Trinidad had

been a time of fantasy and knight-errantry, of brave deeds poetically witnessed, of challenges, of seeking out an ordained enemy – and how well the Spaniards filled that role – in a strange glittering forest full of dangers and wild folk.

The fullest account of the adventure remained in manuscript until 1899. It is by Captain Wyatt, of whom nothing else is known. Wyatt saw Dudley as the greatest hero of chivalry and Wyatt saw himself as Dudley's squire. He aimed at a style that matched the adventure and his role. A storm at sea was like 'a seconde enundacion of the whole worlde'. Wyatt's journal, always straining after effect in this way, is the first that catches the excitement of an Atlantic crossing to Trinidad: the crews spending Christmas Day below Teneriffe, 'a verie hott day', the men 'swimminge from ship to ship' to make 'greate cheere to each other'; the twenty-two-day journey; the flying fish rising from the sea like a flock of frightened larks; the new climate.

Until Wyatt's narrative, in these Trinidad documents, the sea was the sea, climate was absent from the New World, and Virginia, Newfoundland, Guiana rain-forest and the Antilles were one. Landscapes were formal. Columbus had seen gardens like those of Valencia in March, and no one had seen more. Wyatt, full of the London plays he had seen (he could recite parts of *The Spanish Tragedy*, a new play), set out to write romance. But in his relishing of the natural world, wonder bursting through his words, the New World as medieval adventure can be seen to be coming to an end. And Berrio, the unnatural enemy in his forest clearing, is seen to be doubly imprisoned in his quest.

Dudley had a hundred and forty men and two experienced sailors. Captain Benjamin Wood knew Trinidad well. The chief pilot, Abraham Kendall, was one of the best English navigators of the day. He had sailed in the West Indies with Drake nine years before and had taken part in the month-long, house-by-house destruction of the great city of Santo Domingo. Once, in this very Gulf of Paria, Kendall had deserted with his two pinnaces from a round-the-world expedition; the expedition had presently ended in scattered shipwreck. Kendall had this sort of ambiguous connection with terror; he wasn't much liked. The story about him was that no one was allowed to die aboard his ship. It was Kendall who, to prevent such a death, had set down the Robinson Crusoe figure on the island of St Helena.

With his force Dudley could have captured Trinidad. But he didn't want any fighting. He didn't know how strong Berrio was, and he didn't want to antagonize Ralegh any more. He had come, really, only for the experience, to test the stories about Indians, Spaniards and gold; and as soon as he anchored in the Gulf of Paria, near the Pitch Lake, he sent one of his captains with 'divers gentlemen' to see whether they could pick up 'anie of the salvages or at least have conference with them'. The Indians were brought. They took away knives, bugles, beads, fish hooks and hatchets. It was hoped they would return with gold. They brought back nuts and fruit and tobacco.

One of the Indians spoke Spanish. A warning sign; but Dudley asked him whether there wasn't a gold mine in the neighbourhood. The Indian said he would lead them to it right away. He led them on an eight-mile walk along the shore to the place where foreigners usually dug for gold. Wyatt and his friends dug up quantities of sand and marcasite. Each man shouldered a load and walked back eight miles to the ship.

The next morning Dudley ordered his land force ashore. A little later he went ashore himself. There was a salute from the ship; and the soldiers, 'reansweringe the great ordenance', let off a 'vallew of small shott'. They marched to the mine, in such good order, Wyatt thought, that 'if wee had bin charged with ten thousande Indians, they coulde not have harmed us'. Wyatt had marched sixteen miles the day before and was doing another eight now in full armour; but he was concerned for his general.

'Thus havinge marched viij longe miles through the deepe sandes and in a most extreme hott daie, our Generall, unaccustomed, God he knows, to walk one foote, leadinge the march, wee at length came to wheare this ore was, and havinge placed our courte of garde in a convenient place and set forth our centronells all the rest were appointed to the geatheringe of ore. And havinge allmost in a moment geathered such a quantitie that after everie one was equallie lodende yeat wee left almost a quarter of a hogshead behinde us, that our men weare not able to carrie, by this time it flowed soe fast that we weare forced to staie untell midnight, at which time the full sea was past.

'In the meanwhile our Generall, perceaving a most filthie miste to fall, caused an armefull of boughes to be cutt and laide on the grownde, wheareon he himselfe lay downe; over whom Ancient Barrow helde his collers and Wyatt, chusinge some of the best of our men, made his stande rounde about him.

'Thus havinge reposed himselfe some ower hee awaked, and not longe pausinge after, wee had alarum given us, which I rather impute to the ignorance of our centronells then anie way unto the charginge of the enemie. For theare is a certaine flie which in the nightime appeareth like unto a fire, and I have seene at the least two or three score togeather in the woods, the which make resemblance as if they weare so manie light matches, the which I perswade myselfe gave occasion of some soden feare unto the centronells which gave the alarum . . .

'Thus after our men had rested themselves and the sea began for to ebb, our Generall gave commandement for our marchinge back againe; the which beinge signified both by his noyse of trumpetts and drome, wee of all handes marched alonge. And for that the waters weare deape up to the girdlesteid [girdle-place, the waist] of our men, our Generall himselfe first through the water up unto the verie twiste [the fork of the body], an unusuall thinge for him, beinge a courtier, but not unfitt for him, beinge our Generall in India, carryinge soe great a majestie in his march with such unremovable resolucions in his proceedings that wee all that followed him concluded in the idea of our consaites hee without all doubte woulde prove the onlie mirrour of knighthoode. For when hee determined of anie thinge, he sett it downe with the great consideracion and advice of the masters, and, beinge concluded what shoulde be done, he would have it accomplished with such expedition that he might saie with Caesar, *veni, vidi, vici.*'

They got back to the ship between two and three in the morning. A blank place, that Gulf shore; but they had made it yield the drama of late hours and a midnight wade in full armour. They had had two adventures, of fireflies and the tide; and they had got a lot of sand. No Spaniard had appeared; and when Dudley rose later that day he set himself – *veni, vidi, vici* – to preparing a suitable plaque. On a 'peece of lead' he had the Queen's arms incised and, below, a Latin sentence in which he claimed the island for Queen Elizabeth and himself. It was dusk when the plaque was ready. Dudley gave Wyatt his sword and asked him to set the plaque up on a tree near the gold mine.

Wyatt understood the gravity of his commission. He went ashore with his company at once and in the dark – further drama – they walked the eight miles to the mine. They decided to spend the night in the woods above the shore. They chose a place where wood and water were at hand, 'two greate necessaries for all souldiers marchinge to anie service', as Wyatt explained. They spent an hour fortifying. When they were satisfied that their camp was 'unvincible', sentinels were appointed and the company lay down to sleep.

Wyatt slept well; he had marched forty miles in less than three days. In the morning he heard from the sentinels that a dog had barked once during the night and that a fire had been seen several times. This gave Wyatt 'some suspition of the enimies scowtes'; and now, after the salvoes and the trumpets, he thought the time had come for caution. He took 'two or three good shott' and, 'as secret as we coulde', went a hundred paces into the wood. They saw footprints in the sand. Wyatt thought it was where the enemy's scouts had been during the night. The knowledge satisfied him; he didn't think there was any further need for secrecy. Back in his camp, he marshalled his company; and they marched 'in good order' to the mine, where the 'service was to be accomplished'.

'First wee caused the trumpetts to sownde solemlie three severall times, our companie troopinge rownde; in the midst marched Wyatt, bearinge the Queenes armes wrapped in a white silke scarfe edged with a deepe silver lace, accompanied with Mr Wright and Mr Vincent, each of us with our armes, havinge the Generalls collers displaid, both with the trumpetts and the drome before us . . . thus marchinge up unto the top of the mounte unto a tree the which grew from all the rest, wheare wee made a stande. And after a generall silence Wyatt red it unto the troope, first as it was written in Lattin, then in English; after kissinge it fixed it on the tree appointed to bear it and havinge a carpender placed alofte with hammer and nailes readie to make it fast, fastned unto the tree.

'After wee pronounced thease wordes that "the Honorable Robert Duddeley hath sent us heather and in his name to accomplish this honorable acte and this with his sword, God favoring his intent, doth he sweare to make good against anie knight in the whole worlde". This beinge ended the trumpetts and drome sownded, the whole troope cryed "God save our Queene Elizabeth"; and havinge thus, as solemlie as wee coulde, accomplishte this committed to our charge, wee marched downe the mounte.'

Wyatt saw a chance for a further service. He loaded his men with marcasite, 'equallie', and they marched the eight miles back to the ship.

The next day they had an idea. They sailed to where the mine was. Dudley called the place Port Peregrine. From the sea, though not from the shore, they could see the 'fortified and garrisoned' Port of the Spaniards, which Abraham Kendall remembered as the Indian village of Conquerabia. Kendall was nervous, but Dudley thought it was a good place to 'water, balliss and trim' his ships. He sent his land force ashore. Wyatt admitted now that the 'unvincible' fortifications of the previous day had been 'builded in haste'. They were pulled down and replaced by fortifications 'impossible to be assaultid'. Dudley himself remained aboard his ship. He came ashore once for a little to talk kindly to the 'salvages'. He persuaded two or three to go back with him to the ship. It was dangerous for them: at least one was detained. It was also dangerous for Dudley: these Indians spoke Spanish and had Spanish names.

At midnight – Wyatt's narrative jumps and becomes obscure – there was a message from Dudley to Wyatt and the others. They were to make haste and get the ships ready. The Spanish-speaking Indians, the scouts in the wood: Berrio's Spaniards, as Kendall feared, had been in touch from the start. Captain Benjamin Wood had gone to an Indian village to parley with them; he had not returned. The village would have to be attacked. There would, after all, be fighting.

'The next daie Cap. Jobson was determined to march to Parracow and to have taken the towne, but as he had commanded Wyatt to make readie a companie to march alonge withall wee might discrie to com from the cliffs out of the wood two or three with a flagg of truce, waving unto us that it might be lawfull to com and speak with us. The which Cap. Jobson did praesently grawnte, and, beinge come in presence of him, he uttered these wordes, *Vinie en pais ou con gero*, which is as much to saie in our languish, "Com yow in peace or with war?", and withall delivered him a letter.'

It is so, his nationality suppressed, the Spanish enemy appears, waving a flag of truce and speaking barbarously. The letter must have been from Berrio. Dudley said afterwards that Berrio had three hundred men and was 'provided' for him. It was Berrio's bluff, based on the reports of his Indian spies. Berrio had less than fifty men in Trinidad, and they were divided between St Joseph and the Port of the Spaniards. Dudley sent another message to his men on shore that evening. After all the marches, they were to be secret; they were not to reveal their numbers. If any Spaniards turned up they were to be told that Dudley despised them. But the next day Dudley sent his three caravels back to England.

They were waiting for another letter from Berrio, perhaps about Captain Benjamin Wood and the conditions for his release. The letter came two days later, at dusk. Two Indians were the messengers; they had also brought presents. Dudley took the letter. But, displaying the disdain he had urged on his men, he refused to talk to the Indians or to take their presents. The next day he withdrew all his men from the shore; and throughout that night a boatload of musketeers lay off the shore 'to chardge on the backs of those the which would give anie assaulte unto the baraskado'. In the morning – Benjamin Wood no doubt with them again – they were ready to go.

There was time, though, for one more gesture. A second lead plaque had been prepared. This stated that Robert Dudley, Englishman, son of the Earl of Leicester, had landed on this part of the island, named it Port Peregrine and had stayed and done as he pleased without let or hindrance. One man alone, without Dudley's sword, without accompanying trumpets or drum, took the plaque ashore, set it up – or down: he had no 'carpender' – and hurried back to the ships. They made for the south of the island, far from Berrio's port and his prowling men.

The adventure wasn't over. They still had Baltasar, the Spanish-speaking Indian captive; and they had picked up another Indian. They asked Baltasar about El Dorado. He didn't want to talk. He was 'threatned unto death'; he talked. He said he would take them to El Dorado. The other Indian required no pressing; he said that all the stories about El Dorado were true; 'the salvages theare hanged rich peeces of golde aboute their neckes in the steed of brestplates'. Wyatt and the others remembered later that the Indian had only 'confirmed' this, and 'by signs'.

But it was enough for Dudley. He said he would go with Baltasar to El Dorado. There was some opposition. 'It was generallie thought verie unfitt that the person of so worthy and hopefull a gallant, as an unfeathered shafte, should be hazarded in so small and simple a vessell.' Dudley saw the point. He also saw that the men were terrified of being left under the command of Abraham Kendall; they 'something feared' his 'villany'. Kendall himself refused absolutely to go. The man chosen to lead the party was the man who had taken the second lead plaque ashore. He wasn't happy about it. Wyatt heard him say that 'in his dreame the night before he did senciblie perceave himselfe drowninge'.

He took 'the two masters mates, the boatswaine, the gunners mate, the corporall and his mate, the armerer, a carpender, two proper younkers sailers, and two painfull and able Dutchmen'; and the two Indians. They went across to the mainland and nothing was heard of them for a week. Wyatt and the others 'did dailye aborde make sacrifice to God, in great devotion callinge upon Him in hartie prayer for them'. A fortnight passed. Kendall gave them up. He was already muttering about a dangerous 'current and indraught' near the ships and his previous 'disastrous experience thereof'. Anxious as always to cut his losses, he was for getting out of the Gulf and out of the way of Berrio's Spaniards.

Baltasar had led the El Dorado party to an Indian village just on the other side of the Gulf. There they heard tales about gold from the villagers. Then Baltasar led them up a creek so encumbered with fallen trees and forest debris that for stretches they had to carry their boat. While they were thus 'pusled' in the South American jungle Baltasar, 'the subtell villaine', slipped away one night into the woods. 'Much amazed', they tied up the other Indian. But that didn't help because, as they now discovered, he didn't speak English or Spanish. He just kept on pointing and saying, '*Paracoa, paracoa.*' He was trying to show them the way back to the open water, the Gulf, but they paid him no attention.

And then even 'this wretch, when we thoughte him most safelie bounde, much about the same season in another night made escape overborde, but, the river being bigger, wee gave him chase and had thearein good sporte; but I think he hardlie ever returned to his countrey, for that he was stricken with a browne bill'. The rivers of Guiana, so 'faire, spatious and broade' when first seen, with birds of white, vermilion and 'a perfect blew', with 'banks munited naturallie with such uniforme and beawtifull exornacions and oftentimes allsoe yealding a pleasante savoure', now became a setting for nightmare labour, 'both in rowinge, towinge and caryinge the bote'; and by a miracle, for which they ceaselessly prayed, they found themselves in the Gulf.

In their stupefied state – they had had no water for three days – they began to row in the wrong direction. They had to row back. And then, when they came to where they had left Dudley and Kendall, they found no ship. They decided to risk the Spaniards and to row back to Port Peregrine. There they saw their ships at anchor, with another. The new ship was English, out of Plymouth; its arrival five days before was the miracle that had saved them; that alone had given Kendall and Dudley heart to stay. Dudley, welcoming back his men, 'almost dead for famine', had ordenance and small shot fired off for 'a whole ower'.

On the following day Dudley suggested that, with the experience gained and the extra security of the new English ship, they might make another attempt on El Dorado. He asked for volunteers. He got none, 'no, albeit I had had commission to hang or kill them'. This time he would have to go alone and nobody would talk him out of it. Still, Dudley wanted to do something, to end the adventure with a flourish. He was beginning to have his doubts about the sand and marcasite (he said later he had always known it was just sand); and he wanted to impress the newcomer, who knew the region and wasn't a fool. He decided on a march through Trinidad. He chose an area well to the south of St Joseph, the Port of the Spaniards and those treacherous Arwacas Indian villages.

It began in the old style: it was a demonstration to the newcomer of what they had been doing. Wyatt landed first with thirty men and was ready to greet Dudley as he came ashore with a 'vallew of small shott'. They then seized some Indians to act as guides.

The Indians at once pledged their allegiance to Queen Elizabeth. The Indians were asked about gold. They said there was an Indian near Port Peregrine who was an expert in melting down marcasite into gold. He was a friendly Indian, 'being accustomed', as Wyatt interpreted it, 'unto our sounde of trumpetts and shootinge of our peeces at the setting and dischardginge of eaverie watch'. But Baltasar's story must have got around. The Indian gold-expert fled into the woods with seconds to spare. He 'so hardlie escaped us that he was driven to leave his victuals seethinge on the fyre readie to be eaten, of the which labour our men eased him'.

They marched through the thick woods over 'high and unpleasinge mountaines' – which do not exist – and through 'deepe and dangerous rivers'. It wasn't as bad as getting a boat through a choked Guiana creek, but Wyatt thought that only people who had done such a march could appreciate the labour, since Trinidad and like countries 'differ from all the worlde beside with the strainge growth of their woodes'.

The Indians fled before them in the night, leaving their houses and their suppers. Dudley, still making a point about the marcasite, thought he discovered a lot of melting-pots with dross in them. Wyatt thought the Indians ran because of the trumpets and the continual musket-shots, 'the which wee did of purpose that wee might still give notes unto the Spaniard which way wee marched, with our collars displaide in honoure of Englande and maugre the Spaniardes berd'.

After twenty miles they camped in an empty Indian village. They heard the pipes of the dispossessed inhabitants all around them. War-pipes, Wyatt and the others thought. They pinioned the arms of their Indian guides and with a 'naked dagger threatned their throates'. It didn't help; one of the Indians slipped his bonds and disappeared. Nothing happened that night, but in the morning they decided to make a dash back to the shore as silently as they could, without trumpets or musket-shots. They went aboard the ships that evening. The adventure was over.

The seething supper, the war-pipes in the night, the empty houses and the cooking bowls: it is as close as we will get to Indian life. When next these high woods are visited by someone open to the natural world – Charles Kingsley, in 1868 – those Indian villages, that thick silent population continually on the move between Guiana creek and Trinidad forest path, will have disappeared. It is the absence of the Indians that distorts the time-scale in these parts of the Indies. Dudley's adventure, which Wyatt's narrative brings so close, can also appear, and only partly in the manner intended by Wyatt, to be set in a land of myth, part of the historical night.

The newcomer who had taken part in Dudley's night march was Captain Popham. He wasn't as impressed as Dudley had hoped. It was Popham who had 'surprised' Domingo de Vera's dispatches about the discovery of El Dorado. Popham knew about Sir Walter Ralegh's plans for Trinidad and Guiana. Those plans depended on Indian support. Ralegh had for some years been training Indian interpreters; he would not have approved of Dudley's manhandling and terrorizing of the local Indians.

Popham must have given Dudley the message. As soon as Dudley got back to England he wrote a cringing letter to Robert Cecil, the Queen's chief minister, who had invested in Ralegh's expedition. The account of his journey that Dudley wrote later for Hakluyt, after a lot of pressing, was modest and elided: no loading up with sand, no lead plaques ceremoniously raised, no Indians threatened unto death or driven out of their houses by trumpets and muskets. 'This Captaine and I', he wrote, 'stayed some sixe or eight dayes longer for Sir Walter Ralegh (who, as wee surmized, had some purpose for this discovery), to the ende that by our intelligence and his boates we might haue done some good; but it seemed he came not in sixe or eight weekes after. So Captaine Popham and I helde it not convenient to stay any longer.'

The six or eight days of waiting referred, in fact, to the length of Popham's stay in the Gulf; Dudley and Popham didn't wait at all. They got back to the ships in the evening; they left next morning. They were just in time. Ten days later – not six or eight weeks, as Dudley well knew when he wrote – Ralegh entered the Gulf of Paria from the south.

RALEGH'S FORCE wasn't as big as he had planned. He had arranged to meet Captain Amyas Preston at Teneriffe; but Preston, who had once been swindled out of some prize money by Ralegh, preferred to go raiding on his own. And Ralegh had been separated from two of his ships on the Atlantic crossing. So he felt his way into the Gulf of Paria. For four or five days he stayed at the south-western tip of the island. He saw no Indians and no Spaniards, though once he saw an Indian camp-fire. He thought the Indians didn't come to the ships because they were afraid of the Spaniards. The two Indian interpreters he had brought out from England went ashore. They recruited two Indian agents, from the Cumaná side of the Gulf.

While his ships rode at anchor Ralegh took out a boat and coasted the land. At low tide he saw oysters on the exposed mangrove roots in the creeks. Like Columbus, he referred to classical authority, to Pliny's *Natural History*; not to the ninth book, though, where it was said that pearls grew from drops of dew falling into open oysters, but to the twelfth, where Ralegh thought a plant like the mangrove was described. Ralegh wrote later that in Trinidad oysters grew on trees; this was considered one of his lies. He studied the Pitch Lake. Abraham Kendall had noted that the pitch was 'good to patch vessels'; Ralegh thought the same. After twelve days the two ships he had been separated from arrived. They made for Port of Spain, three ships of some size, seven smaller vessels and three hundred soldiers.

Under a white flag – Spain and England were at war – Captain Whiddon went in the flagship's boat to the 'landing place'. Berrio's nephew was in command; he had eight Spaniards and twenty-five Arwacas archers. Whiddon must have been recognized from the previous year. He said in explanation that the English ships had come to Trinidad only for *refresco*, 'refreshing'; they were on their way to the English settlement at Canaveral in Florida. Whiddon had a letter for Berrio from Ralegh; the Spaniards said later that Ralegh also sent a ring as a mark of friendship. They were taking lots of arms and munitions to Florida, Whiddon said; if Berrio was short they could spare him some to pacify the natives.

Ralegh's letter was sent off to Berrio in St Joseph and Whiddon invited Berrio's nephew and the eight Spaniards to have some wine aboard the flagship. The Spaniards hadn't tasted wine for years; but they didn't trust Whiddon. Whiddon pressed and in the end Berrio's nephew and four soldiers went aboard 'on pledge'. They looked over the ship with interest; they offered to buy linen and other things. They feasted. Ralegh spoke to them about Virginia and Canaveral and he was convincing: it was his intention to call in at Virginia on his way back to England. A little wine made the Spaniards 'merrie'. They 'vaunted of Guiana and of the riches thereof, and all what they knewe of the wayes and passages'. Presently the entertainment was over. The Spaniards were not allowed to leave.

Ralegh's interpreters and their agents had been busy. A canoe with two Indians, one of them a chief, came alongside the flagship that evening. More Indians came. They had many complaints. They said that Berrio 'had divided the yland and given to every souldier a part, that hee made the ancient caciques which were lords of the countrey to be their slaves, that he kept them in chaines, and dropped their naked bodies with burning bacon, and such other torments'. Arwacas Indians had been brought over from the mainland and resettled in Trinidad 'to eate out and wast those that were naturall of the place'. Two Indians had been recently hanged and quartered for trading with English ships.

Raleigh asked about Berrio's strength. The Indians said that Berrio didn't have many soldiers but was expecting to get more any day. There were two ways of getting to St Joseph. One was up the Caroni river; but the river was narrow and could be easily blocked. The other way, through Indian country, was over the hills from Port of Spain.

Eight more of Berrio's soldiers came to Port of Spain the next day with gifts from Berrio to Ralegh: fowl, venison, fruit. Whiddon invited them aboard to drink wine and 'to amuse themselves'. They declined. Whiddon sent some wine to them on shore. It was now dark. Two more Spaniards came and began to drink with their fellows.

Another boat left the flagship; it was full of soldiers. There was a signal from the flagship. The fourteen Spaniards on shore were stabbed to death. At the same time Berrio's nephew and his four men on the ship were killed. Soon there were a hundred and twenty English soldiers in Port of Spain, and Ralegh's interpreters went among Guanaguanare's people and the other Carinepagotes to tell them that the time had come.

Late that night, the Indians roused, the Spanish Indian auxiliaries lying low, the march began. Captain Calfield went ahead with sixty English soldiers; Ralegh followed with forty more. At sunrise English and Indians came to St Joseph. 'After a fewe shot' the fight was over. They entered the plaza, the English crying, '*Paz! Paz!* Peace! Peace!' They found about a dozen Spaniards and killed all except Berrio and the old man who had been Berrio's deputy on the third voyage.

Sixteen of Berrio's soldiers, the rest of his Trinidad garrison, had fled down the Caroni river during the night. Some had got to the Pitch Lake, where there were friendly Arwacas Indians and canoes; some were hiding in the swamps. The Spanish women who had been left behind had run to the forest. Ralegh said of these Spaniards that they 'had escaped killing'. He aimed at the extermination of the Spaniards in this part of the world, and he wrote of the massacre as he felt a man of action should. 'To leave a garrison in my backe interested in the same enterprize, who also dayly expected supplies out of Spaine, I should have savoured very much of the asse.'

Guanaguanare's tribesmen repossessed the site of their village; and Berrio was a prisoner in his city where, on the day of its founding, Domingo de Vera had put up a gallows and pillory as a symbol of the law that had come. In the prison there was a ghost. 'In the city after I entred the same,' Ralegh wrote, 'there were five of ye lords or little kings (which they call caciques in the West Indies) in one chaine almost dead of famine, and wasted with torments: these are called in their owne language *acarewana*, and now of late since English, French and Spanish are come among them, they call themselves capitaines, because they perceive that the chiefest of every ship is called by that name. Those five capitaines in the chaine were called Wannawanare, Carroari, Maquarima, Taroopanama and Aterima.'

Ralegh was exact where he appeared most fanciful. Wannawanare: a name in a barbarous roll, to be corroborated and given meaning three hundred years later, when the Spanish documents were recovered. After the foundation of Berrio's town, according to the visiting Spanish Judge of All Irregularities, 'Guanaguanare moved elsewhere'.

Guanaguanare's tribesmen sacked St Joseph and at their request Ralegh burnt the town two days later: the straw houses, the thatched church, the Franciscan convent. With his two Spanish prisoners Ralegh then went to Port of Spain. He stayed there for three days. He called the chiefs and spoke to them through one of his interpreters.

'I made them understand that I was the servant of a Queene, who was the great casique of the North, and a virgine, and had more casiqui under her then there were trees in that yland: that shee was an enemie to the Castellani in respect of their tyrannie and oppression, and that she delivered all such nations about her, as were by them oppressed, and having freed all the coast of the Northren world from their servitude, had sent mee to free them also, and withall to defend the countrey of Guiana from their invasion and conquest. I shewed them her Majesties picture which they so admired and honoured, as it had been easie to have brought them idolatrous thereof.' The Indians said that Ralegh's Queen was *Ezrabeta Cassipuna Aquerewana*, 'which is as much as Elizabeth, the greatest princess or the greatest commander'.

Then Ralegh took Berrio and Berrio's deputy to the south of the island. He left no soldiers in Port of Spain.

The first Spanish survivors reached Margarita that day. The governor of Margarita at once sent off a canoe to Port of Spain with twenty Indian paddlers, six Spanish soldiers and an officer. They arrived the next day; Port of Spain had become Spanish again. The Spaniards, more lucid in defeat than in victory, collected the facts: the number of the dead, the flight of Berrio's soldiers, the hostility of the Indians. Ralegh's name gave them trouble. They called him Monsieur Raeles, Guaterral, Guatarral and sometimes Count Guaterral, *el conde milor Guaterral*. They got the titles Ralegh had used as his credentials with the Indians: Earl of Cornwall, Captain of the Guard of the Queen of England.

They heard from the Arwacas that he was at the south-western tip of the island, felling trees and building a fort. He had landed three pieces of artillery. He was still addressing the Indians, promising them liberation and getting them to acknowledge the Queen of England. The Queen's arms were displayed on a tall pole.

And Berrio did not understand that this was more than a raid, that he had been finally dispossessed. He had lost thirty men who had cost their weight in gold; he had lost his nephew; but he behaved like a soldier who had only lost a battle. 'This Berrio is a gentleman wel descended,' Ralegh wrote, 'very valiant and liberal, and a gentleman of great assuredness and of a great heart. I used him according to his estate and worth in all things I could.'

It was to the courtier in Ralegh that Berrio responded, after the years spent among 'men born in the Indies'. Ralegh was interested; Ralegh asked questions; and Berrio spoke to Ralegh as he wrote to his King. He told him of his military service in Europe, his retirement to the Indies, the beginning of the quest. He told of the great third journey, the slaughter of the horses, the building of the canoes; of Albujar's stay in the Inca's palace in the golden city of Manoa; of the jealousy of Spanish officials and the trouble with the Indians.

Ralegh got all the hard names right, and all the complex intrigue. He had to draw the facts out sometimes, the concrete details of landscape and Indian customs Berrio had noted but didn't think worth mentioning. Berrio converted a journey across an unknown continent into a shortage of food and water, sudden illness, a strong current, a high mountain hard to climb. Ralegh, who wanted to see and smell, began to feel that Berrio was 'utterly unlearned' and not 'curious in these things'.

To Berrio, very devout, screened from the world by the completeness of his faith, the only wonder beside gold, the body was a mystery. Illness was illness, 'almost like the plague', an act of God. Ralegh wanted more; he got truth mixed with medieval fantasy. 'This province of Amapaia is a very low and marish ground nere the river; and by reason of the red water which issueth out in small branches thorow the fenny and boggy ground, there breed divers poisonfull wormes and serpents; and the Spanyards not suspecting, nor in any sort fore-knowing the danger, were infected with a grievous kinde of fluxe by drinking thereof.'

The talk touched Whiddon's expedition of the previous year and Berrio's killing of eight of Whiddon's men. Berrio said simply that Whiddon had been too 'inquisitive' about El Dorado.

Ralegh said that he too was interested in El Dorado. That was why he had come; that was why he was building that fort on the shore. The talk about Virginia and Canaveral had only been talk.

Berrio went foolish. He was 'stricken into a great melancholy and sadnesse', Ralegh wrote, 'and used all the arguments he could to disswade me'. Even canoes with a draught of twelve inches shoaled on the sand-banks; the season of floods was at hand; the

Indians were hostile. He tried a bluff; he said he expected his son any day with reinforcements from New Granada. And he refused to give any more information. He didn't know the names of the rivers or the tribes; he just knew the Orinoco river; 'he had no meanes to discourse with the inhabitants at any time'.

One month after the burning of St Joseph the governor of Margarita heard from his Arwacas spies – two of them were used to going among the English – that Ralegh was still treating Berrio well, entertaining him at banquets and asking him to be a pilot to El Dorado through the 'broken islands and drowned lands' of the Orinoco estuary. Ralegh said he knew a lot already; he had all the letters Berrio and Vera had written to the King of Spain.

A week later the spies reported that Berrio was to be handed over to the Indians to be killed by bowshot. Berrio's seventy-five-year-old companion, Alvaro Jorge, was to be hanged. The two men were dragged ashore 'with much fusillading'. Still they didn't talk. The spies said that two days after this Berrio and Jorge were taken up the Orinoco by Ralegh. But this is uncertain. At this point, for reasons that will presently appear, Berrio and Jorge drop out of Ralegh's narrative.

RALEGH WAS AWAY for thirty days, and he spent half that time getting from the Gulf of Paria to the main Orinoco. The first Indian he picked up was polite. The Indian said he would pilot them, but after some days it became clear that he couldn't; he had last gone to the Orinoco twelve years before, when he was a boy, and he had forgotten the way. 'And if God had not sent us another helpe, we might have wandred a whole yere in that labyrinth of rivers, yer wee had found any way, either out or in.' The other help was an Indian captured by chance; a second captive brought them into the Orinoco.

As an explorer Ralegh was as unskilled as Dudley and even more timorous. He never felt he had enough men. He longed for the new but was nervous about the unknown. The sight of the falls on the Caroni river from twenty miles away was good enough for him. He said he was 'a very ill footeman'. It was his companions who urged him on to the next valley and the next, and then he was glad to find 'the deere crossing in every path, the birdes towards the evening singing on every tree with a thousand severall tunes, cranes and herons of white, crimson, and carnation pearching in the rivers side, the aire fresh . . .'

The Indians on the Orinoco had heard about the killing of the Spaniards in Trinidad. In Moriquito's territory they welcomed Ralegh as a liberator. He spoke to them as he had spoken to the Indians in Port of Spain; he added some details about the defeat of the Spanish Armada seven years before. He heard the old stories about El Dorado. He heard about 'mines' and a diamond-bearing mountain was pointed out to him in the distance. The Indians wanted him to march on El Dorado right away. But he put them off; he didn't have enough men or supplies. Next year, he said. Then with a thousand men from England, with fifteen hundred men, he would march, together with all the Indian 'borderers'.

He distributed what the Spanish Judge of All Irregularities later called 'curious things he had brought from England'. They were golden sovereigns, 'the new money of 20 shillings with Her Majesties picture', which the Indians were to wear in token of their new allegiance. He left two young Englishmen, one a boy of sixteen, with the chief; and the chief in return gave one of his sons to be taken to England. Such mutual trust; yet Ralegh had spent no more than six days among the Orinoco Indians.

It rained on the way back to the Gulf. Ralegh suffered; no unusual journey was easy for him. The Indian spies in Trinidad reported that he came back 'very pleased'. This is where Ralegh's story of his 'discovery' of Guiana and El Dorado ends. 'Now that it hath pleased God to send us safe to our shippes, it is time to leave Guiana to the sunne, whom they worshippe, and steare away towards the North.' This is how, with poetic elision, Ralegh begins to lie. The adventure wasn't over.

Berrio was still a prisoner. From Trinidad, from Ralegh's ship or Ralegh's fort, he now began to write to Margarita for a loan of 1,400 ducats, his ransom and Alvaro Jorge's. It wasn't excessive; a Negro cost between 500 and 800 ducats. 'It became not the former fortune in which I once lived, to goe journeys of picory [from the Spanish *picaro*, a rogue],' Ralegh wrote, 'to run from cape to cape, and from place to place, for the pillage of ordinaries prizes.' But much money had been invested in Ralegh's expedition; and he had begun to think of money.

But he was divided. He was also thinking of El Dorado and the following year. He thought he might build a fort at Port of Spain. He sent two launches to take soundings; the news at Margarita was that Ralegh's men had begun to dig foundations on a sandy beach at a spot well provided with fresh water. The governor of Margarita sent a boat to Trinidad to find out more. The boat didn't get to Trinidad. It turned back with news. Guaterral was raiding.

The next day Ralegh's ten ships appeared off Margarita. He made an attempt on the pearl-fisheries but gave up after he had lost one of his men. He sent Alvaro Jorge ashore to arrange the ransom money. An agreement was made, but then the Spaniards quarrelled among themselves. Ralegh moved on to Cumaná. Cumaná he intended to attack. The two Indian agents his interpreters had recruited came from Cumaná. They said they knew secret ways to the town; they might also have promised an Indian uprising as at Trinidad. But neither they nor Ralegh knew that Captain Amyas Preston had passed that way just four weeks before and that the Spaniards were ready.

What followed was a massacre: a spirited English landing, just like that, a swift Spanish withdrawal to higher, prepared positions, a fusillade on the raiders who found themselves on an unprotected hillside. Ralegh's men turned and ran back to their boats. The Spaniards and their Indian auxiliaries chased. Only the pricklypear plants, the governor of Cumaná wrote, kept everyone from joining in the chase; 'and I don't blame them'. The Indian archers peppered the raiders with poisoned arrows as they tried to climb into the boats. Forty Englishmen were left dead on the shore. The Spaniards gave some of their names: Carofilde, who was Captain Calfield, leader of the march on St Joseph; Thechen, who was Captain Thynne; Glenfilo, who was Ralegh's cousin, Grenville.

On the ships the agony began. The poisoned men were 'marvellously provoked' by thirst; but Ralegh thought that drink made their condition worse. Berrio couldn't say what the poison was made from; the Spaniards used garlic-juice as an antidote. But it was too late. Keeping the occasion of his knowledge secret, Ralegh wrote with accuracy ('a digression not unnecessary') of the effects of the poison. 'The partie shotte indureth the most insufferable torment in the world, and abideth a most ugly and lamentable death, sometimes dying starke mad, sometimes their bowels breaking out of their bodies: which are presently discoloured as blacke as pitch, and so unsavoury, as no man can endure to cure, or to attend them.'

Ralegh himself didn't. There were two Dutch merchant ships standing off Cumaná. Ralegh spent his days aboard the Dutch ships, returning only at night to his own ship and his cabin with the green silk hangings. The governor of Cumaná, watching, thought that Ralegh acted as he did because he was heartbroken. Berrio said later that twenty-seven men died in the ships.*

There was no longer any question of getting a ransom for Berrio. It was unlikely that the governor of Cumaná would pay; he was Berrio's old enemy; he had sworn to kill Berrio. And if Berrio were taken back to England he would talk. It was agreed that Berrio and Alvaro Jorge should be exchanged for a wounded English boy.

Some distance away from the town of Cumaná was the house of a Spaniard called Fajardo. Fajardo was the friend of anyone,

* See note, p. 359.

English, Dutch, Indian, who wanted to trade. Fajardo had been Moriquito's slave-trading partner; Fajardo had handed over Moriquito to Berrio's men to be executed. It was to Fajardo's house that Ralegh led Berrio and Alvaro Jorge. They dined together. Keymis, Ralegh's lieutenant, thought that Berrio, 'having lost his men, was left . . . all alone, as forlorne' and was now capable of 'minding nothing else but his solace, and recreation'.

Ralegh had lost too. But he and Fajardo talked of their travels. Fajardo wanted to know whether Ralegh had seen the tribe beyond the Caroni 'whose heads appeare not above their shoulders'. Fajardo, 'a most honest man of his word', said 'hee had seene many of them'. Ralegh put this conversation in his book. He didn't give Fajardo's name, not wishing, he said, to compromise him with the Spanish authorities; and he said that the meeting in Cumaná occurred 'by chance'. Nine years later, when Ralegh was in the Tower of London, this conversation gave Shakespeare a line for *Othello*: '. . . the Anthropophagi, and men whose heads do grow beneath their shoulders'.

The governor of Cumaná watched Ralegh go and added to the report he was writing: '*Postscript*. Today, Friday the 30th, the Englishman sailed away . . . The report is that he is going back to England. He is not leaving as tall (*parado*) as he would have liked.' A fortnight later, off the western end of Cuba, Ralegh met Amyas Preston, a friendly enemy, who had successfully raided Margarita and Cumaná. 'We met,' Preston wrote, with irony for those who knew, 'with the honourable knight, Sir Walter Ralegh, returning from his paineful and happie discovery of Guiana, and his surprise of the isle of Trinidad.'

THERE HAD only been victims: Guanaguanare in chains in St Joseph, 'those poore souldiers' at the Port of Spain landing place who had been 'many yeeres without wine', Berrio 'stricken into a great melancholy', those bodies among the prickly-pear plants at Cumaná, the rotting men in the ships. The sixteen-year-old boy

Ralegh had left behind in the jungle had already died; his English clothes, the Indians said, had astonished and maddened a tiger. And the Indians of St Joseph, roused but unprotected, were presently to be repacified.

Ralegh went back to London and within weeks wrote a book of victory, celebrating the land and the people. Of the churls of his own country Ralegh nearly always wrote with resigned exasperation, as though they had been sent to try him alone. In Trinidad and Guiana it was always such a labour, 'a very impatiente worke to keepe the meaner sort from spoyle and stealing'. Even death did not save them from sarcasm: Whiddon's eight men who had been killed had acted 'like wise men in the absence of their leader'. For the Irish Ralegh had nothing but contempt: the food, the way they ate it, the whiskey, the drunkenness. But he loved the Indians for being 'the greatest carousers and drunkards of the world'; and he encouraged his gentlemen to drink with them. The Indian cassava liquor – the soaked cassava chewed by women and squirted through the teeth, the acids of the female mouth helping fermentation – he found 'cleane and sweete'. His eye rested with approval on a chief lolling in a hammock, with two women serving him 'with six cuppes and a little ladle to fill them'. It was with pure pleasure that he studied one of the wives: 'In all my life I have seldome seene a better favoured woman: she was of good stature, with blacke eyes, fat of body, of an excellent countenance, her haire almost as long as herselfe, tied up againe in pretie knots.' And not only the chief's wife: his approval extended to the girl being taken to market, to be sold or bartered for a few knives: 'as well favoured', he wrote, 'and as well shaped as ever I saw any in England'.

To be received among them as a liberator: that was part of the dream. In Ralegh's memory those six days of Indian welcome on the Orinoco blended with the memory of a magical forest, of a 'mountaine of christall' seen from a distance, 'like a white church-tower of an exceeding height', over which a mighty river poured, touching no part of the mountain. To this there was added the knowledge of a 'mine', never seen. In the end it drew him out of the Tower of London, which was his perfect setting, perhaps subconsciously sought, where, liberated from his inadequacy in the role the age imposed on him, he reached that stillness where the fact of life and action was reconciled with the fact of death. This was what he had plundered, this latecoming to the quest that destroyed so many.

'Would to God El Dorado hadn't been discovered!' the first Simón de Bolívar wrote from Caracas, after Ralegh's raid.

2. Fathers and Sons

1595–1618

TO CUMANÁ there eventually came about a dozen of Berrio's soldiers, refugees from Trinidad and the scattered garrison in Moriquito's territory. They were still willing to serve but there was nothing for them to do. Berrio and Alvaro Jorge stayed on vacantly in Fajardo's house. Then Berrio began to believe that the governor of Cumaná, his old enemy, was plotting to kill him. Berrio got his people together and they went inland, to the territory of the very old chief who had been helpful on the third journey and had given a pilot. But the chief had become Ralegh's man; his Indians were inflamed against all Spaniards. Berrio and his men hid on one of the islands in the Orinoco. There wasn't much to eat.

It wasn't the Indians who attacked. It was a party of Spaniards. They were led by a man called Felipe de Santiago. Felipe had grown up in Berrio's household in New Granada and had been on the quest with Berrio for twelve years. He had made the third journey and was among the twenty-eight men who had witnessed the foundation of St Joseph; he had later signed the pledge of loyalty to Berrio. He had escaped from St Joseph just before Ralegh's raid and had gone to the mainland. There, some weeks later, paddling in a canoe with some Indians, he had had another shock. He had been spotted – 'a cavallero', in Ralegh's account – by Ralegh's boats and pursued 'with no small joy'. Ralegh offered £500 for his capture; Captains Thynne and Calfield had given chase. Felipe had got away then; but, worn out by defeat, he had decided to change sides, to offer his services to those Spanish officials, enemies of Berrio's, who looked like winning.

Felipe's orders might have been to kill his former leader. But the Spanish Judge of All Irregularities said that Felipe, in attacking Berrio, acted out of some 'passion' of his own. The fight was inconclusive. A man was killed on either side; and Felipe, after capturing the second Englishman Ralegh had left behind (he spent seven years in Spanish jails), went to Trinidad to repacify the island and to found, on the site of Berrio's city of St Joseph de Oruña, the city of San Felipe de Montes, 'three leagues from the sea and the port which they call of Spain'. Montes was the name of the official to whom Felipe had transferred his allegiance; Montes had provided the soldiers.

Nothing more was heard of Guanaguanare or his Indians. The Spaniards classified Indians as Indians of work, war or peace. Felipe described his Indians as being of work; it suggests what happened after the pacification.

BUT FELIPE had changed too late. At this moment of defeat Berrio had become a name and his quest was famous in Castile, especially in Toledo, Extremadura and La Mancha, soon to be known as the land of Don Quijote. It was because of Ralegh. The news of his raid (and the Spanish victory) was like proof that El Dorado existed. And it was also because of Domingo de Vera, who had been Berrio's advocate in Spain for more than a year.

The news of Berrio's capture by Ralegh aided Vera's cause. Vera declared himself still the campmaster for El Dorado and the loyal servant of Berrio. If Berrio had been taken back to England, Vera wrote to the King, then all the English prisoners in Peru, Havana, Lisbon and other places should be exchanged for him. Berrio was meritorious, important to the royal service; through Berrio the faith might yet be spread in those provinces of El Dorado. Berrio was heroic. 'Hardships so dire and grave, when they are known, appear fables in the telling.' Berrio was the victim of envy; his enemies should be put down and all intruders expelled from his province. 'Because it is not just, after he has laboured so long and expended his fortune, that another should benefit, especially when there are nine honourable and deserving children. I only ask for justice.' Berrio could not be said to have been defeated in a fair fight. At St Joseph he had no fort, no munitions, no artillery, no horses; and when the attack came his soldiers ran away. All this would be known one day, Vera said. Time was 'the discoverer of truth'.

Vera found an audience. The King was near his second bankruptcy and willing to gamble; he contributed 70,000 ducats to Vera's expedition. The city of Seville gave 5,000. Retired infantry captains joined, and many first sons; people sold their farms and houses to go. The expedition grew from 500 to 1,000 to 1,500 and, according to some, 2,000. There was a setback. The English – Ralegh again – raided Cadiz; they achieved little, but Keymis, Ralegh's lieutenant, reported that the ships which were to have taken the expedition to Trinidad 'were converted into ashes'. Flyboats were obtained from the Flemings on credit. And, in the meantime, to secure Berrio in his province and to punish the King's enemies, the Judge of All Irregularities was sent out.

Fajardo fled to the mountains behind Cumaná, Fajardo who traded with the enemy and encouraged them to come, as the Judge said, 'with so little Christianity, living in their errors, which they seek to propagate here', openly making drawings of ports and taking soundings, openly landing contraband Negroes from Angola, Guinea and Cape Verde. The governor of Cumaná, Berrio's enemy, became violent when the Judge's men tried to dig up some buried contraband. 'I blame him,' the Judge of All Irregularities wrote, 'for all these irregularities. I hold one of his officials prisoner. He bartered away three pearls of price to English ships.'

The other Spanish officials understood; they said they were on Berrio's side. The governor of Margarita said he had always thought that time was all that was needed to complete the conquest of El Dorado.

Berrio was still on his river island. It had come too late for him, the destruction of his enemies, the King's support and, presently, Vera's mighty force, twenty-eight ships, the largest Spanish fleet that had ever entered the Gulf of Paria.

EIGHTEEN MONTHS later, from the city of St Joseph, Vera, about to die, his gift of rhetoric and even of language gone, wrote a confused and hysterical account of his failure. For twenty years and more afterwards survivors of the expedition, scattered now in many parts of the Empire, cursed Vera's name. In Venezuela and Trinidad the failure became a Spanish folk memory of horror. It is this folk memory that is preserved in the eighteenth-century ecclesiastical history of the region by Fray Antonio Caulin.

The ships anchored in the Gulf, Caulin said, on the Sunday or Monday of Holy Week 1596. A hundred soldiers were detailed to occupy Port of Spain and evict Felipe de Santiago from St Joseph. This was easily done. But there was no shelter in Port of Spain for 1,500 people. Straw huts were put up on the beach, and the friars straightaway found themselves consoling the sick and the despairing. They worked through the night and through the next day. Even when they retired to some secluded part of the beach they were followed for the consolation of their holy words by women, many with babies. The women said they could tell from the way the adventure had begun that it would end badly.

There was, however, another, remote witness: Laurence Keymis, Ralegh's deputy, who had come back to the Orinoco to tell the Indians why Sir Walter Ralegh wouldn't be coming to them that year. Keymis heard of Vera's twenty-eight ships; ten were still at anchor in Port of Spain, 'some of them at Conquerabia, the rest off the small ilands neare the disemboging place'. Disaster was still far away. Felipe de Santiago was in prison in St Joseph, awaiting execution; and Felipe's soldiers, 'actors in this enterlude', had gone back to Cumaná and Margarita in canoes.

Vera wrote nothing about the arrest and execution of Felipe de Santiago; that was no longer important when he wrote. Vera said that soon after landing, no doubt after the 'fortifying' Keymis saw, he got together a number of canoes and piraguas and sent over eight hundred and seventy men to Berrio. This was where the trouble started. Vera didn't know, but Guiana had changed since Ralegh's visit. The Indians were withdrawing from the areas of Spanish control. The Spaniards, even in extremity, never planted; they depended on the Indians for food. When the Indians withdrew, when no crops were planted, the Spaniards starved. Keymis, writing before the disaster, observed that Berrio, even when he had a few men, had had to spend much time 'in purveying of victuals, whereof there is such scarsitie, by reason that the Indians forsaking their houses, have not this halfe yeare planted any of their grounds, so that the Spaniards are inforced to seeke their breade farre off and content themselves to live with little'. The arrival of eight hundred and seventy men was a disaster.

There must have been raids on distant Indian villages and provision grounds, and trouble with the Indians. The assault on El Dorado led by Alvaro Jorge, 'old, blind and weak', as Vera said, was ambushed. The Indians killed Alvaro Jorge and some three hundred and fifty Spaniards. After this everything went wrong. The supplies Vera sent from Trinidad didn't get to Berrio; they were taken off to Caracas by people who no longer cared about El Dorado. Caracas should have sent supplies; they had been paid for; but the supplies never came. The new governor of Caracas was the man who had led the mutiny on Berrio's second journey; it was too late now for Vera to protest to the King.

Men rebelled in Trinidad and Guiana, deserted in groups of ten and twenty and were killed by Indians. Spanish officials lured away others. 'It is a great work of mercy according to them,' Vera wrote, 'but God restores His cause.' The friars encouraged disaffection and despair. 'I serve them,' Vera wrote, 'and I pay them due respect. Beyond this I do not like to have any dealings with them.'

A relief party sent across the Gulf by Vera met a fleet of man-eating Caribs from the northern island of Dominica. There were three hundred Caribs. They killed and ate the men and took away the women. According to Caulin, it was the friars, somehow surviving, who had to bury the remains: 'the inhuman carnage, with chests torn open and hearts eaten up, others cut up into joints, among them a poor woman from San Silvestre near Madrid, from whose womb they tore out the baby, leaving it with its mother's entrails next to the head'.

When Vera heard he left Port of Spain with a hundred men for the well-known spot across the Gulf where the Caribs met after manhunts to share their catch. A storm blew up, Vera said; and he lost forty men. He got to the mainland with the others, but gave up the rescue attempt. He thought then that as he was already half-way there he would go and see Berrio.

It was their first meeting in three years. Vera hoped at least for some acknowledgement of his services. He found Berrio withdrawn. 'Berrio,' Vera wrote, 'didn't even say for civility's sake, "I will do as His Majesty wishes".'

'Sir,' Vera said, direct speech occurring at this point in his letter, 'you have canoes here. Order them to go to Trinidad for supplies and barter goods. Get the men together. I myself will go to friendly Indians here on the river. They will give us food and keep us supplied. Then we will join forces. At the beginning of the summer everything and everyone will be ready.'

'We are trying to do too much,' Berrio said. 'If we try to do too much we will end by doing nothing at all.'

That was all: the only spoken words of Berrio's that are recorded. Vera waited for three days but Berrio had nothing more to say. He had always wanted men, and men who were not of the Indies. Now they had done too much; they had destroyed themselves by their own numbers. Vera went back to Trinidad. No further message passed between the two men.

Vera said he continued to send men to Berrio, but they always rebelled. He sent a friar with one party. It didn't work. The soldiers tied up the friar, beat him with their swords and threatened to drown him. They set him down on a deserted beach, cannibal food; miraculously, he survived.

The starving Spaniards of Guiana plotted to kill Berrio. It was the hatred of men of Spain: Berrio was lunatic and already dying. Eight months after his meeting with Vera he was dead.

And now, six years after he had left his father, and as though he had been waiting for his moment, Berrio's nineteen-year-old son turned up in Guiana to claim his father's province. Vera went to see him to report and hand over, and Berrio's son assumed his title: 'Don Fernando de Oruña y de la Hoz, Governor and Captain-General by the King our lord of the provinces and kingdoms of El Dorado, Guiana and the Great Manoa, and of the island of Trinidad'. He remained in Guiana and Vera returned to St Joseph.

Vera said he had pacified the Indians of St Joseph and Port of Spain. 'They plough the land,' he wrote, 'and make it fertile.' But there was still not enough food for the three hundred men in Trinidad. The eighty horses were an extra burden. Within the new fort of St Joseph, with its ten pieces of artillery, men waited to die.

Vera wrote his letter from St Joseph in October 1597. He was dead – of a urinary complaint, according to Caulin – when his letter reached King Philip II. The King was himself about to die. The paperwork of Empire was like ritual now, automatic, absorbing failure and grief. The King wrote: 'Let all the papers relating to this affair be put together.' And the papers were forgotten for three

hundred years. Time, the discoverer of truth, swallowed Berrio up. No portrait remains of the man who sought the third marquisate of the Spanish New World.

RALEGH CONTINUED to send a yearly ship to Guiana. But for the Spaniards, and especially for Fernando Berrio, the quest was over. Fernando was two when he came out to the Indies with his father and twelve when he started on the great third journey. When he was fourteen he had gone home to New Granada, and there he had stayed. Now, as governor and captain-general, Fernando appointed a lieutenant for Trinidad, and the lieutenant paid 4,000 ducats for the post. The lieutenant was to give himself a salary out of the revenues he could raise in Trinidad.

Fernando stayed in Guiana for three years; he was living with an Indian woman. He developed one settlement in Guiana, San Thome, and founded another. The Indians withdrew; for thirty leagues around no Indian grew any crops. Fernando said he had been defeated by the worst sort of Indian war, famine. He 'dis-peopled' the new settlement and went to his father's unlucky city of St Joseph. There were only fifty people there now, and the lieutenant was grumbling. He had made a bad deal and wanted to call it off. He couldn't raise his salary. The Royal Chest in St Joseph had only 1,652 pesos, and that meant he was entitled as lieutenant to just sixteen pesos and a half. Fernando gave him that and freed him.

Sixteen pesos and a half, an official's salary: it gives a scale. After the El Dorado failure this part of the Spanish Main was on the periphery of the Spanish Empire. Margarita, the nearly exhausted pearl-island, had fifty-one houses; nineteen belonged to priests and widows. And Margarita was the brightest spot in the region. The region held nothing for officials, and when they found out they complained to the King like children.

'Your Majesty wished to reward me. But my luck didn't last too long. I was given this petty post, which I nevertheless hold in high esteem inasmuch as it is Your Majesty's pleasure.' – 'Give me another job,' the first Simón de Bolívar wrote. 'Anyone can handle Venezuela, even if he has very little ability.' No ships came from Spain; salaries were not paid. 'I swear before God that for twenty months I haven't been given a real. I have got to eat, and if it weren't for the few Indians I have – free men – who grow a little maize on my little patch, neither they nor I would have anything to eat. I am compelled to do this to provide something for my family, and I trust Your Majesty will consider it well done, seeing that I can do nothing else.' – 'Now I am being asked for rent. Does a governor pay rent? Besides, how can I pay rent if I don't have any money? Send me a decree so that I can live in this house and not pay rent.'

The life of the isolated official was yet full of alarms. 'In one of my letters I begged Your Majesty for the favour of the governorship of Caracas. But now I beg Your Majesty not to give it me, because there is a rumour that the last governor was poisoned by herbs. A few days ago the bishop, who was visiting, died in the same way; and I hear that the people there are in the habit of using these herbs. Some strange deaths have occurred in that province and I beg Your Majesty to look at me with eyes of pity.' Foreign corsairs raided the small settlements at will and sometimes just for fun. Some Dutchmen captured a group of pearl-gathering Spaniards off Margarita one day and asked them how big Margarita was. The Spaniards said it was very big. The Dutchmen laughed; they knew that when the pearl-fisheries were busy there were only about thirty-five people in the fifty-one houses of Margarita.

The Spaniards never had enough to eat. They were also in danger of being eaten. Man-eating Caribs were increasingly on the prowl. 'They eat the Indians they seize and they kill the Spaniards in the most cruel way possible . . . and when these are not available they nourish themselves with Negroes.' One report suggests that Negroes were castrated and 'held in perpetual servitude' until they were eaten.

The Caribs might have left the Spaniards and their precious Negroes alone, as they left the Dutch and English alone (and were, indeed, their friends). But cannibalism was never a joke to the Spaniards; it aroused the same wish to mutilate, destroy and enslave as did sodomy, another open Indian practice, and the Indian habit of casually pissing during conversation, without turning aside. 'Their crimes are so notorious and of such gravity that there can be no hope of reducing these people by means of the Gospel. Your Majesty must dispeople these islands of Caribs.' The Caribs must be declared slaves and hunted down; plans were sent again and again to Madrid for extermination raids by Spanish soldiers, for a galley patrol, the galleys manned by enslaved Caribs. 'If something isn't done about this, it will be impossible to maintain any settlement in Trinidad, Cumaná, Margarita and other places.'

But there was seldom any reply. The Empire was too big. Mexico, Peru, the guarding of the treasure fleets, the difficulties in Europe: the islands and the eastern Main were not important. There were a lot of Indians in Trinidad, a Spanish historian said, but it wasn't a 'good' place. Sometimes, after years of correspondence, the armada of the treasure fleet made a sweep. But it didn't help. The Caribs continued to raid, the foreigners continued to come.

The foreigners no longer came to raid. They came to barter; it was big business. The Dutch got their salt from Venezuela. The English came to Trinidad for tobacco, to satisfy the craze started by Ralegh. Trinidad had almost dropped out of the Spanish Empire; but it had become an English word. Trinidad, Trinidade, Trinidado: it was the word used in England, before Virginia, for tobacco. It was illegal for Spaniards to trade with foreigners. But there was no one else to trade with. No Spanish ship called at Trinidad, and few called at the settlements nearby. 'Although guards may be placed in the mess-room and the Negroes sleep under lock and key, as soon as a barter ship is sighted, even if it is two leagues away, everyone goes out at night to barter with them. Some have even taken passages to Flanders and England in the said vessels.'

Every Spanish official broke the law; every Spanish official complained of his helplessness and complained about every other Spanish official. 'I weep in my heart with tears of blood that Your Majesty has appointed me to a place where there are so many enemies and I am in no position to attack them or even to make a show of hostility. I beg and implore Your Majesty to do me the favour of transferring me to another governorship where I will not have to bear this daily pain of powerlessly looking on at the activities of our enemies.' – 'I tell you with truth that this treasurer I have is the worst man you can find in the world. You hardly have time to punish one set of derelictions before he starts on another.'

Sometimes there was an investigation. 'The licentiate Pedro de Liaño, judge commissioned by Your Majesty, has arrived here to acquaint himself with the irregular dealings and barter which some towns have been shamelessly carrying on. He is a highly gifted man and a true Christian acting without any personal interest.' Five months later the same official wrote to the King about the same judge. 'I did what I could to help this man. I was firm with those who dealt in contraband. I punished the guilty myself. When the aforesaid licentiate saw that he had been forestalled and that there was no room for his cupidity in that direction, he began in his ill-intentioned way to go far beyond the terms of his commission as laid down by Your Majesty. He sent his law officers all over the place, paying them enormous salaries to pry into all sorts of private details . . .'

When everyone was guilty, when even an old Indies hand like Fajardo could become a governor, the law couldn't be enforced. 'The governor sent me to arrest two alcaldes. They escaped while I was at mass. Some of the guards were accomplices. I managed to recapture one alcalde. But the other got away. I am so grieved I have had to take to my bed, where I still am. The man who got away has no fear at all of God or his King. Even the priests are involved in this business.'

God and the King: the isolated Spanish official had no other allegiance, no other idea of association. He was an individual; Spaniards were as much his enemies as foreigners. 'Your Majesty knows that the governors of Cartagena, La Havana and Puerto

Rico have been investigated and found guilty. I beg Your Majesty to grant me one of those governorships. No complaint will be heard against me.' It was part of the Spanish waste; it could be exploited by others with a more developed idea of community. 'There is in these parts a Spaniard proscribed for well treating some English fallen into his hands,' an English diplomatist wrote from Port of Spain. 'He, with divers Spaniards his followers, are fled into the mayne as open enemyes of the kyngs proceedings. I have sent my shallop to seeke him. I know if myself may confer with him . . . he may offer good service to your lordship.'

'I dare presume to say,' another English trader-explorer wrote, 'and hope to prove within a few yeares that only this commodity, tobacco, will bring as great benefit and profit to the undertakers as ever the Spaniards gained by the best and richest silver myne in all their Indies.' But to the Spaniards the tobacco of Trinidad was only a liability, like the salt of Venezuela. If the tobacco grounds were destroyed there would be no illegal trading, and the Indians would once again grow food crops and work the mines. And tobacco grounds were destroyed; but it didn't stop the trade.

As for the salt of Venezuela, the Council of War of the Indies decided one winter that it was 'of no use whatsoever to these kingdoms or to the Indies'. The salt-pans were therefore to be destroyed. To deprive the Dutch of salt would also be to apply the most powerful sanction (*el mayor torcedor*) against the rebels in Flanders; it would bring that draining war to an end. The salt-pans might be flooded; an engineer was sent out to report on the possibilities. 'Send me poison,' another official wrote to the King. 'By poisoning the water the salt would be poisoned and would cause such harm in Holland, Zeeland and England that I am sure they wouldn't care to come back for more. Let the poison be sent to me with all possible secrecy.'

Among the engineers and officials sent out to examine and report there is, unexpectedly, a famous name: the Duke of Medina Sidonia. Not a descendant: it is the admiral himself, the unwilling commander of the Spanish Armada, the Enterprise of England. In the imagination he disappears to his estates, broken and ill, after the great defeat. Knowledge adds the humiliation of the English raid on Cadiz eight years later, when he was governor of Andalucia, and the ships in Cadiz harbour that were to have taken Vera's El Dorado expedition to Trinidad were 'converted into ashes'.

But the imagination could never add this, sixteen years after the Armada, this survey of the province called New Andalucia, the pacing of the Araya salt-pans, the survey of the Gulf of Paria and the seas between Trinidad and Margarita: the enemy now unnamed Dutch and English traders and man-eating Caribs in canoes, and the difficulties still the same. 'I told Your Majesty how necessary it was to send men and money,' he had written after Cadiz; 'and I never even got an answer.' And now again this was the substance of his report; and again the answer was that there was no answer.

No ay que responder, no ay que proveer, there is nothing to reply, nothing to do: it was the royal formula of silence. It was fact: there was little that could be done. The Empire stretched across the world; it was too big. Fernando Berrio was different from these complaining, anxious officials. His inherited appointment was for life; he never asked to be released or transferred; he divided his time between Guiana and Trinidad and never complained. He was still officially looking for El Dorado, but he never wrote a report. Others wrote about him, though. 'Don Fernando is not at his post. And considering where he is at the moment he won't find El Dorado in five hundred years. I give Your Majesty my word that he has bartered off and sold more than 8,000 Indians.' – 'He is not looking for El Dorado. He is trading in Indians. He has sold more than 10,000 Indians now. Your Majesty must understand this: where this man is, El Dorado is not.'

'He is in trouble as usual, for the usual reasons: not enough cattle or horses. I myself think the whole thing is absurd. The soldiers are fed up. They regard it all as a joke and they feel they have been tricked.' Sometimes the criticism was ambiguous. 'I have had standing orders since 1598 to look into this El Dorado affair,' the governor of Cumaná wrote in 1605, replying to a reminder of 1603 (everything now moved more slowly). 'I sent our notary public and an ensign with four soldiers to make secret inquiries. I didn't ask the soldiers to bring back slaves. I merely ordered them to bring back those Indians who had been dispossessed for good reasons by Fernando Berrio.'

'Tobacco crops have been uprooted in all these provinces except in San Thome and the island of Trinidad. In Trinidad there is much bartering of cloth, and there are always English and French ships there for that purpose.' The governor of Margarita said it was 'like a trade fair' in the Gulf of Paria and on the Orinoco. The river of El Dorado was now a recognized contraband route. 'All the contraband cloth enters there and goes straight up to Peru, which does the Royal Treasury no good.'

'The head and fount of these and other crimes is the governor. He acts without any sort of Christianity and without any regard for the fact that he is a vassal of Your Majesty. He behaves like an absolute monarch; he is like an infidel barbarian; there is nothing Christian about him.'

'We don't hear much about or from this man. But from what I hear it isn't much of a conquest. Although this conquest isn't being carried out at Your Majesty's expense, or perhaps because it isn't, Christianity is in some danger. The pursuit of the chimera of this discovery has to be paid for in the unregulated and licentious life of the soldiers who obey the laws neither of God nor of the state and give free rein to every sort of vice. So that place attracts and welcomes delinquent seculars and monks, apostate friars; and is generally a seminary for the damned. To all this it is said by way of excuse that the gentleman doesn't enjoy the best of health, that his health is in fact poor, if not shattered. The reasons for this lack of health are public.'

Fernando Berrio lived with an Indian woman. She was his guide, one Spanish official wrote, to El Dorado. Fernando's illness might have been syphilis. Syphilis was an Indian disease; it had been taken to Europe after Columbus's second voyage, the only revenge of the new world on the old. 

Fernando never wrote about his illness. He never wrote about anything. The picture is of a middle-aged, decaying man of thirty, content in his kingdom without the law. But, foolish, corrupt, Fernando was still a Spaniard, as capable of swift, stinging action as the lean house-wasp which in Trinidad continues to be known as Jack Spaniard. He carried, in the Spanish way, the surname, de la Hoz, of his cousin Rodrigo, who had gone down that day to the Port of Spain landing place to meet Ralegh's men, had been lured aboard the flagship with a promise of wine, and killed. Fernando had a number of things to avenge.

THE REGION was becoming better known. The legends were going. Samuel Purchas, who had inherited the papers of Hakluyt of the *Voyages*, asked Keymis, Ralegh's lieutenant, whether it was true about the men with heads below their shoulders. Keymis said it was only rather that they 'lacked necks'. The Indians were being used by the English and Dutch against the Spaniards, by the Dutch against the English. The Indians were getting guns; an English visitor wrote that they had 'learned to handle their peeces very orderly, and some of them are good shot'.

Ralegh, a prisoner now of his King, had his own memories of the region; in the Tower of London these memories were turning to fantasy. He continued to send or subsidize ships. But he was less interested in exploration than in keeping in touch with his Indians. And there were still Indians who remembered him.

An Englishman called Robert Harcourt came to Guiana with plans for a colony and plantations. He told the coast Indians, falsely, that he had been sent by Ralegh. The name drew an Indian chief and some of his followers out of the jungle; they were dressed in English clothes, now tattered, which Ralegh had sent them years before. Harcourt had to explain why Ralegh hadn't come, after fourteen years. Ralegh's old Indian interpreter and servant, Leonard, who had been to England, made a long journey to meet Harcourt and to entertain him, 'not after the ordinarie rude manner of the Indians, but in a more civill fashion'. Leonard wanted the English to settle. He showed a site and said it was good for *houses*, and the English word in the South American jungle startled Harcourt. There was an eclipse of the moon. The Indians shot flaming arrows at it. Martin, an Indian who had recently come back from England, explained the custom, 'laughing at their simplicity'.

It was like Ralegh's dream of Arcadia; and there were still the old stories of gold and the golden city of Manoa. Harcourt asked for a guide to Manoa. One was provided. But when they came to the spot the Indians had described there was nothing, and 'our guide was then possessed with a shameless spirit of ignorance'. Harcourt had always thought that the London stories of mines were exaggerated. Still, he left thirty men to look for the Great Manoa; and went north to Trinidad, Fernando Berrio's tobacco kingdom.

Three English ships were anchored in the south of the Gulf of Paria. There was some uncertainty: it was a fortnight before Harcourt got to Port of Spain. Two days later Fernando Berrio's lieutenant and some of his men came aboard and were entertained. Harcourt wanted tobacco. The Spaniards had other problems. 'They plainly confessed that they are much molested by the Charibes, and knew not how by any means to suppresse them.' Eight Spaniards had been killed during a recent Carib attack, and many wounded. Harcourt's surgeon attended to some of the wounded.

The three English ships in the south had followed Harcourt up to Port of Spain. But there was still no 'good tobacco amongst the Spaniards'. It was unusual; it occurred to Harcourt that the 'delays and faire words' were part of a plan. 'Which wee perceiving, departed thence upon the seaventh day about one of the clock in the morning, leaving the other shippes to attend their trade.'

The *Diana* was owned by a Dutchman who lived in London,

the *Penelope* and *Endeavour* by a London merchant named Hall. Hall was a friend of Ralegh's; some of Ralegh's men were on those two ships. Not long after Harcourt left, thirty-six men from the *Penelope* and *Endeavour* who had gone ashore were seized by Fernando Berrio's lieutenant in Port of Spain. They were tied back to back and their throats slit. The Berrio-Ralegh account was settled. Harcourt had been lucky; he had actually been using Ralegh's name.

The memory of the killings was still fresh when an English courtier and diplomatist came, again partly at Ralegh's expense, and explored the Amazon-Orinoco area for a year. He fetched up afterwards in the Gulf of Paria. He found fifteen English, French and Dutch ships loading tobacco, 'freighting smoke', at Port of Spain. He had a quarrel with the Spaniards about the killing of Hall's and Ralegh's men, 'whom they used worse than Moores'; but it ended 'with quiett'. There was much Spanish activity. Cattle and horses were being gathered in Port of Spain for a new attempt on Guiana. 'But it will vanish, and be turned all to smoke, for the governor is lazy, and unapt for labour, and hath more skill in planting tobacco and selling yt, than in erecting colonies, or marching of armyes.'

The diplomatist who wrote this was Sir Thomas Roe. Four years later, as the first ambassador from the King of England to the Mogul court in India, he was making the slow, dusty journey from the western Indian port of Surat to Agra in North India. It was a more glittering empire. But its weakness was the same: the King, only the King, his subjects only mercenaries, not a nation. Its intellectual concerns were fewer; its fall was to be swifter and more complete. Roe was as unimpressed by difficult, nervous officials in the open marble halls of Agra as he had been by Fernando Berrio's busy Spaniards in the straw huts of Port of Spain. 'The Spaniards here are equally proud, insolent, yet needy and weake: theyr force is reputation, theyr safety opinion.' There was weakness even in that activity in Port of Spain. Roe saw that it was only because 'the Justice of the Kyng is dayly expected'.

THE KING's investigator was expected. It had taken time. The Trinidad tobacco trade, worth £60,000 a year to English merchants and as much to merchants on the Continent, had become a scandal. There had been ambassadors' reports. There had been warnings from Spain to Fernando Berrio ('. . . otherwise, what ought to be done will be done': it did not become royalty to threaten more directly). Even after an investigation had been decided on there were complaints. Indians and Spaniards in Trinidad had been boasting that they had enough contraband cloth to last them fourteen years; letters had been found on a captured English ship from Fernando Berrio, his lieutenant and even from a Franciscan friar. Fernando himself was saying nothing; he wasn't even making an excuse. There was a rumour that he was receiving some sort of medical treatment in Margarita.

It took two years to set up the investigation; and it was almost a year after Sir Thomas Roe's visit that the investigating judge, a former governor of Venezuela, 'dayly expected' for so long, at last left Margarita for Trinidad. He left with three launches and a piragua. He had thirty Spanish officials and soldiers and more than a hundred Indians and Negroes. The crossing to Port of Spain took a fortnight. From there the judge went to St Joseph, a city of thirty-two straw houses with an adult male population of forty. Fernando Berrio was not in residence; he was across the Gulf in Guiana.

The judge put up at the inn – never described – and presented his letters of commission to the local council. Then he went to hear mass. All the citizens of St Joseph, even 'the principal women', followed the judge back to the inn. They had a petition which they wanted the notary to read out, if the judge gave permission. The judge gave permission. As soon as the notary began to read all the citizens dropped to their knees. The petition was for mercy.

The citizens said they were all guilty without exception; they had been bartering with foreigners for years; if the judge wanted to start hanging he would have to start with the children. The judge was affected by 'the pitiful scene'. He asked men, women and children to rise and he tried to console them. He said he was going to recommend a general pardon.

He spent a month taking down their confessions. His feeling at the end was that Fernando Berrio was 'seriously guilty'. It was clear, though, that Fernando wasn't going to come to the judge; the judge decided to go to Fernando. But then there was an alarm. The Caribs were raiding again. 'I am now in a city where at all hours of the day we carry arms in our hands for protection against the Caribs,' the judge wrote. He was full of sympathy for the local Spaniards; he agreed with them that the Caribs should be destroyed or enslaved.

The judge's men beat off the Caribs and the judge went down to Port of Spain to cross over to Guiana. He found that even while he had been in St Joseph, collecting evidence about illegal trade, foreign ships had called at Port of Spain. The judge raised the number of charges against Fernando Berrio to thirty-eight. Fernando, when examined in Guiana, was cool. He said he was poor and needy and had been poor and needy for all the sixteen years of his governorship. The judge – never describing Fernando or the setting – raged; he said Fernando deserved the death penalty. He banned the growing of tobacco in Guiana. Then he went back to Trinidad.

There were more foreign ships in Port of Spain. 'But Flemings and Englishmen are in and out of this port as though they are in the English channel,' the judge wrote. 'There are so few Spaniards here and so many enemies that it is less a place for walking about with a pen in one's hand than with a musket on one's shoulder.' He 'ambushed' one English ship and made the captain a prisoner. 'And before I had him hanged' – just that, no more – 'I asked him many questions.' The captain said there were other foreign ships on the way.

Ships appeared: warships, a whole armada. The judge prepared to meet them. But the ships were Spanish, part of the armada which for fifty years had been protecting the treasure fleets with complete success, although the routes and sailing times were fixed and known. The Council of War in Spain had decided that the armada should make a two-day sweep in Trinidad waters. But now, after all the correspondence, the visit didn't seem necessary. There were no foreign ships to be seen. There was a reason: they had been warned by their Indian allies. Information about this warning system had been sent to Spain some time ago; but the papers hadn't yet been read.

The Spanish admiral was for moving on. Time was precious and the treasure fleet was more important than foreign barter ships. The judge compelled him to stay for six days. No foreign ships appeared. Words passed between the two men. The judge said he had only been anxious to serve the King and put down heresy. The armada went away. The judge suspended Fernando Berrio from the governorship of Trinidad, appointed a lieutenant-governor and went back to Margarita to write his report.

He took his time. He made the usual recommendations: more settlers, a permanent garrison, more Spanish trading ships. He added a memorandum about Negroes who had been illegally landed in Trinidad in exchange for tobacco; and he ended with something about himself. 'I am not complaining about the six ducats a day I am supposed to get during the time of this inquiry. It matters not to me that a judge of the Audiencia gets ten ducats a day, or that I had to take soldiers with me, who would have received nothing at all if I hadn't given them something. But there are many foreigners about, and I am happy to do what I can and spend what I don't really have for the pleasure of knowing that in this way I am serving Your Majesty.'

The governor of Margarita wrote a supporting letter. Both

documents went to Madrid. Nine months later the King minuted the letter from the governor: 'Let this be put together with the other papers about tobacco, until such time as a decision is taken; *y no hay que responder*, and there is nothing to reply.'

THE DECISION was taken two years later, when Fernando Berrio went to Spain and raised the matter of his joblessness and deprivation. Until then he lived in Guiana. Trinidad, without him, was more troubled than usual. The lieutenant-governor had too much energy. The first thing he did was to send twelve Spanish soldiers and some Arwacas archers to seek out and destroy a Dutch tobacco plantation in Guiana. The Dutch had artillery. The Spaniards suffered, until the archers let off flaming arrows at the thatched Dutch fort. Six Dutchmen and all their barter goods were destroyed in the fire; the tobacco grounds were trampled down. The victory brought retaliatory raids by the Caribs, allies of the Dutch; a corsair threatened to seize St Joseph; and the Spaniards of St Joseph rose against the lieutenant-governor for the 'vexations and annoyances' he was causing them.

It was then, like a man washing his hands of a disagreeable situation which others had needlessly provoked, that Fernando Berrio went to Spain and laid his 'just causes' before the Duke of Lerma. The Duke ruled Spain in the name of the King; and the Duke's favours had a price. Fernando was deprived of his governorship of El Dorado and Trinidad, but he was given some compensation. He was given a loan of 2,000 ducats (it turned out to be a gift), a grant of land in New Granada and an allotment of unclaimed Indians. So, six years after it had begun, the case against Fernando Berrio ended. The judge wasn't paid; presently he died.

It was felt by the Council of War of the Indies that the new governor of Guiana and Trinidad should be a man of parts, a soldier, and experienced in the ways of the Indies. Three men were considered and Diego Palomeque de Acuña was chosen. He knew nothing of the Indies; but he was a man of birth, a relation of the

Spanish ambassador in London. He and Fernando left Spain in the same ship, Fernando bound for his estates in New Granada.

Palomeque was tall and corpulent; he stood out among the leaner Spaniards of St Joseph and Port of Spain. He was severe; he had soldiers from Puerto Rico at his disposal. He stopped contraband. He examined the accounts of people he suspected and he fined anything that looked fraudulent. When people said they couldn't pay he made them write promissory notes. After two years the Spaniards began to plot to kill him or to send him off the island in a canoe.

It was then, after many warnings, that the news came from Spain that Sir Walter Ralegh was coming.

It was an act of madness. The Spaniards no longer looked for El Dorado. The Dutch had found nothing; the French had found nothing. Robert Harcourt had ridiculed the idea; Sir Thomas Roe had found nothing. Guiana had given up its mysteries, of tobacco and Indian tribal antagonisms, to scores of merchants. Ralegh himself no longer spoke of El Dorado and the Great Manoa; but in the Tower of London he had continued to dream of mines and a crystal mountain.

Twenty years before, during his week on the Orinoco, he believed he had seen such a mountain; the mine or mines he hadn't seen. Yet no expedition was more publicly canvassed; and when, at the age of sixty-four, he was released from the Tower, after thirteen years, so complete had his conviction become, of 'finding the Guiana gold as . . . of not missing his way from his dining-room to his bedchamber', that he accepted his freedom on conditions which were absurd, as in a parlour game. The mine was in Spanish territory; the Spaniards would be informed of his movements. He would have to find the mine without disturbing the Spaniards; and the penalty for failure would be death.

As soon as he was released his conviction weakened. The will to action dropped away. He threw all the responsibility for finding the mine on to Keymis, his old friend, who claimed to have seen the mine. His thoughts and half-plans for action were wild: Guiana, the East Indies, the West Indies, employment in France, piracy. After the reconciliation and peace of the Tower, the contemplation of death, he had re-engaged himself in the world. It was an act of self-violation. It is possible, from his easy irritation with his son, with the churls with whom he had once more to deal and later even with his Indians, dwellers in Arcadia, to infer his self-doubt, his sense of deflation and futility. He was like a man committed to a course of events; events now carried him along. Bad luck: there was much of that. But luck, good or bad, is often suggested by the spirit of the man concerned, and with Ralegh there is now no suggestion of spirit attempting to control events. He is withdrawn; the action is around him.

It was like a comedy of false starts, on Ralegh's side and on the side of the Spaniards who watched him and jumped whenever he jumped, both sides like amateurs in adventure, both sides anxious about defeat and worrying about money. In March 1616 Ralegh was released from the Tower. In November the first news of his plans reached Madrid. Ralegh knew that the Spaniards knew; he told a friend he was 'nothing appalled'. In December his ship, the *Destiny*, was launched. The Spaniards, far from being ready for him, hadn't even decided what to do. It was only in January that the Council of War of the Indies decided they could do nothing. There wasn't enough money; the information from London ought perhaps to be checked; the governors of Margarita, Trinidad and Venezuela couldn't do much with the forces they had, but they might be alerted.

Two months after that the Spanish ambassador in London wrote more urgently to Madrid. Another warning, and nothing else, was sent out to Margarita, Venezuela and Trinidad. Three weeks later there were two more letters from London. And three weeks after that a paper was prepared about what action might be taken: the Ocean Fleet might be reinforced, the island of Jamaica fortified.

Two months later, in June 1617, after new information had been received, it was decided that there was no need to fortify Jamaica or to collect a fleet to pursue Ralegh, since he had already left and no one knew where he was going. Fresh warnings, the third set in five months, were sent out to Trinidad, Venezuela and Margarita; this time they went in duplicate.

Within days it began again. The Spanish ambassador wrote from London that Ralegh had been delayed in Plymouth. He didn't have enough supplies, he was short of money and in a state of exasperation and despair. Then at last Ralegh left. But the bad weather he always ran into forced him to put in first at Falmouth, then at Cork. There were 'contenuall quarrels and fyghting' among the men on the ships; many were seriously wounded. It was eight weeks before Ralegh was on the open sea.

'I know,' he wrote to his friend Keymis, 'that, a few gentlemen apart, what a scum of men you have.' His irritation broke into the journal he began to keep, brief, full of blanks, inelegant, words loosely strung together, records of mileage, compass directions, bad weather. There was trouble with the Spaniards at the Canary Islands; one of his captains deserted and went back to England. In the Cape Verde Islands he lost a pinnace. All the men were asleep; no one was at the watch; and the pinnace drove under the bowsprit of Ralegh's ship and sank. 'But the men were saved though better worthy to have bin hanged then saved.' Then the 'sickness' came. The deaths were at first noted in the margin of the journal; then they formed the substance of the journal, mixed with accounts of bad weather.

'29 *Sep* . . . Munday being Michelmas day ther died our master surgent Mr Nubal to our great loss, and our saile maker, and we had 60 men sick and all myne owne sarvants amongst them that I had none of myne owne but my pages to serve mee . . . *Octob.* 1 . . . a hurlecano fell uppon us with most violent rayne . . . 2 *Oct.* . . . Fryday one of my trumpeters and one other of the Coockrome died . . . 6 *Oct.* From Sunday 12 to Munday 12 we made 28 L. this Munday morninge died Mr John Haward, Ensigne to Cap: North, and Lieutenant Payton and Mr Hwes fell sick. Ther also died to our great greif our principall refiner Mr Fowler. *Oct.* 12. From Saterday the 11 day at 12 to Sunday att 12 we had all calmes . . . so as we made not above 6 L . . . This Sunday morning died Mr Hwes a very honest and civile gentleman having lyen sick but 6 dayes . . . *Oct.* 13. From sunday noone to munday noone we made not above 12 L. observe we could not for the darck weather, a lamentable 24 houres it was, in which we lost Captayne John Pigott my Lieutenant G: by land; my honest frinde Mr John Talbote one that had lived with mee a leven yeeres in the tower, an excellent generall skoller and a faithfull trew man as lived. We lost also Mr Gardner and Mr Mordant two very faire conditioned gentlemen, and myne owne cooke Francis . . .'

The bad weather continued. 'I observed this day, and so I did before, that the morning rainbow doth not give a faire day as in England.' On the last day of October Ralegh himself fell ill and for a fortnight he did not keep his journal. For twenty days he could eat nothing except 'now and then a stewed prune'; he sweated all the time and had to change his shirt 'thrise every day and thrise every night'. He was still ill when they came to the Guiana coast. He was unable to move, but he sent at once 'to inquire for my old sarvent Leonard the Indien who bine with me in Ingland 3 or 4 yeeres'. Still not able to hold a pen properly, he wrote jealously in his journal of the assistance Leonard had given nine years before in Guiana to Robert Harcourt, who had used Ralegh's name. Leonard didn't appear.

The ship was 'unsavoury, pestered with so many sick men which being unable to move poysoned us with a most filthy stench'. It was like this, with men putrefying from poisoned arrows, that he had last seen the continent. He had himself carried ashore. He sent to find out about his other Indian servant, Harry. Harry sent his brother and two chiefs and they stayed with Ralegh all that night. He wrote to his wife the next day, 'God that gave me a strong heart in all my adversitie, hath also now strengthened it in the hell-fire of heat.' He had lost forty-two men by the sickness. 'To tell you I might be here King of the Indians were a vanitie; but my name hath still lived among them. Here they feed me with fresh meat, and all that the country yields; all offer to obey me.'

But Leonard didn't appear; and Harry, when he came to see Ralegh, 'had almost forgotten his Inglish'. It was the end of the dream of Raleana, his Indian kingdom. He stayed on the Guiana coast for more than a fortnight, but he wrote no more about the Indians. When, in Trinidad, he wrote about them again it was as of an anonymous aboriginal mass. In twenty-two years Guiana and Trinidad had changed. The Indians had been worn out by the alliances, rivalries and pacifications of the Spaniards, English and Dutch. Even as Ralegh was writing to his wife there was a Captain Janson from Flushing off the coast; he had been trading with Guiana for a dozen years.

Ralegh buried his dead: Captain Pigott, who had died five weeks before, and Captain Hastings, who had died ten days before. The ships' guns fired a salute; there were three volleys from the companies on land.

It was better now, after all the years, after the journey out, not to know about El Dorado, Manoa, the mountain of crystal or even the mine. Keymis knew where the mine was. Keymis was to go to look for it, with five ships and four hundred men. Ralegh's son went with Keymis.

Ralegh himself went with the others to Trinidad, to wait. The morning rainbow did not give a fair day. As he came to the southern coast of the island there was a fearful portent: fifteen rainbows in one day, 'and one of the rainebows brought both ends together att the sterne of the shipp making a perfait circkell which I never saw before nor any man in my shipp had seene the like'. He anchored at the south-western tip of the island, where twenty-two years before he had raised Elizabeth's arms, built a fort, addressed the Indians and listened to Berrio's story of the quest.

No Indians came now to his ships, and it was dangerous for Ralegh to go ashore. The Spaniards were few and nervous, but ready. The governor, Diego Palomeque, was in Guiana. But his lieutenant in Trinidad had felled trees to block the land road from Port of Spain to St Joseph. This was the route Ralegh and his Indian allies had taken in 1595; now those allies had been pacified.

For a fortnight, making no entries in his journal, Ralegh stayed where he was. On the last day of the year he 'turned up north towards Conquerabo, otherwise called the port of Spayne'. He anchored at the Pitch Lake and the next day he wrote in his journal. He observed the lake, 'all of ston pitch or bitumen which riseth out of the ground in little springs or fountaynes and so running a little way, it hardneth in the aire, and covereth all the playne; there are also many springs of water and in and among them fresh water fishe'. They ate fish; they also ate 'many of the country fesants . . . exceeding fatt and delicate meat'.

He recorded nothing more for nineteen days. Keymis's Orinoco party had now been away six weeks. Ralegh became irritable. A preacher who was on his ship said he didn't speak much about the mine; when he did 'it was with far less confidence than formerly'. He talked of going away and leaving the Orinoco party. It didn't matter, he said, whether they returned or not, since 'they were good for nothing but to eat victuals, and were sent to sea on purpose that their friends might be rid of them'. He said there was a lot of tobacco in Trinidad. He played with the idea of landing at Port of Spain and marching on St Joseph, as he had done in 1595. But he did nothing.

He sent a ship to Port of Spain to trade for tobacco. The Spaniards waited until the ship's boat was forty paces from the shore; then they opened up with twenty muskets, and shouted abuse as the boat turned back. No one was hurt. But Ralegh talked no more of tobacco-trading or of landing at Port of Spain. He sent a ship back to the south-western end of the island to wait for news from Keymis. A few days after this three men and a boy went ashore at the Pitch Lake. They were 'boyling of the country pitch' when they were fired on. One man was killed, one began to swim out to the ships, one ran to the woods for cover; the boy was captured. The ships raised the alarm, boats were lowered. The Spaniards got away, leaving their canoes, cloaks and other 'implements' behind. The Pitch Lake wasn't safe. Ralegh went back to the south-western end of the island.

On the following day the sentinel ship sighted a piragua coming up from the south with some Spanish soldiers and Indian paddlers. The Spaniards got away, but seven of the Indians were captured. They didn't speak Spanish; by signs they made Ralegh understand that they were from Trinidad, from a village sixteen miles to the east, a day's journey. Ralegh kept three of them aboard and sent twelve of his men with the others 'to see their towne and to trade with them'. They were well on their way when one of Ralegh's men thought he recognized one of the Indians. They had met two years before on the Orinoco, and Ralegh's man remembered that the Indian had then spoken Spanish. He twisted the Indian's arm. The Indian confessed and said that one of the Indians on Ralegh's ship also spoke Spanish. The news was taken back to Ralegh.

The Spanish-speaking Indian on Ralegh's ship declared himself and answered questions. He had heard, he said, from Guiana Indians who had been visiting his village, that there had been some trouble between Englishmen and Spaniards on the Orinoco. The English had taken the town of San Thome. The governor, 'Diego de Palmita', had been killed with two of his captains; the other Spaniards had run away. On the English side two captains had been killed.

If this was true, it was the end. It was the act of piracy for which Ralegh had always known he would have to pay. Unless Keymis had found the mine; unless Keymis could bring back even 'a basket or two' of the ore, just to prove that the story was not an invention. And the two dead English captains: Ralegh did not write in his journal for six days.

The men came back from the Indian village with an Indian who told the same story about San Thome and added 'divers other particularities'. This vagueness was now Ralegh's only magic. He saw a camp-fire on shore; the boat he sent to check found no one. Two days later he sent a skiff up the Orinoco for news; one of the captured Indians went as pilot.

A pinnace from the Isle of Wight came that day to the Gulf of Paria. The meeting refreshed Ralegh. He wrote up his journal. He got the month wrong. It was mid-February; he wrote January. He questioned the two Indians on his ship again and again. Their stories changed. One said he had been in San Thome during the fighting. Ralegh behaved like a distracted man. He sent sixteen musketeers to the Indian village to pick up more Spanish-speaking Indians. The musketeers came back without any Indians; all those they had captured had run away.

Ralegh allowed one of the two Indians to go ashore to trade knives, perhaps for food, with a tribe in the east of the island. The condition was that if he didn't come back within four days the Indian on board would be hanged, as well as that other Indian who had gone as pilot to the Orinoco. The Indian who was to be left behind 'condiscented' to the arrangement.

The four days passed. The Indian who had gone to trade didn't come back. 'I went ashore and tooke the Indien with me well fastned and well bound to one of my men, so carried him with me to shew the trees which yeild balsemum of which I had recouered a nuttfull of that kinde which smells like angolica and is very rare and pretious, and after it was 10 o'clock and very hott, the wood also being full of musketos, I returned and left my Indien in charge with one of my masters mates and three others, but I was no sooner goun but they untyde him and he att the instant tooke the woode and escaped, notwithstanding that I had told them that if the Indien gatt but a tree betweene him and them and were loose that all the Inglish in the fleet could not fetch him agayne. I had now none left but the pilott sent to Orenoke and I feare me that he also will slipp away by the negligence of the mariners who (I meane the common sort) are dilligent in nothing but pillaging and stealing.'

The interest in the rare balsam, the quick physical discomfort, the exasperation with 'the common sort' who had been sent especially to try him: it is as if, almost at the end, accommodating himself to misfortune, preparing at once to act and to withdraw again from the world, he had recovered his spirit.

The next day he came to an arrangement with the captain of the pinnace from the Isle of Wight. The pinnace was to follow him for six months. In the afternoon he sent three gentlemen and sixty men to the Indian village to see whether they could pick up either of the runaways. Later that day a launch from the Orinoco expedition appeared. The launch had among its passengers a dandified Indian in Spanish clothes. He had been liberated from the prison in the Spanish governor's house; he was treated by the English with exaggerated respect. It was the whimsicality of frightened men: they had news.

Everything the Indians had said was true. There had been an attack on San Thome six weeks before and the Spanish governor had been killed. The Indians had got his name reasonably right. It was Diego Palomeque; they had made it Diego de Palmita. They had even got the names of the two Spanish captains who had died with him: 'Erenetta' for Arias Nieto, John Rues for Juan Ruiz Monje. And the 'divers other particularities': Mr Harrington, 'the Countess of Bedford's kinsman', had been wounded, and two English captains had died. One was Captain Cosmo, who had led the 'forlorn hope'. The other was Ralegh's son, Wat.

There was an Indian witness of this moment of news. He was an Arwacan, a Christian, and his name was Francisco; he was either on Ralegh's ship or on the launch that had just arrived. He told his story to a Spanish official, who repeated it at the Spanish inquiry six months later. 'And this Indian told witness that while he was held prisoner on board the ship of the general, whose name was Guatarral, he had seen a launch arrive with news of what had happened, and that the General, on hearing it, began to weep for the death of his son.'

The arrival of the launch was not mentioned in Ralegh's journal. The journal was closed; there were no further entries.

AND NO ONE need have died. If there was a mine, and if the garrisoned settlement of San Thome had to be taken before the mine was discovered and worked, it could have been done without conflict. The Spanish garrison and the Spanish settlers were prepared to surrender without a fight. They wanted to be rid of Palomeque; they wanted to recover the promissory notes and the pledges (including a large collection of silver plate from Doña Andrea Maria de Berrio) that had been extracted from them in lieu of fines and kept under guard in the Royal Chest in Palomeque's house; and in the arrival of Keymis's party they saw a perfect opportunity for an 'accident'. Six days before there had been an attempt to kill Palomeque; it was suggested later by some Spaniards that Palomeque had been killed even before the English came.

The attack occurred after midnight. In the morning Palomeque's body was found stripped naked under a silk-cotton tree in the square. The left side of the head was 'split down to the teeth with a sword slash'; the frank Spanish eye, which might also have been the Indian eye: the Indian women who saw the governor's body said they burst into tears 'for his sake'. But it is uncertain. There was some subsequent rivalry between the Guiana officials and the Trinidad officials, and the Trinidad officials wished to discredit the Guiana officials. What is certain is that the garrison deserted; and that the English night attack was on an abandoned settlement guarded by no more than three men – the governor, perhaps, and the two captains he had brought over a short time before from Trinidad.

Ralegh's son precipitated the action. He left his division of pike and ran ahead, 'where he was unfortunately welcomed with a bullett', as an English witness wrote, 'which gave him no tyme to call for mercye to our hevenly father for the sinful lyfe he had ledde'. After this there was no communication between the English and the Spaniards. The English pillaged and burned. The Spaniards, from the island to which they had retreated, saw that they were outnumbered seven to one; they prepared for a siege.

And then, like every Indian guide to El Dorado, Keymis knew nothing. Nothing about gold, nothing about the mine. He might have been expecting another St Joseph, and the rapture of liberated Indians. He found an almost empty town: a crippled priest, two Negroes who had been turned loose by their owners, an Indian in chains in Palomeque's house, Palomeque's Indian servant, a Portuguese youth, and on the following morning three Indian women. The women were taken to Keymis in the bedroom of Palomeque's house, where he had set up an office of sorts. They found a tall slim man of sixty, with a cast in one eye; he held a baton of polished wood about a yard long. He told them they were not to be frightened; they had only to cook for his men. Later he asked them to identify the dead Spaniards and to bury them. The women said they didn't know how to bury people. So Keymis's men tied the bodies together and put them in the hole the governor had had dug the day before when he was preparing his earth-fortifications. The day after, the English dead were buried. The shrouded bodies were carried shoulder-high on planks; the procession went twice around the square with lowered banners.

The Negroes moved about the settlement freely, but Palomeque's servant had a narrow escape. He said for some reason that he was half-Spanish; and the English soldiers would have hanged him if the Negroes hadn't said that he was lying, that he was a full-blooded Indian from New Granada. The chained Indian in Palomeque's house had got into trouble for openly abusing the Spaniards and saying he was glad the English were coming. The English now treated him with honour. They called him Señor Don Pedro, dressed him in fine Spanish clothes – were they the outsize clothes of the dead governor? – and invited him to eat with them. The Portuguese boy was led through the town and whipped; when it was clear that he couldn't tell them about gold he too was allowed to move about freely.

That was the trouble. There was no gold. Keymis appeared to know no more than the people he led. He went out one night and brought back a little 'ore'. It was found worthless and he talked no more about it. Six days after the capture of San Thome he composed his letter to Ralegh and sent it on a launch with the two Indians from Palomeque's house, a parcel of papers from the treasury, a roll of tobacco, a tortoise, some oranges and lemons. He went exploring up the river and ran into a Spanish and Indian ambush; six of his men were killed. Then he went upstream for more than two hundred miles. Neither he nor Ralegh had been on this stretch of the river, and his ignorance and blankness were now clear.

'Captaine Alley,' wrote Captain Parker to the man Ralegh had sent back to England from the coast, 'your goinge from us was verie fortunate in that you prevented the undergoinge unspeakable miseryes . . . When wee were possessed of the towne Captaine Kemish tooke divers gentlemen with him to fynde the mine, and tryfeled up and downe some 20 dayes keeping us in hope still of findinge it, but at last we found his delayes meere illusiones and him selfe a mear machevill, for he was false to all men . . . I will speke no more of this hatefull fellow to God and man.'

From Keymis there was only silence. His expedition ended in near-starvation. He lost control. The town, already thrown open to Indians hostile to the Spaniards, was sacked and fired. Then it was time to go to meet Ralegh in the Gulf of Paria. His ship flew two white flags.

'He sent the heretic to have his cry answered in hell.' This is how Fray Simón, who published his history just eight years after the event, describes the death of Ralegh's son. And this is the moment of news: 'But their joy was well watered by the weeping that straightaway began in every ship for the death of the general's son.' It was the brutality the defeated had to endure. It was the brutality Ralegh himself had dealt in twenty-two years before, when he wrote of the Spaniards who looked for El Dorado: 'They [the Indians] slewe them and buried them in the country so much sought. They gave them by that means a full and complete possession.' It was the brutality Ralegh could still deal in. But now its object was not the Spaniards but Keymis, his lifelong friend, who in 1603, because of his association with Ralegh, had been shown the rack, Keymis who twenty-one years before had pledged: 'My selfe and the remaine of my fewe yeeres, I have bequeathed wholly to Raleana, and all my thoughts live onely in that action.'

The responsibility, in Ralegh's mind, was all Keymis's. Keymis arrived in the Gulf of Paria three weeks after his letter; and in that time Ralegh's case against Keymis had taken shape, had become hard, something in which Ralegh could pretend he believed, something to which he could add. Incapable of action, as he had been since his release, doubting the value of action, a man withdrawn, prepared for the end, this became all his activity. The mines existed: his faith in this was like vanity, no more.

There was gold. There were mines, two mines, three, seven, eight. That was why the Spaniards had fought. Keymis had been 'obstinate', had refused to follow instructions (he wrote them out later in the Tower, safe again from geography). If Keymis had stayed two days longer he would have been helped by an Indian chief who was Ralegh's old friend. (But Leonard hadn't come, and Harry had forgotten his English.) He threatened to go to the mine himself; but the ships were in poor shape and the men were mutinous. He suggested again that they should land at Port of Spain and march on St Joseph. But he was only talking. Keymis had destroyed them all. And Ralegh's credit with the King had been destroyed, and his fortune wasted, and his son was dead, and his health bad.

He taunted Keymis. He made him act. He wrote three careful

accounts of Keymis's death. 'He then told me that he would waite on me presently, and give me better satisfaction: but I had no sooner come from him into my cabin, but I heard a pistoll go of over my head, and sending up to know who shott it, word was brought that Kemish had shot it out of his cabin window to cleane it; his boy, going into the cabin, found him lying on his bed with much bloude by him, and looking on his face saw he was deade. The pistoll being but little, the bullet did but cracke his ribb; but he, turning him over, found a long knife in his bodie, all but the handle.'

All the accounts Ralegh wrote were gruesome. They were meant to be. Suicide condemned a man; and Ralegh, the sceptic, knew how to exploit theological prejudice. 'He was false to all men and most odious to himselfe,' Captain Parker wrote of Keymis, 'for most ungodly he butchered himselfe lothinge to live since he could doe no mor villany; I will speke no more of this hatefull fellow to God and man.'

As they sailed away from the Gulf of Paria, the expedition breaking up day by day, Ralegh begging people to leave him and then complaining of their desertion, Keymis's 'obstinacy' grew in Ralegh's mind and in the letters he framed. The obstinacy became perverse, inexplicable. Palomeque's servant helped the cause. He was going with Ralegh to England. He would tell people – Ralegh always being his interpreter – that there were gold mines in San Thome. He hadn't told Keymis because Keymis hadn't asked him.

And the story grew. There had been a treacherous Spanish night attack (the Spaniards were outnumbered seven to one). He had been betrayed by the King to the Spaniards from the start. Guiana wasn't Spanish anyway. And he always remembered that he was very ill. His sight was going, his pleurisy had returned, he was in the hands of death. He insisted there was gold in Guiana. He even made up the names of people who owned gold mines: Pedro Rodrigo de Parana (a South American place name); Hermano Fruntino (*hermano*, brother, and Fruntino one of the names he had picked out from the papers Keymis had sent from the San Thome treasury); Francisco Fachardo (Francisco de Vides was the governor of Cumaná who had defeated Ralegh in 1595, Fajardo was the Spaniard with whom Ralegh had dined in Cumaná and talked about the men whose heads grew below their shoulders).

Ralegh never forgot Palomeque's servant, the only guide now to El Dorado. 'To tell you I might be here King of the Indians were a vanitie.' This Indian, who stayed in the Tower with Ralegh until the end, was all that remained of the dream of carousing Indian kings and their beautiful women. Ralegh hoped that the Indian might find service with some English nobleman.

And Ralegh never forgot Keymis. On the day of his execution he condemned him, speaking from the notes he had made. 'But he that knew the head of the myne would not discover it, when he saw that my son was slain, but made himself away.'

It was the end of the quest. It had begun as a dream as large as the New World itself; it had ended in this search for a mine no one had seen, in an action of amateurs, in which all the great ones, and few of the lesser, perished.

For more than three months the body of Diego Palomeque rotted in the shallow hole where he had been dumped by Keymis's men. When the time came for him to be buried he could be recognized only by his height. When the King of Spain heard of Palomeque's death he wrote to Trinidad: 'I am sorry to have lost so loyal a servant. It is my intention to honour his memory and show favour to his heirs. Let me know whether the governor left any debt or obligation in your country, so that I may order it to be discharged in a manner that is fit. I the King. San Lorenzo el Real, September 18 1618.'

Seven weeks later Ralegh was executed in London. The execution was witnessed by Diego Palomeque's servant. He later went to Madrid, and from there he made his way back to the Indies, where he told Fray Simón, the historian, his story.

The mystery of the final adventure lies in Ralegh's book about his first Guiana journey, *The Discovery of the Large, Rich and Beautiful Empire of Guiana*. This is a book about the discovery of Arcadia; it suggests mines and gold, spaciousness, enamelled forests, a world in which the senses, needs, life itself, can be extended. The book is part of the world's romance. But its details are precise and true. It catches part of the New World at that moment between the unseeing brutality of the discovery and conquest and the later brutality of colonization. It was the swiftly passing moment when romance could be apprehended. But the book was written by a man with much to hide, a courtier whose gifts never extended to the action the code of his court required; and in the details of action it is, fatally, imprecise.

Ralegh's account of Arcadia and victory is really the story of a defeat and of a nervous six-day journey of exploration. No one had seen a mine: that was part of the imprecision. These men, Keymis and Ralegh, saw themselves as actors in great events, classical figures, even as Vera saw Antonio Berrio and himself. And the quest was heroic. But their world was as small as the classical world, and the world was changing by their own efforts. The Indians had changed. They had been dulled by defeat and disappointments, and there is no trace in their stupefied descendants today of that intelligence and quickness which attracted Ralegh and made them such feared enemies, masters of the waters.

The ships from Europe came and went. The plantations grew. The brazil-wood, felled by slaves in the New World, was rasped by criminals in the rasp-houses of Amsterdam. The New World as medieval adventure had ended; it had become a cynical extension of the developing old world, its commercial underside. No one would look at Trinidad and Guiana again with the eye of Ralegh or Robert Dudley or Captain Wyatt.

As ONCE BEFORE after disaster, Fernando Berrio turned up to claim his province. His claim was legitimate and his attitude one of weariness. He more or less said that as soon as he turned his back everything was bound to go wrong. But officials in other territories weren't so happy. The powerful Audiencia of New Granada said they intended to be firm this time; they wanted no protests, delays and prevarications (*réplica, causas y escusas*).

The insult was too great; Fernando wrote to the King. This wasn't the sort of treatment he expected, he said, after thirty years of continuous service (he was under forty). He received an indulgent, almost fatherly, reply. 'You know the heavy expenses that have been incurred. The Treasury is short and cannot meet all the demands made on it. So you must try to do what you can, as you have done in the past.'

It was some time before Fernando was missed. On 30 June 1622 the Audiencia of New Granada reported angrily to Spain that Fernando was not at his post. But Spain had heard three weeks before. Fernando, on his way to Spain from Trinidad without anybody's permission, had been captured by Moorish pirates in the Mediterranean; and Fernando, lifelong dealer in slaves, had found himself taken, at the age of forty-four, to the busy slave-market in Algiers. His travelling companion, his twelve-year-old nephew, was also up for auction; and the Bey of Algiers was dropping hints to Spaniards going back to Spain after being ransomed that he thought he might do better if he sold the boy, who was a good piece, in the Turkish market. What the Bey felt he could do, for the sake of people in Spain, was to place a 'second ransom' of 4,000 pesos on the boy. Word got back to the King; he paid the double ransom. Fernando died before he could be ransomed.

Three years after he died there was a brief, appalled letter from Trinidad about a further peculation of Fernando's that had just come to light. And a year after that a new governor reported that he had found three hundred and fifty quintals of tobacco among Fernando Berrio's possessions. He asked Madrid for instructions, saying at the same time that the tobacco was beginning to go bad and he had 'lent' it to local citizens of substance. The reply came two years later: the tobacco was to be sold and the proceeds sent to Madrid by the galleons from Cartagena. The governor had another idea: why not pay the soldiers with the proceeds? Very well, was the reply, in the fifth year of this correspondence, pay the soldiers; but send the rest.

The name of Berrio lived on in Fernando's nephew, ransomed from Algiers: Martín de Mendoza, to which he sometimes added de la Hoz, sometimes Berrio, and sometimes de la Hoz y Quesada. A hundred years later, in the derelict city of St Joseph, once the base for El Dorado, there is a record of a Martín de Mendoza. He was almost certainly a descendant. So the great names of the conquistadores disappeared in the lands of the conquest or the pretended conquests. It may not have been local romance alone that, at the end of the eighteenth century, made people on the mainland point out a ragged shepherd boy to the traveller Humboldt as a descendant of the conquistador Gonzales Ximenes de Quesada, who had won for Spain the wealth of the Chibchas, had founded the Kingdom of New Granada and had bequeathed to the husband of his niece the quest for El Dorado and the dream of the New World's third marquisate.

PART TWO

The Spanish Capitulation

3. The Ghost Province

1633–1776

IT SENT LITTLE TO SPAIN; it received little from Spain. After 1633 no Spanish trading ship called for twenty years. But it remained a province of the Empire: the great river which Columbus thought flowed down from the Garden of Eden, the drowned lands of its estuary, the Gulf, the island. And for some time the name survived, 'these provinces of El Dorado', the capital still Antonio Berrio's city, 'this humble city of St Joseph de Oruña', as one petition said: some straw huts, a church nearly always in disrepair, often without wine for mass or oil for lamps.

The development of Virginia and the Carolinas killed the Trinidad tobacco trade. But Guiana continued to torment the Spaniards. Quicksilver, of which the Spaniards already had enough, was discovered, and the foreigners continued to come. Until the French and English combined to destroy them, the foreigners were mainly Dutch; and they always threatened to settle. The Dutch married Carib women and at one time had alliances with seven Indian chiefs in Trinidad. They sacked St Joseph twice. The second time they took away the city's few Negroes, fifteen pieces, and all the Spaniards' clothes. The Spaniards hid in their huts until clothes were sent to them from Margarita to 'cover themselves and go and hear God's word' in the burnt-out church.

The province was a liability. But it was not like those Caribbean islands which the Spaniards were willing to dispeople and leave to the foreigner. This strategic province on the Orinoco the Spaniards feared to lose; its weakness made officials nervous. Raids, complaints of neglect, peculation and contraband, threats of another lost province, requests for ships, men, money: in the end the King lost his temper. The Contractation House, which handled the Spanish Indies trade, had prepared a memorandum about Trinidad. 'You write about money,' the King replied, 'as though I had taken yours or some other person's, or as though, if I had not taken it, much of Milan, Flanders and all Burgundy would not have been lost.'

In this area it was no longer open to the individual Spaniard to act. Resolution and enterprise, one governor of Margarita said, were more important than numbers. He ruined his career. With a scratch force of less than eighty men from Margarita and Trinidad he surprised the Dutch and French settlements in Trinidad and Tobago, one after the other, and took a hundred prisoners. Thirty-six were Negroes and valuable booty; but the others were a problem, if only because they were almost as numerous as the Spanish troops, many of whom were Negroes, mulattoes and mestizos, 'people who run after toys, are facile liars and of little constancy'. The governor had the prisoners, all except nineteen boys, strangled on the Margarita beach early one morning and buried.

Then he was frightened. He ordered his people not to talk; the nineteen Dutch boys were to be hidden in private houses and instructed in the Catholic faith. 'I command you,' the King wrote, when he heard, 'upon finishing your accounts of office, to come to this my court for special matters of my service. Do so and I shall consider you serve me well.' In time the governor went to Spain. He was expecting a grant of unallotted Indians or the habit of a knightly order; he found that both he and his son were to be punished and degraded. The King was also afraid. Enterprise and resolution in any area of weakness added to the black legend of the days of power; they invited reprisal.

The Caribbean was no longer a Spanish sea; and now, more than before, every Spaniard was on his own. A Spanish official who went out to report on the defences of Trinidad didn't get to the island. He was chased among the Leeward Islands by a French pirate, captured and taken to Dieppe, where he was abandoned. He wrote to the Spanish ambassador for help: he said he was sure his wife and children were starving in Spain. He got no reply.

'I am sick, in bed,' the governor of Trinidad, Diego de Escobar, wrote. 'I am surrounded by the enemy and hostile natives. I have asked four times for help, but no governor here wishes to help me. I don't believe anybody in the world has ever had to put up with such hard luck or such labours.' He hadn't been paid; his soldiers, all ten of them, were barefooted; they needed sandals (*alpargatas*) and shields against Indian arrows. It was one of many letters.

'Tell them in Santa Fé that the church is more a doorway than a church. Tell them we have nothing to celebrate mass with and that the friars are as a result disconsolate. Tell them our bodies show through our rags; that the dead are buried without shrouds; that at night we don't have a lamp between us; that we daren't stir outside the city. Tell them that the whole thing is now like a joke, that the Dutch are telling the Indians that we are dead, that no one is ever coming to help us.'

'The people want to go away. I haven't been paid my salary. The enemy have robbed me four times since I have been here. I walk about barefooted and virtually naked. The whole thing is incredible.'

He succeeded in frightening the authorities at Santa Fé in New Granada. They sent him clothes, soldiers and supplies. Many months later some of the soldiers returned penniless and wretched to Santa Fé. Diego de Escobar had met them in Guiana. He had taken the supplies and told the soldiers to wait while he went to Trinidad. They didn't see him for five months; and then he came back with Dutch goods which he offered to sell to the soldiers. He had spent the five months in Trinidad trading the relief supplies.

In 1641 Madrid ordered an investigation and six years later sent a reminder. 'No report has been received. You have surely had enough time.' The issue vanished, like many others. The man ordered to report was Fernando Berrio's nephew, who had been ransomed from Algiers. He was like his uncle. He never complained. He ruled Trinidad for ten years and at the end asked for an extension. Once he threatened to resign if he didn't get some help from Spain. His resignation was accepted; but somehow he never heard, and Madrid forgot. It was the ghost province, remoter than it had been a century before. 'To Don Juan Muñoz,' a letter from the King began some years later, 'who it seems is, or has been, our governor . . .'

The time came when no one wanted to be governor. The Council of the Indies put up the names of three men to the King and outlined the qualifications of each. 'I name Don Lorenzo de Cienfuegos,' the King's secretary wrote, and the King affixed his rubric. 'Sir,' the Council of the Indies wrote back, 'Don Lorenzo de Cienfuegos has been informed of the favour of the governorship of Trinidad and Guiana which it has pleased Your Majesty to bestow on him, and he has excused himself.' Eight months later the Council tried again. 'Sir,' the Council reported, abridging the form, 'Don Francisco de Santillan has been informed of the favour Your Majesty has shown him, and he has excused himself.'

THERE WAS a new danger: the buccaneers, French and English, human debris of the Caribbean, clad in skins and caked in dirt and animal blood. Their unpoliced grounds were on the island of Hispaniola, which the Spaniards had dispeopled. The cattle and pigs they hunted were feral descendants of the domestic breeds the Spaniards had left behind; and the hunters themselves had grown as wild. Now they found leaders and patrons and became gangsters of the sea.

Five shiploads of French buccaneers came to Port of Spain in 1684 to look for the gold of El Dorado; they had heard the stories from the Indians in the north. The governor hurried over to Guiana. His Spanish soldiers locked him up in the chapel of San

Thome, threw their guns in the Orinoco and ran off into the bush. The governor and some of his officials were captured by the raiders. Three Spaniards were tortured; one died. The governor was set down later, starving and full of sores, on the Trinidad coast. The raiders took away the governor's silver inkhorns and all the Negroes. 'Oh, the most malignant influence of that city of Guiana,' the governor wrote, 'destroyed and sacked so often, a ten-hut place, its reputation its misfortune, and its citizens hardly with a shirt on their backs.'

Sixty years before, Fernando Berrio's successor had complained about his escribano or legal clerk. 'The man scarcely knows how to write, which is no small handicap if Your Majesty's service is to be performed in a manner that is fitting, especially as I myself am so little lettered.' Now Margarita was short of paper; and in Trinidad, since the loss of the governor's inkhorns, there was a shortage of ink. In the province of El Dorado the very paperwork of Empire was about to go.

The islands to the north fell to France and England and became valuable. The slave sugar plantations altered the landscape and the population forever (the French and English, both claiming the island of St Kitts, united to exterminate the Caribs in one swift action). North America was being peopled. But Trinidad had dropped out of history. Nobody came to raid or to trade. The Spaniards lived like shipwrecked people, close to nature, concerned only with survival.

THE SPANIARDS ENDURED. It was the Indians who faded. After the small triumphs of the raids, and after the allies, English, Dutch or French, had gone away, there were the Spanish pacifications. 'I returned by sea, sending Captain Agustín de Santiago with his company by the land way, to punish all the Indians he met and burn their crops; which he did.' It is the report of an early pacification. There were also new diseases; and the Indian population, which Domingo de Vera had put at 40,000 a century before, had dropped to 4,000.

On the mainland and in the Gulf of Paria the Indians were still dangerous and the Caribs still went on their annual manhunts, 'proud, brave, warlike', one Spanish official said, admiringly now, 'and arbiters of peace and war'. But in Trinidad the Arwacas Indians declined from Spanish allies into Spanish servants, and became so amenable that it was proposed to evangelize them.

The Capuchins were keen. Less than a year after the royal decree had been issued for the establishment of a mission in Trinidad and Guiana, the first missionaries came out to St Joseph. The prefect looked around the Indian villages and reported on the 'happy beginnings, the great harvest he expected, and the multitude of souls that had to be saved with the help of our Lord'. A trip across the Gulf to Guiana was less happy. There were twelve missionaries; they met a hundred and fifty Caribs in seven canoes. 'God was served that they should retire after we had fought with them for seven hours. Of those with me only one died; four were wounded.'

The missionaries had come out in a hurry. They didn't have all they needed. They needed a bell, to call the Indians to prayers, censers, chandeliers, vessels for the holy oils and wine, wine itself, oil, flour, wax. They needed paper; they needed almost everything. 'Many conversions of the heathen begin in the finery, ornaments and rites of the Church. I do not have to paint a picture for your Reverence of the conditions of the Indians, a materialist people who respond to what they see. And, as the Apostle says, through what they see they come even to knowledge of the God they cannot see.'

Two years later the missionaries still didn't have the things they had asked for; letters were still being exchanged with Spain. But the missionaries had been working. They had had three hundred Indian slaves freed and had ruled that no Indian was to be called a 'piece': that was the word for a slave. They had built a settlement called Santa Cruz for some of the freed Indians and had settled others in Port of Spain, which at that time had only ten Spaniards. They had set up country missions. These were self-supporting work colonies. The Indians who went in were to be baptized and taught the habit of working for wages, first to buy clothes and later to pay a small tribute to the Crown; they were to be kept apart from non-baptized Indians and Negroes.

The Spanish settlers complained. They said they were being denied the use of the Indians' labour and the Indians in the missions were being pampered and kept in idleness. There was some trouble between the governor and the missionaries. The Indians themselves were not always co-operative, and the missionaries became disheartened. They began to feel that the Indians were wild people who preferred to live in the bush rather than in towns. It was like a final judgement. For the Spaniards civilized life was town life; two centuries before, Columbus had condemned the Indians of central Haiti as bush-dwellers after he had exterminated them.

The Indians in the missions became more restive. In the last year of the 17th century their temper snapped. It was the last Indian rebellion, the last sign of Indian life. It gave Trinidad its first Christian martyrs and its first miracle.

A new church was being built at one of the missions and two Indian labourers were working one morning under the supervision of a monk and a Spanish carpenter. The Indians were clumsy. It seemed to the monk – this is the official Capuchin story – that their clumsiness was deliberate. He rebuked them and said he would tell the governor, who was due that afternoon on a visit. One Indian lifted his spade and knocked the monk to the ground. The other Indian knifed the Spanish carpenter. They both then gave their ancient war-cry and all the baptized Indians came running out of their huts.

The wounded monk dragged himself to the old church and knelt before the image of the Virgin. The Indians transfixed him with arrows; he prayed for them until he died. In a secluded part of the mission grounds another monk was reading his hours: it was a suitable way to die. A third monk was in the kitchen, preparing the monks' midday meal; he took his crucifix, knelt and waited. The four bodies were buried in the foundations of the new church. The old church was desecrated, the mission burnt and an ambush laid for the governor and his party. The governor, the sargento mayor, the treasurer, the escribano and others were killed. They died slowly; the Indians had used poisoned arrows.

In the official Capuchin history the monks died forgiving their Indian charges. But the sixty Spaniards in St Joseph soon found themselves under Indian attack and were full of hate. Guiana couldn't send help immediately; the local captain had gone off twenty months before to New Granada to get help to meet a crisis that had since passed. It was two months before some Spanish infantry captains and Christian Indians came. The rebellious Indians were driven back to the sea. The final battle took place on Trinidad's Atlantic coast, near the point which Columbus, about to make landfall on his third voyage in 1498, had sighted in the late afternoon. His eyes were bad, he hadn't been sleeping well; and the cape, as he felt his way towards it in the moonlight, reminded him of a galley under sail. He called the cape Galera, and the name remained.

Near this point now many of the Indians, men, women and children, drowned themselves in the ocean and the lagoon. But many more were captured. Their offences were too great for hot-blooded execution on the wide beach. They were taken to St Joseph, tortured and tried. Sixty-one were sentenced to death. Some were shot. Twenty-two were dragged through the city, the crier proclaiming their crimes, before they were hanged. Their heads and hands were cut off, their bodies quartered and the pieces spiked on the public road.

A year later an official party went to the site of the mission. When the bodies of the monks were dug out from the foundations of the new church they were found to be still whole; fresh blood ran out of the wounds. The bodies were taken to St Joseph and remained whole for the nine days they lay in state in the church. Someone wrote a poem about the event, 'A Very Sad Story', *Romance muy doloroso.* It was the only piece of literature the Spaniards produced in Trinidad; it was quickly forgotten; people who heard it just remembered that it wasn't much good.

There is a report thirty years later of some Arwacas of the Nepoios tribe helping the Spaniards during a Carib raid. But after the battle on the beach at Punta Galera the Indians ceased to be important. They were pacified and gathered back into the missions and they worked to pay their taxes. The Spanish settlers pressed for the use of their labour; the missions lost their autonomy and came under government control. For a hundred years the Indian population held steady at about 2,000; then in the nineteenth century the Indians all but disappeared.

It was an Indian who in 1885 guided a Dominican missionary to the overgrown site of the massacre and the miracle. The Dominican reported it as an Indian tradition that on Holy Thursday and Good Friday singing could be heard in the bush and Spanish voices raised in prayer: after four hundred years the Indians still told the visitor what they thought he wanted to hear. Orchids grew on the site. The Dominican took some to Port of Spain and planted them near his cell in memory of the martyrs.

THE SUGAR ISLANDS to the north became more valuable; the island of Guadeloupe, six hundred and twenty square miles, was traded for Canada. France and England fought over the islands. They were battles without heroes, over pieces of real estate, fought out by mercenaries from outside, the estates themselves helpless with their swollen Negro population, subject to famine (few food crops were grown) and vulnerable to servile revolt. Trinidad was not valuable; it was safe. There were no internal troubles. The Spanish population rose to a hundred and then a hundred and fifty.

A little cacao was grown and exported to Spain. The affairs of the province were small and domestic.

The carpenter presented his bill to the governor; the governor authorized the treasurer to pay; the treasurer said there was no money; the governor ordered the money to be borrowed; the money was borrowed, the carpenter paid, the loan repaid. The documents, twelve pages in all, everything sworn to and signed, were sent to Madrid. Guiana, still tormented by its reputation, asked once more for help. The St Joseph cabildo or council met and decided it could do nothing. A man was sent off the island: Madrid was informed. The governor inspected the arms and munitions of Port of Spain and St Joseph and found fifty pounds of powder, 'in this time of lively wars'. He climbed a mountain near Port of Spain and suffered in the heat. (He was the first Spaniard to speak of the heat of Trinidad; the year was 1711.) But he didn't mind because he had 'an insatiable desire to serve Your Majesty'. He established a school for grammar and theology 'to dispel the darkness'.

It was Spanish irony and self-satire; it could become perverse. Some missionaries left the island without permission. The governor seized two monks, who were visiting; feverish though he was, he took them off on horseback to Port of Spain and from there had them sent by night in a canoe to the priestless mission. By this action he thought he had saved many souls. 'I haven't been paid, but I would willingly have done more for Your Majesty if I had greater strength. But I am weak and feeble, having wasted the flower of my youth in this hot and humid place, exposed to the inclemencies of the weather and nearly always, sir, in need, because there is a lack of everything in these parts. Many times I have been obliged to eat grass, as though I was in the desert. All this is public and notorious and common knowledge and public property.'

The cacao trees were blighted and the revenue of the province dropped to 231 dollars. A governor went looking for El Dorado and was away for fourteen months. Then there was an administrative shake-up in the Spanish Empire and Antonio Berrio's ghost province of El Dorado at last disappeared. Trinidad was separated from Guiana and both territories incorporated into the Captaincy-General of Caracas. Caracas was growing; it was soon to have a university. Berrio's city – its many names reflecting its insubstantiality: St Joseph de Oruña, St Joseph of Trinidad and sometimes even Trinidad of Guiana – no longer sent dispatches direct to Madrid.

In the year in which the province of El Dorado disappeared there was washed up on the Atlantic coast of Trinidad a small dismasted ship from the Canary Islands, the starving crew stupefied by wine, their original cargo from Teneriffe, which had been their only nourishment for some weeks. And two years later, the parody of the discovery and conquest appearing to continue, three more missionary martyrs were brought to St Joseph for burial from the Orinoco.

Men like these were the new adventurers of the Spanish Empire. Their martyrdoms were celebrated in Spanish engravings as imaginative and full of blood as those in which two hundred years before the rest of Europe had condemned the cruelties of the conquistadores. Ecclesiastical histories like Fray Antonio Caulin's completed the Spanish heroic cycle: Spanish blood now for Indian, the heroism of martyrdom for the heroism of conquest.

THE ISLAND recovered after the cacao blight. The population rose to a hundred and sixty-two and the revenue to 1,218 dollars. Then there was a smallpox epidemic. Even the monkeys died. The morale of the settlers broke. For a century and more they had lived close to nature. Now, ignoring the Spanish code, they left their huts in St Joseph and lived, like the Indians before them, in the bush.

They wanted to be left alone. In 1745 they chained up the governor, who had 'used them violently', in the casa real in Port of Spain. It was eight months before soldiers came from Venezuela to release him. The alcaldes or magistrates of the St Joseph cabildo were imprisoned and some of the settlers banished to Havana. The new governor ordered the cabildo to thatch the church; the cabildo said they had no money; nothing was done. After five years the Havana exiles returned. There had been a petition on their behalf. The whole community, it was said, was suffering from the absence of its elite; there was no one to catch fish.

When a new governor came to St Joseph in 1757 he found the streets full of holes and ditches and overgrown with 'woods and thickets'. Many huts were derelict, and the thatch and mud of others so perished that the building plots looked vacant. A meeting hall for the cabildo had been left unfinished. The citizens lived in the bush; the few Negroes they had had become their companions. The governor could find no house for himself in St Joseph and he stayed in Port of Spain. He wrote to the people of St Joseph. He asked them to clean up the streets, complete the meeting hall, build a chest for the records and get 'a decent book, properly bound', for the minutes of the cabildo.

They replied that they couldn't do as the governor asked. They were few and very poor; they lived on what they could scratch in the woods and net from the sea and many days they got nothing. If the governor compelled them to do what he asked they would leave the island, as many had done. It would take them more than a year to clear the streets and fill the holes, if they had tools. They didn't have tools and couldn't afford to buy any; and there were no tools on the island anyway.

'Notwithstanding all these difficulties, orders will be given to Pedro Bontur, the only carpenter in the island, to make the chest for the records and to accept payment in provisions as and when they can be collected from the inhabitants, who will be required to make a contribution for that purpose. But His Excellency the Governor must provide the boards, the cabildo knowing no one on the island who can make them; and when opportunity offers His Excellency must get the locks and hinges for the same from the Main, nothing of the kind being available here. Orders will be given for the papers of the cabildo to be properly arranged; and a book will be made when paper is available, the members of the cabildo not having a single sheet between them at the moment.'

It was a comprehensive reply. The governor didn't press. He stayed in Port of Spain until his term was over; and that fishing village, never founded, without a council, became the place where governors of Trinidad stayed. The Spaniards there extracted oil from turtles, distilled rum from sugarcane syrup and – the sweet touch of the Spanish Main – bred and sold singing birds.

The citizens of St Joseph, now an ancient New World foundation – the founder's name forgotten: some thought it was Barrero, others said it was Josef de Oruña – continued to live with their Negroes in drunken isolation. They tried to prevent a doctor leaving them; he gave them medicines free and they didn't think they would find another like him. They quarrelled with the priests and had the church closed for a while. They intrigued without art or perseverance against a governor whom they thought too ambitious. They passed resolutions about building a school, regulating weights and measures, calling their fellows out of the bush, building that chest for the records; and did nothing. They plotted against another governor and lost; they took their revenge by scattering and hiding the records. A new doctor came; he died. He was succeeded by a Frenchman who presented some certificates in French, which the cabildo couldn't read; they noted in their records that the new man at least looked like a doctor.

A new governor came. The St Joseph cabildo didn't attend the Sovereign's birthday ceremony in Port of Spain. The governor took the slight seriously. The cabildo was cowed. They said they didn't know they had to attend; besides, it was raining that day and they didn't have horses. In their minutes, though, they protested. It was the duty of the governor, they wrote, to come to the *capital* for the Sovereign's birthday, when 'the royal banner is unfurled to the sound of cannon and muskets'.

Exempt from history, they might have gone on scratching for food, and the eighteenth century would have leaked away. But, abruptly, Spain thought of taking Trinidad in hand; and the Spanish Arcadia was over. Elsewhere in the Empire there had been reorganization and development. Venezuela had once been as poor as Trinidad. After Ralegh's raid on St Joseph the first Simón de Bolívar had begged to be transferred. 'For Venezuela anyone would do,' he had written, 'even if he has little ability.' Now the Bolívar family – with a dash of jungle Indian and a tincture of Negro – was very grand. Caracas had a university and a theatre. Venezuela, if not yet a country, had its own social codes. It was because of the independent life of its provinces that the Empire had endured. Soon the Empire was to be threatened by this life. It was the absurdity of what, in the end, had amounted to imperial success.

So now with Trinidad. It was seen once again to be strategic. It could guard provinces as tempting now as El Dorado had been, not against raiders and pirates, but against the movements of fleets and armies. It was to be populated and fortified; it was to be another arsenal of the Empire, a second Cartagena; it was to be a centre of South American trade. But to be all this Trinidad would have to cease to be Spanish. Spain didn't have the men. She would have to get foreign immigrants. The immigrants would be Roman Catholic; that was a guarantee of a sort.

Such settlers, some Irish but many more French, were at hand, in the slave islands to the north. The French in the Caribbean were used to conquest and foreign, usually English, rule. Some, bankrupt or with their lands, plant and Negroes irredeemably mortgaged, welcomed it. To be conquered was to have French debts wiped out; it was also to have the chance of running up new ones with the English merchants who fell on each captured island, anxious to trade and lend. Trinidad, under a welcoming Spanish government, already on the defensive, offered especial sanctuary.

The Spaniards, self-critical, aware now of lost opportunities, were willing to copy. They hoped, in addition to everything else, to turn this part of the old province of El Dorado into a West Indian slave island, as profitable as those to the north. But it was not the time for imperial resolution in the New World. The royal decree for colonization went out from Madrid to the governor of 'my island of Trinidad to windward' in 1776.

4. The Three Revolutions

1776–1797

NO QUESTIONS would be asked in Trinidad about debts, mortgaged Negroes or other liabilities; and there were about four hundred French families from various islands willing to come. They said that between them they could bring over 33,000 Negroes. This was an exaggeration, but the French were bargaining. They wanted the sanctuary and the grants of land. But they wanted no cramping Spanish trade laws, no taxes; and they wanted to keep those links with France – priests, bequests, travel – that were not awkward. They also wanted laws to ensure property in Negroes; as the law stood there was no means of getting a runaway Negro back from Venezuela.

They said they had been thinking of taking their Negroes to the United States. 'The new American constitution,' the French representative said, 'must enchant the mind of every citizen by its fanatical attachment to liberty.' New England, it was true, was cold and Trinidad warm. But in Georgia, Carolina and Florida the West Indian planter could grow crops his Negroes were used to. Spain would lose by 'this addition to the power of a new government which perhaps before long' – the representative was writing in 1777 – 'will play an interesting role in the balance of power in the two continents, even if the Americans are compelled to be for a few more years under the domination of Great Britain'. Spain, the French representative said, needed to develop her Caribbean islands. But she couldn't do it with Spaniards; they were too indolent. It was the sort of thing foreigners could say to Spaniards now; it was what some Spaniards said themselves.

Perhaps too much was asked. Perhaps there was some question in Spain whether fortresses could protect the great South American continent. Some people felt that the best protection would be an unpopulated coastal strip; others talked about a 'flying camp', *campo volante*. Nothing was done about Trinidad for some time. When the Versailles Treaty was being negotiated the British dropped a hint that they wouldn't mind exchanging Gibraltar for Trinidad. The Spaniards became agitated; none of them knew where Trinidad was. The Spanish ambassador in Paris told them that if they gave away Trinidad they would be giving away South America. Soon afterwards Madrid acted. Everything the prospective French immigrants had asked for was granted.

The emphasis was on land and Negroes. Every immigrant, who had to be Roman Catholic, was to get a personal grant of thirty-two acres and sixteen acres for every Negro he brought in. A free Negro or mulatto would get sixteen acres for himself and sixteen acres for every one of his own Negroes. Immigrants would pay no taxes on their Negroes for ten years, and they could import Negroes duty-free for ten years. If the money was used to buy Negroes, goods could be taken out of the island and sold subject only to a five per cent tax. A Negro Code would be promulgated; in the meantime every immigrant would be required to have sufficient arms to contain his Negroes.

A naval officer, a Spaniard of the new type, was sent out as governor. He was José Maria Chacon, a Knight of the Order of Calatrava; as a captain in the Spanish Royal Navy he had distinguished himself at Mobile during the War of American Independence. His associate in Trinidad was an army engineer of high rank. Mexico was to provide much of the money for development.

GOVERNOR CHACON had some trouble with the Spaniards of Port of Spain and St Joseph. They didn't like being disturbed. They had been used to foraging in the forests and they saw that their ancestral grounds would shrink with the arrival of immigrants. They claimed the whole island; sometimes they sold 'their pretended properties' to immigrants. If what they said was true, Chacon reported, there was 'hardly a spot remaining that can be granted to new colonists'.

He abused them like a foreigner, for being Spanish, poor, indolent and crooked. He rejected all their claims by a decree; and, to isolate them in St Joseph, he ordered the cabildo to meet in Port of Spain. Fish became scarce inland; fish brought in from Port of Spain was too expensive. The Spaniards of St Joseph came out of the bush at last, defeated. They were a minority now. Seven of the ten members of the cabildo that met in Port of Spain were French, and one was Irish.

There was also some trouble about Negroes. Some immigrants, using trusted Negroes and mulattoes as decoys, had been stealing Negroes from other islands in order to claim more land in Trinidad. The contract for 'new' Negroes, from Africa, had been placed by the government with a Liverpool firm, Baker and Dawson. But they were sending their best pieces to Havana. The immigrants complained; and two Irishmen, Barry and Black, set up as Negro-shippers. They didn't deal in new Negroes. Their Negroes were from the other Caribbean islands and not always legitimately obtained. Some were at the end of their useful life; there were ways of disguising age and disease. Out of one parcel of forty Barry and Black Negroes, at just under 300 dollars each, thirty-four died three days after being landed.

Madrid intervened. This and other matters were regulated. The slave colony was already getting its tone, of bustle and acuteness; men like Black were its pioneers and aristocrats in one generation and in one character. Madrid offered a million-dollar loan for agricultural improvement and sent out subsidized tools. Fresh tax-exemptions were granted to immigrants. The urban area was defined, the rest of the island divided into administrative quarters.

Port of Spain was laid out on the grid plan. English fire-engines were imported, weights and measures regulated, prices fixed for bread and meat, lepers cleared out. And the Negro Code that had been promised was issued.

NEGROES WERE to be given Catholic instruction and baptized within a year of their arrival. They had to be fed and clothed adequately. Every Negro had to have a bed of his own and there were to be no more than two to a room. It was to be understood that the chief occupation of Negroes was agriculture 'and not those labours that call for a sedentary life'. Every Negro was to be allowed two hours a day to work on his own plot, and he was to be paid two dollars a year. No one under seventeen or over sixty was to work. No one was to work on holidays. Negroes who were old or chronically sick were not to be turned out; they had to be looked after by their owners.

Negroes were to be guarded against all moral dangers. Women were not to do work unsuited to their sex or work which kept them for any length of time in the company of men. After mass on holy days Negroes were to 'divert themselves innocently' in the presence of their owners or their owners' stewards. They were not to be allowed to drink too much; men were not to mix too freely with women; and Negroes from one plantation were not to mix with Negroes from another plantation. Negro diversions were to end before prayers. Marriage was to be encouraged. The owner of the husband was to have the option of buying the wife at a fair valuation, or he was to sell the husband to the owner of the wife.

Punishments were restricted to prison, chains and the whip. A Negro could be whipped only by his owner or the owner's steward; not more than twenty-five lashes were to be given for any offence and there was to be 'no contusion or effusion of blood'. A Negro who was punished more severely could be confiscated. An owner who broke any article of the code could be fined from 50 to 200 dollars.

It was a good code. It was issued from the Royal Palace at Aranjuez in Spain; but it had been written by a Trinidad French planter who – like Governor Chacon, already – had a mulatto family. At this time in the French islands racial laws were adding humiliation to severity. On the British island of St Vincent the planter-assembly twenty years before had passed 'An Act for Making Slaves Real Property'; one clause laid down that any Negro who struck a white person should 'have his nose slit, or any member cut off'.

Was the Trinidad code followed? The evidence is that in Port of Spain in 1790, before the great French rush, the Spanish practice was milder than the code.

In August 1790 a nineteen-year-old Negro called Francisco stabbed a Dutch-speaking Negro to death early one morning during a wake in a Port of Spain yard. The legal process that followed has been preserved; it gives some idea of Port of Spain Negro life.

A free Negro woman had died, and the wake at her house turned into an all-night Negro party. There was no curfew; but when a Negro went out at night he carried a lighted candle, and this might have been the law, as it was in Port of Spain at a later date. Many Negroes lived in the houses of their owners and moved in and out as they pleased. Many, like Francisco, who was a sailor, had outside jobs; and their owners didn't always know where they were. Sally, Paly and Belchy were at the wake, and the woman known as Pata de Jamón, Pig-foot. Ham was there, and Stan, Scipio, Sui and Samson. Some of them spoke Dutch, some Spanish, some French.

They were all under thirty. Caribbean Negroes began to live long only when the slave trade was abolished. Francisco was nineteen or twenty-three; he wasn't sure. The woman he was going to marry, a slave too, was older. Francisco felt she had trapped him, and he wasn't in a good mood when, after midnight, he stood outside the house where she lived and called her out to go to the wake. At the wake Francisco picked a quarrel with a Dutch Negro who was chanting the rosary. Francisco said the Dutch Negro was ignorant and didn't know what he was chanting. The quarrel ended in a stabbing.

The Negroes at the wake were not all of good character. It was said later of Sally, a prosecution witness, that she was 'a black woman who goes out to work journey work; that she leads a bad and vicious course of life; that her mistress had sent her off the island, not being able to put up with her conduct'. This was a woman slave's punishment: to be banished, to cease to belong to a house. It was said of Pig-foot that 'being a free Negro woman she has not even any place of abode, but passes both days and nights under the sheds of houses or in houses that are building, and that during the chief part of the time she is drunk, and that she gives herself up without restraint to all manner of vice'.

Slavery in Port of Spain was not yet a simple racial attribute. The slave remained an individual, not totally outcast. Francisco was a complete person in Spanish law. He declared that he was 'a native of the district of Curiepe in the province of Caracas, that he resided in this port in consequence of his being the slave of his honour Don Manuel Sorzano, who also resides in this place, that his station or employ is that of a sailor, and is unmarried, that he professes the Roman Catholic Apostolic religion'. Francisco was so much an individual that he resented discrimination. His shipmates, Negroes and mulattoes, refused to eat with him; they said he was a slave and ought instead to be waiting on them. Twice when they went to the south of the island they left Francisco on shore.

Francisco's humiliations were social rather than racial. He was like a domestic slave in the classical world. The point comes out in the final representations of Francisco's lawyer. He rejected all the prosecution evidence because it had been given by slaves. 'For according to law 13, chapter 16, book 3, no slave can be a witness; and in those cases where by this law they are permitted so to be, they must previously be tortured, because slaves are men of desperate minds, a disposition they contract from the servitude in which they exist; and every man ought to suspect them of speaking lightly or falsely, and that they will conceal the truth unless some reward is given them . . . it being well and generally known that there is no person whatever so vile as a slave.'

It is the voice of the classical world. But it is part of a long and careful defence of a slave. The case was referred to Caracas. When orders came that Francisco was to be tortured, to confess, the authorities arranged for him to escape.

The Trinidad Negro Code represented fairly the Spanish mildness, the concern for the individual, the antique Spanish legalism. The mildness was also of Trinidad, of the St Joseph bush that was still unproductive, of the port that was still poor. Here were no mines or, as yet, latifundia.

It was in 1776 that Spain, to protect her Empire, opened her empty Caribbean islands to foreign settlers. It was in 1789, the year of the French Revolution, that the Trinidad Negro Code was issued. The timing was now always wrong; events had passed out of Spain's control. Spain was looking for her own rich sugar islands at a time when the whole eighteenth-century structure of Caribbean wealth was about to go.

The revolution in France was reflected in Santo Domingo, the richest and most hysterical slave colony in the Caribbean. To the local antagonisms of white, mulatto and Negro, rich white and small white (*petits blancs*), metropolitan and colonial, bureaucrat and trader, there were now added the changing political divisions of France. The revolution appeared to offer something to everyone, rich whites, small whites and mulattoes; and they quarrelled among themselves until in August 1791, while Francisco's trial was going on in Trinidad, the Negroes rose and set the north of Santo Domingo alight.

In the following year a republican army arrived from France

and declared for the Negroes. The island of Martinique also came under republican control. Planters, white and mulatto, came from both islands to Trinidad with their loyal Negroes. Some weeks later England and Spain were at war with France. Spain, protecting very little, intrigued with the insurgent Negroes of Santo Domingo. England, aiming at the destruction of France through the destruction of the source of French wealth, the French Caribbean Empire, and risking invasion at home, committed nearly all her army to the conquest of Santo Domingo. The British navy isolated the republican French islands and captured them one by one. And then it was the turn of the French republicans to run. Some came to Trinidad; Chacon couldn't stop them.

Whites, mulattoes, Negroes, royalist and republican: within three years – after all the discussion about terms for settlers – a composite French colony had been assembled in Trinidad, and it was a colony in a state of insurrection and anarchy. The enemy was authority. Authority was England, the government in France, the French slave-owner, the white slave-owner. The enemy was rebellion, the dangerous Negro, the assertive free mulatto, the proselytizing republican, mulatto, white or Negro. Spain was irrelevant to these conflicts; and Chacon, without forces of his own, was an onlooker in the colony he had been sent out to organize and develop.

And Spain, however ineffectually, was still at war with France. The ideology of the revolution was dangerous to the Spanish Empire. Even words like republican and *camarade* were damaging to what Chacon's superiors had described to him as 'the sacredness of religion, public tranquillity and the necessary subordination of colonies'. Chacon tried to keep the non-royalist French out of responsible positions in Trinidad. He showed his pleasure when the British captured republican Martinique. The French, white and mulatto, remembered him for it. They were divided among themselves, but they saved their deepest enmity for the English. This was traditional; it had nothing to do with ideology.

In the Caribbean now was Victor Hugues, Robespierre's emissary of revolution, enemy of the English, a West Indian mulatto but also a Frenchman, a man dramatically right for the role of anarchist and avenger: of poor family, a failed hairdresser, failed innkeeper, failed ship's master, later a lieutenant in the French army, returning now to the islands of his childhood as Commissioner, with a small fleet and a force of 1,500 men. He recaptured the island of Guadeloupe from a British and royalist force ten times stronger than his own and executed three hundred French royalists. He disinterred and exposed the body of the British governor, and the plaque which commemorated the event contained an obscene reference to the English King.

His own brother had been killed by insurgent Negroes in Santo Domingo, but Victor Hugues proclaimed the end of slavery. He recruited Negroes; he armed corsairs; he sent wine, hams, salt and arms to the aboriginal island Indians. He warned the British that he would kill two English prisoners for every French republican, black white or brown, they killed. The Caribbean had known pirates and mercenaries; the revolutionary was new. The revolts Victor Hugues agitated in Martinique and Dominica failed. But there was trouble in St Lucia. In St Vincent and Grenada many whites were killed; in Paris the Convention applauded the news.

Victor Hugues was French, a representative of France; and in Trinidad the white French judgement on him would in the end be less harsh than their judgement on the English who, with the help of French royalists, had liberated the neighbouring island of Tobago. There a Colonel Williams abused the French as cowards and whores. He also called one Frenchman a scoundrel. The word had an unfortunate sound to French ears. Converted to *scondrel*, this British insult lived and nearly fifteen years later was reported to a French traveller, who put it in his book and explained in a footnote that *scondrel* was an English insult so vile he wouldn't translate it. War, servile revolt and massacre threatened the French in the Caribbean. But this was the sort of injury they also cherished and hoped to avenge.

Liberty–Law–Equality: this was the banner over Victor Hugues's many proclamations. In Haiti Toussaint, the leader of Negro revolt, a man of sudden genius, had joined the French republican side. In Jamaica there was a revolt of runaway slaves serious enough to be called a war. And in Trinidad there were signs of disorder among the Negroes. After the code, after the talk of importing Negroes in sufficient numbers at so much a head, tax-free and duty-free, the law seemed unable to assure property in Negroes. Governor Chacon himself lost some of his Negroes. They might have been stolen; they might have run away. It wasn't safe to go looking for them in the interior.

In Port of Spain, on the Coblenz estate, a hundred Negroes died all at once. They had cost between 270 and 280 dollars each; the planter was ruined; later, in calmer times, the estate was sold up. New Negroes, like everyone else, quickly became diseased in strange climates; and Port of Spain, set in a swamp, was especially unhealthy. But the Coblenz Negroes were 'seasoned'. They had been poisoned. It was the way of life of the slave islands, where poison was the last weapon of Negro malice, anger or despair. A hundred convulsed corpses: this was not the slavery and the settlement the Negro Code had envisaged. That now seemed like a pastoral dream of content, of fruitful fields and Negroes innocently diverting themselves between the wholesome labours of the day and their evening devotions. What had been imported with the Negroes was the hysteria in which it could now be seen those slave islands, so rich and in the eyes of some Spaniards so exemplary, had been living for a century. From island after island came the report of fire and massacre.

A man with a Negro concubine and mulatto children in an island tense with racial hatreds, an imperial official among the agents of anarchy, a Spaniard in a French colony: Chacon's powerlessness was complete. He had built, for defence, four little towers of mud and straw. They had melted away with the first rains. No man's heart was less in defence; he could defend nothing and he had nothing to defend.

A peace treaty was signed between France and Spain, and Spain was briefly neutral before reverting to her old alliance with France. Chacon's situation did not change. The French colonists had not forgiven him. And France, as a friendly neutral, was perhaps even more dangerous than as an enemy: there existed in the French Naval Office a paper on the advantages of occupying the island.

A Negro conspiracy was uncovered in the south of the island, where many mulatto planters had settled. Another uprising, near Port of Spain, was frustrated. Chacon estimated that he needed between three to five thousand men to control the island; he had less than a hundred.

When the Spanish admiral, Aristizábal, called at Port of Spain Chacon begged him to stay. Admiral Aristizábal couldn't stay. He was on his way to Spanish Santo Domingo. The Spanish portion of the island Columbus had called Española, the Spanish island, had been ceded to France; and it was Aristizábal's duty to recover Columbus's remains from the cathedral of the city of Santo Domingo, the oldest surviving settlement in the New World. The remains had been taken there from Toledo in Spain by Columbus's daughter-in-law in 1541; now Aristizábal had to transport them to Havana.*

Aristizábal took Chacon's message of need to Havana, and from Cuba there came an offer of help. It came from Jean François, a former slave, one of the early figures of the Santo Domingo insurrection; he had fought with the Spaniards against the French, and after the Spanish–French treaty had moved to Cuba. He offered

* He took the wrong box, the one with the remains of Columbus's son Diego, Viceroy of the Indies. In 1877 the lead box with Columbus's remains was discovered in a vault in the Santo Domingo cathedral; they are still there.

now to bring his black guerrillas to garrison Trinidad. The offer was sincere. It frightened Chacon; he refused. The French ought to have been relieved, but they were annoyed. The guerrillas were black, but they were French; and there were rumours among the French that Chacon intended to hand over the island to the English enemy.

The administration broke down. There was no stone or lime for building. There were no barracks, no prison and, apart from the mole battery and those washed-out mud towers, no fortifications. There were no police. Four Negroes beat their white owner to death. It was a reminder of the greater threat. Chacon had the Negroes hanged at once. It was illegal; but that no longer mattered. The island belonged to the French republicans, rich, poor, black, brown, white; and they fought among themselves. Chacon longed to be free of them all. Negroes wore the tricolour cockade and sang the *Marseillaise*. It was part of the French absurdity: the slave revolt was not wholly a slave revolt, the race war not wholly a race war. All the local hatreds were entangled with the revolutionary politics of France. Paris supplied each side with the same simple vocabulary of revolution, words that were like part of the drama and the promise: even the pretty climatic names – *germinal*, *brumaire* – of a new calendar of the North.

The Gulf of Paria was Spanish and neutral. But French republican privateers came there to refit, and Chacon couldn't stop them. British ships came to hunt them down and Chacon couldn't stop that either. The *Alarm* frigate, thirty-two guns, had already sunk three privateers. The island was really no longer Spanish; Spain had failed again.

THE *ALARM* came one day into the Gulf of Paria with the corvette *Zebra*, twenty guns. The *Alarm*, Captain Vaughan, cruised up and down inside the Dragon's Mouth, sealing the gulf. Vaughan sent a message to Chacon: there were French privateers in the Gulf; the *Alarm* and *Zebra* were taking action. Chacon replied that he would bear no responsibility. Just before dawn the privateers were shot up and sunk. The *Zebra* went back to its Leeward Islands station. The *Alarm* anchored in the harbour at Port of Spain and Captain Vaughan came ashore to call on Chacon, whose house was on the Calle Marina, the strand, just above where the low tide exposed flats of black mud.

Some of the *Alarm* sailors stayed near the jetty. Some of the officers went up one of the short straight streets of the new town to the house of Mrs Griffiths, a Welsh lady with two marriageable daughters. Vaughan joined his officers there after he had left Chacon. They heard shouts outside. The crews of the sunk privateers had just made their way back to Port of Spain, and a fight had broken out between them and the British sailors near the jetty.

Vaughan and his officers went out to their men. They were outnumbered and in a hostile city. They barricaded themselves in a stone house. The French crowd grew; they were mainly people of colour; some were armed. The surgeon of the *Alarm* was wounded.

The Spanish garrison, eighty men, came and put themselves between the crowd and the house. While a Spanish officer argued with the crowd, word was passed to Vaughan that he should get his people out by the back. The Spanish soldiers at last gave way. The French broke in and ransacked the empty house. Then they marched through the city singing the *Marseillaise*. They broke into the arsenal. Tricolour flags and cockades appeared in the streets.

Their governments might decree wars for commercial reasons, but French and English also fought because they hated one another. Vaughan was unhinged by the humiliations of the day; and next morning, leaving the *Alarm* almost defenceless, he landed two hundred and fifty men in Port of Spain and ranged them in battle order on the Calle Marina. He ignored the protest of the officer of the Spanish shore picket. 'I am your prisoner,' the officer said, offering his sword. Vaughan, in no mood for this sort of style, marched on into the city, where four to five hundred armed French republicans awaited him.

Chacon, moving swiftly, put his small garrison between the French and the English. He spoke to Vaughan in English. He said that Trinidad was Spanish and neutral, and Vaughan was breaking international law. Vaughan couldn't hope to capture the island or to hold it. The island was almost all French; if there was fighting the few English residents and all the Spaniards would certainly be killed.

Vaughan listened. He and his officers stood aside and they talked for a little. Then Vaughan came to Chacon, saluted with his sword, turned and led his column back to the jetty. A crowd gathered and followed, whistling, jeering, singing.

There was a riot that evening in Port of Spain. Shots were fired at English people; an English Negro was killed. Chacon wrote a long letter to Godoy, Prince of Peace, in Madrid. He asked for ships and men. Vaughan had no one to appeal to. When he got back to the *Alarm* he shot himself.

Vaughan and the *Alarm* were remembered in the manifesto against England which the Spanish government issued some months later. The manifesto preceded the official declaration of war by a few days. Chacon's allies in Trinidad were now the republican French, who hated him. His enemy was England, whose Caribbean victories he had so recently welcomed.

In Santo Domingo and elsewhere the British army was on the point of defeat. In England naval mutinies were brewing. But the British navy still ruled the Caribbean, in spite of Victor Hugues. On the South American coast the colonies of Berbice, Demerara and Essequibo fell; and then, in easy succession, the islands of St Lucia, St Vincent and Grenada.

SPANISH MILITARY preparations were defensive and fearful. Doubt sapped energy and attracted bad luck. Chaguaramas, to the west of Port of Spain, was a perfect harbour; for that reason it was seen as a place where Spanish ships might easily be blockaded. A fort might be built to protect Chaguaramas. But there were the old doubts about the value of forts. Landings could be made in so many undefended places, the fort could be captured and the Spanish guns trained on the blockaded Spanish ships in the safe Spanish harbour. Every preparation held its own danger, every advantage a disadvantage.

Venezuela sent an engineer and cannon, but because of the British navy the Indian labourers couldn't come across to work on the fort. A corvette bringing money and munitions from Puerto Rico was captured. Five new Spanish battleships called at Port of Spain on their way to Cartagena with troop reinforcements. Chacon wanted the soldiers to help with the fort and he persuaded the admiral to stay. The soldiers, unseasoned, fell ill by the score. There wasn't the money to look after them; some had to depend on private Spanish hospitality.

There was truth in that Spanish vision of defeat, in which every preparation for defence only invited attack. The British had been planning an attack. Now, because of that new squadron in Chaguaramas harbour, the attack was brought forward. It was to be massive; there was to be no mistake. The fort was incomplete; there wasn't even water for the men. Not one of the twenty cannon and three mortars, which the sick soldiers had dragged into place, would ever fire. The engineer's fine drawings, useless, would be taken to London, where they still are, fresh and sharp, as though awaiting execution.

The British forces were to rendezvous at the small island of Carriacou in the Grenadines on or before 13 February 1797. More than 7,000 men had to be picked up from Barbados, Tobago and St Vincent and kept ready in forty transports. On 12 February Admiral Harvey and General Abercromby left Headquarters in Martinique. When they arrived at Carriacou on 14 February they found everything ready. A pilot, a sixty-five-year-old Mandingo Negro, had been found to take the fleet through the Dragon's

Mouth into the Gulf of Paria. It was the sort of detail the Spaniards themselves now sometimes overlooked. Some years before, the Viceroy of Mexico, on an official visit to Trinidad, had turned back after being held up for a fortnight outside the Dragon's Mouth.

Chacon and the Spanish admiral were together in Port of Spain on 16 February, perhaps at lunch, when they heard that the British were coming. There could be nothing like a Spanish plan. Chacon had six hundred men in Port of Spain. Not all of them were fit; some had been in hospital beds that morning. There was the militia, but it had never been reliable. A mole battery, two redoubts in the low hills to the north of the city: these were his defences. The Spanish admiral could try to take his squadron out of the trap of the Gulf. Or – this was discussed – he could remain in the Gulf and attack the troop transports. His own ships would be destroyed, but he might frustrate the invasion. Such an attack called for spirit and finely tuned crews: the Spanish ships were under-manned, the crews sickly.

At about three in the afternoon the British armament began to enter the Gulf: one ship after another: eighteen in all, to the Spanish squadron's five. Their movements were economical and precise.

Chacon ordered two hundred of the militia to reinforce the hundred and thirty men at the naval fort. But the militia had disintegrated. The men left their officers and ran off into the woods. In the Gulf it continued like a naval drill, like the strategist's primary fantasy, in which the enemy, though granted strength, is denied movement. The forty troop transports, protected by two frigates and the corvette *Zebra*, moved down into the Gulf until they were opposite Port of Spain. They had always been out of range of the Spanish ships; now they anchored out of range of any shore batteries, and there was only one.

The bent sails of the Spanish ships suggested imminent sailing. Two sloops and the frigate *Alarm*, under a new captain, remained under sail just inside the Dragon's Mouth, controlling exit. The Spanish ships didn't move. Just before dark the nine British ships of the line anchored in an arc opposite the five ships of the Spanish squadron, blockading them in their very safe but unprotected harbour. It was the Spanish fear come true.

Night fell; lights came on in the ships, marking their positions for the morning's battle. Only the three British cruisers moved between the dark land masses of the Venezuelan and Trinidad peninsulas, which appeared to touch. The Spanish ships and the fort that protected them were silent.

In Port of Spain the French republicans went wild. Chacon was cool. He seemed indifferent to defeat. He was more concerned about the archives and the contents of the treasury; he was having them transported to St Joseph. When the French asked for arms or some sign of action Chacon said, 'All in good time, gentlemen. *Poco a poco, señores*.' In the end he opened the arsenal. The French took what they could, four to five thousand muskets, it was said; and, like the militiamen, disappeared.

Between half past one and two in the morning there were explosions from the west. The Spanish ships, their sails still bent, were burning. They had been burning, unseen, for some time. It was a still night. The sulphur and resin strewn on the decks of the new ships didn't catch easily; the ships had smouldered for a long time before the explosions and the flames. The explosions continued. The ships burned till morning.

At about nine the admiral and some of his staff arrived in Port of Spain. They had come by a ship's boat, staying close to the shore. The decision to scuttle had been taken at a council of war; the officers themselves had spread the sulphur. The fort had also been abandoned, the cannon and mortars spiked. The sailors and the men from the fort had taken to the bush.

The French made this morning meeting between Chacon and the admiral the subject of a story. 'You have burnt the ships!' Chacon said. 'Then everything is lost.' – 'Not everything,' the admiral said, making the sign of the cross. 'I managed to save the statue of St James of Compostela, my patron saint and the patron saint of my flagship.'

One Spanish ship wasn't allowed to burn. It was rescued by the crews of two British ships and claimed as a prize. The fort was occupied. Early in the morning General Abercromby went aboard the frigate protecting the troop transports. Some of the other ships closed on the city and there was a brief exchange at long range with the mole battery. A Spanish cannon blew up and killed a soldier; he was the first and last Spanish casualty.

At midday the British troops began to land a little to the west of the city. A sloop provided cover; it was the end of the navy's responsibility. The troops were landed in deep black mud, hundreds of yards from dry land. They sank to their knees. Abercromby, looking for shallow water, had chosen the worst spot on the island for a landing. But there was no fire from the shore.

The men's equipment was heavy. Their uniforms, it was said, would have done for the Canadian winter. It was the hottest time of day. But at the end of the mud and the rotting smell was a sugar factory with casks of rum and cane syrup. A gigantic rum-punch was mixed; the soldiers drank and rested. Just before five they began to march on Port of Spain, the sun on their backs, one column taking the main road, the other making for the hills to the north.

Chacon had withdrawn from the city to his two hill redoubts. He was cut off from the mole battery. He had about three hundred and fifty men with him; he had also managed – fittingly, for this farewell Spanish display – to muster some Indians with bows and arrows. He sent out a patrol. The patrol returned and reported. The German Jaegers of the invading force penetrated the northern hills and occupied positions above the two redoubts. Chacon withdrew from the redoubts.

'I was still buoyed up,' he wrote later to Madrid (he said he had destroyed 'the greater part of the German regiment'), 'with a faint hope of being able to make a diversion by attacking the enemy on the hills. I therefore sent out messengers in every direction, but without result, for when I repaired to the spot I had named I found only the admiral there.'

It was now night. Presently a British officer with a white flag came to where Chacon, the admiral and their staffs were. The British had ordered a ceasefire; Chacon was invited to do the same. The officer presented his written instructions from General Abercromby. 'State to the governor that I see with sorrow his troops are without hope of being able to carry out his wishes. I beg him to name a place for conference. I offer him an honourable capitulation on such terms as are due to good and faithful soldiers.' It was a generous message. Chacon went to meet Abercromby and that evening they agreed on the terms of the capitulation.

All officers and men of His Catholic Majesty were to 'surrender themselves prisoners of war'. At five on the following afternoon they were to 'march out with the honours of war' and lay down their arms three hundred yards from the positions they occupied. From that moment they would be fed at the expense of the British government. They would keep their personal effects. Officers would be allowed to wear their swords. They would all be taken to Spain as soon as possible, where they would consider themselves prisoners of war; until they were told they had been exchanged they were not to take arms against Great Britain or her allies. Some officers would be released on a six-month parole to attend to their private affairs in Spanish America. All government property, including military stores, had to be transferred, with inventories. Private property remained inviolate. All laws and contracts remained in force. There was to be freedom of worship. The free people of colour were to be protected in their liberty.

The surrender was signed at eight next morning in an estate house some miles to the east of Port of Spain. Under the floorboards the more valuable contents of the treasury had been hidden two days before. Some days later the Spanish military chest was taken to Caracas; perhaps the treasure went with it; perhaps it went with Chacon to Cadiz.

Chacon was an officer in the Spanish Royal Navy that had just dishonoured itself, an imperial governor who had surrendered his province, a Knight of Calatrava who hadn't fought his battle. Abercromby saw him as the representative of 'a sinking nation' and was anxious to spare him personal humiliation. And Chacon liked the English. He had been their prisoner before, during the American war; and the English were the enemies of the republican French who had been his tormentors.

Chacon was no doubt behind Abercromby's order, the day after the surrender, that anyone who considered himself a citizen of the French Republic should take himself and his property off the island within ten days. Transport would be provided to any Dutch, French or Spanish colony. Everyone else was to swear allegiance to George III so long as he wished to live or hold property under the King's government. All arms were to be surrendered, 'except the swords and fowling pieces of gentlemen'. A respect for property, the rights of gentlemen: the words stand out: here, expressed by a busy soldier, were the articles of faith of a new Empire.

The British navy worked to a tight schedule. An attack on Puerto Rico, the other of Spain's recently developed Caribbean islands, was planned; and soon Harvey and Abercromby went away. Abercromby left his aide-de-camp as governor of Trinidad; at thirty shillings a day. He left him 1,000 men, half British, the rest Germans, Negroes and French royalists. No Spanish attack was to be feared, Abercromby thought; and if one came, 'from the nature of the Spanish troops great expectations may be formed of success, even against superior numbers, by an enterprising conduct'.

An enterprising conduct: it is a good translation of *buena disposición y gallarda resolución*. The governor of Margarita – the one who had taken so many prisoners that he had had to strangle some – had used those words a hundred and sixty years before, laying down the Spanish principle of action against intruders in these provinces of El Dorado. 'Experience has taught me,' the governor had written, 'that these battles depend less on numbers than on an enterprising conduct.'

THERE REMAINS the coolness with which Chacon let a Spanish territory go after three hundred years. His enemies said he had been bribed by the English. It was possible. But there is another explanation. In 1797 England looked defeated. Chacon thought that the war was almost over and that the peace treaty would restore the island to Spain. He thought he had saved it from France and the republican French, so dangerous to the Spanish Empire. He collaborated enthusiastically with Colonel Picton, the governor Abercromby had left behind. The presence of Picton's soldiers kept the French and everyone else still; for the first time for years Chacon felt secure in Trinidad. He was even able to recover and sell some of his runaway Negroes.

Picton was a quick-tempered Welshman of thirty-eight. He was a professional soldier who had fought no battle. He was remembered only for what had happened in Bristol when the 75th Regiment was being disbanded at the end of the American war. He was reading out his instructions on the Green when some of the men began to protest. Picton drew his sword, ran to the centre of the disturbance and manhandled the ringleader; order was instantly restored. After that Picton had spent twelve years as a half-pay captain. The idleness had damaged his temper for good. He had seen no action in the recent West Indian fighting; he had only been a member of Abercromby's suite. Trinidad was his first important post.

When he heard Chacon's stories of disorder and republicanism Picton summoned the Port of Spain cabildo. He placed his sword on the table and, his temper rising as he spoke, said that at the slightest sign of trouble he would hang them all. Chacon had a particular enemy, a Frenchman from Martinique, who used to say that he had a guillotine ready and that the first head to go, come the day, would be Chacon's. Picton said he was going to hang *him* right away and burn down his estates. Picton was over six foot tall, with a 'repulsive expression which sometimes hung upon his brow'. The Frenchman pleaded for half an hour. No one was hanged; no estate was burnt. But there were no more French republican demonstrations in the streets of Port of Spain.

A sweet revenge for Chacon, but Picton had news for him too. The British, Picton said, were planning a general war on Spanish possessions. A printed proclamation to the inhabitants had already been prepared: 'Fortune offers the inhabitants of the Spanish Main: LIBERTY entire and complete for all trade. ABOLITION of all import and export duties. FREEDOM to plant and sell the crops of your choice. An ELECTED government. Under the effective protection of British arms.'

Caracas, in spite of its wealth and its university, had no printery. The printed word had authority. Chacon saw the printed proclamation as a new way of making war; he thought it would have 'the most fatal consequences'. The liberty of trade, not the liberty of French republicanism, but its implication was the same: the end of the Spanish Empire. The rich who had grown weak didn't have a choice of friends; they had only a choice of predators. Chacon saw, as the Captain-General of Caracas saw more hysterically, that the British would not give up the island that guarded the Orinoco.

Chacon began to think of reconquest. He began to talk with Spaniards on the island. It was too late. Picton was hustling the more educated Spaniards, and especially the lawyers, off the island. The Spanish admiral had already been sent to Spain. Now Chacon himself was deported to Cadiz.

A YEAR LATER in Cadiz Chacon and the admiral were tried by a Council of War. Chacon was defended by the governor of Cumaná, the admiral by his brother, high and rising in the service of a declining Spain (ambassador in London, and later the last effective

Viceroy of Mexico). Chacon and the admiral were acquitted. But the loss of Trinidad began to be felt more and more. Napoleon resented it, fearing the surrender of other Spanish provinces to England. Spain resented it. The French in Trinidad resented it. They couldn't be sure, besides, until the peace treaty, that Trinidad wasn't going to be handed back to Spain; and they feared Spanish retaliation then.

The French in Trinidad had sworn allegiance to George III, but they were anxious to prove to Madrid that before that they had been loyal to Spain. They put their case to Picton. They said it was the custom for the conduct of an outgoing Spanish governor to be investigated. Picton agreed; a committee of some sort met and the French inhabitants recorded their condemnation of Chacon for surrendering the island to the British. They sent petitions to Madrid; they sent emissaries to Spain by way of New York; they won the ear of Napoleon. Newspapers in Boston and London took up the story of the governor who had surrendered his province without a shot.

Three years after it had been given, the decision of the Council of War was quashed by the Spanish King. The Spanish admiral was stripped of his rank, Chacon banished for life from the Spanish dominions; and perpetual silence about the affair enjoined on both men. Some years later, after France had invaded Spain and England had become Spain's ally, the admiral was restored to his rank. Chacon died in Portugal.

For French and Spaniards in the Caribbean it was a difficult time. The three revolutions, American, French and Negro, had left them confused and divided against the single-minded commercial intentions of Britain and the United States, whose trade with the Spanish Empire was to increase twentyfold in ten years. The harshest words about Chacon came from Roume St Laurent, the Frenchman who twenty years before had negotiated the terms of French immigration. Roume had been much concerned then with the recovery of runaway Negroes. His mother, Rose de Gannes de la Chancellerie, Marquise de Chaurras, had taken over seventy-five Negroes when she settled near Port of Spain. The La Chancellerie estate was still there, with its Negroes. But Roume was now in Santo Domingo, a Commissioner for the Directory of France, a servant of the Negro Revolution.

Roume wrote to the Captain-General of Caracas that Chacon was contemptible and treacherous; that he had tarnished the ancient lustre of Spanish arms; that he should be punished to deter others who might sell Spanish colonies and Spanish ships to England. So much he wrote as an ally. Then, as a servant of the Negro Revolution, he gave his news, in the classical vocabulary of the revolution. 'Our phalanxes have marched with a sword in one hand and the constitution in the other.' Rebels had been executed or won over to liberty. 'Our new brothers, the Africans, know their rights and duties as well as other citizens. Slavery is the greatest crime against divine and natural laws, and is equally damaging to agriculture, industry and commerce .' He alarmed the Venezuelans; they had been having their own Negro troubles; they decided that Roume, ally or not, was to be handled with reserve.

Roume was soon in trouble in Santo Domingo. He had, again, an immigration plan. He suggested that Jamaican Negroes should be revolutionized and if possible stolen off plantations. He ordered a raid. He was arrested by Toussaint, imprisoned for some time and expelled to the United States. Toussaint's supporters were puzzled; but Toussaint knew what he was doing. Roume's master had changed. It was Napoleon who had ordered the raid on Jamaica, to draw renewed British hostility on Santo Domingo. Napoleon's aim, and Roume's now, was to destroy the Negro Revolution.

Commissioner Roume exiled in the United States, Governor Chacon dying in the poor Portuguese inn: with a fourth revolution maturing, the second-hand revolution of Spanish America, with energy but without principles, with leaders but with no true heroes, there was generated just that degree of confusion in which a man would sometimes find it hard to say where he stood.

Governor Picton saw the Spanish American revolution as an opportunity for the military action he had not so far had; he saw it as a more important extension of his duties in Trinidad. He gave shelter to revolutionaries who spoke the high language of liberty. But the island Picton had inherited was a slave island, where he alone was the law. On his island there was to be order; there was to be no revolution. The situation held danger for the revolutionaries. It also held danger for Picton. His disgrace, when it came, was more sensational than the disgrace of Roume or Chacon. Yet out of this disgrace was to come the glory which perhaps the man of thirty-eight, after twelve years on half pay, had ceased to expect.

PART THREE

The Torture of Luisa Calderon

5. The Fourth Revolution

1797–1800

General Picton died, aged fifty-six, at the battle of Waterloo. He had been badly wounded at the battle of Quatre Bras two days before, but he had bandaged himself and kept the wound secret. When Wellington, under whom Picton was directly serving, gave the order to withdraw, Picton lost his temper; he said that Waterloo was a damned bad place to fight a battle.

'A rough foul-mouthed devil as ever lived' was what Wellington said of Picton. But Picton by this time had licence: a Knight of the Bath, a Member of Parliament, one of the heroes of the Peninsular War, unanimously judged by the House of Commons to be 'amongst the foremost in that race of glory', his reputation, won at Ciudad Rodrigo, Badajoz and Vittoria, higher than that of Sir John Moore, of the poem, who in 1797 had also been a thirty-shillings-a-day military governor in the West Indies.

Ten years after Picton's death it was decided to put up a statue in Carmarthen. The King himself subscribed; and Picton's brother, a Pembrokeshire rector – he had just come back from a visit to the Picton estates in Trinidad, where he had been fined £164 for maltreating two of the estate Negroes – sent his abashed thanks through the Home Secretary, Sir Robert Peel. A memoir of Picton was written by Captain Marryat, the novelist, himself the son of a Trinidad slave-owner. In 1835, twenty years after Picton's death, there came a two-volume *Life*, which went into a second edition. There were people then who placed Picton above Wellington; but this was part of the continuing reaction to the long disgrace that preceded Picton's four years of glory.

The military glory Picton aimed at and achieved could not last. It lay in personal valour: the smoke clearing, the hero seen leading his men up the breach at Badajoz; the hero putting himself at the head of the retreating Portuguese battalion at Busacos and, still in his coloured nightcap, crying 'Forward!' and 'Hurrah!' The style – 'That damned fighting fellow Crawfurd will some day get us into a scrape' – was the military style of the age. 'A force more formidable to its friends than enemies': Abercromby said that in Ireland, Picton said it in Port of Spain, but the sentiment is remembered as Wellington's. The reputation of Picton and others was to be absorbed in Wellington's more complex, nation-building myth. Picton's glory abolished his disgrace; when the glory went, the man and his disgrace were forgotten.

It seems to be another Thomas Picton who appears in the *Newgate Calendar*, the popular chronicle of English criminal trials, offered with 'occasional remarks . . . original anecdotes . . . moral reflections . . . confessions and last exclamations of sufferers'. There, among the cases of Richard Ferguson (Galloping Dick), convicted at the Lent Assizes in 1800 for highway robbery, and George Waldron (The Gentleman-Pickpocket), several times convicted and finally transported to Botany Bay, is the case of Thomas Picton Esq (Late Governor of Trinidad), 'convicted February 24, 1806, of applying a most cruel torture, in order to extort confession from Luisa Calderon'.

That was only one trial. The investigation had begun three years before, when Picton was still in Trinidad; the trial could be said to have ended only with Picton's death. The proceedings fill 1,000 fine columns in Howell's *State Trials*. The Picton papers in the Public Record Office in London have been worn thin by handling. The affair was the subject of one-sided books, pamphlets, articles. Pictures were sold in London of Luisa Calderon and the instruments of her torture.

Picton saw Luisa twice. He saw her early one evening in Port of Spain when she was brought to the hall of Government House, accused of theft; he saw her four years later in London at his first trial. But it wasn't just for Luisa Calderon that Picton was being tried. He was really being tried for being governor of Trinidad at the end of the eighteenth century. There had originally been thirty-seven charges; the torture of Luisa Calderon was the only one that had stuck. The trial was soon to look like persecution. Slavery existed; it made many people rich. Yet it was clear that Picton was being tried for being governor of a slave colony. In the United States, England and France there were people willing to exploit the Spanish American revolution; the revolutionaries themselves betrayed the revolution and each other. Yet it was clear that Picton was also being tried for having failed the revolution.

He was the victim of people's conscience, of ideas of humanity and reason that were ahead of the reality. And such a victim: an unemployed soldier of thirty-eight who had come out to the West Indies on speculation, interested neither in slaves nor revolution, looking only for action and glory, as the man who would rally a retreating battalion and give the order to charge.

HE HAD GOT the job as military governor because he knew Spanish – picked up in Gibraltar when he was an ensign – and in the beginning his duties were clear: to maintain order in a conquered and disorderly colony, full of French republican factions, and to defend that colony against attack. Just across the Gulf, on the Venezuelan mainland, there were many French republican refugees, people of colour from Trinidad and other islands. They were less nervous about making war than their Spanish hosts. The British navy had gone and the Spanish and French privateers had come back to the Gulf and the waters around the island. Picton had no naval force; and his garrison was unreliable.

The German mercenaries hadn't been paid; they began to desert. Their major was ill, the other officers useless. The Venezuelans paid each deserter six dollars, twenty if he brought his arms; they also paid the boatmen who took the deserters across the Gulf. Picton offered sixteen dollars for every deserter captured or killed. Fourteen German privates were recaptured and hanged immediately. Port of Spain had seen nothing like it.

The Spanish peons, the former bush-folk, had become a menace, quick with the cutlasses which they always carried. A drunken peon went to the house of a Spanish lady in St Joseph and stood 'in the middle of the hall' abusing her. Soldiers had to be called. The local Spanish administrator thought the peon should be sent off the island; it was what Chacon would have done. Picton didn't think this was 'sufficient'; the man was hanged that day. The peons were in the habit of claiming sanctuary in the church. Picton abolished the idea of sanctuary; the story was that he had a gallows put up just outside the church.

The runaway Negroes in the interior were hunted down. A Negro woman called Present, who had eloped with a black soldier before the capitulation, was brought in one afternoon. Her owner went to claim her next morning. He was too late; his 'valuable slave' had been hanged at sunrise.

A free Negro woman complained to the Chief Magistrate that she had been raped near the magazine by four men of the Royal Engineers. The Chief Magistrate, an Irishman, sent her to Picton, 'to whom I thought it would afford amusement to hear of a rape in the West Indies'. After his early-afternoon dinner that day the Chief Magistrate walked down to the wharf. There he saw one of the accused men about to be hanged. 'Villain!' Picton was shouting. 'You are going to hell with lies in your mouth.' The three other men were sentenced by court martial to 1,500 lashes each.

It was by this system of impartial terror that Picton sought to maintain order. But more important than order and defence was the revolution on the mainland. Much had already been done. The British consul in Cadiz had been supplying general propaganda for some time; and Picton's more concrete proclamation had had some effect. The Capuchin missionaries, whose headquarters had once been in St Joseph (they were still short of some church fittings), hadn't been happy with the Spanish government ever since the Jesuits had been expelled from Paraguay; they promised now to keep their Indians 'out of the business' if the British invaded. And there was a Cadiz-born merchant, interested in the trade the British offered, who was acting as Picton's agent in Cumaná; his aim was to bring Caracas and Cumaná under direct British rule.

The resentments of missionaries and merchants didn't add up to a revolution. That was preparing elsewhere: in the prison of La Guaira, in the cell of a prisoner who had just been transported from Spain.

His name was Picornell. He was a Majorcan who had gone to live in Madrid, where he ran a school. He had written a book about the education of infants. He was also a freemason and a republican and had written a political book. Soon he began to plot against the government; he wanted a Spanish republic on French lines. He hid arms in his school. He was betrayed, arrested, tried and condemned to death with three of his supporters. The sentence was commuted to one of life imprisonment in Panama. He was brought to La Guaira in Venezuela; he was to stay in solitary confinement in the local jail until a ship could take him to Panama.

He was an unusual prisoner for Venezuela. He said he couldn't eat the jail food and didn't like sleeping on the floor and he asked for soap and water to wash his clothes. The jailer became respectful and protective. Picornell asked for a priest. More alert officials wouldn't have seen this as a sign of repentance. Picornell got his priest; in almost no time he had become Picornell's convert.

Soon, through these two contacts alone, the jailer and the priest, all La Guaira was responding to revolution. Picornell, with the co-operation of his guards, moved freely about the port. La Guaira was a good place for a conspiracy. Several hundred French republican prisoners of war had stayed there for some years and preached liberty and equality, words which every man could interpret in his own way. Picornell's supporters came to include a high official called José España, who was also a planter and slave-owner; and a retired soldier called Manuel Gual, who after thirty-three years with the Veteran Battalion of Caracas had only been permitted to reach the rank of captain.

No conspiracy was swifter. In December 1796 Picornell arrived in La Guaira; in June 1797 he was allowed to escape; the uprising was planned for July. The manifesto was simple. America had been usurped from the Indians; it was time that justice was done. There were to be no class divisions, no slavery, no Indian tribute. There was to be unity and equality, without offence to religion. All goods were to be held in common; there wouldn't even be tobacco stalls because everything would be free. Everyone was to call everyone else 'brother'. The flag of the republic was to have four colours representing the four races: white, blue for the Negro, yellow for the mixed, red for the Indian.

A well-to-do man called Montesinos was among the conspirators. He tried to interest his barber, a mulatto. The barber was an officer in the mulatto battalion; he told his colleagues; they told the chaplain. Montesinos's house was searched; twenty-four people were arrested. Gual, España and Picornell had to run. They went to Curaçao. Curaçao was a French island, and Spain and France were allies; but the French republican governor sheltered the conspirators and declared them French citizens. He got rid of them only after Picornell had shouted at a Spaniard in the street: 'You dog of an informer, you enemy of humanity!' and threatened to run the Spaniard through with his sword.

The conspirators went on to Guadeloupe, ruled now by Victor Hugues. He welcomed them. Picornell printed a revolutionary song, which was variously called the American Song, the American Sonnet, the American Carmagnole: 'Long live our people! Long live equality, law, justice and liberty.'

Gual went on to Martinique. He told the British governor that Venezuela was ready for revolution; he asked for military help.

The governor thought that Gual was just the man Picton was looking for. Both Manuel Gual and José España were sent to Port of Spain.

Their revolution was not the simple revolution, the chance for military action, that Picton had in mind. The four colours of the revolutionary flag also stood for the four aims of the revolution: equality, liberty, property, security. The words had special meanings: equality for the mulattoes, liberty for the Negroes, property for the merchants, security for all. It was the American, French and Negro revolutions rolled together. It was an absurdity, a 'shouting', as one Spanish official said, for almost everything; and impossible to combat. True, it had for the moment failed. The Venezuelans had declared an amnesty; and the three mulatto informers had been made captains and rewarded with sixty pesos a month, a gold medal with the Spanish King's head and permission to use the title of Don. But the Venezuelan officials who spoke of the 'iniquitous and detestable plan of Monsieur Pitt to subvert the Americas', of 'countries dominated by irreligion and corrupt manners' and of 'the sweet yoke of Spanish rule' were not using words which could be set against those of the revolution.

The revolution was also impossible to manage. But to Picton it was a revolution. It had leaders and they were at his disposal. He wrote to London that the 'moral revolution' had made progress on the continent; it was now possible not only to subvert the Spanish government in Caracas but also 'to shake their whole Empire'. There was a bonus. The Venezuelan troops assembling at Angostura for a descent on Trinidad had to be diverted to duties of internal security.

Picton ordered a raid across the Gulf. Many people in Trinidad knew the country, and had contacts; the Capuchins were helpful. The French republican refugees were scattered; a quantity of cattle and other provisions were brought back. A second raid didn't end well. The Spaniards and republicans were waiting. They shot up the launches and twenty men were lost, with the church bell that was being taken to the Capuchins. Caution was still necessary all round. Many of the local people of colour remained, Picton thought, 'irreconcilable republicans'. Expulsions and exemplary punishments continued. Martinique sent reinforcements to Trinidad; the British commander-in-chief recommended 'severe police'.

There was order, and even growth. Serious settlers came in with about 1,000 more Negroes. Roads were improved; there were prospects of a good crop. Trade with the mainland was maintained, though some of the British manufactures were too fine for Venezuelan needs; the island was even re-exporting Venezuelan produce to other islands. The French planters who had stayed and were prospering didn't want to go back to the instability of Spanish rule. At the end of the year the British conquest of the island had been consolidated. The revolution on the mainland looked promising. Picton was taken off his thirty-shillings-a-day allowance and given a salary of £1,200 a year.

WITH GUAL and España Port of Spain had become the centre of the revolution. But there were Spanish American revolutionaries in Europe as well, and recent events in Venezuela had at last made them more plausible. The revolutionaries in Europe had also been made anxious; they didn't want to miss the revolution. The most famous of these revolutionaries, the most famous South American of his generation, was Francisco Miranda, sometimes de Miranda. General Miranda, Count de Miranda. He was forty-seven; he had already been out of Venezuela for twenty-six years. In 1797 Miranda was in Paris; but he had been having his troubles, and at the end of the year he crossed to England, disguised by a wig and green spectacles. His trunk had a false bottom; the Russian passport he carried gave his name as Mirandow.

For the second time in eight years Miranda had a plan for the South American revolution to put before Pitt, the Prime Minister. Miranda said he wanted to save the revolution from the 'detestable maxims' of France. He and his friends had worked out a constitution for Colombia, which was to be the name of the independent Spanish American state. It was like the British Constitution, with a House of the People, a House of Nobles and a hereditary Inca. Eight years before Pitt hadn't been civil. Miranda had suffered, but now Pitt appeared interested and Miranda, in his journal, was forgiving.

Picton wrote later of Miranda as of a man he didn't know. But it is possible that Picton had seen Miranda twenty-two years before in Gibraltar. Picton was then a seventeen-year-old ensign; and Miranda, a twenty-five-year-old captain in the Spanish service, had visited Gibraltar and was entertained by the officers of the garrison. For Picton there had followed the idleness of garrison duty, the years on half pay in Pembrokeshire in Wales, years passed, as his brother the rector remembered forty years later, in 'the enjoyment of the sports of the field, in studying the classics'. For Miranda there had followed adventure, esteem and waste: service as a Spanish lieutenant-colonel in the American War of Independence; a scandal about money, Negroes and smuggling in Cuba; arrest, release, the break with Spain, the flight to the United States; and then exile in Europe.

In the beginning exile was glamorous. Miranda was the first South American of culture Europe had known; many doors were open to him. He got as far as Russia. He thrilled the Empress Catherine with his talk of the Inquisition, and she loved him for the dangers that as a revolutionary he might have to pass. The Russian embassies in Europe were thereafter Miranda's.

As a young man in Caracas Miranda had longed for Europe, for a civilization and society more demanding than the plantations and emporia of Venezuela. He loved Europe better than any European because he could never take its graces for granted; he never ceased to prepare himself for it. He glittered. The French talked of sending him to Santo Domingo as governor. They made him a general in their revolutionary army because they thought he had been a general in the Spanish army. A minor military disaster followed, and a trial and a prison term. But Miranda impressed

Napoleon, as later he impressed Wellington. After two decades of talk, disappointments, bungled action, bankruptcy, he never bored.

He gave himself the title of Count. It was his colonial dandyism, which began as his tribute to the metropolis and became an aspect of his insecurity as an outsider in a setting which he yet felt to be his own. He exploited his glamour. The Spanish American revolution was part of this glamour; this glamour became his self-esteem. Were there Negroes in Spanish America? There were none, or very few. South Americans were Spaniards or Indians; and the Indians were descendants of the Incas, a noble people awaiting liberation. There were Negroes in Trinidad and the other Spanish West Indian islands; but they were not a true part of Colombia, and Miranda and his associates were willing to surrender all those islands, except Cuba, in return for English help.

The plan Miranda presented now to Pitt and the United States ambassador in London was for a joint British–American invasion of South America. England would get the smaller and black Spanish West Indian islands, thirty million pounds and commercial advantages in the new Spanish American state; the United States would get commercial advantages; and there would be a defensive alliance of the three great powers against France. Pitt was interested, the United States ambassador was encouraging. And it was agreed that Miranda should first of all send out an agent to Trinidad to give the news of the help to come and to keep an eye on the revolution.

The agent was a Cuban exile called Caro. Spanish intelligence in Paris heard of his mission even before he left, and a description was circulated to all ports on the Spanish Main. Caro, it was said, would be arriving in Trinidad or Venezuela in 'a very singular disguise', with a wig that 'perfectly simulates the wool of the Negro, and he has stained his face and his body in the same colour with a dye so fast that neither water nor sweat can wash it off'. These revolutionaries, and the men who tracked them down, took disguises seriously – even Miranda, an austere man, had his false names and his green glasses – and Caracas sent out orders to officers in all Venezuelan ports that until further notice they should pass their hands 'with deliberation', *con detenida pausa*, over the heads of all incoming Negroes.

Then, as always before, Miranda was disappointed. In the United States Alexander Hamilton said he regarded 'this man' – Miranda – as 'an intriguing adventurer', whose letters didn't deserve a reply. Pitt, more concerned about Napoleonic invasion, went silent. Caro, with or without his disguise, was delayed and delayed. The Americans became encouraging again, then cool again: they were working towards a pact with France. Miranda's military plans, which he had written out for the British cabinet and they had sent on to Headquarters in the West Indies, were captured by the Spaniards; and orders were issued in Venezuela for Miranda's arrest, if he landed. The order was at least like an expression of regard.

'There is a native of Caracas, I understand, now in London who might be useful on this occasion,' Picton wrote to London in May 1798; 'not that he possesses a great local knowledge, or has any considerable connection, being the son of a shopkeeper of Caracas, who left the country at an early period; but as a native of the country who has made himself a good deal talked of, he might fix the attention of the people, and thereby make himself serviceable. For reasons very obvious, I would advise his not being consulted on the business, or acquainted with it, until the moment of execution.'

The shopkeeper's son was Miranda. And Miranda's father wasn't even a Spaniard. He was a Canary Islander, an immigrant who had set up as a draper in Caracas and done well. He was looked down on by the local nobleza and there had been a dispute about his position in the militia, which the King had resolved by imposing perpetual silence on all discussion of the origins of the Miranda family. Who was Picton's informant? His agent in Cumaná? A dissident member of the nobleza? After the years in Europe, the books, pictures and study, after the talk of liberty and constitutions, the colonial world remained, still knowing only about blood and money, cacao and tobacco, the management of Negroes and shops. It was Miranda's simple failure: as an exile his strength and dignity were always in the keeping of others. Only the enemy, the Spanish government, always took him seriously.

EVERYONE HAD EXPECTED early British action. But the months passed and nothing happened. The British army was still tied down in Santo Domingo; England itself was still exposed to French invasion. In Trinidad the German mercenaries, in spite of floggings, were still making trouble about their pay and deserting to Venezuela. Picton became nervous about his revolutionaries in Port of Spain. Picornell, the first mover of the revolution, had been captured by the British and taken as a prisoner of war to Bermuda; there he had got the Irish garrison to mutiny. Picton decided to hide away José España and Manuel Gual in the houses of planters he trusted.

He wrote to London that these men had a price on their heads. But his plans were now defensive. He built a new road over the hills and a small £300 fort on the north coast; they were like preparations for a retreat. He feared a Spanish attack; at Headquarters there was for a time a rumour that Trinidad had been retaken by a naval force from Spain. Picton began to write letters like Chacon's. He needed 2,000 men to keep order; he despaired of reducing the French people of colour to loyalty; he needed proper fortifications if the island was to remain British.

The revolutionaries saw that, like Miranda in London, denied a passport, they had become prisoners. José España preferred – perhaps with Picton's approval – to hide among friends, on his own estates in Venezuela. He went disguised, of course. He dressed like a sailor and wore a black eye-patch. The port officials at La Guaira, no doubt still looking for a false Negro, let him pass.

It was now, when agents were no longer required, that Caro, Miranda's agent, arrived in Port of Spain. And Caro wasn't like a Negro at all; the Spanish people in Paris had been fooled by someone else's disguise. Caro was ill, delicate, complaining; he had had a rough time. His journey from London to Port of Spain had lasted almost a year. His ship had been captured by a French corsair and he had been taken to Algiers and nearly hanged as a British spy. Then there had been delays in Portugal, a very rough Atlantic crossing, delays in Barbados. On the ship from Barbados Caro had been worried about Spanish corsairs; they would certainly have hanged him as a British spy.

His mission no longer had a purpose; the news he brought, of British–American invasion plans, was out of date. And now, landing in Port of Spain, he was arrested and taken to Picton. He was asked to identify himself. But he had lost his papers. He was abused as a Spanish government spy and ordered off the island. Caro said he was a British government spy. Picton said he hadn't been informed. 'As soon as I heard that name *Caro*,' Picton said in Spanish, with his famous, frightening laugh, 'I knew that you were a suspicious character.'

Caro was ill; there was no ship. He was allowed to stay but not allowed to see anyone. Sometimes Picton invited him to dinner. This was the news, of his continuing personal troubles, that Caro sent back to Miranda. He fabricated a few encouragements: Venezuela was still in ferment; all that was needed was a leader and 2,000 men. But Caro soon came to understand the situation of the Venezuelan revolutionaries in Trinidad.

'The Venezuelans have no concentrated plan,' he wrote to Miranda in April 1799. 'They do not work with foresight. They are better prepared to change their masters than to become free. They believe that it is the same to acclaim independence as to be independent, and that independence will be accomplished simply by rejecting the yoke of Spain and placing themselves under the protection of some other nation.'

Picton read all Caro's letters. This one he sent on to the Under-Secretary of War in London as proof of Miranda's untrustworthiness.

Miranda had been trying to leave England for Trinidad. The United States ambassador hadn't been able to help. The Russian ambassador said that if the Empress Catherine was still alive Russia would have given Miranda two frigates and 2,000 men; but now there was the 'odd genius' of Paul I. Two Englishmen had talked of sending out Miranda with warships to South America and setting him down as 'the Washington of that continent'; they thought that 'from such a venture more honour and profit would flow to England than from the bloody and expensive European war'. The idea came to nothing. At the same time Huskisson, the Under-Secretary of War, told Miranda he had 'recently become an object of suspicion to the government' – it was because of Caro's letter – and couldn't be given a passport.

'Behold how despotism always seeks to arm itself in its calumny,' Miranda wrote in his diary, 'in order to find fault with one who is blameless!'

THE FRENCH republican refugees in Venezuela submitted a plan for the invasion of Trinidad. Caracas was never happy about its republicans, and turned down the plan as 'foolhardy'. But the news disturbed Picton. He stepped up the pamphlet war to keep alive the threat of revolution. Some of the pamphlets were Miranda's; some were composed locally.

'Liberty! The philosopher's stone that turns all metal to gold. Look at the inhabitants of the North of our America. You will see that Nature delights in populating the fields of liberty, and looks otherwise, with regret, on the growth of slavery, an institution which is contrary to her laws. Deserts, solitude and silence are the fruits of tyranny. *Nunc atque numquam. Il vaut mieux tard que jamais. Más vale tarde que nunca.*'

'Spain, beaten throughout Europe; begging for peace at the price of honour; deservedly without the esteem of her allies; her navy destroyed; her armies in disarray; her treasury empty – how can such a country compel you to the obedience which she says she must have from her subjects? Nature has given you the fairest and most fertile country in the world. In such a country you need liberty alone to make you among the happiest of men.'

It was the cruelty of the revolution. Thirty years earlier Spain had been for Miranda the country of old churches, mosques, paintings, fine wines (listed and described in his journal), prostitutes of allure, fine clothes, books, learning. He had longed to serve in the country's army; and to show his worthiness he had prepared a genealogy, an *informe de hidalguía*, proof of generations of clean blood and noble living, which was the pattern of the *informe de hidalguía* that Diego de Ordaz, companion of Cortés, had presented when he claimed the licence to conquer that very region of the Orinoco.

The launches came and went between Trinidad and Venezuela. The trade was illegal both ways; it was permitted by both sides. From Trinidad the launches took British goods and Picton's propaganda; from Venezuela they brought cattle, mules, tobacco, salt, dried meat, all contraband, and Spanish government spies. The spies were useful to Picton. Government House on the Port of Spain strand was open to them. Some had standing invitations to afternoon dinner. In the evening Picton was free with claret and madeira.

So Caracas heard that Picton had asked the captain of a neutral ship whether he had seen a British frigate near the Orinoco; and that Picton looked 'perplexed and despondent' when the captain said he hadn't. Caracas also heard that Picton was just pretending to be worried about a Venezuelan invasion, to throw the Venezuelans off their guard. London was secretly preparing its own invasion force; and there were already 5,000 muskets in Trinidad, to assist any uprising in Venezuela.

The officer of the harbour-guard brought a Venezuelan to Government House at six one morning. Picton was already dressed for riding. The Venezuelan said he had come on church affairs. Picton offered breakfast and invited the Venezuelan to come and eat again. The Venezuelan came the next day, Picton had just received the newspapers from England; he talked about the war in Europe and the unhappy condition of Spain. He also talked about Venezuela; he showed the report he had of Venezuelan plans to invade.

Abruptly, Picton ordered the Venezuelan to get off the island. The Venezuelan hadn't eaten anything; he wasn't given any time; he even had to leave his laundry behind. He was, of course, a spy. After his hungry crossing (he complained to his superiors) he reported that there wasn't an event or decision in Venezuela Picton didn't know about in two days.

The governor of Cumaná offered 20,000 dollars for Picton. Picton offered 20 for him.

This was Picton's aim now: once again to suggest imminent action, not only to the authorities in Venezuela but also, for greater realism, to the revolutionaries in Trinidad. He brought them out of hiding. He gave them money and sent them to the Spanish stalls and grogshops near the wharf.

'How can you people be such slaves? Can't you understand this freedom from taxation that the English people enjoy? You are such fine men, and you want to remain slaves?'

A Venezuelan agent heard this in a Port of Spain shop one day. To give himself countenance he bought a cheese. The speaker was Juan Mansanares, a thirty-four-year-old lawyer who had come by way of London from Spain, where he had served a prison sentence. He accosted Venezuelans in the streets and led the talk to the rights of man, freedom from the yoke and his own sufferings in the cause.

'They'll want to know me all right when the time comes, His Excellency the Viceroy of Santa Fé and the governor of Guayana. Oh yes, they have their warrants out, but we'll meet on the day I am dictating the terms of surrender. Study this face well. You'll be seeing it over there soon.'

It was a thin, discoloured, pock-marked face. Mansanares was five foot two, of regular build, with curly black hair; he wore a jacket and pantaloons; he was melancholy by day but jovial at night at Picton's table, where he was a great favourite. This was the description that went to Caracas. Mansanares also acted as impresario for Manuel Gual, the embittered and taciturn old soldier.

'You don't know this man? But how can that be, if you know Venezuela? Before you, my dear sir, you behold Gual, the friend of Caracas.'

One of the Venezuelans who came over at this time was a man of twenty called Manuel de España. He came to see his elder brother Andrés. Andrés had remained in Trinidad after the surrender; he worked for the British on one of the armed launches in the Gulf. It grieved his mother in Angostura that Andrés should serve the enemy, and she sent Manuel to talk to him.

'Brother, you've got it wrong,' Andrés said. 'But don't go away. Something big is coming up. We want men of spirit. This evening we'll talk with two great friends of mine. You must listen to what they have to say, because it means a lot for us.'

That evening at about eight Gual and Juan Mansanares came to Andrés's house. The talk was about the government of America, Spanish America. Manuel said he had always been a loyal subject of the King of Spain. Gual and Mansanares didn't say any more then.

Four days later they invited him to their house and they said, '*Amigo*, you don't know us. You must understand that we are your friends. All of us who are *americanos*' – it was one of the words of the revolution – 'must unite, if we are to stop being slaves.'

Manuel said they should speak more clearly.

'We want about twenty or thirty brave men. To liberate our usurped American land.'

Manuel said, 'I am at the age when I have to think of earning my living, and I would rather be a hewer of wood than work for the enemy.'

'No, *amigo mio*,' Mansanares said, 'you've got us wrong. It is one thing to work for the enemy. It is another thing to work for your country. You are at the age when you can defend your country. You and your brother are men of great spirit. We are positive of that. We believe that we could easily become the liberators of our fatherland.'

'*Amigo*,' Manuel said. 'I know that all those people who have taken up this liberty you talk about have come to a bad end. And they will always do so. I don't want to be one of them. Ever since I was born my father worked to support me, and I have supported myself ever since I was able. It looks to me that I will always have to support myself by my own labour. The way America is governed isn't going to help me one way or the other.'

'Be quiet,' Gual said. 'It is one thing to be a slave, as you are now, to support yourself. It will be quite another story when we get liberty. Then you will be one of the first generals.'

Manuel was confused. This was a definition of liberty that hadn't occurred to him. He said he would have to think it over. When he went back to his brother's house he told him everything.

'Well, what do you think?' Andrés asked.

'What do I think? I think I want to go home and get away from this place. I don't want to think about the impossible.'

'You make me wonder. An *americano*, and you have this low way of thinking.'

'But I don't see how I can believe what those men said.'

'That is because you don't know the forces Great Britain is putting at our disposal when the time comes.'

For two days Andrés worked on him, and in the end he agreed. If the revolution was going to be as easy as Andrés said, and he was going to be made a general, he would join the revolutionaries. Andrés took the news to Gual and Mansanares, and they gave Manuel his first job. It was to deliver some documents to a priest on the mainland.

Picton invited Manuel to dinner at Government House, introduced him to the British governor of Martinique, who was visiting, gave Manuel 300 pesos ('I am obliged to spend considerable sums in gratifications to persons on the Continent,' Picton wrote to London that month, asking for a rise in salary) and promised Manuel the command of a frigate when the time came. London had ordered the invasion, Picton said; there were going to be at least 5,000 men; operations would begin in about four months. It was going to be a bloodless affair, and Manuel could help to keep it so: those papers he was carrying would win over many Venezuelans.

Gual said he knew there were six towns in Venezuela ready to revolt. He said to Picton, in Manuel's presence, that all *he* needed was a hundred and fifty to two hundred men and a couple of warships. Picton said that could be arranged; he would also get a squadron to cruise along the coast, to give Gual support.

The Venezuelan authorities began to look for Manuel de España almost as soon as he had got back to his mother's house in Angostura. Manuel didn't know. He was making his way to the coast to deliver his papers. He lodged with friends and strangers in towns and plantations, three or four days at a time; it was the way of the Venezuelan road. After twenty-four days he reached his destination. It was five in the afternoon. He found lodgings, went for a stroll, bought some tobacco, drank a glass of wine. He passed some young men in the street. He heard them say, 'They are looking for that man.'

He asked, 'Which man?'

'You.'

Early next morning some militiamen rode up to the sugar-estate where he was lodging and Manuel heard them asking for 'a young man who had just come from Trinidad'. The estate people said they didn't know anyone like that, and the militiamen went away.

Manuel left the estate and rode until evening. He found lodging in a plantation and lay down to sleep in his hammock. At about eleven or twelve he heard the horses of the militia. He ran out to a lemon grove and saw the men searching the outbuildings by the light of a torch. All but two of the men then went away. Manuel stayed in the lemon grove until dawn. Then he gave himself up.

He lied at first. But the officials were kind; and Manuel told everything he knew.

The governor of Cumaná studied the transcript of the interrogation and reported to the Captain-General of Caracas that he wasn't greatly disturbed. He thought he understood Picton's 'instruments of deceit and fiction'. He didn't believe that a big expedition was being got ready in London or Martinique; he thought that Picton was lying to Gual and Mansanares as he had lied to Manuel de España. He didn't believe there were six towns in Venezuela ready to rise or that Gual was now at the centre of much of a conspiracy. He thought it just possible that the British might incite and arm the Negroes in Venezuela to start another Santo Domingo; and of course precautions should be taken.

Caracas had, in fact, already won. The first Venezuelan revolution had been smashed. The news of Manuel de España's arrest and imprisonment, when it got back to Trinidad, was lost in bigger news. The tragedy of the revolution had occurred. José España, who had gone back from Port of Spain to the mainland disguised as a sailor with a black eye-patch, had been arrested.

José España was a planter and a slave-owner, but he went back to start – as a first step in the revolution – a Negro insurrection; and he hoped to start it with the Negroes on his own estate. These Venezuelan revolutionaries were as simple as their words. After the first jail-break in La Guaira two years before, two of the revolutionaries had walked to the house of the official interpreter and had hung around until they were arrested; they thought they were in the house of the French consul. And now José España, well known and with a price on his head, hid in his own house. He constructed a hiding place which was somehow concealed whenever the front door opened. He gave up his black eye-patch disguise and walked about the streets dressed like a charcoal-burner.

He gave his Negroes a day for their insurrection. One of them told the authorities. José España's house was watched. One evening the sentinel heard a loud noise. He got the rest of the guard. The maid confessed at once. José España didn't hide in his hiding place. He ran up to his roof, jumped on the roof of the house next door, climbed down the chimney and fell noisily on a trestle table with some plates. He was taken to Caracas and tried six days later. He had forgotten 'the fear of God, the sentiments of humanity and the no less sacred duties of religion and society'. His aim was the 'shedding of much innocent blood, pillage, arson, the ruin of families, disorder, confusion, anarchy, the contempt and degradation of religion'.

It was judged that he 'should be taken from prison, tied to the tail of a beast of burden and led to the scaffold, the common crier proclaiming his crimes; that having there come to the end of his natural life at the hands of the hangman, he should be beheaded and quartered; that the head should be taken in an iron cage to the port of La Guaira and be there affixed to the very top of a thirty-foot pole which should be placed at the Caracas Gate of that town'. The quarters were to be distributed among the places associated with the revolution. The sentence was carried out two days later, on 8 May 1799; that evening the quarters and head were transported on muleback to the places named.

Five more executions followed in the next month. Thirty-three men were exiled, many of them to periods of forced labour. The Negro who had betrayed José España was given 300 pesos a month for life. In Trinidad, before the hangings were over, Gual urgently put up a plan to invade; he asked for just two hundred men and the protection of two frigates for just one or two days. Picton wrote to Headquarters. Gual wrote to his friends in Venezuela. Headquarters didn't have the authority or the troops. Gual's letters were intercepted in Venezuela; people were questioned. The revolution, which was to be known as the Revolution of Gual and España, was over.

PICTON'S DISPATCHES to London became fewer and then stopped altogether for four months. In Port of Spain the distance between the revolutionaries and their patron grew. Every revolutionary felt that España had been betrayed, and by Picton. Caro, Miranda's unhappy agent, was still in Port of Spain, still a prisoner. There had been some talk of Caro going to the mainland in disguise, and Picton had appeared to approve. But now Caro changed his mind. He wrote to Miranda that they should start the revolution alone; it was dangerous to delay; 'the secret will become known'. Picton finally ordered him off the island. The revolutionaries in Trinidad heard nothing more about him, and they assumed that he had gone to the mainland and that he too had been betrayed.

The Captain-General of Caracas was a new man, an energetic servant of the declining Empire. It was he who, with little money and little paperwork, had organized the Venezuelan intelligence service. He sensed the distance now between Picton and his remaining revolutionaries and thought to exploit it. He wrote to the governor of Cumaná. 'As a beginning I am sending you a separate letter, which you might lose or even perhaps arrange for a copy to get to Colonel Picton, in such a way that he might believe that the person who passes it on to him is betraying our correspondence and doing him a service.' The letter was plausible, in the manifesto style of official Venezuelan correspondence. It stated that Gual and Mansanares were abusing Picton's credulity; principles like theirs had separated the United States from England and had recently put Ireland in danger; their propaganda was hardly worth the serious consideration of a man like Picton. Captain-General of a declining Empire to governor of a rising: there was sympathy; the assessment was also Picton's.

'It seems to me an appropriate moment,' the Captain-General wrote to his governors, 'to turn Picton's attention to his own house. We might begin to drop hints of an invasion.'

Picton responded. He wrote to London that a Venezuelan expedition was preparing; he asked for help. He wrote two or three dispatches to London in the next two months, about deserters, immigrants, land grants, accounts. Then for four months he wrote nothing at all. There was nothing to report.

JUST BEFORE he left Trinidad Caro appeared to have met Gual; and Gual took over as Miranda's agent in Trinidad. Gual was fifty-seven, Miranda forty-nine; they had known one another as young men in Caracas thirty years before; and they could both now be said to be prisoners. Gual wrote to Miranda and reintroduced himself. He had 'the glory to be proscribed by the Spanish government as the author of the revolution that was planned in Caracas in 1797'; he told of his wanderings and persecution. He addressed Miranda as the saviour of the fatherland and begged him to come to Trinidad to complete the work of independence.

Miranda took Gual's letter to a British minister to show that the revolution still lived. 'He is a native of Caracas,' Miranda wrote, 'has served in the militia and is popular; he comes from a rich and noble family. General Miranda knew him intimately.' Rich, noble! Miranda was applying the concepts of Europe as words alone, accurate but misleading, to a simpler world: the Negro-worked plantations of Venezuela, the low wooden houses of Port of Spain, the muddy shore, the rough Spanish shops, the one printery. He sent Gual his pamphlets. Gual read them with 'holy enthusiasm' and wrote as a man to whom the high words of revolution had been restored. 'A smile from our native land is more precious than all the favours of tyrants.' – 'I expect that the breach once begun will be made absolute by the lance of Achilles.'

At the same time Mr Turnbull of the London house of Turnbull and Forbes, who had been supporting Miranda for two years, wrote to Miranda about money. 'Really, My Dear Sir, it is impossible to go on at this Rate – the Simple Interest of our advance amounts to £100 per ann. Mr Forbes, I assure you, is equally disposed as I am, to assist and serve you, – but a line must, for your Satisfaction as well as ours, be drawn.'

Once again, though, an English invasion of South America looked likely. General Abercromby, the conqueror of Trinidad, came down from Scotland to see Miranda. Miranda gave maps, facts, figures, advice. 'The generals have begun to see me,' Miranda wrote to Gual in March 1800. Madrid heard, and sent warnings. Gual wrote to his friends in Venezuela: the size of the British expeditionary force grew. Then Abercromby took his army to Egypt instead; it was there that he died.

'In this country,' Miranda wrote to Gual, 'every promise that has been made to us has been broken; I see nothing but perfidy and bad faith.' All the Spanish Americans in London, Miranda said, had gone to Paris, where the principles of the revolution had been reasserted. 'I have asked and asked for my passport to leave the country, and they detain me by treachery.' He hadn't heard from Gual; he suspected that Gual's letters were being intercepted. 'If by any chance you write to me, let it be under cover to Mr King, Minister Plenipotentiary of the United States of America.'

Picton had written nothing about the revolution for a year. He sent this letter of Miranda's back to London as further proof that Miranda was 'not well disposed to the British government'.

It was Gual, in Trinidad, who paid. In his letters to his Venezuelan correspondents he tried to undo the damage: Britain was sending help in a few weeks, Britain was a great country. His letters were opened, those written to him from London, those he wrote to Venezuela.

There were reports in Port of Spain that among the Venezuelans whom Gual knew there was a poisoner with a commission. The governor of Cumaná had provided the pills, which were of opium or crushed glass.

'I wish you the best of health. Hold firmly on to hope and never be disheartened by tyranny, which is always weak. And so goodbye, from your ever loving countryman and servant, Manuel Gual. Trinidad, 8 September, 1800.' It was his last letter; it was intercepted by the Venezuelan authorities.

'People who have taken up this liberty you talk about have always come to a bad end.' Manuel de España had said that; and now he was in a Venezuelan jail. His brother Andrés was also in jail, in Port of Spain, on an unspecified charge. The Trinidad estates of Santiago Mariño were confiscated. But both Santiago Mariño and Andrés de España lived to fight another day. Juan Mansanares, once so free with the money Picton gave, and noticeable in the Port of Spain streets with his European jacket and pantaloons and his wild talk ('the bragging of these resentful or desperate men', the Venezuelan spy said), was no longer seen. He died quietly; the date is unknown; he was thirty-six. Manuel Gual left Port of Spain and went to St Joseph. There, three months after the presence of the poisoner had been reported, Gual died.

The governor of Cumaná may have supplied the poison. But the Spaniards of Trinidad thought that Picton was responsible for the poisoning. No open accusation was made, and Picton said nothing. His Spanish American accusers never looked for the truth. They were content with their resentment; it was all that remained of the revolution for the time being.

Caracas knew more. They knew the poisoner; they gave him asylum. He was Antonio Vallecilla; he had been a friend of Gual's. Two and a half years before he had been reported to Caracas as one of the Spaniards in Trinidad who had taken service with the British. He had raised a company of peons to hunt down runaway Negroes in the interior. The British commander-in-chief had made him a captain and given him 60 pesos a month; and Picton used to tell Venezuelans that he had Spanish soldiers he could call upon.

Vallecilla, waiting for the revolution that never came, had changed sides again. He was like Caro, Miranda's agent, who had disappeared. Caro was someone else the Trinidad Spaniards never bothered to find out about. Caro hadn't gone to the mainland; Caro hadn't been betrayed. He went back to England. He complained about Picton and tried to get money from the British government and from Miranda. Then he went to Hamburg. He continued to write his witty, complaining letters to Miranda, his 'friend and lord', 'friend and countryman'. He had met some Frenchmen the other day, he wrote, and there wasn't a man of principle among them; each was a sort of 'noble-royalist-democrat-jacobin salad'. Almost on the same day Caro was writing hysterically to the Spanish minister in Hamburg, begging for money, enclosing a letter to the Spanish King, begging to be forgiven, asking only to be allowed to live in peace and perhaps to expiate his errors in the royal service. The revolution was a farce, Miranda a fraud: Miranda wanted to be the Inca-Emperor of Spanish America. Caro was not forgiven. He died in poverty in Portugal three years later. In Trinidad he continued to be remembered, with Gual, as a martyr of the revolution and Picton's victim.

The revolution known as the Revolution of Gual and España held much of what was to come: the borrowed words that never matched the society, the private theatre of disguises and false names that ended in blood and the heads spiked in public places. That day in Caracas people had watched in silence when one of José España's friends broke away twice from the hangman and twice was chased about the square. The hangman was a murderer whose life had been spared twenty years before on condition that he performed this duty for the rest of his days. He was now old; he had to fight his victim into the noose; no one moved to help him.

Some years later, in 1808, when Picton was recovering from his disgrace, Miranda and Wellington met in London to discuss the invasion of Spanish America. Wellington didn't go to Spanish America; both he and Picton went to Spain itself, to fight the invading French. But Wellington said later of Spanish America, 'I have always had a horror of revolutionizing any country for a political object. I always said, if they rise of themselves, well and good. But do not stir them up; it is a fearful responsibility.'

6. 'Apply the Torture'

1801–1802

UNEXPECTEDLY, Miranda tried to conciliate Picton. There was a new government in London; they were interested in Miranda's invasion plans. Miranda said that Picton should be one of the generals. Picton at once responded; he said that Miranda was important to any South American venture. A week after Picton wrote, the peace came; and all invasion plans had to be put aside. Picton was forty-three; the invasion of South America, if and when it came, would be without him.

Some years later in London Picton and Miranda became friends. But they could not have worked together in Trinidad in 1801. A lady in England noted the 'boastfulness' with which Miranda the revolutionary spoke about 'great principles'. She forgave him. Picton would have been less kind. He had got to know Miranda's background too well. Miranda, after a lifetime in Europe, had developed the patrician intimations of his youth. Picton, after four and a half years as Governor of Trinidad, had become a colonial. Shaking himself free of the revolution, the revolutionaries and the Spaniards, he had made Trinidad his opportunity. He had become a planter; he owned Negroes. He had become a defender of slavery, vehement, like a convert to the cause. He had the vocabulary and could make the private jokes; he could describe the system as 'the assistance of Africans from the Coast'.

There was a feeling in London that Trinidad should be settled by free men. Picton pretended to agree; but the people he welcomed during the war were French royalist emigrés from Santo Domingo and other French islands each of whom came with a few hundred loyal Negroes: the Count de Loppinot de Lafressilière, the Viscount de Montignac, the Count de Rouvray, the Count du Castellet, the Baron de Montalembert, the Chevalier Dupont du Vivier de Gourville. Picton, and British rule, gave these men a second chance, without any new responsibility; and in Trinidad the principles of their aristocracy, which had set the Caribbean ablaze, were revived.

It was an aristocracy which, in the Caribbean before the troubles, had grown to measure itself against its own Negroes. Between the white and the Negro the French recognized a hundred and twenty-eight shades of colour, from the half-and-half of the true mulatto to the quadroon to the marabou to the sacatra to the sang-mêlé who, with a hundred and twenty-seven degrees of whiteness, was still 'of colour'. The classification had come late – a hundred years or so before, slaves in the French islands were white as well as black – and it came from racially insecure people, penetrated with the blood of their Negroes and increasingly anxious to suppress competition. In the second half of the eighteenth century there was a whole series of racial laws in Santo Domingo. Attempts were made to expel people of colour from their plantations and to prevent them buying houses or keeping Negroes of their own. People who were officially of colour were not to wear swords or French dress; they were not to be educated in France or called Monsieur; they were not to hold dances; they were not to play French games.

Trinidad, with no law or lawyers and only a memory of Spanish forms, was Picton's kingdom. He was the law; the French planters were his barons. For them in 1800 he rewrote the Negro Code. The Spanish code had reduced a Negro to his needs. The new code was concerned only with the needs and the fears of the Negro's owner.

The limit on floggings was raised from twenty-five lashes to thirty-nine. Negroes had to carry passes and were to be whipped, twenty-five lashes, if they were found on the streets after nine.

Negro dances had to end at nine sharp; the sale of rum to Negroes, except in quantities of five gallons and over, was banned; a free man of colour who admitted a Negro to a dance was to be fined. A special Saturday-night patrol enforced these regulations in Port of Spain.

Working hours were extended because, Picton wrote, a new Negro was naturally lazy and 'would rather suffer hunger and enjoy his repose'. 'Laterally', Picton went on (his spelling was always shaky), the 'increasing opulence' of the planters had 'enabled them to augment their forces by considerable purchases of this description of Negro'. The custom of giving Negroes Saturday to work on their own provision grounds – instead of a food allowance – was therefore abolished; and planters would be fined 50 dollars if they didn't work their Negroes on Saturday.

Creole Negroes, plantation-born and bred, were always more amenable; and Negroes, so far from being guarded against moral dangers, as in the Spanish code, were to be encouraged to breed, 'so that in course of time the importation of slaves from Africa may be considerably diminished, if not totally dispensed with'. A woman who had more than three children and kept them healthy was to be given a dollar a year per child; a woman who had seven would be spared all field labour.

Other laws forbade Negroes to sell the crops they grew on their provision plots, and punished them for stealing from their owners. The severest punishment was for witchcraft and sorcery. Negro sorcery, leading to a Negro underground, was the especial French terror. Subordination, the suppression of competition, the suppression of anything that might lead to conspiracy and riot: the code marked the dangers of the slave island. There was no longer a threat of Venezuelan invasion; the Spaniards on the island were negligible. The French free people of colour were bitter but subdued. The danger lay in the Negroes themselves, by whose numbers the prosperity of every slave island was measured.

Every Sunday morning the militia, white and Royal, coloured

and Loyal, drilled for three hours in the sun. Morning and evening at the Orange Grove Barracks the soldiers, black and white, were flogged; a traveller estimated that the garrison was flogged four times round in a year. Sometimes the soldiers were punished on the piquet. Picton had revived this military antiquity: the trussed soldier, suspended by his wrists from a rope, was hoisted up on a pulley and then lowered from time to time to rest the tip of his big toe, not more, on a blunt stake.

LAND WAS CHEAP or free in Trinidad; but Negroes and machinery were expensive, and it cost about £8,000 to set up a 75-Negro estate. Picton had no money of his own; and it was only at the end of his term that his salary as governor was raised from £1,200 to £3,000. His enemies said that Picton made his fortune by hunting down Negroes who had run away into the interior in the Spanish time and selling them locally or in Venezuela; he was assisted in the catching and selling by a Spanish captain, whom he later killed. It would sound like gossip if we didn't know about Antonio Vallecilla, the poisoner of Manuel Gual. Vallecilla had raised a company of peons to hunt down runaway Negroes; he made many trips to the mainland and at last went over to Venezuela for good.

Another charge was that Picton had robbed an orphan of his patrimony of fifteen Negroes; and some transfer did take place, though it might have been that the Negroes were impounded because their maintenance during the years of the orphan's minority – it cost at least 40 dollars a year to keep a Negro – hadn't been paid. Two Spanish prisoners of war complained to London that money had been extorted from them at the time of the capitulation; Picton said they were lying. Someone else said that money bequeathed him had been kept by Picton; Picton made an excuse and sent the money.

Picton supplied his estates with stock and timber and other stores, including salt-fish for his Negroes, by illegal barter with United States ships. There was a sharp letter from London; Picton, like any Spanish governor two hundred years before, replied that he had only wanted to preserve the island from absolute want and famine. Merchants in London complained about the excessive duties they paid in Trinidad. Picton promised to send the accounts but didn't: his accountant was 'indisposed'.

These were modest dealings for a colonial governor; there was never anything like a rebuke or a threat from London. A legitimate source of a governor's income was his fees. Picton estimated the fees of the Trinidad governorship at 12,000 dollars a year. He said he didn't take fees, but that was when he was applying for a rise in salary. The fees from the vendue or auction office were 500 dollars a month. Billiards were popular in Port of Spain just after the conquest and every billiard table paid Picton 16 dollars a month.

This was not excessive. Fees were not paid to the government but to the official. Picton's secretary received a salary of half a guinea a day; he also took fees, a dollar for a pass to the island of Grenada, 16 dollars for a commission in the Royal Trinidad Colonial Artillery, 40 dollars for a lawyer's licence. When a merchant vessel came into the harbour everybody got fees: the collector, the naval officer, the comptroller, the colonial secretary, the searchers, the harbour master; there was even a dollar or two for the officer in the sea fort.

The jailer in the Port of Spain jail, a Frenchman with the good jailer's name of Vallot, got fees whenever he was asked to flog a Negro or – this was the punishment Picton had prescribed for runaways – when he cut off a Negro's ears. Vallot preferred then to get his fees in advance, in case of accident. Once a Negro dropped dead as soon as the knife cut into his ear; no owner would have paid the ear-clipping fee after that. Vallot charged two bits a day, about a shilling or twenty cents, for every Negro in jail. This covered the imprisonment charge and food: salt-fish, dried horse-meat and bread.

A freed Negro came from Grenada to look for work in Trinidad.

He found work but he wasn't paid; he became tiresome, asking for his 70 dollars, and his employer had him taken to the jail – no legal formality was necessary. In time Vallot found out that the Negro was free and penniless and that there was no one to pay his jail fees. Vallot claimed the Negro as his own property in lieu of the fees, and sold him.

Lower than Vallot among officials were the alguazils or policemen. There were six of them in Port of Spain, People of colour considered the job degrading and it was reserved for those free Negroes who had no Negroes of their own. An alguazil earned a fee whenever he picked up and impounded a curfew-breaking Negro or a Negro who walked about after dark without a light; the owner then paid to redeem his Negro. The alguazils did particularly well out of new Negroes, who were in the habit of going to the front of their master's house in the evening to smoke and study the life of the street. The new Negro usually spoke some African language alone; the alguazil pretended not to understand his explanation and took him off to the jail. Some creole Negroes conspired with the alguazils to be caught out after curfew. If the alguazil kept his side of the bargain the Negro got part of his own redemption fee. But he paid a price: his owner was required to give him twenty-five lashes after he left the jail.

PEACE BROUGHT its anxieties to a soldier, and it brought an especial threat to Picton. He had ruled so far as a British governor, the representative of British power, in a foreign colony. Now, with the peace, British immigrants began to come, some from the other islands, some from England. Picton looked upon them as intruders, 'the scum and sediment of the West Indies' or insolvent shopkeepers and adventurers from Liverpool and Lancaster. He couldn't stop them coming; but he kept them out of Government House. It was said that sometimes when an Englishman went to Government House to report his arrival Picton took him upstairs to the mirador or gallery and pointed out the gallows. 'Look at that gallows, sir! If you do not behave yourself properly you may depend on being hanged. Go about your business and let me hear no complaint about you.'

The newcomers had their own objections to Picton. He was born, they said, 'of obscure parents somewhere on the mountains of Wales' and 'bred among the goats'. His brother, also a soldier, had been cashiered at the Cape of Good Hope for 'cowardice and cruelty'. His sister had married an American, 'a peddling broker of the name of Bette, who was originally an itinerant showman or player'. Bette had visited Picton in Trinidad. The visit had produced no scandal, but the English made it the subject of a malicious moral story. 'Little Bette', it was said, was astonished at the style of Picton's living and his title of Excellency, 'which none of the family ever enjoyed before or since the days of Caractacus'. Bette felt out of place. Picton was abashed; one day he broke down and confessed to Bette that it was all much better 'when they lived in *Wales* on twenty pounds a year'.

The kingdom was threatened. But in the beginning it seemed a private fight; Picton's barons stood aside.

THE TRAVELLER nowadays always entered the Gulf of Paria from the north; he saw what Columbus had seen. The Orinoco, the river of Columbus's Terrestrial Paradise, pushed its flood waters far. Even outside the Dragon's Mouth the water was olive with mud, in irregular bands of gradated but distinct colour frothing white at the edges. The traveller saw the South American continent in the distance as a low unbroken mountain range. Then the range broke, the channel of the Dragon's Mouth appeared: Venezuela to the right, Trinidad to the left.

There were still Indians in their piraguas in the Gulf. They were from Venezuela, which in the interior remained Indian country; in Trinidad the last Indians lived in alcoholic ennui in their mission reserves. There was no sign of cultivation on either side of the channel; it was all still the primary vegetation Columbus had seen.

On the rocky islets off Trinidad, thatched with brightest green, monkeys chattered.

The galley Negroes sang, and the traveller dropped down to Port of Spain past the deep-water harbour where the Spanish admiral had burnt his ships, the shallow bays, the swamps. Near Port of Spain there were a number of private wooden jetties. The principal quay was of stone, with the old Spanish battery *en barbette*. The town was laid out in small rectangular blocks. It was full of greenery; it was set between swamps and closed in by the mountains to the north and was hot and unhealthy. A traveller thought the stuffy little wooden houses were 'admirably well adapted to roast human beings alive'.

The heat was one of the punishments in the jail, where there were punishment cells known as *cachots brûlants*. The temperature in these dark windowless rooms was never less than 100 degrees; prisoners there, chained flat on boards, quickly wasted away and became demented. These rooms were separate in their function from the attic of the jail. This was a 'through' room and was reserved for white prisoners of quality who could pay more than the people below. It had also been fitted up recently as a torture chamber with irons, chains, pulleys and other instruments. This had meant more work for Jean-Baptiste Vallot, the jailer; he had bought a Negro to help him. The Negro's name was Porto Rico; Vallot called him 'Bourique'.

The jail was always full. The alguazils were greedy; and the unprotected, black or white, curfew-breaking Negro or 'disguised' – that is, drunken – English sailor, had to walk carefully. Vallot's jail, the military barracks and Picton's house were the three most important buildings in Port of Spain. It was in the jail that the galley Negroes, whose singing the traveller heard, were lodged, as city property, with their driver.

There were still many Spaniards, mostly of mixed race, in Port of Spain; they preserved the Venezuelan flavour of the town and kept it distinct from the life of the French plantations. There were traders and sailors and skilled artisans among the Spaniards, but they were not as rich or educated as the English newcomers. The grog-shops near Government House were Spanish; Spanish shops sold salt and tobacco and peon staples; the shops with finer goods, cloths and wines, were all English. Few of the Spaniards could read. Spanish was the language of the streets and of some official proclamations. The excellently printed four-page weekly newspaper, the *Courant*, was in French and English. The long news dispatches from Europe were usually two months old. The advertisements were mainly about plantations: sales of Negroes, carts and other equipment, descriptions of runaway Negroes, often maimed, one-eyed or 'much marked by the whip'.

The *Courant* came out on Saturdays. On Sunday mornings the white and coloured militia drilled. There were ways for a rich man to get out of this militia drill; but the young indentured English clerks from the English shops always had to turn out. These clerks earned between 100 and 200 dollars a year; they had to provide their own militia uniforms. When the militia parade was over the clerks went back to their shops; there was no Sabbath closing.

Unlike the Negroes, the indentured clerks had no holidays. Like the Negroes, they died young; out of every hundred poor English who came to Trinidad twenty to thirty died within a year. Negroes were expected to die; they were carried off by overwork, bad food and special Negro diseases, like the *mal d'estomac* caused by dirt-eating. A Scottish pamphleteer who came to Trinidad said he had noted the same disease, the product of despair, among the Scottish Highlanders who had sold themselves into slavery in the United States. But it was felt in Trinidad that the young poor whites died because of their vices.

The vices of Port of Spain were billiards, drink and sex. It was said then, and right up to the middle of the nineteenth century, that 'ardent spirits' were 'the bane of the lower order of the British'. Rum, at half a dollar or about two shillings a gallon, quickly turned the immigrant into 'a banquet for land-crabs, despised by the very slaves, breathing his last in a Negro hut'. The English merchants drank what they had been used to in England – claret, madeira, port – just as they always sat down to dinner in 'a long coat made of broadcloth'. It was years before they accepted that the light clothing of the French and the Spaniards might be more suitable to the climate, and that in the tropics madeira and port were not drinks for a mid-afternoon dinner. But their prejudices were justified up to a point: by the time the English merchants came to accept rum they had ceased to be English and middle-class and had become West Indian, culturally neutral, classless in a society too simple for class.

And sex. The European, as soon as he arrived, looked out for a mistress, 'either of the black, yellow or livid kind'. If he liked a Negro woman he bargained with the owner; if he found a free woman of colour he bargained with the mother. Free mulatto women acted as go-betweens, and a mulatto woman, Mrs Perry, ran the best brothel in Port of Spain; it was called 'The British Coffee House'. The Scottish pamphleteer, who gives this information, said that all the taverns in Port of Spain were brothels. The only genuine tavern was 'kept by a worthy little Highlander of the name of McKay. Such is the pitch of West India depravity, that, because he does not keep an assortment of ladies of easy virtue in his house, he does not meet with encouragement.'

Port of Spain was known for the beauty of its mulatto women. An English traveller twenty-five years later explained why. 'The French and Spanish blood seems to unite more kindly and perfectly with the Negro than does our British stuff. We eat too much beef and absorb too much porter for a thorough amalgamation with the tropical lymph in the veins of a black; hence our mulatto females have more of the look of very dirty white women than that rich oriental olive which distinguishes the haughty offspring of the half blood of French or Spaniards. I think that for gait, gesture, shape and air, the finest women in the world may be seen on a Sunday in Port of Spain.'

LITTLE WAS MADE of it by his French friends in Trinidad or later by his accusers in London, but for some time Picton had been living openly in Government House with a free mulatto woman, Mrs Rosette Smith. To the visiting Scottish pamphleteer she was the *aspera et horrenda virgo* of Government House. Picton had given her the fuel contract for the garrison. It was, the Scottish pamphleteer said, a honeymoon present: 'Accept of this bagatelle, my darling. The profits of it will enable you to buy trinkets.'

There was a Mr Smith. All that is known about him is that he owed his wife some money; the fact makes Rosette an adventuress of class. Most of what has come down about her is gossip. Nothing was said about her looks. They must have been good. She was said to have shared Picton's profits from the runaway Negroes. For a fee she could get men thrown into jail; for another fee she could have them freed. She took articles from shops, especially English toys, without paying. She held a levée twice a week and, with Picton's support, required all Port of Spain's English fashion to attend.

It seemed to the English that a chance had come to put Rosette down when she offered to buy the house of Mrs Griffiths, an old Port of Spain resident who, with her 'two amiable daughters', had found herself at the centre of the affray caused by Captain Vaughan and the *Alarm* fourteen years before. The bargain had been settled. Rosette was to pay 300 'Joes' for Mrs Griffiths's house, about £120. She offered a Negro girl and 25 Joes as part payment. She had more Negroes but she didn't want to part with them; she said she would pay the rest as soon as she got the money Mr Smith owed her. Mrs Griffiths signed an agreement of some sort.

Then Mrs Griffiths said she had signed nothing; she didn't know what she had signed; Rosette had tricked her. She refused to leave the house. Rosette complained to the Chief Judge of the cabildo. He was an Irishman; he had had some trouble with Rosette before, when, like royalty, she had wanted an Irish fisherman hanged for not presenting her with a turtle he had caught. Now the Chief Judge said he could do nothing. Rosette, according to the story, took it out of Picton at Government House.

'*Vou pa kalé entré dans couche à moi, jusqu'à tan moi dans case à Mistress Griffith*. You not coming in my bed until you get me inside Mistress Griffith house.'

Picton summoned the Chief Judge, called him a reptile and sacked him. He also ordered a company of black soldiers to surround the house and prevent anything or anyone going in. The soldiers insulted Mrs Griffiths and her daughters and racketed all night. When Mrs Griffiths complained they said the whole regiment was coming the next day. Rosette stood outside and told the soldiers she would have the skin off their backs if they let anyone go in. Water ran out, there were no more candles. A military surgeon who was engaged to one of the daughters was caught trying to smuggle in a kettle of hot water. A mulatto woman, a neighbour, tried to pass some oranges across; Rosette visited her and said she had better look out. After five days Mrs Griffiths surrendered the house to Rosette.

So among the English the Picton legend grew. And the legend went back to Picton's first days in the island. The story of Gallagher, the soldier hanged without trial for rape, was worked over and over. Picton and Gallagher, it was said, had quarrelled in a brothel over a whore. A mulatto woman, whose price was a 'Portugal piece', knew of the quarrel; to please Picton she complained later that she had been raped by Gallagher and robbed of a handkerchief. '*Ly pa kalé volo mouchoie à toi enco*,' Picton said. 'He not going to thief any more of your handkerchief.' He had Gallagher arrested and asked him, 'Did you see the sun rise?' Gallagher said, 'Yes.' – 'You won't see it set.' And Gallagher was hanged.

This was the gossip of English outrage: an exclusion from Government House, a widow insulted by black soldiers, a soldier unfairly hanged. The Negroes in Vallot's jail, the dirt-eating Negroes dying from *mal d'estomac*: that appeared to exist elsewhere.

ENGLISH IMMIGRANTS continued to come. A French traveller thought that the merchants among them, coming to Port of Spain as to the new El Dorado, made 'an interesting and sometimes comic spectacle'. They landed in full English costume but prepared for tropical adventure. They carried rifles on their shoulders. Behind them marched their Negroes with sample-boxes, tents, oilcloth huts. Self-sufficient, ignoring local example, they preserved the full domestic apparatus of their life in England and had solemn secret discussions among themselves about prospects for trade with the foreigners whom they hated and didn't study. Many of them went bankrupt. Ignorant of the Spanish laws that protected debtors, the English merchants competed with one another in those early days to lend money to Frenchmen and Spaniards who had no intention of repaying.

The English were absurd because they were foreign, new and clannish; the French traveller thought them 'degraded by this anti-social sentiment to the level of the half-civilized peoples of Asia'. The English were also absurd because they were more adventurous and gifted than the people they found themselves among. The Venezuelans had their 'marquises of cacao and tobacco'. The French had their aristocracy of the hundred and twenty-eight shades. The English were 'new men' with concrete gifts. They were putting in steam engines on the sugar plantations in Trinidad; they talked of a canal system to open up the interior. The English editor of the *Courant* was a master-printer of considerable education and literary style; his paper was almost too good for Port of Spain.

The English were not yet colonial; they were still a part of England. Their drives were more complex, and the colony offered liberation of a sort. English tradesmen took up duelling; 'the humbler the grade of the duellists, the more sanguinary were their encounters'. And the English fight against Picton in Trinidad soon went beyond gossip and became like an extension of the political agitations in England. The English immigrants claimed rights; they talked of writing to London newspapers and London lawyers. They wanted a British constitution in Trinidad. They planned a petition. They announced a public meeting.

A British constitution meant more than it said. It meant rule by the British in Trinidad. It meant the disenfranchisement not only of the free people of colour but also of the French planters, Picton's barons. The English were not comic at all. Their fight against Picton was not private; the kingdom itself was threatened. And the English were only one danger.

THE SLAVE SOCIETY had its jokes.* The Negro cook-girl burnt the Sunday callalloo, a slimy vegetable dish. Her French mistress ordered a professional whipping *à quatre piquettes*; it was the 'four-poster' method favoured by the French. The cook-girl was stripped, spreadeagled face down on the ground, her wrists and ankles tied to four stakes. Her mistress stood by, smoking a cigar. At every lash the girl cried out, '*Aie, aie, madame! Ça ka brulé dos moué!* That burn my back!' '*Eh bien, ma fille,*' her mistress replied, '*pour chi ou brulé calalou moué?* What for you burn my callalloo?'

Once Vallot flogged the skin off the back of the free Negro he had claimed in lieu of fees. A sympathetic fellow-prisoner, a mulatto man of property, spoke to the bleeding Negro afterwards. The Negro said, 'Gubnah da one debble, de jaila da he broder, and de jail da hell. When jaila say hang um, Gubnah say teek de rope.' 'This exornation,' the mulatto reported, in the careful language mulatto men of property used, 'excited my risible faculties'; he gave the man a dollar.

Even the dirt-eating and the *mal d'estomac* which killed many Negroes was the subject of obscene epigrams. But Negro suicide was never funny to the French planter. Of that, as of poison, he had an almost religious horror. Suicide, poison, sorcery; a Negro *atelier* in frenzy; the whips and the chains of the overseers useless; the secret unsuspected words: *ah, c'est bien dommage*, it might

* See note, p. 362.

be; the flames, the night of revenge: it was the terror of the estate house. At the first sign of that stillness among his Negroes the French planter could act like a man affected by the witchcraft he feared.

In 1794 on the Coblenz estate in north Port of Spain a hundred Negroes had died from poison; the estate had been left derelict. Baron de Montalembert bought half the estate in October 1801 and stocked it with a hundred and forty seasoned Negroes. Now, in the first month of the Baron's ownership, a hundred and twenty of his Negroes died in batches of sixty, forty and twenty. At about the same time, on St Hilaire Begorrat's estate in Diego Martin, west of Port of Spain, more Negroes were poisoned. It began to look like a conspiracy, a Negro challenge to authority. Montalembert was a newcomer; but Begorrat was Picton's closest friend and the Chief Magistrate for that year.

Begorrat was a Martiniquan and one of the earliest French immigrants to Trinidad. He was the planter Picton had threatened to hang, immediately after the capitulation, for being a troublesome republican. Begorrat's republicanism had only been a wish to be free of government interference, and it had long disappeared. He was a man of some education, lucid, precise and with a dry humour; he was the opposite of Picton and the two men had grown to work well together. Begorrat knew more about the management of Negroes than anyone else on the island. He had organized the slave colony for Picton; Picton deferred to him on all Negro matters.

Begorrat gave an example of his skill now. He had one of his dead Negroes opened in the presence of his assembled Negroes; and he and the doctor began to look for traces of poison. This solemn business had its effect on the poisoner. She turned out to be a nurse in the plantation hospital; her name was Thisbe. Without being accused she ran to a neighbouring planter and begged him to help her. He handed her back. Begorrat called some other planters and they examined Thisbe. She lied and contradicted herself. 'In order to profit of the first moment of anxiety and not to afford her time for reflection,' Begorrat wrote later, 'I ordered her to be suspended by the hands about two seconds, five or six inches from the ground; which induced her to confess her crime immediately and declare all her accomplices.'

Picton was for trying the accused Negroes at once. Begorrat thought that a case should first be established. In these matters he liked as he said later, to act with 'delicacy'. He suggested that the Negroes should be taken to the jail, confined apart for five or six days and then examined. Picton agreed. All the suspected Negroes from Begorrat's estate, Montalembert's and others thought to be infected were brought to the jail. There were twenty in all. Vallot put some in irons; he chained some; he shut some up in the *cachots brûlants*; he mortised the legs of others in wooden stocks.

Some days later the Negroes were interrogated by a Frenchman from Martinique who had sat on many poisoning commissions in that island. His recommendation was that the Negroes should be tried, and Picton named seven planters to act as judges. Begorrat was among them. They sat in a room in the jail. The trial took up much of their time but they took no money; it was an example, Begorrat said, of their generosity. It was stated in a London court later that three or four of the Negroes were professionally tortured. But Begorrat said this wasn't so; the torture was used only once, on the hospital wench Thisbe.

THE POISONING commission began to sit in November 1801. Early in December the cantankerous English immigrants met in a tavern to discuss the petition for a British constitution. They soon began to quarrel. It turned out that the people who had prepared the petition were London style radicals; one violent man even boasted of his connection with the Corresponding Society. Most of the indentured shop clerks signed the petition. The more respectable immigrants didn't; they were still close enough to England to be more afraid of London radicals than of Picton. The elderly English tavern-keeper said that 'while he was mixing his liquors he heard some very warm debates'.

One merchant said he thought the whole thing was 'only a scheme for sinister purposes'. A colonel of the militia left because he didn't want to be 'mixed with people of so inferior class'. Another man changed his mind because he saw at the meeting that there weren't enough 'men of experience and science' to make a British constitution work. In the end only six or seven people remained. They decided to try again; they said they would hold a public dinner in a fortnight; in the meantime the petition would be left for signature in Higham's store.

Picton, unexpectedly strengthened, banned the dinner and said he would break it up by force if it took place. He ordered an investigation of everyone who had signed the petition. The Chief Judge and the escribano went about all day taking down depositions. One or two of the indentured clerks stood firm. The elderly tavern-keeper said he hadn't paid much attention; he had signed only for the extra business. But the apparently legal form, with an unreliable Irish judge asking questions and a Spanish-born escribano writing and writing in Spanish (he got a fee for every deposition, and he charged extra for the writing and the paper) – making real the terror of the island's unknown 'Spanish' laws: Inquisition, rack, stake – was enough to make many recant. Mr Winterflood yielded to more direct pressure. He was Comptroller of the Customs; he could get up to 20 dollars in fees from a merchant vessel. Picton said he would ruin Mr Winterflood if he found his name on the petition. Mr Winterflood had four orphaned nephews to look after. He ran to Higham's store and asked to have his name scratched out. Higham did so and Mr Winterflood 'thanked him with tears in his eyes'.

Little was dug up against the ringleaders, but it was enough. One had 'had his gown torn off his back' on another island. To be publicly manhandled was to be discredited; redemption lay only in flight. And this same English radical, fleeing to Trinidad, had confirmed and compounded his disgrace by being caned in public by a French nobleman 'for something dishonest which he did': a Corsican had seen.

As for Dr Sanderson, the man from the Corresponding Society, who had nearly got into a fight with a respectable merchant at the meeting at the tavern, he was said by another Englishman to be 'of no account'. But the only person who had anything to say against Sanderson was Vallot, the jailer. Vallot was to surprise many people in this way. He took his fees and did his job, flogging a Negro in a simple or complicated way, cutting off a pair of ears, branding cheeks with a hot iron, fitting stocks, checking a *cachot*. But this vacancy was deceptive. He didn't deal in pain; he could say, as he did later, that he didn't know whether he applied a torture with severity or not. But Vallot judged.

Vallot didn't approve of Sanderson. Sanderson might be a radical, but 'the deponent believes Dr Sanderson is a very unhuman man and a bad master'. Sanderson, who didn't have much of an estate anyway, had flogged one of his few Negroes on the face: Vallot didn't like that. And there was the Negro wench who had complained against Sanderson. Her complaint of maltreatment was proved; she had been confiscated and lodged in the jail. She was very ill. Vallot sometimes bought an enfeebled Negro in his jail as a speculation; but this girl was too far gone. Vallot begged Sanderson to redeem her. Sanderson said she was government property now and no concern of his. Two or three days later she died.

The radical owned slaves. Quick intellectual confusion awaited the radical from England; and Picton was especially enraged by those whose 'pretended humanity', as he said, 'frequently resides upon the tongue without ever vexing the heart'.

The radicals had been discredited, the petition had failed. But it remained an English affair. A Corsican, a planter, heard that an important document was being signed in Higham's store. He went to sign. Higham told him that foreigners were not allowed; 'at which answer the deponent walked out'. Soon, though, the petition had to be hidden. Higham spent a day and a night in jail; and he and one of his friends were dismissed from their commissions in the militia. The dinner didn't take place.

ALL THIS TIME the seven planters of the poisoning commission sat, intermittently, at the jail. The Negroes were taken from their cells, examined and returned to their respective confinements. They lived on water and plantains.

The planters reported regularly to Picton. They told him about the Negro called Aubinot; from their experience they believed him to be especially dangerous. Aubinot was a master of charms and divination; he had killed a number of Negroes on M. Ladeveza's estate with a poisoned whip. He had been thoroughly investigated but it was felt that he might have more to say and should be tortured. Picton gave the word to Vallot. After the torture in the garret Aubinot was brought down and tied up again to his pole and his legs placed in iron stocks.

In a *cachot brûlant* there was another dangerous Negro, a sorcerer called La Fortune. He had caused sickness among Negroes and had 'dangerous connections with the devil'. He had tried to kill himself to escape arrest. That was another grave charge against him. In the *cachot* he had gone foolish and derelict. He could no longer stand. He was repeatedly examined. Two of the jail Negroes had to drag him out and hold him up while he faced the tribunal.

Begorrat had tortured Thisbe, the hospital nurse from his own plantation, in a rough-and-ready way. He said then that she had confessed everything; but that confession couldn't be taken into account. She was taken up to the garret and tortured. Vallot's assistant, Porto Rico, did the heavy work, pulling on the rope. She confessed again. But, ruptured and swelling, she refused to condemn her husband. It was stubbornness like this, with its suggestion of a supernatural power at work among the Negroes, that the French planters feared.

The jail as a place of horror: it could not be otherwise: the planters of the commission, entering the jail, faced the tortures, confessions and rotting bodies like the African darkness that might overwhelm them all: powder turning to insects to ravage a plantation, charms killing the canes, money turning to dung, Negroes dying in convulsions, the world ending in blood and flames.

Picton could no longer withdraw. He might say that he was still a soldier, that a revolution had failed through no fault of his own, that his ambition lay elsewhere. But Trinidad was his creation; and like the planters in the jail, he could take no risks. On 23 December, while the poisoning commission was doing its work, a country alguazil brought in a Negro as a runaway. The two English immigrants who owned the Negro in partnership hurried to Port of Spain to plead for him. He hadn't run away; he had only been sulking and had 'lurked upon the estate'; he hadn't made for the woods, as runaways always did. But Picton gave the order to Vallot. Vallot's knife cut into the Negro's ear; the blood spouted; the Negro dropped dead.

OUTSIDE THE JAIL the city seemed at peace. Every evening, at about the time when the sunset gun was fired from the Sea Fort, Picton went for a walk; and in the Spanish-speaking area around Government House Negroes, mulattoes and Spaniards came out and chatted on front steps, had drinks at Negro stalls near the Greenmarket or in Spanish liquor-shops. The liquor and chandler's shop near Government House was owned by a Spaniard called Rodriguez. It was there, a few days before, on 7 December, at sunset, that an intrigue had begun.

Luisa Calderon came into the shop. She bought nothing. She hung around and talked with Rodriguez's wife. Luisa was about fourteen, the youngest of the three daughters of a manumitted Venezuelan mulatto woman. For nearly two and a half years Luisa had – on a promise of marriage, according to her mother – been housekeeper and mistress of a mulatto trader called Ruiz. It would have been a good marriage for Luisa. Ruiz, starting from almost nothing, as a clerk in a Spanish shop, had set up in business on his own. He had won Picton's favour and supplied fresh meat to the garrison; he traded in cattle and mules from the mainland; and in his shop – which was directly opposite Government House – he sold salt and tobacco. He was successful, at least in the way Spanish mulattoes understood success. He owned three Negroes, though they were not of the highest quality; two houses; and carts and mules.

Every evening at about this time Luisa left Ruiz's shop-and-house and went to her mother's. The idling in Rodriguez's liquor shop was unusual. She asked Rodriguez's wife to come out for a short walk, as far as the bridge. Rodriguez's wife said she couldn't. Luisa still stayed. Then Carlos Gonzalez came in. Rodriguez asked him to sit down. Carlos said he was too busy. Carlos was a Venezuelan-born mulatto of thirty-six; he now lived in Port of Spain with his wife. He was a trader, a man of substance. Rodriguez asked about Carlos's new schooner, which was in the harbour. Carlos said it was doing well.

Luisa left the shop. Carlos left. He caught up with her around the corner, in front of Ruiz's shop; and they spoke. She entered the shop. He walked on a little up the street, exchanged abstracted greetings with a doorstep group, then made his way back. On the sea side of Ruiz's shop there was a narrow passage, open to the street. Carlos entered the passage and 'stood there, pretending to make water'. A Negro man and a Negro woman passed in the street. The woman shouted at him that that was 'the place where kitchen articles were usually put out'. Carlos went further up the passage, 'constantly feigning as if he were making water', until he came to the side door. Luisa opened it.

Carlos may or may not have gone in; he said later that he didn't because Luisa told him that Ruiz was coming. When Carlos left he took a roundabout route, past the warehouses on the sea front, back to his own house. The next thing he heard – Negroes were running about with the news – was that Ruiz had been robbed of 2,000 hard dollars.

At Ruiz's shop Carlos found a crowd. Picton was there. Ruiz had complained to Picton as Picton was coming back from his evening walk. A bedridden man next door said he had heard the side door being opened and a noise like the breaking open of a trunk. Picton went away. Carlos, no doubt glad to talk to Ruiz on a neutral subject, asked whether Ruiz had checked up on his Negroes. Ruiz said he had. But Ruiz had accused Luisa and a second person, a man, to Picton already. And when the time came there would be evidence: the boards of the side wall would be broken away. Ruiz's Negro said he saw only the broken trunk; but he was a Negro and a known thief – Ruiz had bought him cheap for that reason – and no attention was paid to his evidence.

Luisa Calderon was taken to Picton's house that evening. He examined her in the hall downstairs. Rosette was there but she said nothing. Picton said that if Luisa didn't confess he would get the hangman Ludovigo – he was an English-speaking Negro called William Payne – to 'put his hand' on her; Ludovigo would 'draw' the money from her. Luisa had nothing to say. Both she and her mother – standing in the street outside, listening to the examination – were marched off by four soldiers to the jail and lodged in the women's section. They were not put in chains or irons that night.

The next day Ruiz, in spite of the loss of 2,000 dollars, bought two cargoes of mules and cattle. Picton, occupied with the English immigrants and their petition, didn't notice; and Begorrat, to whom the Luisa Calderon case had been passed as Chief Magistrate, was busy with the poisoning commission. Begorrat was in and out of the jail; he just ordered Vallot to lock up Luisa 'under two keys' and to take her mother to a room upstairs.

It was a busy time for Vallot. Three days later he took in Higham the storekeeper; and then Ruiz came to ask whether it was possible – without his name being mentioned – for Luisa to get something better than the usual jail food. It was possible. Vallot's wife, Rose, fed Luisa from her own table. It was the jailer's life, finding that line between prescribed punishment and the favours people were willing to pay for.

Luisa and her mother had been in the jail for a week or more when a Spaniard came up from one of the Indian missions to Port of Spain. He called on Ruiz, a mulatto but a 'countryman'. They talked about the robbery; neighbours joined in. A woman said she had seen Carlos Gonzalez in the passage on the evening of the robbery. Later, after he had dressed more formally, the Spaniard made his courtesy call on Picton.

'So they've robbed Mr Pedro,' Picton said.

'So they say,' the Spaniard said.

'What do you mean by "so they say"? Does this expression have a sinister or suspicious meaning?'

The Spaniard was cowed. 'Sir, I have just heard a conversation.' He told what he had heard from Ruiz's neighbour.

The next morning Carlos Gonzalez's house was searched. Later that day Carlos was arrested. And then, just a few days before Christmas, Begorrat took the case in hand.

Begorrat's term as Chief Magistrate was to end at the end of the month. He didn't have much time. On 22 December he examined most of the witnesses. Many people had seen Carlos and Luisa on the evening of the robbery. The Spanish-born escribano took down all they said. The case seemed straightforward. All that was needed was Luisa's confession. But when Luisa was examined in the jail she confessed nothing; and it occurred to Begorrat that a little torture, 'a slight torment', such as he had applied to the sorcerers, might help. He needed Picton's permission; he was acting now as Chief Magistrate and not as a member of the poisoning commission.

The next morning he wrote out a torture order: '*Appliquez la question à Luisa Calderon*. Apply the torture to Luisa Calderon.' He and the escribano took it to Government House. Picton read it and signed: *Th. Picton*.

And was damned. That there was no robbery, that Carlos Gonzalez and Luisa Calderon were framed by a jealous Ruiz: of this there is little doubt. But the facts of that backyard mulatto intrigue were soon disregarded in the scandal that grew around that signature and the act of torture that followed.

Begorrat and the escribano examined three more witnesses that day. Late in the afternoon Begorrat went to the prison and examined Ruiz's partner, who had also been imprisoned on Picton's order. At the time of the sunset gun Begorrat was ready for Luisa. She was in the garret. Begorrat and the escribano, Vallot and Porto Rico and two alguazils went up. It was a low room; it ran the width of the jail; the roof sloped at the ends. At one end Luisa sat on the floor, her legs in iron rings. The rings were on either side of an iron rod; the rod was fixed to a wooden pole. Even if the irons permitted, Luisa couldn't have stood upright; the roof sloped too low.

The torture instrument was simple. A pulley was fixed to the ceiling. Over the pulley passed a length of rope with a small noose at one end. Set in the floor directly below the pulley was a tapering wooden stake six inches high. The top of the stake was flat, circular, half an inch in diameter.

One of the alguazils, a former galley slave, whispered to Luisa that she should say that Carlos had taken the money. Luisa had seen two young Negro women tortured in that room; but she had nothing more to say.

At about seven Begorrat took out his watch and placed it on the table: he had an idea that Spanish law didn't permit more than an hour's torture at one time. He gave the word.

Vallot undid Luisa's irons. The two alguazils held her upright, raised her left hand and fitted the wrist into the noose at the end of the pulley rope. Vallot and Porto Rico took hold of the other end of the pulley rope and pulled the noose tight. Then the alguazils, still holding Luisa, bent back her left foot and tied it to her right hand with a separate piece of rope. Vallot and Porto Rico pulled on the rope until they began to raise Luisa's trussed-up dead weight off the floor. The strain on Vallot and Porto Rico was the strain on Luisa's wrist, shoulder, chest, waist.

They raised Luisa and then lowered her until the ball of her right foot just rested on the half-inch point of the stake and carried her full weight. 'In which posture,' Begorrat wrote, 'the said Luisa cried *Ay, ay*, repeating the same several times, calling on God and the Holy Virgin.' Vallot and Porto Rico held the rope tense for about twenty minutes. Luisa didn't confess. Begorrat gave the order to Vallot and Porto Rico to pull on the rope again, until only Luisa's great toe touched the stake. 'In this situation she remained, repeating her former expressions.' Another twenty minutes passed. Then Vallot and Porto Rico pulled until Luisa hung from her wrist alone. This time, after ten minutes, she begged to be let down and to be allowed to confess.

Luisa's mother was in a cell below the garret. She heard everything.

The rope was released. Luisa was unbound and taken down to Vallot's room. She leaned on the table; she was in distress. Begorrat gave her some wine and water 'with his own hands' and she appeared to recover. An alguazil fetched Carlos Gonzalez from his cell and Luisa told him he had stolen the money. He looked stupefied. Then Vallot took Luisa back to the garret and put her in her irons at the end of the room where the roof sloped low.

Vallot wasn't sure what Luisa's name was; in his adenoidal, eliding way he made it Louise Cardon. He didn't know what she was being tortured for. He saw that she suffered but he couldn't say whether the torture was severe or not. He did what he was paid to do. He tortured Luisa – the fees were 60 reales, about 33 shillings or 6.60 dollars – just as, at Ruiz's request, he fed her from his own table. 'She even had coffee in the mornings,' he said later. But Vallot approved of Luisa's spirit: 'I was surprised at her being resolute.'

For Vallot the time had passed quickly. He thought the torture had lasted fifteen or eighteen minutes. According to Begorrat's watch, it had lasted almost fifty-three minutes. The eighteenth-century military punishment, from which this torture derived, was never inflicted for more than fifteen minutes; it had lamed and ruptured many men and for some years had ceased to be an army punishment.

Early next morning Begorrat told one of the alguazils to go and bring the escribano to the jail. Luisa Calderon was to be examined again. It was Christmas Eve and Begorrat wanted the matter settled before the holidays and before his office as Chief Magistrate came to an end. The escribano came with his inkhorn and papers; the two alguazils were there, and Vallot and Porto Rico. Just before eleven the six men went up to the garret. Vallot hadn't had time to give Luisa anything to eat or drink that morning; but it was too late to think of that now. Begorrat asked where the stolen money was. Luisa said she didn't know. Begorrat took out his watch and put it on the table.

Vallot took off Luisa's irons. The alguazils trussed her up. Her right hand was put into the noose this time; Porto Rico pulled on the rope; her right foot rested on the stake. 'In which position,' the escribano noted, writing up the torture even while it was taking place, 'the aforesaid Luisa called on the Holy Virgin several times.' She had nothing more to say. She was taken down, trussed up the other way and raised again by the left wrist, torn from the previous evening.

The last thing she had drunk was wine. Now she asked for 'a little drop of vinegar'. 'I imagine she suffered,' the escribano said later, 'because I saw her cry.' She fainted twice and the second time they thought she wouldn't revive. One of the alguazils held her in his arms. Begorrat sent Vallot down to get some vinegar. Vallot always kept a little vinegar in the jail, to dab on a Negro's cuts after a flogging. He came back three minutes later, poured some vinegar into the palm of his hand and held it under Luisa's nose. She was still suspended, Porto Rico alone taking the strain of the rope. When she revived she found herself untied.

The time had again passed quickly for Vallot. He thought the torture lasted five minutes; Begorrat made it twenty-two. But, as Vallot said later, he had no way of checking the time: 'I was busy about other things.' As soon as Luisa was 'restored' – Begorrat thought there was some 'affectation' in her fainting – Vallot put her in her irons again. It was now about midday. The six men left the garret. The inquiry was suspended for Christmas, which that year fell on a Friday.

On Saturday Ruiz's partner, who had been forgotten in the jail over Christmas, although he was no longer suspected, petitioned to be released; he was released. On the same day Luisa and Carlos were briefly taken out of the jail. With Begorrat, the escribano, the two alguazils and a file of soldiers they walked the three blocks, some 1,500 paces, to Ruiz's house, Luisa 'smoaking a segar all the while'. All the witnesses were assembled. Ruiz's house was searched, Luisa's mother's house was searched and Carlos Gonzalez's, twice. The money wasn't found and Carlos and Luisa were taken back to the jail and fettered.

ON TUESDAY the 29th Begorrat was very busy. On that day his poisoning commission passed its first sentences; and on that day the sentences were carried out.

The Negro called Bouqui had been charged with sorcery, divination and poisoning. He had spent some months in solitary confinement. Now he was taken out of the jail and marched by a guard of soldiers to the church. In religious matters a new Negro was considered a *párvulo*, a child under six, and could be baptized without instruction. The curate of Port of Spain baptized Bouqui. The soldiers put him in irons and took him to the gallows. Fifteen minutes after the hanging the Negro executioner took Bouqui's body down and cut off the head. The headless body was tied to a stake. The head was taken away and spiked on a pole on the mountain road to St Joseph.

In the meantime in the jail the Negro called Pierre François had been ordered to fall on his knees to hear his sentence. He was then taken to the church. He was not baptized; he was already a Christian. Prayers were read to him. He was then 'heavily ironed' and the soldiers led him to where Bouqui's headless body was tied to the stake. Many Negroes watched. Some of Vallot's jail Negroes were waiting with faggots. Pierre François was chained to the stake with the headless body. He was made to put on a shirt. The shirt was filled with sulphur. The jail Negroes built up the faggots. The executioner lit the fire.

It was about three in the afternoon, dinner time. The Negroes who were watching didn't stay. They ran through the streets, yelling. The smell of sulphur and the two burning bodies drove many people out of their houses and there were some whites who feared a massacre. Begorrat and the French planters had devised the punishment and the ritual. They said afterwards it was what they used to do in Martinique.

A third sentence was passed that day, on Leonard, a mulatto. He was banished.

IN THE NEW YEAR, 1802, Begorrat handed over as Chief Magistrate to a Spanish planter. He immediately laid an attachment on Carlos Gonzalez's property: furniture, silver, linen, tallow, some cattle, two Negroes and the schooner. After this he took his time, attending to the case mainly at weekends. He released Luisa's mother. Luisa remained in the garret in irons. Carlos was also still in irons. They were now just prisoners in the jail. Drama had gone out of their case. Drama in the jail had followed Begorrat. He was still a regular visitor. On 29 January, a Friday, Begorrat and his poisoning commission issued their second set of sentences, on five Negroes.

Four of the Negroes belonged to Begorrat. Louison was judged to be a sorcerer's apprentice and banished. Antoine, his mentor, was also banished; he was to be branded on the forehead beforehand. Felix was banished; his ears were to be cut off. Felix was lucky. He was 'violently suspected' of poisoning; but his wife Thisbe, the hospital nurse, had refused even under torture to incriminate him. Thisbe herself was to be destroyed. So was La Fortune, the poisoner and attempted suicide, who came from another estate. He had been in the *cachot* all the time. He couldn't walk or stand now; he was put on a cart and taken to the execution place. Thisbe walked. Before she was hanged she said in patois, 'This is but like a drink of water to what I have already suffered.' She hoped that nothing would be done to her husband Felix; she herself was 'going to God'. Immediately after she was hanged she was heard to call out Felix's name.

He was there, watching, with Antoine. This was the first part of their punishment, to watch. They were then mutilated. La Fortune was hanged. The heads of Thisbe and La Fortune were cut off and the bodies burned on a pile that had been prepared. The next day, Saturday, Thisbe's head was taken to Begorrat's estate at Diego Martin, just to the west of the city, and spiked on a pole. La Fortune's head was displayed at Luzette's estate in St Anne's, just to the north.

AT SIX ON Sunday morning, one or two English strollers about, the sentry at the stone pier found a handbill stuck on his sentry-box. The wafers were still wet.

'*Sanguinary Punishment corrupts Mankind. The Effect of Cruel Spectacles exhibited to the Populace is the destruction of all tender emotions, it more frequently excites Disgust than terror. It creates Indifference rather than Dread. It operates on the lower orders as an Incentive to practices of Torture, etc., for the purpose of revenge; when they have the power of exercising what they have been instructed in they will. Par Ordre d'Alcalde de Barrio.* HUMANITAS.'

One thing was certain. A handbill so literate, abstract and contentious hadn't been put up by order of M. Bernard, the French alcalde de barrio or district warden. Of its English authorship there could be no doubt. Picton issued two angry and sarcastic proclamations ('. . . certain Jacobinical PHILANTHROPISTS . . . the tender feelings of the Negroes . . . POISONERS . . . nefarious conspirators . . .') and offered a 500-dollar reward for the bill-poster.

The sentry helped, and 'Humanitas' was found. He was an English lawyer who had recently come to Trinidad; he was an associate of Sanderson, Higham and the others. A copy of the handbill was found in his possession. He explained that he had copied down the words at the pier on the Sunday morning. Ink? He said he had sent a black boy to buy some from Higham's store. At six in the morning? He began to falter. He said that the other Englishman the sentry had seen on the pier was responsible. The sentry didn't agree. The lawyer was expelled.

The poisoning commission issued its third set of sentences. Manuel, an Ibo Negro, was to be destroyed in the usual way. Thisbe and La Fortune had been executed just ten days before, and it was decided to take Manuel to St Joseph. Vallot's jail Negroes were sent ahead to prepare the pile. When the time came Manuel, who had spent about six months in iron stocks, was loaded with chains and put into a cart.

The shift to St Joseph looked like a concession to the lawyer's protest. The additions to the sentences of the Negroes Yala and Youba cancelled that impression. The charges against Yala and Youba were slight. They had 'made an improper use of the credulity and weak minds of the Negroes' and the commission had ordered them to be banished. Picton decreed that they should first be taken to St Joseph to witness the hanging, decapitation and burning of Manuel, and then have their ears cut off. Those ears were really the English lawyer's.

THE *Courant* printed nothing about the executions. In its obliqueness was a type of truth. For most people life went on. British immigrants continued to come; disappointed immigrants left. A Scotsman was leaving; he had a notice in the *Courant* of 15 February 1802, a week after the execution of Manuel, asking his debtors to settle and his creditors to present their accounts; he also offered 'for Cash, an active WAITING BOY, and a good Saddle HORSE'. Colonel Balfour warned that he was no longer going to put himself to the trouble of catching goats that strayed into his grass-plot; he was going to kill them. Patience Nibbs, a free woman of colour, begged leave 'to acquaint her old Customers and the Public that she will next Week resume her favourite Character and go to Market every Morning where she will procure the best to be found, for SOUPS, STEAKS, ROAST, AND BOILED which may always be had with a good glass of what you please'.

The day before this edition of the *Courant* came out an additional pair of irons had been put on Luisa Calderon and Carlos Gonzalez. Carlos on that day had petitioned to be released. His business was being ruined, his new schooner was 'exposed to the sun, winds and the worms' and his health was suffering from the 'want of exercise, the filthiness of the place of his confinement, and the irons on him'. The petition had encouraged the Chief Magistrate to make the imprisonment of both 'more irksome'.

Carlos still hadn't confessed and Luisa hadn't said where the stolen money was. Two days after the extra irons Luisa, 'lame of leg and swelled', was let out of jail to find a 'defensor', a respectable person, not necessarily a lawyer, to plead her cause; and a doctor was allowed to visit Carlos. The doctor, an old English resident and something of an expert on the Trinidad 'fever', said that Carlos's 'slight indisposition' came from 'the uneasiness of his mind'; and charged two dollars. Early in the afternoon Luisa came back to the jail in tears. None of the four people she had asked wished to be her defensor.

Six weeks later another Negro sorcerer was hanged. His associate was made to watch with a rope around his neck, as though his turn was next. But the sentence that was then read out to him under the gallows wasn't a hanging sentence. His ears were cut off, his right cheek was branded with a hot iron and he was banished.

A week later the poisoning commission completed its work. Aubinot, the man with the poisoned whip, who had spent many months in jail tied to a post, was hanged and decapitated. His body was burnt and the ashes scattered to the wind; his spiked head was displayed near the cemetery. Three Negroes witnessed; then their ears were cut off, they were branded on the right cheek and banished. One of them was named Icare. Icare, Thisbe, Piram: the French liked sometimes to give their Negroes these classical names. It was a colonial aspect of the taste for pastoral.

THE ENGLISH opposition in Trinidad liked to pretend they were in danger. One day, after a man called Redhead had been imprisoned for punching one of Picton's friends in the street, the rumour ran among the English radicals that their ears weren't safe, that Redhead's had been asked for, that those mutilations in the jail might not just be 'Negro's punishment' but might be sanctioned by that unknown Spanish law which Picton, Begorrat and Vallot administered. It was only a rumour. Picton had to handle the English immigrants carefully. He might send one or two to the jail for a short time; if there was a good case he might expel someone. Otherwise he could get at a man only through the man's Negroes. They could be confiscated on a charge of maltreatment; they could be impounded for curfew-breaking; they could be mutilated as runaways.

It was through his Negroes that Picton got at Dawson. Dawson, a Liverpool Negro-shipper (one of his household Negroes was called Liverpool), was a party in an old and complicated property dispute. The Negroes he had sold to an estate hadn't been paid for, and Dawson claimed the estate. Picton had judged against Dawson and Dawson was taking advantage of the radical agitation to make trouble. Picton said that Dawson was 'a damned old blackguard' and sent a message 'that if I did not take great care of myself' – the story is Dawson's – 'he would shop me'. Dawson didn't take the message seriously enough.

Dawson had a devout and faithful Negro called Goliah. Goliah was going to church one Sunday when he was arrested by an alguazil. On Tuesday Dawson rode into Port of Spain to redeem Goliah and to protest. He said his Negroes were always being picked up. Picton said there were extra jail fees this time, two Joes, because Dawson gave 'too much encouragement' to his Negroes. Goliah had a cutlass and had 'rebelled with the constables'. Dawson refused to pay; he said he had given Goliah a pass to go to church and that Negroes were allowed to carry cutlasses.

Two days later some of Dawson's Negroes came to Port of Spain. They went to the jail to see Goliah. They found him under the gallows in the jail-yard, 'dreadfully mangled from his hips up to his shoulders, having been unmercifully flogged with a driver's whip, which cut huge lumps of flesh from his body'. Goliah was taken back to the plantation; he revived just to speak a few words to his master; a few days later he died.

IN APRIL 1802, on the British island of Dominica, the black troops of the 8th West India regiment mutinied and killed their officers; the colonel had for some time been holding back the regiment's subsistence funds for his own use. On the island of Guadeloupe the French, on Napoleon's orders, were just managing, after a bitter war, to re-establish Negro slavery. In Santo Domingo the Negro Revolution continued. Toussaint had been captured by a trick, and the aim of General Leclerc, Napoleon's brother-in-law, was to exterminate the creole Negroes and restock with new Negroes from Africa. In Paris Napoleon presented the fact of the aim as proof of its necessity. More than 50,000 French soldiers were to die.

Picton could say, and the French planters and those of the English who had already become planters, that Trinidad had been spared disorder. The island prospered. Slavery had not only been established; the number of Negroes increased from month to month. Some were imported in the usual way, but many more were brought in by their owners from Curaçao, Santo Domingo, Martinique and other unsettled islands.

Just a few years later it was to be agreed by everyone, French and English, that Picton had been 'the saviour of the colony'. But the English opposition in Trinidad, still full of the political attitudes of England, gave Picton no rest; and Picton was writing to London like a persecuted man. He was accused of brutality towards Negroes. He said such talk was intended to incite Negro rebellion and was seditious. He was wrong. Many of his opponents had already begun to buy and work their own Negroes; and they had their own complaints about Picton's black soldiers, who were 'daily accustomed to inflict the most humiliating indignities on Europeans of every description, under a Governor who attempts to make His Majesty's ministers believe that he exacted the most rigorous observance of deference and submission from the Blacks'. He was attacked for being 'a *British* governor struggling to prevent the extension of *British* laws to a *British* colony'. He said that the demand for British laws was no more than a demand for the 'legal humiliating distinction' of the free people of colour. So, easily, Picton trapped himself. His opponents were English radicals, English humanitarians, English patriots, colonial slave-owners, all at the same time. They occupied every position. In the war of words Picton couldn't win.

His opponents wrote letters to newspapers in the other islands. They wrote to Erskine, the London lawyer. And now, more dangerously, they sent an emissary to London with all their charges. Begorrat and the others rallied to Picton. They passed resolutions of support and decided to send their own man to London. They chose a French nobleman, the Chevalier Dupont du Vivier de Gourville.

The Trinidad government agent in London was Joseph Marryat,

the father of the novelist; he owned land and Negroes in Trinidad. 'De Gourville called on me on the morning of his arrival,' Marryat wrote to Picton some weeks later, 'but no explanation was necessary from him to enable me to form my judgement on the complaints made against your government in Trinidad. Jacobinism is no longer the rage, and whatever outcry her votaries may raise, they will be able to make no impression to your disadvantage here.'

Marryat was too committed to his cause; he expressed his hopes rather than the facts. The British ministers had already, in July 1802, decided that Picton's powers were to be lessened. Trinidad was to be governed by a board of three Commissioners, Picton was to be Second Commissioner, in charge of the military. The First and Third Commissioners were to be sent out from London. The sharp letter from Lord Hobart, Secretary of State to the War Department, announcing these changes, arrived at Government House in Port of Spain at the same time as the letter from Marryat.

IT WASN'T ONLY because of the opposition. Picton had established order; but he had done the wrong job. London didn't want another West Indian slave colony. They wanted Trinidad to be a colony of free settlers: it would be an offering to the abolitionists. There had been suggestions from London about settling Spanish peons. There had been advertisements for settlers in the London newspapers: ten acres for a white settler, implements, rations for a year, a house subsidy. There had been talk of transporting London prostitutes to 'increase the white population'. A naval lieutenant serving in Asian waters had written a memorandum on free Chinese immigration. Slave labour, he had written, was the most expensive; it was a point that people were beginning to make, Picton had ignored all this. The people he had welcomed were the titled French and their Negroes. The ministers in London had been anxious that Picton shouldn't make too many grants of land. But the land was found, the Negro-estates established.

Trinidad was of value as a British colony only because it was going to be the centre of British trade with South America. That was the hope of the merchants who continued to come to Port of Spain. Trade didn't need Negroes. It needed the independence of Spanish America. And independence required that revolution which Picton had given up.

Picton had given up more than the revolution; he had given up the Spaniards of Trinidad. He had expelled most of the rich and the educated. 'Nothing but want,' he wrote of the peons who remained, 'can stimulate them to exertion and their activity never fails to disappear with the cause.' But the revolution still lived, if only as resentment, in Trinidad. That Spaniard from the country who had talked nervously to Picton about the Luisa Calderon case: he was a revolutionary. He, like the others, remembered José España and Caro, both, as was still thought, betrayed by Picton; Juan Mansanares, dead at thirty-six in Port of Spain; Manuel Gual, poisoned in St Joseph; Andrés de España, still in Vallot's jail on an unspecified charge; Santiago Mariño, expelled and his estates confiscated.

In London the news of Picton's demotion had been given to Francisco Miranda as good news. Miranda was once again important. He was having discussions with the man who was to be First Commissioner and was choosing the two men who, with the secret approval of the British government, were to go out as his agents to Trinidad with the First Commissioner, to re-establish the links with London, to prepare the way for a British invasion of the mainland.

A new regime in the new colony: there were many to whom it offered new prospects: the First Commissioner himself, the place-seekers who had attached themselves to him, the immigrants who had answered the advertisements.

And there was someone else: a Scottish pamphleteer in Philadelphia. He left as soon as he was alerted. Young Miss Franks, 'an ornament of the American fair', gave him a volume of her 'juvenile pieces' as a parting gift. He is a mystery man, this pamphleteer.

He might have been the spy of a British minister, or the editor of a 'democratic paper' in London with one naval mutiny to his credit, or he might have belonged to the Corresponding Society. He was one of the earliest foreign correspondents, a 'peregrinator', as he said; it pleased him that as a writer he was described by some officials as a 'pest'. His beat for four years had been the United States and Haiti. His politics were of the radical-humanitarian-patriotic sort. Now he was summoned, by persons unknown, to write up Trinidad and expose Picton.

One man did not hurry. He was the Third Commissioner, and he was very grand. He was Commodore Samuel Hood, a naval hero, Nelson's second-in-command at the Battle of the Nile. He was staying behind in London for a little for discussions about the French war, which seemed likely to start again soon.

BUT PICTON was still governor. His terse instructions at the bottom of petitions were final. The Luisa Calderon papers came to him at last. Luisa had been in irons for eight months. She was released; her wrists were marked for life. Carlos was to pay a fine of 1,800 dollars and the costs of the case. He was deported; his wife stayed in Port of Spain to settle.

A week later Picton wrote to acknowledge Lord Hobart's letter. He began calmly, but calm soon left him: '. . . calumnies and misrepresentations . . . despicable and insignificant . . . characters too notorious . . .' But he would obey. For the Commissioners he had hired 'the best house in the town'. He couldn't ask them to stay in Government House; that had 'a single habitable bedroom which I occupy myself'.

Picton didn't think he had anything to hide, not even Rosette Smith. Decisions cancelled out problems; and his aim was now to clear up, to leave no issue outstanding. There was the question of the costs Carlos Gonzalez had to pay. The escribano totted them up: three hundred and thirty-nine items: the visits, the notifications, the confessions, the two acts of torture, the sentence, the paper, the writing, the estimation of the costs: 313 dollars.

To pay, Carlos's wife sought to recover Carlos's property from the receiver. She had a surprise. The receiver presented his own bill for the repair and upkeep of Carlos's schooner. It came to 1,298 dollars, including 26 dollars for twice chasing and catching one of the schooner's Negroes. Carlos's wife protested to Picton. The schooner was for service in the Gulf, not for voyages to Europe; it had cost 900 dollars when new. The schooner was immediately put up for auction, 'it being first announced by beat of drum and afterwards by the mouth of Silvestre, a black slave, who acted as common crier, there being no regular one'. No bids were made; the receiver himself offered to take over the schooner for 600 dollars; Carlos's wife agreed. And the costs of that auction – from the judge to the crier – had to be paid. For Carlos it had been a bankrupting adultery. He never returned to Trinidad.

He was like Dawson the Negro-shipper, Goliah's owner. Dawson lost two more of his Negroes, including the one called Liverpool. Dawson took the hint; he left the island. All the other trouble-makers were in the jail. Picton was able to write to London that everything was ready for the Commissioners; the island enjoyed 'the most perfect tranquillity'.

Picton overlooked the dissatisfaction of his Negro executioner William Payne, Ludovigo, as he called him. Ever since the hanging, beheading and burning at St Joseph Ludovigo hadn't been paid. Vallot had no supervisor, as in the Spanish days; he was responsible only to Picton. And Vallot wasn't passing on the fees. He must have begun to sense that time was running out both for Picton and himself. And Vallot was getting old; he would have to retire soon. There had been that sign of failing powers: when he cut off that Negro's ears and killed him. That had caused a little scandal. The English owners hadn't stopped complaining of their loss. Vallot cut off no more ears. With the help of Porto Rico he tortured in the garret and did 'fourposter' floggings downstairs and other light jail-yard work. But ears and heavy floggings under the gallows, like the one that killed Goliah, and all the outdoor jobs he left to William Payne. Once he gave William Payne two Joes. But he had given no more; and throughout that busy year William Payne's resentment, at Vallot and at Picton, grew.

And then right at the end of the year, just days before the First Commissioner arrived, there was another outbreak of Negro poisonings, and again on that Coblenz estate of Baron de Montalembert. More bloated corpses among the dirt-eaters whose legs ran with sores: six more poisoners, two women among them, brought to the jail and chained flat in the *cachots brûlants* below the burning shingles: three taken up to the garret – Benoit, Serpent, Piram – and tortured by Vallot and Porto Rico. But not Petit Georges or Rachel. Later, though, Elizabeth went up; Vallot called her Zabeth. Another poisoning commission for Begorrat, another trial in the jail, more sentences. It was seasonal now; it was what Picton had committed himself to; it was, as Begorrat showed him, what used to happen in Martinique.

7. The Executioner's List

January–July 1803

The First Commissioner arrived in Port of Spain harbour on 3 January 1803. He came with his wife, his wife's sister and their personal staff; four young secretaries for whom government jobs with fees would have to be found or made; five surveyors (Miranda's two agents among them); the Secretary of the Commission; a man who had been given the meaningless job of Attorney-General; and a number of immigrants. A warship had transported the party from Portsmouth. It was the style the First Commissioner expected. At forty-eight he knew his way around government departments, the Army, the East India Company. Others still fumbled to define privileges and duties; he knew; people like him were giving the British Empire a style.

It was not yet a style of dress. The First Commissioner dressed like his young secretaries. He wore a windsor uniform, blue with red collar and cuffs, waistcoat and shorts of yellow nankeen, blue hose, shoes with enormous buckles. He wore a dress sword and carried a stick; he took snuff. He was Colonel William Fullarton of Fullarton, a Member of Parliament for Ayrshire in Scotland, a Fellow of the Royal Societies of London and Edinburgh. He had estates in Ayrshire; his wife was the daughter of Lord Reay. He had written a book about agriculture in Ayrshire, and another book about his two-year military service in India where, twenty years before, he had been made a colonel in the East India Company armies and was, in his own description, 'Commander of the Southern Army on the coast of Coromandel'.

It was his Indian experience that had no doubt recommended him for the political duties of the First Commissionership: the conciliation of the foreigner, the extension of British influence to the Spanish American mainland. And the Under-Secretary of State for the Colonies was an old friend, a colleague from the Indian days. Colonel Fullarton trailed this atmosphere of connections, wealth, education (he had made the Grand Tour with William Beckford's tutor), experience, ready service and muffled scandal. In 1794, when he had raised a regiment of light dragoons for service in Ireland, he had been in arrears over the subsistence funds; and forage money had been entered as paid to a non-existent man for non-existent horses. In 1800 he had raised another regiment and the scandal connected with that had not yet died down. The Duke of York had written the Secretary of State that Fullarton should not be allowed to go to Trinidad until he had settled certain 'serious claims'.

But he had arrived; and the day after, he landed in what he liked to call 'regular form'. The two magistrates of the Port of Spain cabildo greeted him on the wharf and led him, black and white soldiers lining the street, presenting arms, drums beating, to Government House, where he showed his commission to Picton, was welcomed and introduced to members of the cabildo and Picton's Council.

The next day a special edition of the *Courant* said that the First Commissioner, in his reply to the speeches, had praised Picton's administration. Fullarton had one of his young men send the newspaper to London with a denial. The evidence, the witness, the covering letter: it was the way of the First Commissioner, the way of a man used to bureaucratic disputes. The next day it was suggested by the Secretary of the Commission that a proclamation should be made that all existing 'laws, usages and employments' would remain in force. Fullarton agreed. But during the night he changed his mind; and at six in the morning he sent another of his young men to the *Courant* printing office to get a proof. It was too late; fifty copies of the proclamation had already been posted in Port of Spain. Fullarton ordered the printer to pull all the proclamations down. When this was done the island knew that there was conflict and that Picton was now officially challenged.

It was a conflict, in the first place, of styles. Picton, the Negro-owning tyrant, lived under the mulatto tyranny of Rosette Smith in Government House; the ambiguity, not unusual, established him as a man among colonial men. He was often to be seen riding around with his 'souple jack'. He spoke French, French patois and a Spanish whose fluency astonished Venezuelans. He kept open house; thirty years later the planters were still telling Picton's jokes, which were nearly always threats, inventively framed.

The Fullartons exhibited a public softness. To his wife, the daughter of Lord Reay, and his wife's sister, 'the ladies of my family', as he always called them, Fullarton was always deferential. It diminished him as a man under 'petticoat government'; and its hint of example in a barbarous land caused offence. Years later, when the issue was dead, and Rosette Smith just a salacious name, both French and English remembered Lord Reay's daughters as 'two of the most accomplished political intriguants that ever came to afflict a West India colony'.

The judgement was unfair; it was part of the coarseness of simple men growing simpler. Wives were seldom mentioned in 1803. People were more concerned with breeding. There were rewards for the Negro woman who produced children who could be bred to plantation ways; if it was the white population that needed to be increased, it could be suggested without offence that London prostitutes should be shipped out. It was not a place for ladies.

THE JANUARY rains continued. The 'best house in the town' that Picton had found for the Fullartons was judged not good enough. It was old and small. Everything in Port of Spain, even meat and vegetables, was imported and expensive; food was always short on a slave island; and within a few days the Fullartons saw that on the First Commissioner's salary of £3,000 a year they wouldn't be able 'to maintain a Table and Establishment on any footing of respectability' – the new words of the new style – unless they raised their own stock and grew their own vegetables. Mrs Fullarton thought she might make her own butter. At once, in spite of the rain, Fullarton began to look out for a piece of land in the country and a new house in the town. His experience helped. He chose a large government house in some disrepair. Carpenters and masons went to work right away; galley Negroes, city property, acted as labourers: and the bill, when it came some months later, some 6,000 dollars, was passed on to the Treasury for payment.

There were not many jobs in Trinidad for Fullarton's young men. There was no structure of government; Picton's one-man rule had been based on *ad hoc* committees and relics of Spanish forms. For one of Fullarton's young men the nonsense post of Provost-Marshal – very roughly, a commissioner of police – had been created. But for the others Fullarton could do little except make them 'commissaries of population' – no duties, small salary – and attach them to himself as secretaries. The surveyors suffered more. Their salary had been fixed at ten shillings a day; in Port of Spain it wasn't enough. The surveyors were Fullarton's special, secret responsibility. Two among them were Miranda's agents of South American revolution.

Colonel Rutherfurd, who had come out as the Trinidad Surveyor-General, had known Miranda for almost thirty years. He was an American from South Carolina who had given up the United States for England even before the War of Independence. It was at Gibraltar in December 1775 – Picton was also there, as a young ensign – that he had first met Miranda; later they had travelled together in the United States. Rutherfurd had been at the back of some of Miranda's invasion plans and he had helped with introductions.

Rutherfurd at least had a job in Trinidad; land-titles were

chaotic and a surveyor was necessary. But his assistant had no job. Fullarton described him sometimes as a linguist, sometimes as a Spanish lawyer, sometimes as a botanist. The assistant's name was Pedro Vargas, though in the Spanish American way he had also given himself a spy name: Smith. He had been involved in a conspiracy in New Granada in 1799 and had fled to England where, fresh to exile and revolutionary pride, he had described himself in a letter to Pitt as being descended through his mother from the natives of America, 'whom the Spaniards call Indians'. He had later acted as a courier between Miranda and Napoleon. Vargas, like nearly all the Spanish American revolutionaries, had deteriorated in exile; the racial pride had worn thin; he endured poverty and disappointment badly.

He wrote to Miranda now that on ten shillings a day he could only live in a Negro hut; he couldn't afford to live with white people. It was another example of British malevolence towards Spanish Americans and the revolution. Still, he tried to do his agent's job. He sent exhortations to his leader and wrote disingenuously about Spanish government spies in Port of Spain. But mainly Vargas collected Spanish American injustices in Trinidad: his own discomfort, the death, imprisonment, betrayal and expulsion of revolutionaries, the hostility of Picton, the hanging of Spanish peons and sailors.

The reports didn't help Miranda in London. But they helped Fullarton in Trinidad. They added to his 'materials' for that 'report' which was always in his mind. And the Spaniards in Trinidad learned that at last, after the Picton years, they had an audience in the island that had once been theirs. They came forward; it pleased Fullarton to think that he could talk to them in their own language.

One of the Spaniards who came forward had been an army engineer in the Spanish time. He said he had been imprisoned by Picton on a false charge of robbery. It was at the time of the Luisa Calderon affair; he had many facts about the imprisonment and torture of Luisa Calderon. Fullarton thought the Spaniard would be useful and ought to be employed. It was decided that the nonsense job of Provost-Marshal took in the job of Alguazil-Mayor or Head Policeman; the Spaniard was appointed Deputy Alguazil-Mayor.

The free people of colour, too, saw the Fullartons as protectors. 'Whenever I went out ,' Fullarton wrote, 'or any of my family, the inhabitants marked their respect and regard in the most flattering manner.' The English opposition saw Fullarton as their champion as well; they began to talk about another public meeting.

This was the line-up. On Picton's side, now as always, were the planters, French and English. But it was still the time for courtesies. On the Queen's Birthday Picton gave a ball at Government House. The Fullartons thought it 'splendid'. It is not known whether Rosette Smith was there.

BUT THERE WAS the jail. Fullarton had heard about it almost as soon as he had arrived. The young Provost-Marshal had visited the jail and reported. The jail couldn't be ignored for much longer. Fullarton did not wish to appear to be prying. He thought he would first of all pass a message on to Vallot. The message was that people shouldn't be taken into the jail just like that; the offence had to be specified; and before Vallot whipped or mutilated anyone he should make a report.

It was a simple message. But it did more than complicate the jail routine; it virtually abolished the jail. Fullarton and his Provost-Marshal hadn't understood about the jail. The jail had its legal side. But it was more important as a centre for Negro discipline. It was a public utility, with an element of the co-operative; it was subsidized by the planters' jail fees and managed by Vallot. To ask for regular reports, for jail-books, for offences to be specified, was to ignore the function of the jail and the rights of the people who paid to keep it going. Vallot's usefulness to the community would be destroyed once it got to the Negroes that he wasn't a free man in his own jail.

It was as Vallot had feared. After thirteen years in the jail, six of them under Picton, his job was coming to an end. He began to talk of leaving the island and going to the United States.

The rumour that ran through the French estate houses was that the First Commissioner had banned the whipping or chaining of Negroes. The magistrates who had welcomed Fullarton made a formal protest. The First Commissioner didn't know what he was doing; he was undermining order. The undermining of order was a serious charge. Fullarton was conciliatory. He said there had been a misunderstanding; the magistrates should write at once to Vallot. Of course Vallot was to continue flogging and fettering as before, if the magistrates asked him; all the First Commissioner wanted was that the chained Negroes in the jail shouldn't be punished without permission. That was something. But it was still interference, the thin edge of the wedge, and Vallot and everybody else who owned a Negro remained anxious.

Three days later, at the weekly cabildo meeting, Fullarton raised the subject of the jail again. He said that perhaps what was needed was a new jail. Begorrat didn't agree. But one of the magistrates knew of some land where a new jail could be built, and later that afternoon they all went to look at the land. Afterwards they called in at the jail.

William Payne, the executioner, was in an ugly mood. He had heard of Fullarton's reputation as a defender of the oppressed and he at once began to complain that he had been paid just two Joes for a year's work. Fullarton asked him to put his complaint in writing.

Vallot took the party round. The prison stank; Fullarton thought the small overcrowded cells 'pestilential receptacles'. In the larger downstairs room, twenty foot square, there were fifty or sixty Negroes, men and women, riveted about the neck or waist to chains. Some of them were naked; at least a dozen were starved and skeletal, 'spectres who had hardly anything of human resemblance'. Vallot didn't always know who a Negro was or who had sent him in or when he would be released. Many of the Negroes, Vallot said, were a burden on him because there was no one to pay the jail fees. Fullarton thought that was because the jail fees were unreasonable. But he didn't say anything. Vallot was doing all the talking. He pointed out one of the 'spectres' and said that she was his; he had recently bought her as a speculation for two Joes. Fullarton objected to the 'transaction'. Vallot didn't understand. He knew he had nothing to hide. But he had an instinct for danger; and when they were in the back of the jail he tried, too clumsily, to get the party past a door. Fullarton asked to see.

It was the corridor of the *cachots brûlants*. In the low windowless cells were five of the poisoners from Baron de Montalembert's estate, naked in the heat and darkness, 'some of them stretched on their backs with both legs fixed in irons not moveable'. They had been there for weeks. Vallot had originally taken in six; he had tortured four; one must have died.

Begorrat, who was president of the tribunal that was trying the poisoners, answered Fullarton's questions. He told Fullarton what they used to do in Martinique; he promised to show him the Annals of the Council of that island. 'The natural frankness of my character,' Begorrat wrote two months later, 'induced me to believe that the Colonel's intention was to procure information on subjects foreign and unknown to Europeans who have not resided in the colonies. I conceived it therefore a duty incumbent on me to give the Colonel every information and every insight on the subject that had come to my knowledge.'

Fullarton was especially anxious to know whether the Negroes he saw had been tortured. Begorrat said there was no other way of getting the truth out of the 'villains'. But his instinct warned him too, and he said that the torture had been applied only once in these poisoning investigations. He told how he had had one of his dead Negroes opened and how the hospital nurse Thisbe had run to the neighbour for help. He told of the mass poisonings the previous year, of frantic mules and Negroes dying by the score.

Fullarton noted down the fearful figures. The Negro as a victim and also as menace: slavery as a double horror, providing its own justification: it bared an unstable point of sensibility. Fullarton said that even if they had been found guilty, the five Negroes in the *cachots* had already been sufficiently punished. Begorrat took the hint; he decided that the demented Negroes were to be released; the evidence was insufficient. The tour was over.

When the party was about to leave the jail William Payne gave Fullarton his written complaint:

Hanged and burned at St Joseph's, and head cut off	1 man
Ears clipt off at ditto	2 ditto
Ears clipt and stampt	4 men
Flogged under gallows	1 ditto
Punished at pillory	1 ditto
Led through town and pilloried	1 ditto
Ears clipt in market	1 ditto
Ditto in jail-yard	1 ditto
Mulatto man and one Negro man flogged through town	2 ditto
Ears cut off in the jail-yard, of two black men	2 ditto

Received in part (payment) 2 Joes

William Payne

Fullarton said he reflected much that night. He tried to be rational about what he had seen, trying to balance 'ill-regulated Negroes' against 'over-strained speculation, improper food, and bad management of planters and overseers'. The next afternoon he went back to the jail; he saw again what he had seen. He made up his mind. He said that if a new jail wasn't built he would take it upon himself to have the prisoners moved to a hulk in the harbour. He insisted now on a list of prisoners, offences and punishments. He wanted a weekly report on all impounded Negroes.

Picton called on Fullarton the next day and protested. The visits to the jail appeared to be a criticism. Fullarton said criticism wasn't intended. He thanked Picton for being so open.

MRS FULLARTON churned her own butter and thought it was as good as Cambridge butter. She was beginning to love the country and the people she ruled. She overwhelmed the oppressed, and especially the responsive Spaniards, by a courtesy they had never known; she involved them in her idea of the romance of her position. Fullarton too had his idea of his role. Twenty years before, in India, he had found himself among the corrupt and pushing new men of England and had thought then that he lived in a time of national decay. His campaign against Picton was touched with the hysteria, self-righteousness and even the self-cherishing that came from this vision.

His enemies said later he had come out from England determined to prosecute Picton. It was possible. But his campaign started from that moment of shock in the jail. He always went back to that, to William Payne's bill and Begorrat's precise explanations which yet had nothing of wilful cruelty. Logic should have taken Fullarton to the abolitionist cause. But he was an administrator, anxious to prove himself; he was not a reformer. Negroes were to be slaves and kept in order; in the jail they were to be chained and whipped; but they were not to be punished too severely. Like Picton, Fullarton became entangled. He could never adequately define or defend his cause, to him so obvious and reasonable; and the cause – humanity sometimes, the 'British national character' sometimes – dissolved to self-justification and hate. He grew to hate Picton; he lost sight of his job as First Commissioner; he forgot the reason for his hatred.

Now he wanted evidence. His young men ran around and took down statements. The Spaniard he had made Deputy Alguazil-Mayor began to investigate the Luisa Calderon case. And there was at last employment for Pedro Vargas, Miranda's useless agent. Vargas was the interpreter, the go-between, the man who knew both Spanish law and the ways of British ministers. The case against Picton became Vargas's cause and employment, his return to the real world from the fantasy of revolution, and remained so until Vargas died.

In a fortnight much information was collected. A case could be made out. For Fullarton it was only the beginning. The endeavour, with its repetitions, its stops and starts, its detours and humiliations, was to last five years. It deranged, dishonoured and killed him.

THE SCOTTISH pamphleteer from Philadelphia, P. F. McCallum, arrived in Port of Spain at last. He had fallen ill in New York, 'with an intermitting fever, of the semi-tertian kind, which Galen said was compounded of a continual, quotidian and intermitting tertian'. He thought the fever unfair. Already during his travels he 'had surmounted incredible hardships, exposed to every malignant blast that blew'. Toughness was not yet part of the journalist's myth or the Briton's; to complain was to display sensibility. The young Misses Franks came from Philadelphia to nurse McCallum; and the illness turned out to have been a 'wonderful interposition of Providence in procrastinating the author's life', because the ship in which he was to have sailed to the West Indies sank with everybody on board. He thought he had been spared 'to bring the crimes of a second Nimrod before the face of day'.

McCallum disliked what he saw of Picton's Port of Spain from the start. He landed on a Sunday but saw no sign of the Sabbath. The gaming-houses were full of people playing billiards. (One of his fellow passengers had brought out a billiard-table and 'other gambling apparatus' and was hoping to start a gaming-house; he was a former London man, 'a sort of chemist or vitriol manufacturer', who had eloped with an actress and had wandered about France and the United States for many years.)

The passengers were taken to Government House. They waited an hour and a half and McCallum began to detest the sight of Picton's secretary. The 'biped', as he thought (and we begin to recognize McCallum as one of the ancestors of Dickens), 'couched and re-couched himself, at other times viewing his delicate features in a looking-glass; frequently grinning eastward and grinning westward, admiring his grinders; when he strutted about he gabbled like a goose'.

Picton came out. 'The Don,' McCallum thought, 'the upstart Don.' McCallum was longing for Picton to insult him or threaten him or at least to point out the famous gallows. But Picton didn't speak to McCallum, didn't look at him; and McCallum, consoling himself during his neglect with a meditation on virtue, found that he was dismissed.

As soon as he found lodgings – next door to the military barracks: floggings night and morning – he went to work. He visited an Indian mission. He envied the Indians 'their harmless minds' but 'pitied the blindness of their ideas'; he thought the missionary was a lecher. He saw Negro women loaded with chains linking neck to ankle and thanked God he had a white colour. He assembled facts and figures. He inquired about crops and local fruit. (In 1803 the banana's shape and colour told against it: it was said 'to excite urine and to provoke venery'.) He called on Fullarton and 'spent an hour with this excellent man in his study'. And he got in touch with the English opposition.

They were in trouble with Picton again. They had advertised another meeting to press for English laws. But Picton had shown that he still didn't like the idea, and the meeting had been called off. The opposition decided now to meet every Saturday evening in McCallum's hotel. They formed a club which they called the Ugly Club. The club had written rules. McCallum, as secretary, was to keep the minutes and 'papers'. But McCallum was cautious. If the Inquisition, as he called Begorrat and his friends, 'only knew that my pen is so devoted to the cause of humanity, they would soon torture the hand that holds it'.

McCallum had arrived in a week of crisis. Fullarton and the French planters had continued to astonish one another, and the French were nervous. The news had gone around that Fullarton had objected to Vallot's buying a jail-Negro as a speculation, and the news had caused great anger: a man could sell his own Negroes to anyone he chose. Someone else had complained to Fullarton that a French baker 'flogged and lacerated' his seven Negroes to such an extent that 'their cries became a disturbance'; one had already been whipped to death, one had lost an eye. There was anger that Fullarton should even have listened to such a domestic complaint. The baker himself 'flew into a paroxysm of rage' when he heard.

Fullarton had done more. The French commandant or warden of the Carenage district, west of Port of Spain, had been having some trouble with a mulatto planter. The mulatto was a known trouble-maker. Because of his 'pranks' he had already been excused from the Saturday-night patrol that picked up drunks and stray Negroes and broke up after-curfew Negro parties. Now the mulatto was refusing to send any of his Negroes for the commandant's road corvée. The commandant said he would send the mulatto to Vallot. The mulatto said he had the money, cash, on him, to pay Vallot. So he had gone to the jail. But the commandant, ignoring Fullarton's order, hadn't specified the mulatto's offence; and Fullarton had had the mulatto released.

The commandant was outraged. For thirteen years, since the Spanish time, he said, he had served as commandant and everybody he had sent to the jail had gone to the jail. Now he was humiliated, the mulattoes were rejoicing and there was a danger of insurrection. The released mulatto had run to his neighbour, a man with a revolutionary past, and the neighbour had gone to the sea shore and 'vociferated' that whites and coloured were equal, that the First Commissioner was for the people of colour and against the whites.

This happened on the Tuesday after McCallum's arrival. Worse was to follow. On Saturday morning an old French woman of colour came to Port of Spain from one of the other islands. She had been expelled some time before by Picton; but she had petitioned Fullarton and he had given her written permission to come back for a week. At nine in the morning she reported to Fullarton. At half past two she returned to his house with an alguazil. Picton had told her to leave the island at once and had personally written out a deportation order. Fullarton dismissed the alguazil and told the woman she could stay. He took the deportation order and sent it by one of his young men to the Secretary of the Commission.

The Secretary said that Colonel Fullarton should act cautiously, 'as such proceedings would give General Picton's enemies a triumph'.

'I am not authorized to answer,' the young man said, and returned to Fullarton.

Later they all dined together, the Fullartons, Mrs Fullarton's sister, the young men. There were also three Spanish guests: the new Deputy Alguazil-Mayor, the escribano who had acted in the Luisa Calderon case and Pedro Vargas.

At about eight, when they were having tea in the drawing-room, the escribano and the Deputy Alguazil-Mayor submitting to the unusual drink as part of the unusual ritual, Picton entered and asked to speak to Fullarton. They went through the open doors to the adjoining gallery or verandah. In no time Picton was shouting and Fullarton was shouting. The sentry heard; the servants heard. Picton was banging the verandah rail; Fullarton was banging it back. Then the storm was over. Picton left.

Pen, paper: Fullarton asked his young men for a statement. While they worked it out – '. . . undersigned gentlemen . . . dined . . . sitting at tea . . . on a sudden the whole company was surprised . . . menacing and vociferous intonations . . .' – Fullarton apologized to the Spaniards for not asking them to write as well. He had 'motives of delicacy'. The statement was signed and Fullarton looked it over. It was incomplete. He wrote: 'They have however omitted to state the violence with which Brigadier-General Picton struck the rails of the gallery with his hands, while addressing Colonel Fullarton, which, of course, induced Colonel Fullarton to strike the rails with superior vehemence.'

On Sunday morning Fullarton went with his family to church. Afterwards, with the help of his young men, he prepared his documents, Vargas's reports, the Deputy Alguazil-Mayor's reports. They made copies of everything. Mrs Fullarton might also have helped; she sometimes acted as an additional secretary. Fullarton intended to lay all his charges against Picton at the special Council meeting the following day.

But there was disturbing news that evening. Picton, acting as Military Commissioner, had withdrawn all guards and sentries from the city. The military had always been the effective police; the alguazils dealt only with drunks and strays. Fullarton saw his danger: more mulattoes, perhaps, rushing to the beach and shouting: an insurrection: and it could be shown that he had given them 'encouragement'. He had no military power; there were objections when he exercised his civil power. It was as though he had no job. The thought of a duel with Picton, 'the ordinary personal means between gentlemen' came to him. It was impossible, of course. But after this Fullarton often solaced himself in moments of stress with that fantasy of personal violence.

The next day in the Council he detailed his charges against Picton. He asked for a certified list of all, regardless of race and colour, who had been 'imprisoned, banished, fettered, flogged, mutilated, tortured to extort confession, hanged, burned or otherwise punished'.

He created a sensation. It was partly Begorrat's fault, volunteering all that information. But no one rebuked Begorrat. And Begorrat himself was shocked. 'I never could have conceived,' he said later, 'that information, given with so much candour and ingeniousness to a person who ought to know how to appreciate the delicacy of a magistrate, should from that moment be destined to produce that monstrous act of accusation laid before you, which this day rendered publick, astonishes all minds, suspends all opinion and causes individuals to regard each other in silence petrified with horror and amazement.'

The members of the Council begged the two Commissioners to be reconciled. After a three-hour discussion Fullarton said he was willing, for the sake of public peace. The documents were torn up by the Council clerk; it was fortunate, Fullarton wrote later, that he had copies at home. Picton wrote an apology to Mrs Fullarton. It was kept as further evidence; copies were made.

Pertinacious when he was on the defensive, so, in the temporary relief of reconciliation, Fullarton grew more demanding. He said that the Secretary of the Commission had made mischief between Picton and himself and ought to be suspended. He repeated the demand three days later and made it a condition of his willingness to be reconciled. He wanted his own Provost-Marshal to take over the Secretaryship; he wanted his other young men to be also attached to the office; he wanted an interpretership for Pedro Vargas; for himself he wanted it clearly stated that he 'should attend to the daily executive detail'.

It was too much; the quarrel had been restated. The next day, the sixth anniversary of the conquest, Picton wrote his letter of resignation. The handwriting was neater than usual, the spelling was as before. 'I now clearly see the difficulty, if not the impossibility, of acting with a man of his faithless astrocious character. It has been a scene of dark misterious intrigue since the first moment of his arrival.' And the words tumbled out: 'specious philanthropy . . . showing off his great humanity . . . great anxiety of property owners . . . cunning artful misrepresentation . . . most selfish, interested motives . . . painful to the feelings of a man of honour and candour'.

That evening, well after curfew, the patrol under Fullarton's Deputy Alguazil-Mayor found a Negro asleep on a soldier's knapsack, blanket and greatcoat in the sentry-box on the pier. At the same time some sailors, always suspect, were seen guarding a canoe. The patrol was 'already encumbered with the Negro'; the guard at the Fort refused to help – Picton's standing orders – and the sailors escaped. A small event; but to Fullarton it was proof of his powerlessness and perhaps even danger.

His hope was that within a few days the situation might change. Commodore Samuel Hood, the Third Commissioner, had been detained for almost two months in Barbados, where he had become interested in the governor's eldest daughter. But Hood was at last on his way. Fullarton had met Hood in London and admired him as an officer and a true gentleman, a naval hero, a scholar, a man of 'high professional and public character'. For Hood Fullarton had hired 'the best house to be found in Port of Spain', pleasantly situated, with a view of the Gulf and the ships. He had detailed one of his young men 'to make the most comfortable arrangements' for the Commodore.

He was also determined – whatever Picton might say – to go aboard the flagship to greet Hood first; and he had decided to take Sir James Bontein with him. Sir James's distinction was that he was the only titled Englishman on the island. He was a place-seeker who had come out the year before with a recommendation from Addington, the Prime Minister, that something like a receiver-ship might be found for him, if he was thought suitable and if such a post existed. Picton hadn't found anything for Sir James; and Sir James was willing now to put himself on Fullarton's side.

AND HOOD failed Fullarton. He declared for Picton from the start. He made it plain that he didn't care for Fullarton, or the too-big house Fullarton had chosen for him, or the obsequious young man of Fullarton's who wanted to wait on him, or Mrs Fullarton. And Fullarton could never understand it. Hood was a busy man, looking beyond Trinidad to the commitments of a major war. But for Fullarton the rejection was a permanent sorrow. The anger came unwillingly. It was months – the war on again, Hood absent, promoted – before Fullarton could allow himself to think of fighting a duel with Hood.

After all the preparations, the welcome had been confused. Fullarton and Sir James Bontein had gone aboard the flagship, as they had planned, leaving Picton with his soldiers on the wharf. When the official party landed, Picton, ignoring Hood, went to Sir James and said, 'I hope your Excellency has arrived in good health. I beg leave to congratulate you on your landing safely in Trinidad.'

Sir James was puzzled.

Picton explained: 'I understand your Excellency has been appointed a Commissioner.'

Sir James saw only then that he was being insulted and that Picton, very angry, was ready for a full public scene. It presently exploded; and was of such violence that Sir James lay low for many weeks until, seeing that nothing was coming his way, he went back to England.

Hood loved his fame, even down to the articles about him in the *Courant*, and the wharf-side scene ought to have told against Picton. But it didn't. And after that nothing went right. Hood drove away Fullarton's young man. With Mrs Fullarton he was civil in the beginning. They had friends in common, like Sir Thomas Trowbridge in London and poor Lady Mitchell who was soon to die 'of a decline' in the Bermudas; and Hood was attached to Lord Seaforth's daughter in Barbados. But Hood, a bachelor of forty, wasn't only a drawing-room sailor; he soon made it plain that Mrs Fullarton irritated him and that he thought her a dangerous, intriguing woman.

The British Commander-in-Chief, who had come from Barbados with Hood, also made his irritation with the Fullartons plain. The Commander-in-Chief was staying in Fullarton's house. He was a busy man, concerned with surveys, fortifications and plans for defence; he couldn't endure 'interruptions to official business' from Fullarton and Mrs Fullarton; and after a week he moved to the hotel where P. F. McCallum, the pamphleteer, was also staying.

Fullarton expressed his 'delicacy' by staying away from military parades. He explained that he didn't want it said either that he 'interfered in any military matter' or that his observations were responsible for any fault the Commander-in-Chief might find with the local military. The feminine excuse compounded the discourtesy. The Commander-in-Chief was furious; and at the end of the week Fullarton found himself isolated and on the defensive.

Hood, the Commander-in-Chief and Picton shared more than a service loyalty and a detestation of 'papers', intrigue and lawyer-types. They were not interested in having free settlers in Trinidad. Some weeks before, the Commander-in-Chief had dropped a hint to Fullarton; but Fullarton had not responded. The generals and the admirals wanted the land themselves. Maitland, the defeated general of Haiti, Admiral Cochrane and others were looking forward to getting grants of land as rewards for their services; they were hoping to build up Negro estates. Nothing had been done for the English immigrants who had come out with Fullarton. They were getting poorer. They had had to pay for their passages out, and Trinidad was expensive. Butter cost six shillings a pound; one immigrant was paying 100 dollars a month in rent. No one had got any land or implements. One Welshman who had begun to clear a little land was frightened off with threats of Vallot and the jail, 'thirty-nine lashes and Negro's punishment'.

But when they had talked in London Hood and Fullarton had agreed about free white settlers. Fullarton didn't feel that Hood had really changed or that Hood and the Commander-in-Chief could really be on Picton's side. He tried to tell them so. He offered evidence. Someone passing Government House had heard Picton and Hood quarrelling; someone else had heard from an officer in the Commander-in-Chief's suite that the Commander-in-Chief had said that the local soldiers were twenty years behind.

Fullarton felt sure that if he could talk privately to Hood he would make Hood see. But Hood didn't want a private meeting, and Fullarton had to put his case at the meetings of the Council and the Commissioners. His two visits to the jail had caused offence, Fullarton said; but the Spanish laws said that a governor should visit the jail once a week and that a jailer should keep jail-books. Porto Rico, Vallot's assistant, came to give evidence. It wasn't true, Porto Rico said, that Colonel Fullarton had ordered all Negroes to be unchained and had banned the whipping of Negroes. The Colonel had only asked him, and not even in writing, not to punish chained Negroes too severely.

It didn't help. Hood was on Picton's side; the two men were always together. The military were still under orders to offer no help to the civil power. Sailors broke into a store on Sunday afternoon and there was no one to stop them. Garbage rotted in the hot streets; the Intendant of Police, who supervised the collection of garbage, came under the military. There was talk of prosecuting Fullarton for interfering with the judiciary and misusing city funds: the Port of Spain cabildo paid Vallot twenty cents a day to lodge and feed each galley Negro, and Fullarton had used the galley Negroes as building labourers on his house and Hood's and also, after the withdrawal of the military, as emergency policemen. The charges were absurd. But Fullarton answered them carefully; Pedro Vargas and the Provost-Marshal helped.

The public attacks on Fullarton became more personal. He was, Picton said, 'an artful cunning man under the absolute direction of an intriguing woman'. He was, literally, mad. Picton said it; Hood said it. At the same time the Attorney-General hinted to Fullarton that all that was required of him was an apology. Fullarton, weakening out of deference to Hood, but still stubborn. and indulging more and more in the fantasy of 'the Toledo', the sword-duel with Picton, played for time. He said he would write to London. The Secretary of State, if he agreed, would dictate the terms of Fullarton's apology to Picton.

Hood and the Commander-in-Chief had been in the island for just over a fortnight. It was time for the Commander-in-Chief to leave. The English opposition, perhaps through McCallum the pamphleteer, presented him with a petition. He passed it on to Picton. Fullarton gave the Commander-in-Chief some documents.

The Commander-in-Chief returned them with thanks the following day and went aboard his ship.

Fullarton got to know that minutes of Council meetings had not been sent to London. He became nervous; he felt that anything could happen. He announced that he would no longer attend Council or Commission meetings regularly. He wished to abstain from the daily 'tone of contest'. Also, he wanted to travel about the island 'to prepare materials for a report'.

The statement was ambiguous. Hood and Picton jumped on it. Was Colonel Fullarton withdrawing from the Commission? Could he absent himself without permission? Could he write a report without the consent of the other Commissioners? The brief letters went back and forth, four in one day. An irony was that it was the young Provost-Marshal, whom Fullarton had made Secretary of the Commission, who wrote on behalf of Hood and Picton.

FULLARTON'S supporters were the English opposition and McCallum's Ugly Club. Fullarton was employing McCallum as an agent and paying him out of 'secret service moneys' drawn on the Trinidad Treasury. McCallum thought that Fullarton's heart was 'dilated with the milk of human kindness'. Yet neither Fullarton nor Mrs Fullarton could have been wholly at ease with McCallum and his Saturday-evening friends of the Ugly Club. They were not well-educated; and their pretensions were literary as well as political. McCallum himself liked using French and Spanish words he couldn't always manage; and his vocabulary could be archaic and Latinate: *lancinated, facinorous, siderated.*

There was a political gap as well. Fullarton, defining his cause, spoke of the British national character and the principles of justice and protection. McCallum spoke of his rights as an Englishman. McCallum's objection to slavery in Trinidad was an objection to the further enriching of 'a few individuals in Liverpool', Negro-shippers, who would 'continue to ride in their coaches, eat turtle, and drink port or claret'. It was an objection to those generals and admirals who were depriving poor British immigrants, and especially Scottish Highlanders, of land and hope. It was also, logically, an objection to the presence of Negroes, which was indistinguishable from an objection to Negroes. McCallum loved Toussaint, 'one of the best of men'; but at the same time, remembering Haiti, he could never see the black Trinidad troops in the barracks next door 'without abhorrence'.

The earliest English opposition to Picton had split into the respectable, who were mainly merchants, and a very few radicals, who were thought to be encouraging Negro insubordination. Less than eighteen months later that division had blurred; the opposition had increased. The radical-humanitarian aspect of the opposition, the aspect derived from the arguments and doctrines of London, had weakened in a colony where a Negro could so easily be bought and hired out, investment and income for less than £100. It was now the merchants who spoke, quite simply, for the opposition. They wanted British laws to ensure rule by Britons.

Fullarton, McCallum, the merchants, the radical remnant: they had a common enemy and they used the same words, but the words represented four distinct attitudes. So that even here, among his supporters, the issues of justice and protection which in the beginning had appeared so easy – an order to a jailer, a request for jail-books – became fogged. Where, between slavery and abolition, did the humanitarian stop? How were the French people of colour to be handled? They were constantly humiliated; but there were also many experienced revolutionaries among them. Fullarton recommended firmness without great severity; it was saying nothing.

He was not only on the defensive. He was confused; he couldn't define his cause. Three days after the exchange of the four letters Hood and Picton summoned him to a meeting of the Council to discuss finance. Finance was not discussed. Fullarton heard Picton withdraw his apology for the scene in Mrs Fullarton's verandah. 'He spoke as he felt, and as he will always feel and speak on similar occasions.' Fullarton heard that he had surrounded himself with 'a set of artful, intriguing, ill-designing bankrupts in fortune and reputation'. And Fullarton heard Picton state, with brutality, the principles of the slave colony.

Picton no longer talked of the 'assistance' of Africans or compared the comforts of the Negro with those of the European peasant. 'The laws, in all countries where slavery is established or tolerated, allowed the master to secure the obedience of the slave by reasonable and moderate punishment. But the First Commissioner, by ordering that no punishment should be inflicted without his order, has superseded the power of masters and magistrates; and in a certain degree rendered the slave independent of both. The misery which has laid waste many of the neighbouring colonies ought naturally to guard us against such dangerous innovation.'

Quite apart from the abuse, the cause could now be defined by negatives. Conciliation was impossible. Fullarton decided that he was the First Commissioner and that, Hood or no Hood, it was time to act. He told his young men that from now on he was going to collect evidence openly. To examine witnesses, he appointed two Englishmen who practised as lawyers (three years later it was discovered that one of them wasn't a lawyer at all) and he appointed Pedro Vargas as his Spanish assessor. Most of the work had already been done. In two days Fullarton was able to prepare an interim paper which specified thirty-seven charges against Picton, of execution without trial, false imprisonment, torture and one burning-alive. The trial of Picton had to follow; the only problem in Fullarton's mind was where.

A ship was about to leave for England. But among its passengers were some military people friendly to Picton; and Fullarton, who already distrusted the posts, thought it safer to send one of his surveyors to England as a courier.

Other letters went by the same ship. One from Picton attacked Fullarton and praised Hood. And there was one from Pedro Vargas to Miranda attacking Picton, Vargas returning for a moment from his assessorship to the half-forgotten private world of revolution. He wrote in the old style, using the words that cost nothing. All the Spaniards in Trinidad and Venezuela, he wrote, looked upon Miranda as their redeemer.

Fullarton went to the jail that day and released a mulatto man of property who had been there without cause for two years. It had been in Fullarton's power to do so all along. Vallot and his wife, Rose Banier Vallot, were co-operative. They always recognized authority; they carried out orders. It was none of their business, but they judged; and they were always ready to talk. Vallot said it had always seemed to him that Picton was 'particularly vindictive' against the mulatto; but both he and Mme Vallot had done what they could for the mulatto. Mme Vallot thought that Picton had acted with 'malice and hatred' in this case.

In the Council three days later Fullarton read out the charges against Picton that he had sent to London. Picton went wild. 'The outrage,' Fullarton wrote, 'with which he received the communication, if addressed to any person of as ill-regulated a temper as his own, would have occasioned his immediate death; for I was armed and he was not. I put my hand upon my sword, but did not draw it.'

Hood was very angry. He said that Fullarton's paper was a 'libellous production'; and that day, thirty days after his arrival, he resigned. So that two of the Commissioners had now resigned. The third, Fullarton, was frightened and had plans for flight. A schooner, hired with Treasury funds, was waiting in the harbour.

Fullarton had bad news from London at this time. Two of the ministers in the previous government, Picton's patrons, were trying to unseat him as a member of parliament; they had decided that the Commissionership was an office of profit under the Crown. But Fullarton didn't have time to think of that now; he wasn't even replying to Hood and Picton's angry queries about his plans. There were still a few things he had to get in a hurry: the reports of Begorrat's first poisoning commission, Vallot's evidence about torture.

And again Vallot was co-operative. He sat down in his room at that table on which Luisa Calderon had leaned after her torture, and in his phonetic French wrote the history of torture in Trinidad. '*Je déclare que . . . à leurs arrivée en prison . . . pour tâcher davoirs deux la verité . . . less quatres nègres . . . ont étés mis au piquet par moi et mon nègre nommé Bourique . . . Je déclare en outre que quand Louise Cardon ou Calderon aité mise aupiquet . . .*'

Louise Cardon or Calderon: she was on Begorrat's mind as well that day. He thought he would look over the record of that process 'to see that no infidelity had been committed on the papers'. He went to the escribano. The escribano said he had given all the criminal records of the island to Colonel Fullarton, who had asked for them just a few days before.

The news, announced at a special meeting of the Council, created dismay. They attacked Fullarton. Fullarton's Provost-Marshal protested. They decided to suspend the escribano. The Provost-Marshal protested. They decided to arrest the escribano.

It was late afternoon, the Fullartons still at dinner with their young men, when the Provost-Marshal brought the news that the escribano was a prisoner in the house of Judge Black, one of the cabildo magistrates. Under Spanish law it was the privilege of an official to be imprisoned in a private house and not in the common jail. For some reason – perhaps his evidence-taking, perhaps his impending flight – Fullarton was in full uniform: the blue windsor coat with red trimmings, the dress sword. His carriage was ready. He took his stick and drove with the Provost-Marshal and one young man to the house of Judge Black. It was nearly sunset. Fullarton hurried up the flight of steps to the landing on the upper floor and called, 'Is Mr Castro here?'

Castro was the name of the escribano. He and Judge Black were sitting at a table talking over certain legal matters. At Fullarton's 'magisterial intonation' they both rose.

'Is Mr Castro here? In prison?' Fullarton asked, going inside.

'Yes,' Judge Black said, 'Mr Castro is here. There he is.'

Fullarton went to Castro and took his arm. 'Mr Castro, *mon ami, venez avec moi.* Why or by what authority, I demand' – turning to Judge Black – 'do you keep Mr Castro in prison?'

Judge Black said he was acting on the orders of the Commissioners and Council.

'Is he at liberty? Can he go out? Mr Castro, are you at liberty?'

'I am a prisoner,' Castro said.

'You see, sir. Mr Castro is a prisoner. It is an illegal proceeding. *Eventuellement il y va de la potence.* This is a hanging matter. I will carry Mr Castro with me.'

Judge Black said Castro was in his charge. 'If you take him by violence I cannot prevent you.'

'Well, *puisque c'est ainsi*, Mr Castro, *je vous nomme commissaire de population de cette colonie.*' A commissary of population was immune from arrest. '*Voyons à présent,*' Fullarton said to Judge Black (whose dialogue of course this is). '*Si vous leur retiendra prisonier –* ' Fullarton broke off to ask the Provost-Marshal to send to the house for the other young men. 'Bring a Bible, bring a Bible,' Fullarton said to Judge Black.

Judge Black refused. He didn't want to make a statement.

'A Bible is unnecessary,' the Provost-Marshal said. 'Mr Black is a Roman Catholic and can be sworn on the cross.'

Judge Black said he was a Protestant, but it didn't matter. He wasn't going to be sworn.

'It is not necessary to write,' the Provost-Marshal said, and tore up what he had begun to write.

Fullarton's other young men arrived, the 'affidavit men', Picton called them. They didn't awe Judge Black. He was middle-aged, impish, renowned for his meanness and admiringly feared for his crooked dealing ever since, as a Negro-shipper, he had landed and sold, at scarcity prices, a parcel of forty diseased Negroes, thirty-four of whom had died within three days.

'Remember, sir,' he said to Fullarton, just after the young men arrived, 'you have told me I should be hanged.'

The affidavit men were thrown off balance. Fullarton saw that that piece of idiomatic French – *il y va de la potence* – so unnecessary besides, since the escribano was Spanish and Judge Black Irish, had taken him too far. He said he hadn't threatened Judge Black; what he had said was that the documents the escribano gave him dealt with hanging matters.

'Gentlemen,' Fullarton said to his young men, 'listen. I said that this is an illegal act. Is it not true, gentlemen, that this act is illegal?'

'Very illegal,' they said, and to Judge Black it seemed that they spoke in recitative.

'Be that as it may,' Judge Black said, 'remember you have told me I should be hanged.'

'The public report,' Fullarton said, remembering his original case, 'is that you have threatened to imprison, exile or hang all those who would give evidence against General Picton.'

Judge Black said, 'I will be answerable that none of those punishments will be inflicted on Mr Castro.'

It was as far as the argument could go. Castro sat silent. Perhaps, as a newly appointed commissary of population, he couldn't be arrested; but Fullarton gave up the rescue attempt.

THE NEXT DAY Fullarton went aboard the waiting schooner. Flight, or just distance, was urgent; in that alone, as he thought, lay safety. Pedro Vargas and two of the young men went with him. But the schooner didn't sail that day or the next. The people on shore wanted their criminal records back. Hood said he would seize the schooner or sink it, if Fullarton attempted to sail. The city – including McCallum and the members of the Ugly Club – watched the schooner and waited.

Aboard the schooner Fullarton was adding to his serial letter to the Secretary of State. 'Whether I am to consider myself as a prisoner or not is at this moment uncertain. I am detained by the application of naval force to prevent me from fulfilling your Lordship's instructions; and while I remained on shore I was at the mercy of the military force under General Picton.'

Mrs Fullarton visited her husband. One of the young men also went on board and in Mrs Fullarton's presence reported – he 'felt it a matter of duty' – what Hood was saying. Fullarton thought it a departure from Hood's 'former modes and character'; it was less 'the language of a Chief Commander' than 'the phraseology of a drunken boatswain'.

Through the Provost-Marshal, still Secretary of the Commission, Hood and Picton sent a more formal letter to Fullarton. They expressed their surprise at his flight and asked for the criminal records back.

A resolution condemning Fullarton was being read in the Council when the Provost-Marshal returned with Fullarton's reply. He read it out.

'I request you to inform the Commissioners and Council that anyone who would carry criminal records off the island must either be extremely ignorant of public duty or must act in direct violation of it. In the present instance, all the criminal records to which your letter refers were safely deposited by me on shore.' The records would be returned as soon as Fullarton had the assurance that copies would be made by his lawyers, who – and this was his final surprise – 'at this moment do not know where the papers are'.

Anger failed Hood; his sarcasm failed Picton. They were reduced to astonished calm. Then the Provost-Marshal read out his own resignation as Secretary, dropped the Commission papers into the lap of a clerk and joined Fullarton on the schooner, which presently – no point in seizing or sinking it now – sailed away to the Grenadines.

There the Provost-Marshal was put aboard a ship bound for England with Fullarton's serial letter of outrage and all the other papers. And Fullarton, First Commissioner, went prowling about the Antilles looking for the Commander-in-Chief, the only man, he thought, who could protect him and his wife against the Second and Third Commissioners, both of whom had already resigned. Momentarily in Port of Spain their calm turned to a sense of injustice. They began to send letters as distressed as Fullarton's, with enclosures as well, to London, to the Secretary of State and even to the Prime Minister.

THEY WROTE to London. They also acted. They sacked the harbour-master (he had helped Fullarton with the schooner). They sacked Fullarton's Deputy Alguazil-Mayor. They kept the escribano Castro a prisoner, and they moved to scatter all those who had given evidence to Fullarton's affidavit men. They banished a Spanish mulatto to England and a Spaniard to Venezuela; they allowed the Spanish lawyer who had acted for Carlos Gonzalez to leave for good. They had Andrés de España, the revolutionary, sent away from the jail.

And there was the mulatto who had refused to send his Negroes for the road corvée, had been imprisoned and had then been released by Fullarton because the offence hadn't been specified by the local commandant. The mulatto was picked up again, the offence was specified and he got seven months. But he was released again; his arrest had only been for the form, to re-establish the commandant's authority and to damp down mulatto excitement. The commandant, in his French way, had gone on to such a degree about his humiliation that the free people of colour had begun to take him at his word. It was known too that Zozo, Barrou and Stanislaus de Colaux, mulattoes who had organized uprisings in other places, had come back to the island. The released mulatto, no doubt feeling especially protected now, talked of bringing an action against the commandant. The lawyer he went to not only advised against legal action; he told the mulatto to use the little time he had to get out of the angry commandant's way. The mulatto understood; he sold up in a hurry and moved.

Picton and Hood acted politically as well. They killed the idea of settlement by white smallholders. About a hundred discharged soldiers, Prussians and Dutch, had arrived as immigrants. They didn't get the plots of land that they were expecting; instead, 'so as to economize their rations', they were distributed among the estates as additional plantation labour.

To weaken English support for Fullarton, the principle of white unity against Negroes and mulattoes was stated. It was Begorrat's idea. He had been talking about a Canadian-style constitution to protect French interests; but now he said that the French would accept a British constitution provided Negroes and mulattoes were exempt from its 'clemency'. Otherwise the island could become another Haiti, 'where the invincible armies of Bonaparte have been defeated and destroyed by this cast of mankind, whom the powers of Europe that have colonies in America must unite to subjugate'.

And attempts were made once more to detach the rich or respectable English from the English who were radical or riff-raff. Notices were posted up in the town assuring British merchants that Hood and Picton had 'their interest under consideration'. At the same time action was taken against English troublemakers. A Negro belonging to one of McCallum's friends was impounded and mutilated. And the Ugly Club was broken up.

Picton and Hood both wanted McCallum out of the way. Picton knew that McCallum was writing a book; he also thought that McCallum had been sent out as a spy by some British ministers. Hood remembered that his brother, now dead, had been abused in a London 'democratic' paper which McCallum had edited. Hood also thought that that paper had been responsible for a naval mutiny.

They got at McCallum first of all by requiring him to serve in the militia. He refused; he said he was a visitor, due to leave in a few weeks. He also explained to his friends that the militia was a self-constituted volunteer force, no commission in it was 'worth a farthing' and that he intended to 'shoot the first man who attempted to lay hands on him'. Some of his friends stayed away from the Sunday parade. On Wednesday morning McCallum was invited to meet some of the militia officers at a private house. They gave him a chair and asked him to explain. The news got round. Spectators began to turn up.

McCallum made a speech about the liberties of the British subject. He said that if they wanted to make a Star Chamber business out of it they would find him a bitter enemy. He was dismissed then, but he knew that his 'doom . . . must now be near at hand'. Five days later he was arrested early in the afternoon and taken before Hood and Picton, in Hood's house.

'You must give us an account of yourself,' Picton said.

'On my return to London I intend to publish all you wish to know of me, and if you are *spared* to read it, I feel confident that you will find it interesting.'

'It cannot be interesting to me, sir. You are a common disturber of the public peace.'

'Permit me to tell your Excellency that there is no truth whatever in that assertion. Though I cannot vouch so much for some of those who are immediately under your command; for this morning I observed three officers of one of the black regiments with bludgeons, in the act of murdering an English gentleman.'

'What are your views in this colony?'

'Being a British subject, I presume no one will dispute my right of residence in a British colony. However, there is no mystery. During my travels on the continent of America, I heard so much of Brigadier-General Picton's renown that I became very desirous of seeing him.'

Picton gave his famous grin.

McCallum asked 'a few legal questions' about the Sovereign, authority and natural rights. He was proving that his arrest was illegal.

'Silence, sir!' Picton said.

'Very well, gentlemen. I trust it will not be long before I shall be heard fully, at the fountainhead of Justice.'

'Hold your tongue, sir!' Hood said, speaking for the first time.

An order was made out.

'We commit him for contempt,' Picton said.

'Then I consider myself a state prisoner. Consequently I claim the privileges attached.'

Picton ignored this. 'Tell Vallot,' he said to the officer in Spanish, 'that he mustn't let anyone speak to the prisoner or see him, except his servant.'

At half past three McCallum was in the jail. He called it the Bastille, but his cell was large, nearly twenty feet long and ten wide, and he had it to himself. He was watched by two Negro soldiers. The spiders in the cell were 'as large as the crabs in Europe', but perhaps there were not also 'scorpions, centipedes, blindworms, moschetos'. In the *cachot* above was an old black woman, a poisoner, who looked seventy or eighty. In the room below there were fifty or sixty chained Negroes; their chains clinked and clanked, and the 'contaminated gas . . . they copiously emit from their secretions' came up through the gaps in the floorboards.

Vallot was a 'most dismal ill-looking monster'. That is all: it was McCallum's incompleteness as a pamphleteer: he had no gift for portraiture. Vallot was talkative as usual. He talked about the United States and said he was thinking of going there. He offered rum-and-water when McCallum said he was thirsty. McCallum began to drink. He thought of poison and stopped. He waited for a drink until his servant brought dinner. Pen, ink and paper also came with the dinner. McCallum began a jail journal.

He had dysentery the next day and kept dozing off. He was convinced he had been poisoned by Vallot's rum-and-water. He knew that the 'publicity' of his travels was dreaded; and he was comforted by the thought that he had a duty to his profession. Ill as he was, he noted the flogging by Vallot of four Negroes, a woman, a boy and two men. They were 'fourposter' floggings, *à quatre piquettes*. The whip was four feet long, thicker in the middle and cutting three to four inches at each lash. 'When the victims made a noise, which is almost constantly the case, or struggled to get loose, Vallot, who stood at the head, kicked them without mercy on the face.'

McCallum couldn't sleep that night because of his dysentery. The next morning he sent a note by his servant to one of his friends (the one whose Negro had been mutilated and was still somewhere in the jail), asking him to see whether he could arrange a visit by Dr Parker. At eleven some soldiers came to take McCallum to Picton and Hood. He said he couldn't walk.

Vallot was concerned; he was on everybody's side. 'Oh, sir, they will soon force you. You must find feet.'

They made him walk to Hood's house, with a view of the Gulf and the ships, and he stood in the sun for three hours at the bottom of the steps. Dr Parker, whom McCallum wanted to see, came down; he was in tears. McCallum went up. Picton had the note McCallum had written that morning. McCallum had given his address as 'Bastille, Felon Side'.

'Did you write this note?'

'Yes, sir. It was not intended for the gentleman to whom it is addressed, but for your Excellencies. It makes no difference as to the address; the contents are a true parallel.'

'What is a parallel?' Picton asked, questioning McCallum's vocabulary in the way Fullarton had sometimes questioned Picton's own pronunciation.

'I hope you do not take me for a lexicographer,' McCallum said, using an even bigger word.

'What is your name, sir?' Hood asked. He was probing what remains a mystery: McCallum's first names were Pierre Franc.

'Your Excellency is no stranger to that.'

'Pray, sir,' Hood pressed, 'where was you born?'

'I really cannot exactly say, though I was present at the time. It was somewhere in the island of Great Britain.'

'Where was you baptized?'

'I must have been present at the time the ceremony was performed, yet I do not recollect it.'

'Did your parents ever tell of the circumstances?'

'They might.'

'What school was you educated at?'

'Have you perceived that my education has been neglected?'

'Stand up, sir! Do you, sir, know who you are speaking to, sir?'

'I have already informed you I was not able to stand. And with regard to knowing who you are, I am perhaps better informed than you would ever wish me to be.'

'Silence, sir!'

McCallum took out his snuff-box.

'Pray, sir!' Hood exclaimed, 'how long have you been a snuff-taker?'

'I really cannot recollect, though I was present at the time I took the first pinch. Perhaps you now imagine yourself on board your ship, interrogating your cook. Remember I am not so much under your control, therefore not afraid of receiving a *dozen*, as you call it.'

Hood, nagging at one point, could reduce a man to tears.

'I despise your scribbling,' Hood said. 'Commit him. Take him away.'

McCallum, going down the steps to the bright yard, saw McKay coming up. McKay was the 'worthy little Highlander' who was attempting to run a Port of Spain tavern without prostitutes and wasn't meeting with encouragement. He was a member of the Ugly Club; he was taking up the box with the Club's 'papers'. McCallum didn't report any conversation.

He was exhausted, in a state of shock after Hood's bullying; and quite ill when he got back to the jail, four hours after he had left it. Vallot was going about his duties. McCallum was in time to see him stake down two Negroes, one after the other, and whip them. An hour or so later McCallum's servant brought dinner. The

Negro soldiers at the cell door 'tossed it about', looking for a letter. McCallum objected. One of the Negroes 'growled' and showed his bayonet. McCallum lost his appetite. The Negroes ate the dinner; they didn't thank him.

The Council was meeting that day. Picton made a long statement defending his administration. A proclamation was made that militia service was compulsory. Another proclamation offered a 100-dollar reward for the missing criminal records; they hadn't been found among the papers of the Ugly Club.

Early in the afternoon – it seemed to be the time for arrests – another English prisoner came to the jail. He was put in the cell next to McCallum's. This cell was as deep as McCallum's, just under ten foot, but it was only seven and a half feet wide; and it already held two Englishmen, an Indian, two French mulattoes and four Negroes.

The new prisoner was Dr Timbrell, a surgeon of the Royal Artillery. Three years before, Dr Timbrell had helped Mrs Griffiths, the widow with the 'amiable daughters', when she was besieged by Picton's black soldiers in her house, the one she said she hadn't sold to Rosette Smith. Dr Timbrell had since married one of the daughters. She came now to see her husband in the jail, but she couldn't offer much comfort. A Negro soldier stood beside her and McCallum thought he was 'ready to plunge his bayonet into her bosom if she opened her lips'.

The gossip was that Picton had tried to buy off Mrs Griffiths. But the case against Dr Timbrell was more serious. At seven in the morning he was taken away to Hood's house. He came back at two and told McCallum – who had forgotten about his own poisoning and dysentery – that he had been imprisoned because he had given evidence to Fullarton's lawyers about the artilleryman who, six years before, had been hanged without trial for rape. Timbrell had spent the morning denying that he had given evidence. He wanted, he said later, to protect the lawyers. Picton and Hood had decided that Timbrell was to be court-martialled for 'volunteering secret information against his commanding officer' and – a French West Indian offence – for 'keeping company with coloured men and Negroes'. The second charge, as Fullarton said later, stretching the facts a little, 'was very fully established, for Dr Timbrell was confined in a room about twelve feet square, in prison, along with nine persons of those descriptions'.

Timbrell's story depressed McCallum. So did the airlessness and stench of his cell and the sound of the Negroes' chains below. At about four Vallot, never idle, found some fault with the Negro jail-boy who waited on the paying prisoners. He was only a little boy, but Vallot, automatically professional, staked him down, stripped and whipped him and dabbed lime-juice on the cuts.

An hour later a letter came to 'Mr P. McCallum, Prisoner in the Jail of Port of Spain'. It was signed by the Secretary of the Commission whom Fullarton had sacked and Hood and Picton reinstated. 'Sir, I am commanded to inform you that you are to be shipped off tomorrow evening for New York, from whence you came.' The turn of phrase was familiar. McCallum placed it, and saw, as he thought, what Picton and Hood wished wasn't missing: . . . *to New York from whence you came and from thence to the place of execution* . . .

But there was a delay, a haggle about money with the American schooner captain, McCallum said. He stayed in the jail. The next day his servant brought a letter, 'concealed like a quid of tobacco' in his mouth. The letter was from another Scot, who had been arrested, examined and released. It was high-toned, a relic of the Ugly Club fellowship; it contained no news. 'Writers who have deigned to employ their talents in exposing the depravity of monsters have, perhaps, contributed no less to the happiness of mankind than those who exhibited only their virtues.'

McCallum's spirits lifted. But he had to spend yet another day in jail – three Negroes staked down and whipped by Vallot in the morning, salt, vinegar and jail-dust applied to the cuts afterwards – before the alguazils came for him, marched him off to the harbour-master, who marched him to his lodgings next to the barracks to get his trunks, took him back to the pier and handed him over against a receipt to the American captain. McCallum said later that the Commissioners, anxious to get rid of him and in that particular vessel (some of the crew had yellow fever: there was an epidemic in New York), bribed the unwilling captain with 700 dollars. The Secretary of the Commission said he paid fifty-six dollars.

A FORTNIGHT BEFORE, at Union Island in the Grenadines, Fullarton had put his second courier, the Provost-Marshal, on a ship going to England. Then Fullarton had gone north, chasing the Commander-in-Chief from island to island, to ask for help. The Commander-in-Chief, acting like a chased man, went steadily north and then made a swift dash south to Headquarters in Barbados. Fullarton turned back south. He behaved like a man who had received a message; he gave up the Commander-in-Chief.

He and Pedro Vargas talked of the need for an association for 'scientific' inquiry that would cover South America and all the islands. The fantasy, which appeared to give a purpose to their idleness, grew. Fullarton began to refer to Vargas as a 'scientific man', and Vargas began to accept the role of naturalist. He was already Miranda's revolutionary agent and, for Fullarton, a surveyor, an official interpreter and an assessor in Spanish law (he said he had acted as secretary for three viceroys in New Granada).

In this way they idled down to Trinidad waters, which they had left a month before. They cruised along the north coast, hidden by a mountain range from Port of Spain and other settled areas. Then they cruised along the Atlantic coast. From time to time Fullarton went ashore to test reaction from a public he had to look for. He said he was received with 'attention and regard' in all those areas 'not immediately within the influence or apprehension' of Picton. But at the south-eastern tip of the island someone showed him a proclamation. Picton and Hood had declared that Fullarton had absented himself from his post against King's Orders and could no longer be considered First Commissioner.

It had been Hood's last act as Third Commissioner. He had gone back to Headquarters in Barbados; the French war was about to start again and he had been made Commander-in-Chief of the Leeward Islands Station. Picton was once more in sole command in Trinidad. He withdrew the sentries from Fullarton's house and personally dismissed the galley Negroes who were working in the grounds, filling in the trenches that had been dug to drain away the stagnant floodwater after the rains. Mrs Fullarton and her sister heard Picton shouting. They came out to the gallery in time to see two cartloads of rubble dumped in front of the gallery. Then all the Negroes went away.

Fullarton knew that Hood had left. When he entered the Gulf of Paria he also learned that Picton had issued detailed orders for martial law; that Hood had placed the Royal Navy brig in the Gulf under Picton's command; and that the lieutenant had orders to seize Fullarton's schooner if it anchored at Port of Spain. Fullarton 'frustrated' Picton's schemes, 'for instead of anchoring at Port of Spain and proceeding by violent measures to reassume the Government, I sailed from Point Icaque' – he had some trouble there, from the local commandant – 'across the Gulf of Paria, directly for Barbados'.

ON THE DAY that Fullarton and Pedro Vargos began this flight to Barbados Miranda was writing a memorandum in Spanish in London. The French war had started again the day before. Miranda wanted to leave right away for Trinidad; he wanted an immediate British attack on Venezuela with the black troops of Trinidad. The force was small, but 'it will be sufficient to give the necessary impetus on the Continent. Most of the inhabitants are impatiently awaiting us, and most of the Spaniards in Trinidad want to join us, as may be seen by an extract from the letters of Commissioner Vargas. This simple exposé will suffice to convince the ministers of His Britannic Majesty of the necessity in which I find myself of obeying the voice of the Motherland that calls me to her succour at a moment which is really dangerous'.

HOOD WAS fortunately away from Barbados on a cruise. Fullarton got in touch with the Governor. But he stayed away from the Commander-in-Chief. He drafted a letter to him. 'Nothing could be more gratifying to me than to meet Brigadier-General Picton, either individually in action, or to attack him in a military post with an equal force; but in the present instance I should have engaged *non equo marte*, with as little conduct as a peace officer, who, trusting to the baton of a constable, should singly charge an armed battalion. Had I been employed to take Port of Spain from an enemy by assault, I hardly know any general, of any service, whom I should wish more sincerely to command against me than the Brigadier.'

Fullarton didn't immediately send this letter. The next day he wrote another letter, much longer, to the absent Hood. It was the substitute for that private meeting Hood had never wanted. 'I trust that our intercourse with Brigadier-General Picton has not made us forget the conduct which becomes officers and gentlemen.' Fullarton gave all the explanations Hood had never listened to, all the evidence; and reported all that had been reported to him. He wrote with sorrow. 'Your panegyric was my constant theme.' Yet Hood had been heard to say loudly in the streets of Port of Spain that Fullarton's conduct was 'infamous, most infamous'. 'As for you and me, our characters, in the mere business of fighting, are long-established. I am quite aware, that while you and I remain in our relative situations, to give or to accept anything like a challenge would, in the highest degree, be improper on either side.'

Fullarton didn't immediately send this letter either. But then he had some luck. The mailboat with dispatches from London to Trinidad arrived at Barbados. The Secretary of State had accepted Picton's resignation; he confirmed Fullarton's executive powers as

First Commissioner and explicitly gave him command of the Royal and Loyal Trinidad Militia. The original dispatches went on to Picton in Trinidad. Fullarton sent copies to the Trinidad garrison commander, the officer commanding the Militia, the governor of Barbados and the unfriendly Commander-in-Chief. He received a prompt and correct acknowledgement from the Commander-in-Chief, and an invitation to dinner.

The mailboat reached Trinidad three days later. Picton decided that fresh dispatches from London 'on this important subject' should be awaited, and that in the meantime Fullarton was not to land. Martial law was declared; ball-cartridges were issued to the troops, the guns in the Sea Fort shotted. But at the same time Picton was getting ready to leave. He had appointed Begorrat his estates-agent; and Begorrat had organized an address to Picton from the 'principal proprietors', who had also subscribed for a presentation sword, 'to be prepared in London'.

Two days later Fullarton's schooner entered the Gulf from the south. The schooner wasn't alone. It was protected by a warship, the one in which Fullarton had travelled out from England.

Picton sent an officer aboard the schooner with a letter. Fullarton was no longer First Commissioner and would not be allowed to land. To prevent Fullarton smuggling himself ashore, the boats from the schooner and the warship were searched. Mrs Fullarton was allowed to visit the schooner only under the protection of the warship captain.

Fullarton transferred to the warship, which for three days cruised about the Chaguaramas peninsula west of Port of Spain. Cruising, 'surveying', Fullarton composed a letter to Picton and prepared a proclamation. He also prepared a letter to the Commander-in-Chief in Barbados, with enclosures. Vargas and the others were kept busy, making copies of everything. The cruise ended, and the disturbed commanding officer of the garrison sent an emissary to Fullarton. Fullarton gave the assurance he was asked for. He didn't intend, he said, 'to put the military under your command to the necessity of disobeying your orders or of forfeiting their allegiance to the King, which requires them to support the Civil Government'.

On the same day Fullarton sent one of his young men ashore with a letter to Picton. 'I beg you to be assured that if it were a mere question of your personal insults or resistance to me in the execution of my public duty, I should desire you to oppose my landing on the Mole, and in the event of your doing so, in person, I should draw my sword and run you through the body.'

They were all getting letters now. Fullarton sent his letter to the Commander-in-Chief and, three weeks after it had been written, the letter to Hood. Fullarton got a letter from the commanding officer of the Trinidad garrison. He was concerned at Fullarton's 'disagreeable situation', but thought that Fullarton showed 'judgement' in appealing to the Commander-in-Chief rather than the 'troops immediately under the Brigadier-General'.

Then suddenly the crisis was over. The Commander-in-Chief had decided that Picton was to be replaced, and the brig with Picton's replacement arrived in the Gulf. That very evening, 14 June 1803, 'after taking an affecting leave of his darling copper-coloured Rosette' – the imaginative touch is McCallum's – Picton boarded the brig and sailed for Barbados. After nearly six and a half years Picton's rule had ended; and it had ended in what looked to Fullarton like flight. 'The multitudes of individuals whom he had personally aggrieved and outraged,' Fullarton wrote later, 'rendered it unsafe for him to embark by daylight, or to hazard himself in the colony one moment after he was divested of authority.'

Picton never returned to Trinidad. Rosette Smith disappears.

IT WAS THREE DAYS before Fullarton landed. He wanted it understood what the privileges of the First Commissioner were and what were the limitations of the military power. This meant more letters. Then he issued his proclamation, which was a definition of his authority; and at nine on the following morning he landed 'in regular form', not from the schooner of his travels, but from the warship to which he had transferred some days before. He noted a general rejoicing among the people of colour and Negroes. 'It required my own personal interference and positive injunctions to prevent general illumination, which is highly dangerous in a town built entirely of wood.'

His triumph was spoiled only by the knowledge that Picton had already been employed by Hood and the Commander-in-Chief on the expedition being planned against the French islands of St Lucia and Tobago; and then by Hood's letter, written from his flagship, the grand realm of the naval hero. 'Sir, I have to acknowledge the receipt of a voluminous epistle from you, which is at an instant I am occupied with a duty more material to my country than the first and last pages (the only part I have been able to peruse) appear to require.'

Fullarton presently had another sorrow. One of his young men died; death came suddenly here to the unseasoned. But there was much to be done. It was Fullarton's turn now to reinstate (the harbour-master, the Deputy Alguazil-Mayor, the escribano) and sack (the Council, the Attorney-General, the unfriendly commandant at Icacos) and to receive addresses. He received one signed mainly by the British merchants, the indentured clerks, the former members of the Ugly Club and the immigrants who had become poor whites. They congratulated him on having conducted his government 'at the moment you chose . . . at a distance'; they looked to him to establish a 'system of British jurisprudence'.

This system was what the free people of colour feared, and in three days the British people of colour, separating themselves from the French people of colour, who had a revolutionary taint, prepared and presented their own anxious address. Looking beyond the local British community, they thanked the Sovereign, 'he who sways the British sceptre . . . for making all British subjects think and feel that they live in a British colony'.

Britishness as an ideal of justice and protection: this was in mimicry of Fullarton's own language. But Fullarton was now concerned to prove himself as an administrator. 'It has been my earnest wish and endeavour ,' he replied, 'to introduce the principles of conciliation, and to afford inviolable security to the property and person of every individual. On the other hand, it gives me the utmost satisfaction to bear this public testimony, that in no instance have I ever found either the white or coloured population of Trinidad inclined to deviate from due order and subordination.'

Fullarton tightened up on Negroes. The alguazil patrol had been suspended during the recent disturbances and Negroes were running about a little too freely, especially near the wharf, without passes from their owners; their drumbeating, dancing and jumping-up at night had already become a nuisance.

Still the balanced administrator, Fullarton issued precise instructions for the collection of the three and a half per cent customs duty on imported goods. The British merchants protested. They wanted British laws, but only up to a point. With Picton out of the way, loyalties were already shifting. Fullarton was no longer necessary to all his supporters.

Anxious now to answer every criticism of himself and at the same time to build up as complete a case against Picton as possible, Fullarton was adding to his own confusion and ensuring his isolation. In his reply to the British people of colour he had, however ambiguously, stated the racial principle of the slave colony that Picton and Begorrat and the others had stated just three months before. Fullarton went further. He heard that a number of planters in the Bahamas had some time before changed their minds about moving to Picton's Trinidad and had taken their Negroes, five to six thousand, to the United States. This became something for the Picton file. Yet the bond between Fullarton, McCallum and the Ugly Club was their patriotic-humanitarian-radical wish for free white smallholders in Trinidad and the suppression of the Negro plantations.

Principle and generous anger had become impossible. At the heart of the difficulty was slavery. The principles of justice and protection: only the free British people of colour spoke like that now, in mimicry. And the people of colour, British and French, were remembered, long after abolition, for their severe management of their Negroes, this overlordship their only distinction.

LETTERS CAME to Fullarton from London, from his friend the Under-Secretary and from the Provost-Marshal. A new governor was to be appointed. But a judicial investigation of Picton's acts was likely. Witnesses and documents would be needed. Fullarton called on Sir James Bontein, lying low ever since Picton had insulted him on the pier the day Hood had arrived; and Fullarton gave Sir James some documents to take to London. (Sir James paid in London, again in public insult from Picton's supporters, for the favour of the free passage back to England.)

Pedro Vargas also took the opportunity to send a report to Miranda. It was his first in three months. He had been at sea with Fullarton much of this time, copying out documents, 'botanizing', chasing and being chased. But he managed to find things to say. Caracas, Vargas told Miranda, was ripe for revolution; the Venezuelans were ready to sacrifice their lives and – Englishness breaking in – their property for the cause. Vargas himself was leaving nothing undone in Trinidad to ensure success. 'Do not forget that you were born in America and she calls you with open arms.'

Then Vargas went back to his work: the Picton prosecution. Time was pressing; the new governor would be arriving any day. It was becoming clear that only two charges could be made to stick: Begorrat's poisoning commission with its tortures and its ritual of burning the living and dead, and the Luisa Calderon case. About the poisoning commission Vargas had his doubts, since under Spanish law a slave's evidence was valid only if given under torture. Luisa Calderon was a free woman, however; and a bonus could be her age. It was Vargas's opinion that Spanish law forbade the application of torture to anyone under fourteen. Luisa Calderon was fifteen when she was tortured. Vargas thought she should be made thirteen. He persuaded the old Spanish curate of Port of Spain to make an alteration in the books and to issue a false certificate. Luisa Calderon's mother had to be coached in her daughter's new age. She was more than willing; she was willing to say that Luisa was ten when she was tortured.

The birth certificate, the details of the legal process: these were the documents. London had also asked for witnesses. This was no trouble. They were all willing to go to London with Fullarton and – this was in Fullarton's power – be kept there at the British government's expense. The two alguazils who had tied up Luisa; Castro the escribano who had written up the torture while it was taking place; Porto Rico, Vallot's assistant, who had pulled on the rope; Vallot himself, always on everybody's side; and Luisa. Everybody, then, who was in the torture chamber, except for Begorrat: torturers and victims, together on the London excursion. The deputy Alguazil Mayor was also willing to go; he had helped in getting much of the evidence, always ready to swear witnesses on the cross, which was sometimes simply two slips of paper fastened with a wafer to the cover of an ordinary book.

Fullarton was also busy clearing up certain slanders against himself which he had found in the Council minutes. He read for instance, that at dinner one day Mrs Fullarton had seated a dark mulatto next to the Baron de Montalembert, and that news of this 'extraordinary phenomenon' had dangerously exalted the 'fervid imagination' of the mulattoes. Fullarton wrote to the Baron. The Baron replied that he would have risen from the table at once. Fullarton's informant had lied, and the Baron undertook to challenge the informant at any time and at any place. Fullarton passed the letter on and left the two men, as he said, to 'adjust' the matter.

There were the charges of insanity and of entering Judge Black's house and threatening to hang him. But time was now very short and it was only on his last morning in Port of Spain – the new governor expected, the ship in the harbour ready to sail to join the wartime convoy to England, everything packed, Mrs Fullarton, her sister and their servants ready, and the young men and the witnesses – it was only on the last morning that Fullarton was able to examine Judge Black.

An especial irritant for Fullarton was that he had been represented in the Council minutes 'as expressing myself in an almost unintelligible jargon of barbarous French'. He had said *il y va de la potence*; Judge Black had made it *pend tous*. Fullarton also objected to the statement, in Spanish, in the minutes that he had entered Judge Black's house *con la espada en una mano y el bastón en la otra*. He said he had nothing more than his sword and his stick.

Judge Black said: 'One is a literal translation of the other.'

'It sounds much worse in Spanish. You have now a large stick in your hand. Would I be justified in giving the impression that you came here to intimidate?'

'Certainly not. This cane which I now hold in my hand is the distinguishing mark of a magistrate in ordinary, being generally called the Bar of Justice, on which we are sworn.'

The examination of Judge Black lasted four hours and ended only when the arrival of the new governor was announced.

Fullarton welcomed the governor and made a more than ceremonial speech in which he explained everything he had done.

At one stage he felt he needed supporting evidence and sent for Castro the escribano, packed and waiting with the others on the wharf. The news brought back was that, as soon as the new governor had been sworn, Judge Black had arrested Castro. Judge Black had also tried to arrest the Deputy Alguazil-Mayor. But he, more nimble than Castro and perhaps more willing to escape, had managed to get to the sanctuary of the ship.

Judge Black was summoned back to the Council. He said that Castro had been arrested because the rumour was that Castro was about to sail for England, and he hadn't handed over all the papers of his office. It was true that Castro had appointed a deputy. But Judge Black wasn't sure that the deputy was eligible. The deputy looked white but it was possible that he had 'a portion of mulatto blood in his veins'.

Fullarton was still First Commissioner, entitled to a salary; but he was now without any executive power. Judge Black's impertinence was no longer impertinence. Fullarton saw that he had stayed too long 'adjusting matters' with the new governor when he should have been thinking of getting away. His party was large, nearly twenty, including witnesses and servants. But he didn't give himself time to count or check now. He barely allowed himself to be detained by one of the immigrants who had come out with him. The man was now destitute; he had spent his savings of £300; his wife and daughter had died. He regarded himself as being under the protection of 'Colonel Fullington'. The cause, of free white settlement, had been Fullarton's. But it wasn't the moment for causes. Fullarton told the destitute widower to take land where he could get it, and hurried aboard the tender. He left without the keys to his trunks and without some of his servants. He left without Vallot.

To deal with Vallot and Castro, keys and servants, Fullarton left Pedro Vargas behind. Vargas was still an official and inviolable. The matter of the escribano's papers could be cleared up in a few days. But Vargas couldn't get Castro to go to England now. Castro had been too badly frightened by his second arrest by Judge Black. To go to England he would require at least the protection of a royal subpoena.

And Vargas couldn't even find Vallot. For the first time in thirteen years Vallot wasn't in his jail. He was hiding. He too had been badly frightened. Judge Black hadn't tried to arrest Vallot – impossible to jail the jailer – but he had told Vallot what the English would do to him in England with their English laws. Vallot saw the trap he had nearly fallen into: the torturer tortured, the flogger flogged, the ear-clipper earless, the jailer, so close to retirement, jailed in somebody else's jail. Vallot, already shaken by the disloyalty of his Negro executioner and by Fullarton's intervention in jail matters, decided to run. He ran from Fullarton as Fullarton ran from Judge Black. Vallot ran from the wharf, from his jail, from the city; and for eleven days hid on Judge Black's estate, until Vargas had left and the danger of the trip to England had passed.

Fullarton had left on 20 July 1803, just twenty-eight weeks after he had arrived. Now the jail was without its jailer and the jailer's assistant was on the high seas. The executioner had disappeared weeks before. There was nothing for him to do anyway. It was the price of his list.

8. The Victims: I

July 1803–February 1806

THEN, AS HAD HAPPENED after Fullarton's other departure, within two or three days everything went back to normal. The new governor was anxious to conciliate. He sacked half the Council Fullarton had appointed and reinstated half the Council Fullarton had sacked. Vallot left Judge Black's estate. He didn't return to the jail; someone else had taken over. But the new man was inexperienced and when, just a few days later, there was a mulatto to torture – possibly a sorcerer: underground Negro life going on – Vallot was temporarily recalled.

The mulatto had been pestering a black woman to sleep with him. He had at last offered just his friendship, and a handshake. He pressed his thumbnail against her palm and she screamed. Her little finger went crooked, her arms jerked and began to swell. Negroes in the street ran up; they were frightened and angry. They complained to a passing city official.

The mulatto, taken to the jail, said what he had used wasn't a poison. Its base was an aphrodisiac he had got for a dollar from a wise old plantation Negro, now dead, and it had already made two women love him 'passionately'. He usually mixed it with quicksilver, nail scrapings and grease. Perhaps the dose had been too strong; the old Negro had warned him about that. He went up to Vallot – Judge Black's orders – and was tortured. He gave the antidote: 'attarnise infused in rum'. It didn't work. Vallot came back. This time the mulatto passed out and lay for a little in a pool of cold sweat. He changed his story about the dead plantation

Negro and the dollar; he said he had got the potion from a Negro who had been banished for sorcery.

This was serious. And the woman's neck was beginning to swell. Two doctors examined her. They found her hands 'callous from labour' and quite unscratched; they doubted whether she had been poisoned at all. And, indeed, as soon as her menstrual period was over her hysteria subsided and she became well again. It was felt, though, that she had suffered more, from her fear of being poisoned, than the mulatto during the torture. One official, speaking 'as a friend to truth', even thought that the mulatto 'might have suffered more without fainting'. The mulatto was banished – herbs were herbs, and Negro magic was Negro magic – and they told him he was lucky not to be hanged.

Fullarton and Luisa and the others were probably still in Caribbean waters. At Tortola in the Virgin Islands Fullarton had waited for his keys and servants and Pedro Vargas. Then the party, eighteen now, without Castro and Vallot, joined the British convoy to Europe. Picton too was on his way to England. The expedition with Hood hadn't lasted long. Picton – it seemed to be his luck – had seen no action. The fighting at St Lucia was over in a day, and the regiment Picton was attached to was in reserve; at Tobago there was no fighting at all, and he had served for a week or so as military governor, again.

While Picton and Fullarton were racing each other to England, Francisco Miranda in London was frantic to get out to Trinidad. Pedro Vargas's early letters, full of personal complaint, hadn't been encouraging. But Vargas's recent reports had made the revolution real again and urgent. Miranda was willing to give up his £500 allowance from the British government in return for a lump sum of £1,500, to be considered of course as a loan. This would take him to Trinidad and help him raise a force to invade Venezuela. 'The object of this proposition is to offer my country in the last act of my devotion all that I possess, as I am thoroughly convinced that a cause more just, more important and more honourable has never been presented to mortal beings. It would be inexplicable if a nation so powerful and rich as England . . .'

The British reply was that the ministers were busy with Irish affairs. The ministers in London also knew more about Trinidad. Miranda himself must have begun to learn a little when some two months later Fullarton and Picton arrived in England within days of one another, Fullarton with his assorted Negroes and mulattoes and his new expert in Spanish law, the former secretary to three viceroys, Pedro Vargas.

The Fullarton party arrived first. They landed at Port Glasgow and spent a few days of the autumn on Fullarton's estate in Ayrshire. Mrs Fullarton was unwell, the effect, the doctor said, of the tropics and the long sea voyage. Luisa Calderon, unremarkable in the Port of Spain streets, was suddenly an exotic, a Spanish-speaking 'creole' of 'an interesting countenance' and 'genteel appearance', 'slender and graceful', with a muslin turban tied in the West Indian way. She and the Negroes who had helped to torture her, including Vallot's own Porto Rico, were sent to London in the care of two of Fullarton's servants. Fullarton was wasting no time in preparing his case for the Privy Council. But the story was also that in Ayrshire Mrs Fullarton had taken Luisa about in her carriage. Mrs Fullarton said later that the story was a libel, and sued.

Fullarton and Luisa made an effect in London. And Picton, when he landed in October 1803, found himself a public figure. 'The bloodstained Governor of Trinidad,' one newspaper said, 'is in England, and the friends of humanity are preparing to bring him to the bar of offended Justice, there to expiate his crimes.'

Picton wrote to Addington, the Prime Minister. He didn't write about Trinidad. He wrote about the threat of French invasion and suggested a strategy: a people's militia served by strategically placed supply depots; plain grey uniforms; light irregulars harassing enemy columns, with cavalry falling on pursuing detachments; regular troops disputing 'advantageous posts' alone, never hazarding 'a general affair'. It was the type of guerrilla warfare, the condition of total war, by which the Negroes of Haiti had virtually destroyed the British Army between 1794 and 1798. The letter didn't lead to an interview. Scores of people were writing to the Prime Minister on defence strategy. Picton's letter was acknowledged by a secretary. It was the beginning of his long disgrace: the general who in the time of a great war had never fought a battle.

For Luisa Calderon it was also only a beginning. How often now, before Privy Council and courts, before lawyers who managed even after five years still to be incredulous or pained, she would describe, raising this hand and bending that leg, the way she had been tied up and suspended in the Port of Spain jail on the two days before Christmas. Begorrat and the watch, Porto Rico and the rope, Begorrat and the wine, the irons for the night, Vallot and the vinegar: the torture would become an act of ritual and these would be its stations: the questions always the same, in the end the responses, words and postures communicating nothing, yet the drama fixed and heightened with each re-enactment, and the setting itself, Vallot's jail, like the setting of so many court cases, becoming a place of myth, to be constructed by each man in his imagination. No plan exists of the jail; it is known only from its individual, unrelated rooms; long before the trial Picton's friends on the Trinidad Council had it pulled down.

LESS THAN a week after he had left, it was discovered that Fullarton had cleaned out the Trinidad Treasury, which on his arrival six months before had been 100,000 dollars in balance, the savings of six years. Money remained on the island after Fullarton, with the British merchants and the planters living on credit from the merchants. But the government was bankrupt for years.

When the Governor's house, formerly Fullarton's, fell into ruin – 'scarcely a dry spot to stand upright under in heavy rains', and the floor calling for continuous 'caution' – it couldn't be repaired.

When the adjacent lots were acquired the government paid partly in galley Negroes; and when fresh Negroes were bought for the public works, at £60 each, the government had to get a three-year credit from the local shipper. Nothing could be done for the barracks when the hammock-rails collapsed, the walls caved in here and there, and the soldiers slept on the broken floor. But by then the soldiers themselves, irregularly supplied from London, were in rags.

Picton ran his government on £8,000 a year. Fullarton and his young men alone had got through that sum in six months, in salaries, travelling expenses and 'secret service moneys'. To this there had to be added the 6,000 dollars for Fullarton's house; the 1,600 dollars for the stores taken aboard for the passage of the party of eighteen to England; the salaries of all the commissaries of population Fullarton had appointed (Vargas and some of the surveyors among them); and the expenses, as great as all the others put together, of the surveying department (Vargas again, and McCallum the pamphleteer).

A letter detailing these expenses went to London from the Trinidad Attorney-General. Fullarton had sacked this man, but he had returned to his post as soon as Fullarton had gone. Fullarton, busy now at the Privy Council, quoted the opinion of Pedro Vargas, Trinidad's official assessor in Spanish law, that an Attorney-General had no financial authority. But Fullarton also had all his financial answers ready. He had not only acted legitimately, he still had claims on government money. He was still First Commissioner at £3,000 a year. All his commissaries of population were still commissaries of population; some were claiming their salaries nine years later. Ten years later the Provost-Marshal was still claiming his fees. And the lawyers and the Negro and mulatto witnesses and Luisa Calderon: they were all entitled to their expenses. In the beginning Pedro Vargas collected for Luisa and the others; but Mr White, solicitor to the Treasury, soon decided to deal with them directly. For the Deputy Alguazil-Mayor lodgings were found in Soho; and he was given a guinea a day.

Fullarton couldn't be touched by the Attorney-General and his friends. But the Deputy Alguazil-Mayor could be broken, at least as an example to Castro the escribano or Vallot or anybody else who might think of going to London to give evidence. The Deputy Alguazil-Mayor was a man of modest property. He owed money; he was owed money. The money he was owed was forgotten; within a fortnight his creditors began to make trouble. His copper-bottomed cutter (copper sheathing, to protect ships' hulls in tropical waters, was new and expensive) was put up to auction with its Negro and knocked down cheap; then the house Negroes went; then, at the end of the year, the house.

In the new year, 1804, the news came to Trinidad that early the previous December Picton had been arrested. The Privy Council had ordered a King's Messenger 'to bring the said Brigadier-General Picton before them,' to answer seven charges of illegal execution and one of torture. Picton was imprisoned in a private house. Bail was fixed at £40,000. A sum so high presumed guilt. There were seven other charges, connected with the poisoning commission, to follow; and after that, perhaps, the mass hanging of the German mercenaries in the Port of Spain barracks. But sureties were found. Marryat, the father of the novelist, helped.

IN LONDON, against the ritual and courtesies of the law, everything reduced to statements, principles, words, the case was startling and looked hopeless. In Trinidad it looked like persecution. There was old Baron de Montalembert trying to make a new life after many disturbed years and losing a hundred and fifty of his Negroes. Someone less well off would have been ruined. One English immigrant said that a friend of his in Martinique had had to burn four of his Negroes. Someone else knew a Guadeloupe planter who had burned two Negroes even when the island was occupied by the British. Begorrat said there had been many more cases like that, and no British subject then 'dared to oppose or comment on the exercise of the French laws'. It was only in Trinidad that 'the enemies of government did not fail to exclaim' at 'imaginary crimes'. In Martinique at that moment, he said, there was a new poisoning commission.

And poisoners were not the only *scélérats*, Begorrat said. There were all those recent cases of arson. One Port of Spain man, looking below his floor, had found his house prepared for firing, and not long after he had again made the same disagreeable discovery. Mr Patrice had caught two runaway Negroes trying to set fire to his canes. Apart from 'this infernal race', there were many French people of colour about, known murderers of white people. Banished, sometimes even to London, they always crept back. People spoke of torture. But Vallot's piquet was 'well known in cavalry regiments'; and Begorrat said sarcastically that an 'accurate' description of it should be sent to London.

After the surprise and the anger the response to the news of Picton's arrest was to tidy up. Many people – they had been sacked from small offices, their property had been confiscated – were beginning to come forward with claims against Picton. Brigadier-General Hislop, the new governor, wanted to conciliate; he judged fairly. He had been almost ten years in the West Indies and had given up military ambition. He liked a good dinner; his enemies, in the cruel way of eighteenth-century caricature, gave him 'the character of a sot'. He had been at the siege of Gibraltar twenty years before and that had been his last battle. Now, at forty, he looked only for employment and security.

He didn't want to take sides in the Fullarton-Picton dispute, but he had an interest in having everything cleaned up, if only because he had some anxiety about that mulatto, the one with the aphrodisiac, who had been tortured almost in the first week of his administration. An Italian sailor, a prisoner in the jail at the time, had seen the torture, and the news had got around to the remaining English radicals. They prompted the Italian so much that he lied. He said that Vallot pulled on the rope and Porto Rico held it. Everyone knew that Porto Rico had gone to England with Fullarton. The Italian was imprisoned again; and the English storekeeper who had prompted him, one of the earliest English radicals on the island and now one of the last, was glad to be allowed to get away to England.

At the same time there was a general inquiry into torture and Negro-burnings, and Begorrat and the others put on record what they or their friends on other islands knew and said about these disciplines. Begorrat had even found some Spanish law-books, to show that suspected criminals, who were not under fourteen, over sixty, or pregnant women, could be suspended by pack thread for an hour.

The jail was pulled down. Vallot was finally released from his suddenly turbulent service.

All this was done just in time. The next news from London was that, even while the Privy Council was going through the other charges, the Grand Jury of Middlesex had found a true bill against Picton 'for a misdemeanour, in causing the torture to be inflicted upon Luisa Calderon, a free mulatto'. A court was to be held in Port of Spain to examine witnesses; a writ of mandamus had been issued by the court of King's Bench. And not many weeks afterwards copies of Fullarton's newly published book came, *A Statement, Letters and Documents, Respecting the Affairs of Trinidad*.

IT TOOK ABOUT two months to get to Trinidad from England. The writ of mandamus was issued in the middle of May 1804 and filed in the Trinidad court at the end of November. The delay might have been caused by the war.

In May a French fleet had been reported near the island; and a squabble had gone on all year between the Royal Navy and the planters and merchants about what was being defended. The planters and merchants said property; the Navy said the Navy, 'the floating property of His Majesty's government'. The Navy wanted Chaguaramas harbour fortified. The planters and merchants wanted a fort to protect Port of Spain and the surrounding plantations. Governor Hislop wavered. He withdrew the Negro labourers from Chaguaramas after £75,000 had been spent and built a small £10,000-fort on a Port of Spain hill. He pacified the planters, who didn't like having their Negroes requisitioned, whatever the cause, by using mostly Negroes owned by people of colour. It was strange. These colonials spoke of property and rights. War secured both, and war was never far away; but war was always someone else's duty.

The dispute must have taken up a good deal of Begorrat's time and delayed the filing of the mandamus writ. Fullarton's barrister-at-law, the unqualified one – some years before, he had paid Picton's secretary forty dollars for a lawyer's licence – was back in Port of Spain and coaching Luisa's mother and other friendly witnesses in the matter of Luisa's age. The mulattoes were enthusiastic. Some of them thought that the younger they made Luisa the more illegal the torture would be. Begorrat had more to do. He had to establish Luisa's age; he had to coach Vallot; he had to rewrite the record. That had been recovered. Begorrat had had it at home for some months.

The torture had been a rough-and-ready business, part of the Christmas rush of 1801. To write out all the illegalities wasn't easy. An extra awkwardness was that at every stage the signature of Castro the escribano was needed. Castro was now like Vallot, very frightened of everybody. He refused to sign; he signed; he threatened to confess in court. Begorrat began to bully. He accused Castro, before witnesses, of 'omissions' in the record. It worked. There were genuine omissions. Castro broke down.

Luisa should have had a 'defensor' before she was tortured. Begorrat wrote it in, in the order for the torture: not the appointment of a defensor, but his intention to appoint one. It was all he could do, because a true defensor would automatically have appealed against the torture order and delayed it for a long time. There should have been five days between the order for the torture and the torture; Begorrat had tortured immediately. He wrote in an explanation in the order now. The torture had to be immediate, 'to obviate further delays that may prejudice this cause'. The Spanish laws forbade torture twice within twenty-four hours. Begorrat had tortured Luisa at seven in the evening and then at eleven the next morning, Christmas eve, after breakfast. He switched the times. In the 'act of torment' itself Begorrat wrote in all the Spanish preliminaries: the oath on the cross, the three admonitions, the magistrate's self-absolution: 'that in case she should sustain any hurt or injury, or that should she die, the same must be on her own head, and not to be attributed to his honour, who only endeavoured to investigate the truth'.

Confessions made under torture had to be ratified within twenty-four hours in a room without any instrument of torture. Begorrat covered himself as best he could in the final plea for the defence. This Begorrat rewrote completely. The original plea had been made by a man who had acted as interpreter in the case. He was an impoverished Spaniard of no importance; he didn't object.

'But when,' Begorrat wrote, 'the order for torture was put in execution, no considerations, either of love or fear, could restrain her any longer; but rendering due homage to truth, she immediately unveiled the mystery.' He came to the second torture. 'His honour the judge, however, not yet satisfied, and who being desirous of knowing who were the accomplices, and to get at the truth, thought proper to inflict the torture a second time; which she endured with patience, and constantly maintaining and steadfastly repeating her latter deposition; during the second, violent pain she suffered, enduring with heroic spirit all the torments, from her regard to truth, which was highly extraordinary in a girl of so tender an age as that of fourteen years.'

So it was all in: Luisa's torturable age, the confession of guilt, the explanation and defence of the procedure. As a defence of Luisa this final plea wasn't very good, and as a defence of Begorrat even the emended process had its contradictions. The ratification without torture, for instance, had been immediately followed by torture. But Fullarton's lawyer was no more a lawyer than the Attorney-General an attorney-general or the escribano an escribano.

The emended record was returned to Castro and the mandamus writ was filed: . . . *and that he the said Thomas being so employed as aforesaid but unlawfully wickedly and maliciously intending to aggrieve and oppress one Luisa Calderon of Port of Spain and to expose the said Luisa to great ignominy and shame and to great anguish of body and mind with force and arms unlawfully cruelly and inhumanly and without any reasonable or probable cause under colour of his said station did cause and procure the said Luisa (being a young woman under the age of fourteen years in the peace of God and of us then and there being) to be unlawfully cruelly and inhumanly tortured by means of fastening and affixing to the wrists of the said Luisa a certain rope passing through a certain pulley then and there annexed to the ceiling of a certain room in a certain prison . . . By means of which said cruel and inhuman torture the hands wrists arms and feet of the said Luisa were cruelly and severely bruised strained and wounded and the said Luisa was thereby rendered sick weak and distempered To the great injury and oppression of the said Luisa In contempt of us and our laws In manifest violation of the liberties of our subjects To the great perversion of public justice and in breach and violation of the duty of his station aforesaid To the evil example of all others in the like case offending against our peace our crown our dignity.*

Justice, duty, dignity: they were big words in the setting. The said Thomas, the said Luisa: the equation offended, and in Port of Spain was dangerous. The conduct of the people of colour was 'deteriorating'. A week after public notice of the mandamus court was given – five printed handbills and an advertisement in the *Courant* – the Council extended the nine o'clock curfew to the people of colour. But the court was delayed for many weeks.

Fullarton's lawyer was absent; then the Attorney-General, acting, curiously, for the defence, was absent; then Governor Hislop, who was to preside, fell ill. It wasn't until the new year, 1805 – Picton in London petitioning the Privy Council for speed, and to be allowed to surrender his £40,000 bail after thirteen months – that the first witness was examined.

HE WAS CASTRO the escribano. He was sworn in Spanish and English. He presented the much-emended process to the court. The Attorney-General asked whether it was the original record. Castro said it was. Neither Castro nor the lawyers had had time to read all Begorrat's corrections. None of them knew that Begorrat had explained why Luisa had been tortured as soon as the torture order had been signed. When the Attorney-General prompted Castro to say that Begorrat had waited the statutory five days, Castro agreed; he said he had forgotten to write that in. Fullarton's unqualified lawyer enjoyed the idea of cross-examining but didn't know what he wanted to establish. He asked circular questions. He didn't unsettle Castro. Castro behaved well all that day.

But then Begorrat had an alarm. He heard that after the court had broken up Castro had gone to see Fullarton's lawyer; and he also heard that Castro was beating about for a competent person before whom he could swear an affidavit.

Castro didn't attend the second sitting of the court. He sent to say he was sick. His examination was suspended. Luisa's mother was called. Fullarton's lawyer ran into trouble right away.

'State the day and year of the birth of Luisa Calderon as correctly as you can.'

'I do not rightly remember when she was born, but what I can say is that she was born in the month of August on St Louis's day and she was ten years old when she was in prison.'

Fullarton's lawyer tried to get a more reasonable answer: all he had asked the woman to say was that Luisa was thirteen. 'Was Luisa Calderon more than ten years old when she was in prison?'

It was a provocative way to put the question.

'No,' Luisa's mother said. 'Rather less than more.'

The Attorney-General took over.

'What is your age?'

'Forty years.'

'How do you know that you are forty years old?'

'I know it because when I came from my country I had a certificate of baptism.'

'Can you read or write?'

'No.'

'Did you ever see the register of your daughter's birth?'

'Don Pedro Vargas showed me a copy.'

'Who is Don Pedro Vargas?'

'He was the linguist of the governor who carried away my daughter.'

'How old is your daughter this day?'

'Between fifteen and sixteen.'

A simple trap: Luisa had been in prison just three years before.

'Do you know why your daughter Luisa was sent to jail?'

'Because Don Ruiz charged her with a robbery she never committed.'

'Before Luisa was sent to jail, was she not living with Pedro Ruiz as his mistress?'

'Yes. On a promise of marriage.'

'How long had Luisa and Ruiz cohabited together before Luisa was charged with the robbery?'

'Two years and five months.'

In prison for theft at ten, a mistress at seven: the Attorney-General had no more questions. It was left to Fullarton's lawyer, out of his irritation and incompetence, to discredit his witness finally.

'If your daughter was only ten years old when she was in prison, and as only three years have elapsed since then, how can she be between fifteen and sixteen now?'

'No, I said that Luisa had fourteen years.'

This was worse. She had misunderstood his anger. She was approaching the truth.

'Do you mean to say that Luisa was fourteen years old at the time of her imprisonment?'

'Yes. Not quite completed, going to it.'

This was all he had wanted. It had wrecked his case but he had got it in the end. He sat down. The interpreter presented the record of her examination to Luisa's mother and she signed it with her mark.

The court reopened after five days. Castro came. Fullarton's lawyer said Castro wanted to take back everything he had said on the first day. Castro read out an affidavit and it was filed. He said he had lied because he had feared for his freedom and property, 'from the subtilty of some men and whom it might be equally dangerous for him, the deponent, to point out'. He wasn't going to say any more; he would give evidence now only 'before the honourable Court in Europe'. He had hardly finished when Fullarton's lawyer, without warning, collapsed. He was always collapsing; it might have been his health or it might have been drink.

The next day Governor Hislop, as president of the court, asked Castro to explain and name the persons he feared. Castro said he couldn't, for the reasons he had given. The Attorney-General pressed. Castro refused to answer. He was committed to the common jail, the new one, for contempt. Two years before, he had been considered a gentleman, someone who could not be imprisoned in the common jail; and while in jail now he heard that he had been sacked from his post as regidor of the cabildo. He had bought the job in the Spanish time and it was an important part of his property. But he had no proof. Fullarton's lawyer was no help; he was ill again. Castro began to compromise. He said he would answer questions in court, but he wanted first to take the questions home and give his answers in writing. Governor Hislop agreed. Castro was released, after a week in jail.

Begorrat was present when the court reopened in the Council chamber. Castro refused to take the oath in Begorrat's presence. Begorrat left, but he had made his effect. Castro began to weaken again. He told the Attorney-General he didn't know who had been 'underscoring' the record. He began to repeat much of the evidence he had given on the first day.

Fullarton's lawyer was silent throughout the sitting. When Castro said that Luisa was fifteen at the time of her torture Fullarton's lawyer just asked for the statement to be repeated. And right at the end of the day, when Castro was about to say that Porto Rico and the others had gone to England with Fullarton, Fullarton's lawyer, for reasons of drama rather than law, objected.

The court adjourned. Fullarton's lawyer fell ill for almost a month. And then martial law was declared.

SPAIN HAD entered the war on the French side and Governor Hislop had heard from London that the Spanish admiral, Gravina, was at Martinique, planning an attack on Trinidad. Hislop was glad he had fortified that hill west of Port of Spain. He moved up there with the archives; the merchants moved up with their books; the people who stayed behind in Port of Spain were advised to make the best peace they could with the enemy in the event of a defeat.

Flour went short. So did gunpowder. The garrison was small, and the coloured or Loyal Militia turned out to be a liability. ('My lord,' a militia captain wrote to the Secretary of State afterwards, 'the command of a battalion of foreigners must always be irksome to the mind of a man who has served with unblemished reputation in His Majesty's service, but to command these people in English and to give the necessary explanations in drill and manoeuvre in the French and Spanish languages is peculiarly difficult and embarrassing.') Governor Hislop thought it worth his while to enrol a company of Negro Rangers. He was careful to choose only 'faithful and well-disposed Negroes'. But the planters didn't like the idea either of arming their Negroes or of losing them. Hislop

got Vallot to say right at the start that there had been no instrument of torture in the jail in the Spanish time. But this was a lucky hit. The important fact was left there and in no time Fullarton's lawyer had lost himself in his usual indiscriminate inquisitiveness. He asked about the jail routine, the rations of the galley Negroes ('Never less?' – 'Never less'), the irons, the staff. And Vallot relived the jail years.

'How long is it since you saw the piquet?'

'I saw it the whole time of the old jail, but since the building of the new jail it has been taken down.'

And in the new jail, still only a building, there was a new jailer, not yet even a name. Vallot was Vallot. The new name would never have that weight; it remains unknown. It was Vallot's last public appearance. His own Negro, Porto Rico, Bourique, had been taken away two years before to the strange streets of London ('Where is he now?' – 'I do not know, but believe he is with Mr Fullarton'). And now he himself, a figure for fifteen years, disappears.

The court had done its most important work. The man called Ruiz recorded his outrage at the suggestion that he would sleep with a girl of four or seven or ten, as some said, whose breasts hadn't grown. Begorrat protested at being called by his friend the Attorney-General as a witness. This was just for the form. His answers were fluent, precise and detailed. He overwhelmed Fullarton's lawyer. He destroyed Castro the escribano.

'I have known him since the year 1784. He was in the service of Captain Barritto, the then governor of this island. At the arrival of Mr Chacon he was made an escribano, to the great disgust of the community, as he had been a common soldier in the veteran corps of Margarita, and went to Angostura, where he enrolled himself in the guards of the coast; and he was the servant and barber of Captain Litemondi at Margarita. Which makes me believe he was not brought up to the study of the Spanish law.'

This was really all that remained to be done now, this punishment and public degradation of Castro. Begorrat and his friends worked at it in the mandamus court over the next three months, through two long interruptions of martial law.

THIS TIME the alarm was real. The French fleet had eluded Nelson's Mediterranean blockade and raised the blockade of the Spanish fleet; and it was known that the combined French and Spanish fleets had sailed for the Caribbean. On his little fortified hill Governor Hislop had his archives and five hundred barrels of biscuits. He found, though, that he had forgotten to lay in water kegs and kettles. The Commissary-General of the militia, who was also a merchant, was making a little fortune, successfully claiming for supplies he wasn't delivering.

Early one morning thirteen warships appeared off the north coast. The soldiers on that coast set their little mud fort on fire and ran. In the afternoon the warships, mightily prepared for battle, entered the Gulf of Paria and sealed it off. There was no battle. The visitor was Nelson, at the end of a twenty-four-day crossing of the Atlantic, pursuing, on a gamble, the French fleet he had lost three months before. In the West Indies he had been misled by an American brig; by a private Trinidad schooner: the signal had been made by a merchant's clerk, watching for the enemy; and by the firing of the mud fort. Nelson thought the island had been captured and that the French and Spanish fleets were in the Gulf of Paria. He found he had wasted three days. At seven the next morning – no messages exchanged with the shore – he sailed back to Europe, the disgrace of Governor Hislop's militia recorded without comment in the log of the *Victory*. Trafalgar was four months away.

It was six weeks before the island recovered from the alarm of Nelson. The mandamus court, when it resumed, became ragged. Fullarton's lawyer asked for extensions and didn't turn up. It was ruled that he was 'trifling' with the court, and the court was closed. It had been known for a year at least that he wasn't a qualified lawyer. But it was only now, after he had almost destroyed Fullarton's case, that a fuss was made and he was banished.

IN LONDON the case was keeping everybody busy. Fullarton was writing to the Treasury about the salary owing to him since he had left Trinidad (it came to £5,250) and the expenses of his young men. Only London could settle; it was known, he wrote, that the Trinidad Treasury was empty. Picton decided to claim too. Commodore Samuel Hood, the Third Commissioner, came back to England and Fullarton thought that the Privy Council should investigate him as well. The mulatto man of property whom Fullarton had released sued Picton for £40,000 for wrongful imprisonment. There was a new Colonial Secretary, Lord Castlereagh. He wasn't a friend of Fullarton's friends; he revoked the Trinidad Commission, cutting off Fullarton's feeding link with the Treasury; Fullarton protested. Picton wrote to Lord Castlereagh that the Spanish curate who had made out the false birth certificate for Luisa Calderon should be punished. The Privy Council decided that another commission was to be sent out to Trinidad, to investigate Picton's poisoning commission.

And the book of McCallum the pamphleteer, announced the previous year, but then delayed by the threats of Picton's friends, was at last published. *Travels in Trinidad* was bulked out to three hundred and fifty pages with pieces about the horrors of Barbados, Haiti and the United States, 'the fag-end of the world', a land of slavery, fraud and vanishing Christianity, where 'what constitutes a city is a tavern and a blacksmith's shop', and where on 'the swampy shores of North and South Carolina' Scottish Highlanders, McCallum's own people, suffered in servitude like Negroes. The New World as blood, fraud and make-believe: McCallum had been paid to plead a cause, but his passion, like his style sometimes, anticipated Dickens. He said in his preface that some people might feel that 'in reciting the atrocities of which the island of Trinidad has unhappily been the theatre, I have indulged too freely the style of asperity'. But he claimed an excuse. 'I was myself the victim of oppression.'

So MUCH was written about Negroes. But the Negroes of 1800 remain as anonymous as the Indians of Las Casas three centuries before. It is the silence of all serfdom. Even Porto Rico, Vallot's assistant, is only a Negro and a name. The poisonings, a love-potion given to a woman with hands calloused from labour, a wise old sorcerer, the obeah, the drumming and the jumping-up at every opportunity: this is what comes to the surface. It suggests a whole underground life of fantasy, linking creole Negroes and new Negroes, French Negroes and English Negroes.

The New World as make-believe: this Negro fantasy life changed and developed. In Trinidad, an immigrant island, it had become many-featured, a dream beyond labour and more real than labour, of power and prettiness, of titles, flags and uniforms, kings and queens and courtiers. The planter, looking at his Negroes and seeing only Negroes, never knew. He might know that certain Negroes dressed up in cast-off clothes and received other Negroes, fed and danced and jumped up together: a mimicry in the Negro-yards of white entertaining. But he didn't know that that Negro carter – belonging to Rosette Smith, now called Rosette Picton – now taking on a load from the Port of Spain store of Mr Rigby, a merchant and Negro-shipper, the planter didn't know that that Negro carter, an especially stupid Negro, was a king at night, with twelve courtiers and a uniform of his own: a black coat with a scarlet collar and a green ribbon over one shoulder, a hat with a black cockade.

Only the Negroes knew; and the knowledge would have frightened any planter who had come from Santo Domingo, Martinique or Guadeloupe. Negro insurrection, which seemed so sudden in its beginnings and endings and so casual in its betrayals, was usually only an aspect of Negro fantasy; but an adequate leader could make it real. The moment would occur when secrecy became its own assurance, when fantasy submerged and ridiculed the world of labour and property. As it appeared to be doing now, this second week in December 1805, in broad daylight, outside Mr Rigby's store.

Dagueville, the old French clerk, was abusing the carter, the king. The carter was abstracted, loading badly. The king was alert.

The king's companion said, 'They are treating us very badly at these stores now. The other day, now, a little white boy beat me.'

The king said, 'If Mr Dagueville was on the road now he wouldn't manage so cockle to beat you.'

Cockle: what was that word? The king didn't lower his voice. Dagueville heard.

Early in the morning Mr de Gannes de la Chancellerie was bathing in the river that ran through his property in one of the cool valleys just north of the city. Twelve Negro women, balancing plantain baskets on their heads, came by on the path. They shook chac-chac pods, sang a patois song and danced. *Pain c'est viande béqué*, the women sang. And the chorus was *San Domingo!*

Vin c'est sang béqué.
San Domingo!
Nous va boire sang béqué.
San Domingo!

'Bread is white man flesh; wine is white man blood. We going to drink white man blood.' It was an old song, from another island. Mr de Gannes didn't take it personally. He saw only the pastoral, the re-creation of the life that for many like him had vanished.

Mrs Metiver, wife of a planter who was also the garrison surgeon, was ill. Two ladies came to see her in the evening, and Dr Metiver took them to his wife's bedroom. While they were there they heard the rhythmic shaking of the chac-chac pods. Presently Mrs Metiver said, 'There is the song.' Dr Metiver went to the window and listened.

Pain nous mangé est viande béqué.
Coca!
Vin nous boire c'est sang béqué.
Coca!

Dr Metiver was spotted at the window. A Negro voice called out, '*Paix! Paix donc!*' Dr Metiver ran out into the darkness. He found no one.

He interrogated his Negroes. And now, and it was so absurd after the songs and the drama, they spoke freely. But it was part of the fantasy that they should, when the time came, like magicians, reveal the real world. They said there was to be a gathering of Negroes at Carenage, west of Port of Spain. There were at least three Negro convois or regiments, each under its own king. For three years the Negroes of Port of Spain had been contributing two bits a week, about twenty cents, to a central fund. The Negroes didn't know who the treasurer was.

One of Dr Metiver's Negroes then asked for permission to go to Carenage.

'I wonder at your impudence,' Dr Metiver said. But the illogicality of the request had given him a fright. He had been in Trinidad only eight years. He began to bluster; he said he knew all about Carenage.

Dr Metiver went to warn his neighbours. Some of them remained cool, even Mr de Gannes de la Chancellerie, whose head had already been drunk to. But Governor Hislop listened. A cotton plantation overseer had recently been killed and the killer had disappeared into the deep woods of the interior; in Port of Spain a black soldier had killed a sergeant. Governor Hislop got the troops out as soon as he heard Dr Metiver's story, and sent them to various estates to pick up the Negroes who had been named by Dr Metiver's Negroes. They got King Noel, the carter, that night; they got the Negro called the Congo King; they got King Samson and King Edward and King Herold, King Simon and King Baptiste;

they got a number of queens and princesses, dauphins and dauphines. But Old Michel, the 'Judge' of the Sans Peur regiment, and two other leaders got away.

The inquiry, which was also the trial, began the next day. It was felt that 'a summary mode' was needed rather than 'the dilatory process' of Spanish law. A Spanish lawyer was consulted. He said that necessity and Justinian's Code both justified the summary mode. King Noel, the carter, turned King's evidence.

The play was over. But not all the Negroes knew. There were some who continued to warn and to mock. That day, the first of the trial, two French ladies sitting out on their balcony watched a Negro in a white shirt ride into Port of Spain on a white mule. He stopped below the balcony. A Negro came to him. They talked; they mentioned the name of a Frenchman whose head they wanted. One of the women ran down the steps; the Negroes hurried away.

Four days later – the inquiry well advanced, the underground Negro kingdoms like exposed anthills, the whip and the chains and worse waiting – Lieutenant Whitsun of the Royal Militia passed a Negro in the street. The Negro, speaking to be heard, said, 'Suppose they kill *bacara* (whitey) good dis time, dey come no more.'

Lieutenant Whitsun hit the Negro with his stick and seized him. The Negro said he would take the lieutenant to a place where other Negroes were saying the same thing. They began to walk. The Negro broke and ran. Lieutenant Whitsun chased, shouting for help. A militiaman threw himself on the Negro and brought him down. This was all that remained of the fantasy of the night: the threat, the surrender, the whip in daylight.

The inquiry established that an uprising had been planned for Christmas day. The heads of Mr de Gannes and Mr Rochart were to be cut off first, and the Negroes were going to eat pork – a collection had been taken for the feast – and dance in the windmill on Mr Shand's estate. Afterwards they would go to Mr Melville's estate and drink holy water.

It came out in the Council chamber as a confused Negro story, unrelated fragments of an extended, confused fantasy. Between curfew and sunrise these kings and courtiers, generals and judges, so many suffering from sores, visited and exchanged courtesies. They blessed, they punished. France, England and Africa, the plantations themselves, the church and the Council provided the ritual, the titles, the ceremonies of power.

A king had his flag. King Baptiste kept his hidden in an 'Indian basket'. A free black woman had charged twelve dollars to make it, and at the time of the arrests she was making a flag for King Samson of the Macacque or monkey regiment. These kings liked to keep up with one another. The uniform of King Edward of Carenage was 'a brown holland jacket and trousers with blue ribbons and coat capes, binding and lacing'; his officers had wooden swords painted white and green. When Samson quarrelled with Edward and left to form his own regiment he had the same uniform made for himself and his officers. Samson could do this because he was a powerful man. He was a doctor; he also had a store of gunpowder. Yet by daylight Samson liked to pretend that he was just a foolish old Ibo Negro.

A regiment could be purely creole; an African regiment might insist on 'one colour' and reject mulattoes. There were the loyalties of the older islands, Martinique, Guadeloupe, Grenada; there was even a Danish regiment. Everybody who joined got a title. It might be 'major de dames' or 'capitaine de dames'. When Scipio joined the Carenage regiment he was offered the title of 'My Lord St John'. He said no; he just wanted to be 'Secretary'; and at gatherings he 'made a show of scribbling'. He belonged in real life to the Attorney-General, who was not really an attorney-general: one make-believe mingling with another.

The kings exchanged polite messages: there were Negroes who could write. Messages were delivered by young women, sometimes even by Negroes in the chain gangs. Their anonymity in daylight helped. A Negro whose legs ran with sores might say that he had a splinter in his foot and had to bathe it in the stream to prevent lockjaw. He would disappear for the night. In the morning he might be glimpsed, a comical Negro, returning in a greatcoat to his plantation. A greatcoat, because these visits of kings and queens were formal. King Noel, the carter, in daylight so especially stupid, sent four deputies to meet and carry a king, because that was 'the ceremony of receiving a king'; kings 'use no form of exercise'. A king could be offered plaintains and wine; one feast was of callalloo, beef and rum.

The night might have other formalities. Old Michel, the Grand Judge, punished offenders by beating them like a plantation overseer; or he fined them, or made them kneel for two hours, knocking stones together; or he expelled them from the regiment for a fortnight. Sometimes King Noel and his queen, Marie, levied a subscription. Then a large loaf of bread was baked and pieces were sent to all the king's subjects and sometimes also to another king. Sometimes a 'communion', a biscuit without salt, was administered to a king and queen; King Samson's subjects paid two dollars each to attend the ceremony. Money was always important to a king. Samson sold rum at twenty-seven cents a bottle.

The kingdoms of the night grew; fantasy overflowed. An owner might observe a 'perturbancy' in his Negroes; but it was the owner, without secrets, without prettiness, who was becoming the phantom. Then it was the owner who was to be mocked, for his ignorance and simplicity, with 'enigmatical songs' and direct warnings. Certain words, like *c'est bien dommage*, held all the mystery. But only Negroes knew.

At midnight now the fantasy suddenly contracted. After the chac-chac and the song outside the lighted window, soldiers came and searched and made the flags and uniforms useless. The kings and courtiers, awakened, captive, said they had only been playing. They were willing to talk. It was only later, when they were fully in the other world, that this turned to conscious betrayal. Samson's queen, the free woman who had made the flags, reproached them:

'Now that the business has gone wrong you wish to say you had nothing to do with it. But formerly when everything was smooth and easy you all thought it nice fun and wanted to be in it.'

For some, though, the play went on. Dominique Rivieu brought some 'papers' to the Council to prove his innocence. Mr Rigby, the merchant and Negro-shipper, read them out. Among them was a letter from one of the kings who had got away. Dominique Rivieu couldn't understand why his papers hadn't saved him.

The inquiry began on 11 December 1805. On 19 December the first executions took place. Three Negroes were hanged and beheaded in the main Port of Spain square. Their bodies were hung in chains, their heads spiked; it was the end of their mockery. A free Negro lost his ears and was returned to slavery; he was sold out of the island. Other 'principals' lost their ears and received a hundred lashes each. Those who received fifty lashes were to wear iron rings for ever. Samson's queen was 'to work in chains for ever' and to wear 'an iron ring of ten pounds to be affixed to one of her legs'. All the queens and princesses and dauphines, even those described as artless or playful or innocent, were to be whipped, thirty-nine lashes for some, twenty-five for the rest. 'Marie, Bonavita, Marie, Marie Ursule and Jeanrose to receive twenty-five lashes each': this was the last sentence of the long judgement. So many Maries: it was hardly a name.

The blasphemy of the Negro communion aroused particular horror, especially at this Christmas time; and in the new Protestant church in Port of Spain Mr Clapham conducted a thanksgiving service.

The inquiry went on beyond Christmas. The underground had been extensive; nearly everybody's Negroes were in it. Another Negro was hanged and beheaded. Six more had their ears cut off and were sold out of the island.

From London Lord Castlereagh sent his approval. He didn't need to be told, he wrote Governor Hislop, that 'this class of the community' had to be watched. The Trinidad Attorney-General had just been telling him, in fact. The Attorney-General was in London to give evidence for Picton and 'to thicken the matter upon Fullarton' (the words were General Maitland's, the defeated general of Haiti, still angling for a grant of land in Trinidad). The insurrection, the Attorney-General had added, could really be attributed to 'a set of men of *white* complexions'.

Locally the story improved. The 'monsters' had planned 'to get rid of all white men by grinding them in Mr Shand's new windmill'. The 'scoundrels' had said that there was going to be only 'one colour'.

In this atmosphere of frontier thrill – Old Michel, the Judge of the Sans Peur regiment, still uncaught, with 200 dollars on his head – the Privy Council lawyer arrived to investigate the burning of the living and the dead that had followed Picton's poisoning commission four Christmases before. The lawyer stayed a month. He missed the surrender of Old Michel, forced out by hunger 'from his skulking places'. But he talked to Begorrat, Black and the others and decided that Picton had no case to answer. The issues in Trinidad had been simplified. In three years the confusion of philanthropy and Jacobinism among the English settlers, London talk from London people, had disappeared.

BUT THE CAUSE of protest still lived in London. The set of men of white complexions were all there: Fullarton, Fullarton's unqualified lawyer, banished and angry, McCallum the pamphleteer, the radical store-keeper, and now the court-martialled and banished Commissary-General of the militia.

To Governor Hislop, looking only for peace, his house growing damp and derelict, and the Treasury without a farthing, the criticisms of these men were the added harassments of a busy year. Problem followed problem; inquiry was following inquiry. The inquiry now was about the mulatto who was suing Picton for £40,000 for unlawful imprisonment. He was a notorious character, Hislop said; he had been expelled from other islands. In Martinique he had been pilloried and a placard hung about his neck: 'Mulatto who hit white man'. Hislop didn't like the inquiry; he thought it would have 'very furious effects'.

And always there was Hislop's anxiety about the law he was administering. The legality of almost everything he had done was being questioned by those men in London. From infancy, Hislop wrote, he had been bred up as a soldier in the virtues of obedience to his 'lawful superiors'. It was hard now to be 'dragged forth to the public as an oppressor'. Until his powers were unambiguously defined he wasn't going to execute anyone any more even for 'the most sanguinary murders'.

Hislop, in fact, had had a nasty shock. Lord Castlereagh had approved of the Christmas hangings and mutilations. But other news had since come; and it had been made worse by the arrival at the same time of many copies of a gleeful pamphlet by P. F. McCallum, individually addressed to people in the island. The news was that the Luisa Calderon case had come up before Lord Ellenborough, the Lord Chief Justice, at the court of King's Bench, Westminster on 24 February 1806. It had lasted the whole day, from nine in the morning to seven at night. Picton had been found guilty.

WHAT HAD been established at the mandamus court in Port of Spain – Luisa's torturable age – had been less a defence of Picton than a defence of Begorrat and Vallot. Much of the evidence was set aside as trivial both by Lord Ellenborough and Picton's lawyer. The lawyer wasn't defending Begorrat or Vallot. If an official went beyond the law in carrying out an order, the lawyer said, that was the responsibility of the official. It would have given Vallot a nasty moment, if he had known.

Picton paced the hall of the Four Courts, tall, sallow, looking his fifty years. He was dressed in black. Luisa Calderon – was it Mrs Fullarton's idea? – wore white on this winter's day; she looked about eighteen. In a white dress and a white muslin turban, according to the reporter of the *Newgate Calendar*, she described her torture, speaking through an interpreter. The Negro alguazil who had helped to torture her – after two years in London they had grown close: she called him Mr Rafael, his first name – then told his own story. He used large illustrative gestures.

'A sort of acting,' Picton's lawyer said, 'has been introduced by the gentleman upon the floor. But I do not complain. I wish the case to be presented to you in any manner which to my learned friend might seem advisable.' All that mattered, however, was the torture order itself. The laws of Trinidad were Spanish, not English; and it had to be remembered that the laws of England were not always the laws of a British colony. In the British colony of St Vincent, for instance, noses could be legally slit and hands lopped off. The piquet itself was not a rare instrument of torture; it could be found in any dictionary of the arts and sciences. It was a military punishment; it had been used 'upon those brave men who shed their best blood and risked their lives in the service and for the defence of their country'. Even if the torture of Luisa Calderon was assumed to be unlawful, it couldn't be said to be malicious. 'Here was no quarrel between the parties, here was no – '

'You cannot go into this,' Lord Ellenborough said. 'The act, if unlawful, is presumed to be malicious.' He was as alert and precise as this all day. And now, simply, he stated the issue. 'The question is, was the act authorized by the law of Spain or not?'

What were the torture laws in the Spanish Indies in 1801? Were they the old laws Begorrat and his friends had dug up? Lord Ellenborough dismissed them one by one; they were too 'remote' or 'far too questionable'; he knew more about Spanish codes than he appeared to. And Picton was not well served by his witnesses.

The Trinidad Attorney-General didn't know Spanish law. He said he saw people in Trinidad turning over old law-books and he assumed they were the laws of the country. He didn't know Spanish himself, and he hadn't attended many courts in Trinidad. He had overdone the coolness; he had said nothing. Worse followed. The

Chevalier Dupont du Vivier de Gourville, who had come to England as Picton's emissary four years before and had stayed, was asked whether he knew of torture in the Spanish time. He misunderstood the question. He cried, '*Jamais! Jamais!*' He astonished prosecution and defence. He saw, and began to talk of the thumbs of criminals being tied together. But the damage had been done.

There was one witness who knew the Indies, had practised Spanish law there and had a copy of the correct Spanish law-book, the *Recopilación*. Spain and England were at war, and this was the only copy of the *Recopilación* available in London. The Spanish lawyer from the Indies who had it was Pedro Vargas.

'Are you acquainted with the contents of that book?'

'Yes. That is to say, more or less. I may have forgot part of them.'

'Is there anything that justifies or alludes to tortures?'

'No, sir. According to my knowledge of it, there is not anything.'

'Did you, in any of the islands, or in any part of the Spanish West Indies, hear of the practice of tortures?'

'No, I never heard that it was practised.'

'Do you know any law authorizing the infliction of torture?'

'Yes. There is an ancient law of 1260 or 1266 or thereabouts.'

That was the case for the prosecution. The defence lawyer asked Pedro Vargas to turn to the parts of the *Recopilación* that dealt with theft. Vargas fumbled with the three volumes, turning over pages, finding nothing. 'There are three volumes,' he said. 'It will be something difficult.'

'When did you arrive in this country?'

'I arrived in 1799, I believe.' He was the revolutionary then, the proscribed conspirator from New Granada, proclaiming his Indian ancestry to Pitt.

'Did you give in your name at the Secretary of State's office under the Alien Act?'

'I think I cannot answer that question.'

'You must not ask him that question,' Lord Ellenborough said. 'He may subject himself to penalties. It should not be put.'

'Did you at any time pass in this country by the name of Smith?'

'Yes, I did.' As Mr Smith he had been the courier between Napoleon and Mr Martin – Miranda – in London. But that was five years ago.

'Have you been at any time employed by Colonel Fullarton in taking examinations against General Picton?'

'I believe not. I was not employed officially.'

Picton's lawyer pressed. Vargas retreated, step by step. The defence lawyer sneered – 'this experienced jurisconsult, this ingenious advocate' – but Vargas's evidence stood. It condemned Picton.

IT WAS the end of the public drama. 'Humanity is satisfied,' Fullarton said. But it was the limit of his success. The case was to go on; there was a motion for a new trial. And things had already begun to go badly for Fullarton. He had been seriously ill for two months. The Trinidad Commission had been revoked and his salary had gone. Lord Castlereagh had been obstructive; the Privy Council had postponed the investigation of the other charges against Picton.

The motion for a new trial was granted. The Marquis of Lansdowne's books came up for sale and Picton's lawyer found a *Recopilación* among them. Vargas's evidence was questioned. An army officer who had served in Trinidad published a book in support of Picton. He was sued by Fullarton. The former Colonial Under-Secretary, Fullarton's friend, also sued. So did the Deputy Alguazil-Mayor from Trinidad, who did as he was told. The book was withdrawn, but issue had been joined in all three cases.

The Deputy Alguazil-Mayor, whose evidence in the end hadn't counted, was already a ruined man, a foreigner adrift in Soho. He had lost his Port of Spain property, his house, his boat, his Negroes; and now he heard that Begorrat and the others were planning to prevent him returning to Trinidad. The old Spanish curate who, at Vargas's request, had made out the false birth certificate for Luisa Calderon, and that hadn't counted either, was ill. He was soon, at Picton's insistence, to be tried for perjury.

In London someone played a trick on McCallum, inserting this advertisement in the *Globe* newspaper: 'If Mr J. P. McCallum, author of *Travels in Trinidad*, does not, within 14 days from the date hereof, fetch away the few effects he has left at No. 40 Suffolk-street, Charingcross, they will be sold as part payment of his rent, and legal steps taken to recover the remainder.'

McCallum would survive. But Pedro Vargas was in trouble. He had changed causes, had given up Miranda for Fullarton, and he was sinking with Fullarton. He had no skills. For a while he passed himself off as a botanist and had got a little work in Kensington; but it hadn't lasted. He had lost his jobs as assessor, surveyor and commissary of population. He pleaded with the Treasury for money. His request for his salary as commissary of population was passed on to a former colleague and fellow-agent of the revolution, the Trinidad Surveyor-General, a life-long friend of Miranda's. The request was turned down. In London Vargas was nothing; and he had nowhere else to go.

9. The Victims: II

1806–1808

'VARGAS DIDN'T ATTEND TO his obligations in Trinidad,' Miranda had written to his friend, the Trinidad Surveyor-General. 'And now he is busy with botanical work and has had himself put down on the list of Picton's accusers!'

It was four months after Vargas's return from Trinidad that Miranda realized he had lost Vargas. Miranda wasn't looking for a defection here; he had to be told, by a British minister; and then he felt he couldn't condemn Vargas without hearing him. Soon he went silent about Vargas, as he had gone silent about Vargas's predecessor in Trinidad, Caro, who had also reneged, the man the Spaniards said had disguised himself as a Negro.

And then Miranda had heard about Vargas from Fullarton himself, at dinner. Fullarton, obsessed with the Picton prosecution, had given the news as good news; he was working to get Miranda on his side as well. In Trinidad, to get English support against Picton, Fullarton had declared for a British constitution. But the issues had since been racially simplified on the island; alliances had changed; and now, to Miranda, Fullarton spoke of the demand for a British constitution as a 'machination' of the Pictonians. Its aim, he said, was to defeat the revolution and Spanish interests in Trinidad.

Miranda dined every few weeks with Fullarton. Once they met at the Crown and Anchor tavern in the Strand and went on to a dinner of the Society of Arts, Miranda the guest, Fullarton the member with the tickets. The detail was Fullarton's; he wrote to

Miranda almost proprietorially of the Society. It was another way of presenting himself to Miranda, who was known as a collector. Books and papers and pictures filled two rooms of Miranda's rented house in Grafton Street; he owed thousands to London booksellers.

Miranda was always friendly. But he didn't commit himself. His interest in the Picton case was not an interest in Luisa Calderon or Fullarton. It was an interest in Trinidad as the base for South American revolution. And, as it happened, Miranda was not in London at the time of the trial. He had left five months before. He had himself become a liability to the British government in its complicated European–South American manoeuvrings, and had at last, in September 1805, been allowed to leave. He was sent to the United States, with £6,000, to invade South America if he could.

One of the letters he received ('My dear General') was from Fullarton, attentive to the last, wishing him success. He noted down Fullarton's address on a scrap of paper. The scrap of paper survived all the adventures of the succeeding months. But it was the end of the relationship.

THE PRIVY COUNCIL lawyer, sent out to look into Negro poisonings, had gone. Old Michel, the Grand Judge of the Sans Peur regiment, had come out of the bush and given himself up. There was still anxiety at the news of Picton's conviction when Miranda came to Port of Spain, defeated.

He had – fantastically – tried to invade Venezuela; and had failed. He had been defeated without landing in Venezuela; and this arrival in Port of Spain, in June 1806, was like a homecoming, after thirty-five years. When he had left Venezuela in 1771 Trinidad could be said to be part of his country, a neglected part, with the Spaniards of St Joseph living alcoholically in the bush with their Negroes, and Port of Spain a collection of fishermen's huts. Like Ralegh in the security of the Tower, Miranda in exile had planned this return for many years. The arguments had been gone over again and again; the messengers had brought hope; the doubters had been won over, not to the dream but to the commercial risk; and the action, when it had come, was like fantasy, simple, obvious and grotesque.

It had in the end been a confused, mercenary venture, secretive but well-publicized (the *Richmond Enquirer* gave Trinidad as the rendezvous), trailing diplomatic and legal scandal in the United States: the ship and arms, not of the best quality, provided by an American merchant; the two hundred recruits, not all trained, picked up here and there in New York; at sea, the printing press on deck striking off proclamations to the South American people, the red, blue and yellow flag of the independent republic displayed, the recruits, the liberators, consulting military manuals; Miranda physically restless, continually picking at his very white teeth, quick-tempered, 'impatient of contradiction', quarrelling loudly with his difficult American captain; Miranda tall, just under six foot, squarely built, with grey hairs sprouting from his ears, but still at fifty-six the European, even English, dandy, with his powdered grey hair 'tied long behind', wearing a red bathrobe even when the bath was from a bucket on the deck; Miranda talking, lecturing, intelligent, abstemious, drinking mainly sweetened water; Miranda, the patrician, the disciplinarian liberator inviting the democratic ridicule of his American recruits.

And so, through delays and quarrels, the expedition had come to Puerto Cabello in Venezuela. They were awaited: forty minutes of firing, confusion and panic among the invaders, two schooners and sixty men abandoned, forty of them imprisoned, ten others shot, beheaded and their heads spiked, by the same energetic official who had destroyed the revolution of José España seven years before. It had happened again: the revolution that seemed for so long to be just words, the action that was like play – flag, uniforms, parole (it was 'America') – and then the real blood on the beach and the heads on the highways.

FULLARTON, trying to win over Miranda to his side, and to show him that their causes coincided, had spoken of the hostility of the English in Trinidad to the revolution and their persecution of the Spaniards who remained in the island. Fullarton had given the news that Governor Hislop had imposed militia service – 'voluntary' but expensive: uniform and equipment cost about 100 dollars a year – on all Spaniards, and had in this way driven many of the poorer Spaniards, potential revolutionary recruits, off the island. And when the invasion was being discussed in London, and it was suggested that the governor of Trinidad should be the commander, Miranda had not been able to contain himself. It would be 'unendurable and infamous', he had written to a British minister, for any expedition he led to be under the control of the governor of Trinidad, especially after Picton's rough handling of the revolutionaries.

But now, when his fantastic invasion attempt had failed, and he ought to have been absurd and disgraced, he was succoured by the British in the Caribbean, all acting unofficially. He was still important; great things were still expected of him. Governor Maitland of Grenada gave fresh supplies; in Barbados there were new recruits and Admiral Cochrane helped with ships. And it was as a hero, a man with 30,000 Venezuelan pesos on his head, that Miranda was received by Governor Hislop in Port of Spain and lodged in the derelict house, formerly Fullarton's, which was now Government House. Miranda, still with a sense of command and military style, called it 'Headquarters', and was immediately busy, planning his new invasion. Governor Hislop was enthusiastic. He promised five hundred recruits, seven hundred recruits; and, dramatically, he closed Port of Spain harbour to traffic with the Main.

In Port of Spain a letter had been waiting for Miranda from one of his new American supporters. 'I find every person in this island is a Pictonian and Pittite, 'tis therefore necessary to be very guarded on these subjects.' It was what Fullarton had said in London. And it was true. In three years there had been a change. Picton no longer had enemies among the English; he was no longer a despot, an opponent of English laws; he was only a British governor being persecuted on behalf of some mulattoes and Negroes.

But that was an irrelevant issue now; the fight against Picton and the Pictonians was Fullarton's alone. To Miranda, planning his new invasion, everything in Trinidad was as it should be. He was in command of the invasion; he was staying at Government House; and Governor Hislop was helpful.

In fact, it refreshed Hislop to be host to Miranda, a distinguished London man who was above colonial squabbles and colonial fortune-making. Hislop was barely on speaking terms with his secretary when Miranda arrived; Miranda noted that the dispute was 'at its acme'. They had quarrelled over one of the secretary's more scandalous business deals; and the secretary (soon, his fortune made, to return to England and a seat in parliament) was writing to London that Hislop was a drunkard and a lecher. Enmities like this poisoned Hislop's bachelor life in Government House. The welcome he offered Miranda was heartfelt; and Miranda's influence showed in the dispatches Hislop now sent to London. Miranda had much support on the Main, Hislop wrote; nothing but good could come of the venture.

To Governor Hislop, and to the English in Trinidad, Miranda was a celebrity. He was not only the South American revolutionary who could keep the French out of South America and open up the continent to British trade. He was also a distinguished London man, given glamour by his culture, his contacts with the great, and his foreignness. In the minds of the English there was a distinction between Miranda and the local Spaniards – the peons, shopkeepers and launch-captains – who were like the people he had come out to liberate. 'Nothing but want,' Picton had written of the Trinidad Spaniards, 'can stimulate them to exertion, and their activity never fails to disappear with the cause.' And this English attitude to the Spaniards still held. Miranda was more foreign than the local Spaniards; in Trinidad he was an exotic.

And there was something in the English attitude. Miranda had spent thirty-five years away from Venezuela, and few South Americans understood him now. To some of the simple he was the leader, the magician-figure of the oppressed. Others saw only the European social success (extending it with hints of sexual triumph; Catherine the Great *perhaps*, Lady Hester Stanhope *perhaps*) and saw it, either with resentment or admiration, as an exploitation of the South American glamour that was also theirs. They saw their disabilities as economic and political alone, and it was what Miranda himself said. They could not conceive the deeper colonial deprivation, the sense of the missing real world, that Miranda had spent a lifetime making good. No South American revolutionary had lasted as long in exile or had remained so whole; none had shown that constant intellectual self-cherishing. For John Adams, Miranda was 'an Achilles, hurt by some personal injury, real or imaginary'. The generous judgement was beyond most Venezuelans; to them Miranda could easily be absurd, a man of words and affectations, a farce and a fraud, a would-be Inca-emperor with a private cause.

In Trinidad he had been betrayed twice. But loyal people had died, like old Manuel Gual, a Caracas boyhood friend, abandoned by Picton and reportedly poisoned. To Gual, rather than to the American adventurers abandoned at Puerto Cabello, Miranda showed piety. He gathered all the information he could about the revolution and deaths of seven years before; and, in final tribute, he went to St Joseph to get Gual's death certificate.

There were others who had remained faithful to the revolution. Like Andrés de España, who had won his brother over to the revolution, and very swiftly to a Venezuelan jail, with the promise of a general's uniform, and had himself been imprisoned by Picton. Andrés had afterwards become a 'surveyor' in Trinidad's ever-expanding survey department. 'He thinks of nothing but storming redoubts,' the Trinidad Surveyor-General had written approvingly to Miranda. Andrés was loyal; but he was on bad terms with other revolutionaries. The revolution in Trinidad, languishing for lack of action, and now even without its borrowed ideologies, had become a matter of these personal ambitions and clashes.

There was that man, French or English, who had come out to Trinidad and had gone silent almost at once. Prodded, he gave the reason. He had married the Chevalier de Gourville's daughter, 'a distant connection of Baron de Montalembert'. He thought Miranda would understand that this was 'one of the first connections in this part of the world', and that Miranda, understanding, would also recommend him, and speedily, for the clerkship of the Trinidad Council; just the day before, the clerk had had a nasty accident and wasn't expected to live.

There was that shaky, barely literate letter from an old Trinidad Spaniard, offering Miranda support and admiration in the name of a former acquaintance with Caro. Caro had betrayed the revolution; but the myth still lived in Trinidad that Caro had been betrayed by Picton. And Miranda learned more about Pedro Vargas and his relationship with Fullarton's Deputy Alguazil-Mayor. Miranda heard only now that the Deputy Alguazil-Mayor might have been a Spanish government spy.

America, Vargas had written, was waiting for Miranda with open arms. But Vargas had written that when he had himself given up the revolution; and many of the Spaniards of Trinidad were like Vargas. They paid sincere homage to Miranda as a great Venezuelan, but they had little faith in his cause, and some had changed their minds about it. Miranda was an honoured guest of Governor Hislop's, and that was as it should be; but the Spaniards of Trinidad considered themselves a dispossessed and disregarded community and many had begun to hope that the island might still somehow be returned to Spain. Such a rumour was, in fact, going around; and few local Spaniards were willing to take up arms against the Spanish Empire. As for the richer Spaniards – 'despicable contraband traders' Miranda called them – they were absolutely hostile to the idea of invasion and revolution. Miranda was finding out what Vargas had found out: these were some of the things that had helped to break Vargas's spirit.

The Spanish recruits were few. And among the English, French and American recruits there were continual squabbles. An American objected to serving under an Englishman; Count Loppinot de Lafresillière dropped out because he refused to serve under an American. One night the crew of Miranda's ship became drunk and mutinous; they fired a gun and hoisted three lights; the affair ended in the Port of Spain jail.

The debts were accumulating in New York, Port of Spain and London. A London bookseller was pressing for his money; there was a threat of the books being taken away from the house in Grafton Street. There was a threat to the lease of the house itself. And there were disturbed letters from the housekeeper, who was also the mother of Miranda's two baby sons.

As a young man Miranda had preferred prostitutes, noting, as with wines, descriptions and prices; and this undemanding relationship in late middle-age with Sarah, to whom he was yet totally committed, even in his will, which he had made before leaving London, was like an area of privacy in his English life, matching the other privacy, of his cause. Someone might write: 'Will you put yourself alone in a coach and come . . .' He ignored the disapproval and cultivated the acquaintance; he went alone.

Sarah's letters, with their omitted words and elisions, were full of love and joy, especially joy in her first baby Leander, aged two. But the darkness was always close, the received wisdom about false friends and the fear of the abyss.

'My dear little Leander is everi day getting pen and ink to write to the Gen to send him toys and pretti things and when [ ] is angry – I will leave you Mammy and go to the G he takes a book and will read for half an Hour abought you and himself telling you what a good boy he grows a very fine Boy, and I am flatter by every body saying he has an understanding twice his years.'

'Everything is only for a moment Leander like his Mother not much thought of, now you are not near – I will as longe as I live Encourage him to think of all of them as I do they are snake's in the grass to boath of our – I see trow there deseat more since I have been alone.'

Port of Spain must have been like the void itself, the gateway to the homeland and at the same time like the limit of the world he knew.

A month after he came to Port of Spain, Miranda left for his new invasion. It was a time for words. A farewell message to Governor Hislop: 'I hope that Providence, reinforcing the pure intentions which animate us, will grant us success; and that, when better informed, posterity will pass an equitable judgement upon the events which flow from a devotion as patriotic as it is honourable.' And a proclamation to his troops: 'The glorious opportunity now presents itself of relieving from oppression and arbitrary government a people who are worthy of a better fate, who ought to enjoy the blessing of the finest country in the universe which bountiful Providence has given them, but who are shackled by despotism too cruel for human nature longer to endure. The Gulf that Columbus discovered and honoured with his presence will now witness the illustrious actions of our gallant efforts.'

Three months later he was back in Port of Spain, hissed in the streets by Spaniards. His expedition had broken up in dissension, in demands for money, in stories of mismanagement and brutality. Andrés de España, who had gone as a captain of infantry, spoke of soldiers starving during the withdrawal and being beaten with ropes. The accusation and the messy facts would come out at an enquiry.

But Miranda had nearly succeeded. He had captured the town of Coro with little trouble; and a Venezuelan dispatch that Governor Hislop intercepted suggested that further success was likely. Coro, the Venezuelan official said, could be like another Gibraltar, if the British decided officially to help Miranda; Coro 'could end by setting the whole continent ablaze'. But the help Miranda asked for didn't come. The Venezuelan people, apart from two runaway Negroes, didn't respond to his proclamations; there was greater local interest in a bishop, who was visiting. After ten days Miranda withdrew.

His return to Port of Spain was without ceremony and was masked to some extent by a local sensation. A fortnight before, two hundred Chinese immigrants had arrived. They had been recruited from the Chinese community in Calcutta by an agent of the East India Company and shipped out with great secrecy – no one wanted the Chinese government to know. They had been brought all that way to work on the Botanical Gardens Governor Hislop was planning in Port of Spain; and to grow vegetables. Vegetables were perennially short in Trinidad. The Spanish peons didn't grow a lot of anything; and Negroes couldn't be spared from the plantations, which were of cocoa, cotton, coffee and sugar. There wasn't much money in vegetable-growing, and it was vaguely hoped that the Chinese would be the foundation of a free Asiatic peasantry in Trinidad, a buffer between the whites, to whom they would be linked by interest, and the Negroes, from whom they would naturally segregate themselves.

For the moment, however, to whites, mulattoes and Negroes, the Chinese were only objects of an affectionate but puzzled scrutiny: the costumes, the pigtails, the little trotting walk, the dainty parasols. They didn't look like people who could grow vegetables or make the Botanical Gardens flourish; they didn't look like a peasantry. Parasols! Perhaps the wrong Chinese had been picked up in Calcutta.

ENOUGH HAD happened to prove to Miranda that his cause was an illusion, that after the years of exile he was a man alone, and that there was no longer a side to which he could attach himself. It was from English people, individuals, that he received the only regard that mattered. But England he never trusted. The Americans told him nothing new when they told him that England aimed to turn South America into another India. Once he had been interested in the United States; after the War of Independence he had gone visiting the battlefields with the man who had become the Trinidad Surveyor-General. But Miranda's eye had since grown colder. He now saw the Americans as adventurers and doubted whether the confederacy could hold together.

On the way out he had met President Jefferson and his cabinet in Washington. Jefferson, speaking of the war in Europe, said, 'We will feed them all while they fight.'

'If they pay for it,' a secretary said.

'To be sure,' Jefferson said.

And Trinidad itself, visibly corrupt, where the English immigrants had already gone as colonial as the French and had reduced the complex drives of their culture to the simplicities of money and race, no longer referring their actions to any ideal, where the Spanish revolutionaries squabbled and some were treacherous, where there were all the makings of a caste or race war, Trinidad itself, though no longer part of Venezuela and the Spanish Empire, was like that Venezuela from which Miranda had run away thirty-five years before.

But Miranda held fast to his cause. An American who had come out with Miranda from New York and had witnessed the tragedy of Puerto Cabello wrote with bitter irony of Miranda's failure. 'He loves freedom; admires candour; esteems wise men; respects humility; and delights in that noble and beautiful integrity and good faith which distinguished the golden times of antiquity.' Miranda, with his colonial sense of deprivation, had prepared himself too well for the world and his role; after all the years of exile he dealt in romance. In Trinidad, for instance, he preferred not to see the Negroes. They formed no part of his revolutionary romance, no part of his vision of a world made classically pure and beautiful. The Indians did, noble and not savage, descended, in his fantasy, from the legendary Incas; and Miranda lamented their degradation in Trinidad. This Indian romance he had passed on to his friend the Surveyor-General, who spent so much time with the decayed and alcoholic Indians of the missions that he was called *Indio*, the Indian.

Two invasions had failed; an enquiry was about to begin into the disaster of the second. Government House was no longer Miranda's home or his 'Headquarters'. But Miranda had lived long with disappointment; and as soon as he could he sent someone to London – not a Spaniard – to ask for more help. And he wasn't modest: he wanted four thousand troops. He himself stayed behind; he could do nothing now but wait.

For a whole year, from October 1806 to October 1807, Miranda waited in Trinidad. It was a year of double exile, the fixed exile from Venezuela, the new exile from England. It was a time of his greatest dependence, and his London reputation was all he had. His creditors pressed; he was exposed to the anger and ridicule of people who felt he had betrayed them; and the letters from London brought news of his own betrayal by others.

He had been given £6,000 by the British government to invade South America. But someone else, an Englishman, a close friend, who had been sent out to seize the Cape of Good Hope, had afterwards taken the opportunity, perhaps with the approval of London, to attack Buenos Aires. The British capitulation at Buenos Aires had coincided with Miranda's withdrawal from Venezuela. It was what Miranda had feared: a British attempt at the conquest of South America rather than a British liberation.

There were other letters. Turnbull of Turnbull and Forbes, harassed by Miranda's creditors and especially by the London bookseller, had been threatening to turn Sarah and the children out of the house in Grafton Street. 'He behaved in the coolist manner to me . . . I was might sick and my heart allmost broke.' Turnbull had supported Miranda for many years; and Turnbull was expecting Miranda to deliver. He had sent his firm's export circulars and a list of Venezuelan merchants; Miranda was to distribute the circulars after independence, with his personal recommendation.

But Miranda also looked upon Turnbull as a friend; in his will he had left his pictures to Turnbull.

'My ever dear General, I embrace every opportunity of writing to my dear friend, for wile I am a night it seames as if I was speaking with you, I thrust the time his not far distant when I shall see or hear of your happiness, my anxiety encreses every day for your safety I hourly pray to God to Protect you from the many dangers that surround you – and to bless you with glory and success – I feel the love of you very much, it is only my two lovly Babis that can give me comfort, and when I look at them my anxiaty for your safety encreases – my dear Leander has every look or action of my dear Sir – he trys continuly speaking of you, and embracing me and promesing your return and you are to bring him a meny pretty things – and when we sett together he [ ] tell me of the General mamma we talk for hours of you – then he wants to by a ship and come to you his conversation is so Ino-cent and delightfull – that I wish sometimes never to hear among others – My uncle is drawing his Picture There is no making him sett a moment.'

In the heat of Port of Spain Miranda would read – his instructions being carried out – of fires lighted in mid-July to air the two library rooms of Grafton Street. His books and papers were precious (he had willed them to the University of Caracas, after independence) and they were never to be let out of the house except to certain specified people, and against receipt. Colonel Rutherfurd, the former Trinidad Surveyor-General, who had gone back to London, had called and played with the children. Rutherfurd himself, who had so recently sat in on discussions about South America with ministers and generals, was without a job now and, in late middle-age, desperate for money. These new men of England, individuals, with a developed sense of the self, were without the protection of clan or community in England; it was the other side of the English aggression and money-frenzy in a place like Trinidad. The void was real; in the early work of Dickens it will be like a child's fear of the dark.

'My dear Leander has been scribling this Hour to his papa, and telling him he will not tease brother so much, that he will learn his book, but his fonder of his hoop and his top, we have had a fair in the Road, he has bough[t] a gun a sword and drum, so that you can hardly hear one another speak, these are his happiest days my dear Sir.'

Home news from Mayfair, but always in Sarah's letters swamped by panic: the effort of writing, and the concentration, turning manageable anxiety into sudden terror. Immediately after one of these letters of Sarah's, among Miranda's Trinidad papers, there is this invitation from the Attorney-General, back in Trinidad after the Picton trial: 'Mr Gloster will be happy in the honor of Genl Miranda's company at Dinner en famille, on Thursday at 4.' It is like the light again. It was the side of Miranda that was known; it was all that the English settlers in Trinidad saw. The anguish came out in his letters to London. In Trinidad he was concerned to show strength. Whatever the betrayals of London, whatever the racial lessons that Sarah, with her special allegiance, was anxious to teach, it was on the goodwill of English people in Trinidad that Miranda depended.

But, for all his caution, Miranda could make a mistake. Lieutenant Alexander Briarly of the Royal Navy had ideas for an attack on Angostura in Venezuela. In Trinidad Briarly enforced the Navigation Acts, which restricted British trade to British ships. Once afloat, Briarly was independent of Governor Hislop, and his powers were wide. Briarly was a friend of Admiral Cochrane, who had been so helpful to Miranda; and Briarly was a man of substance. He had a 10,000-dollar Port of Spain house, and his country estate, with thirty-three Negroes and eleven mules, was valued at £13,000.

Miranda borrowed from Briarly and lodged, at Briarly's invitation, in Briarly's estate house and in his Port of Spain house. They talked business. Miranda wanted to raise money to pay off some of his debts, and Briarly agreed to buy Miranda's ship, the *Leander*. Then Briarly picked a quarrel. Miranda's servants were making too free with 'the mules and the Negroes at different times to the prejudice of the place'. It was an abrupt notice to quit. The business deal was off.

Miranda's London reputation was like a bluff which it was open to anyone to call. But the English were anxious to explain away Briarly. Briarly was a rogue, a known tormentor of Governor Hislop, like Governor Hislop's secretary, with whom he was in league. Briarly's naval command was nothing more than an abandoned hulk in the harbour, a jail for prisoners of war, which he had himself bought for almost nothing and then passed on, at an inflated price, to the Navy Office. In four years he had made a fortune from splitting with contraband American and South American traders whom he protected, and from prizes. (Out of spite against Governor Hislop, he had seized the ship that had brought the Chinese.)

So the English explained away Briarly. Miranda was gracious. He said he would think 'with pleasure' of Briarly's good qualities and 'forget his inconsistencies'. And for most of the English his London reputation held. He couldn't stay with Governor Hislop at Government House; that would have looked like official British approval of the invasion attempt. But he was in demand. Judge Black sent a whimsical, English-Spanish, showing-off invitation for Christmas ('Dear General, Christmas times *con nosotros* are times of feasting and merriment'). There was a ball at Government House. There was a month-long tour of country estates with an English party, Miranda the lion, someone keeping a journal to present to the General afterwards.

The countryside had changed. There were more English planters, many overreaching themselves and in debt; and they had established what, with all its dilutions, could be recognized as a type of English life. People rode over to friends' estates for dinner, for the night, for weekends. The estates were modern; the new steam engine on Low's estate produced as much cane juice in a day as three 'cattle mills'. '*Thursday the 6th March 1807*. Remained at home all day: – the General giving Miss McLurie some French lessons; – after dinner walk'd toward Evening with the ladies, for a mile, looking at the improvements. *Friday the 7th March*. Stood at home all day, and after dinner took a ramble round the Estate with the ladies.'

With Miranda the English tried. They used their best manners and their best vocabulary. He responded; he did what was expected of him. He assessed one old planter (a great enemy of the English opposition in the old days) as an Epicurean; the word was noted. He noticed that the ladies at another estate were 'thinly clothed' and that one even wore 'a transparency'.

The English in the party were outraged on Miranda's behalf at the exploitation of the eight hundred Indians by the Spanish priest of the Savannah Grande mission. 'He has taken care to squeeze as much labour out of them, as to cut down and draw out of the woods as much cedar wood, as would build him a spacious house of an innumerous size.' A Spaniard 'of the lowest order' sold the Indians rum and shared the profits with the priest. Miranda was 'gratified with the ride and the country, but disgusted with the manner the Indians were treated'. But Miranda made no comment when on one estate the two hundred Negroes were mustered in their Sunday clothes and made to sing their hymns.

One estate they went to was the Union Estate. It was owned by Picton in partnership with a man called McDonald. No one was at home. Everything was scattered about; there were many books; Miranda noted that none belonged to McDonald. Miranda wasn't entering the house of the enemy. He had learned much since he had arrived. If in London Fullarton and Pedro Vargas and the others were sinking – the Provost-Marshal petitioning for his fees, the Deputy Alguazil-Mayor stripped of his guinea-a-day allowance and begging for a return passage to Trinidad and a grant of land to make up for his losses – if in London Fullarton was sinking, in Trinidad Fullarton no longer had a side.

A subscription was being raised for Picton. The committee was giving a dinner that day at Mrs Perry's tavern in King Street in Port of Spain ('Dinner on the Table at 4 o'clock'). One of Miranda's country hosts was going. He had left the day before, by water, but couldn't make it; he returned, baffled by the wind. It was assumed by everyone among the English, from Governor Hislop down, that Miranda was on the right side. Miranda himself had been invited to the dinner 'to meet Colonel Picton's friends'. He didn't go. But he was on the right side.

A WEEK AFTER Miranda returned to Port of Spain from the country there was a second mandamus court about the Luisa Calderon case. Fourteen months had passed since the trial in London. The Privy Council had thrown out Fullarton's other charges; Picton was soon to be presented to the King by Lord Castlereagh (Fullarton raging in a broadsheet); but Picton was still on £40,000 bail and his retrial was a year away. The evidence required by this second mandamus court, about torture and the Spanish laws of Trinidad, had been submitted voluntarily to London eleven months before. But it had been submitted as an anxious resolution of the Trinidad Council ('Whereas . . .') and had been rejected by the prosecution lawyer as 'a sort of *manifesto*, in opposition to what was done at the trial'. Now the same witnesses were to be called, the same facts established.

Castro the escribano was the key man. He had no doubts now about the legality of torture. He had already remembered that when he was a boy in Córdoba in Spain he and some friends, passing the local jail, had heard the 'cries and lamentations' of two men, suspected murderers of a priest, who were being tortured in 'a private apartment of the jail'. The evidence Castro gave the mandamus court now was more direct. It was about the Negro Francisco who, on trial in 1791–2 for the murder of another

Negro, had been condemned to be tortured. Castro had acted as escribano in the case; he had managed to find an old copy of the process, the original of which had been sent to Caracas and not been returned.

A few weeks later the Spanish curate who had made out the false birth certificate for Luisa Calderon died in the Port of Spain jail. He had been curate of Port of Spain for twenty-one years; he was about to be tried for perjury and forgery. At the same time the Deputy Alguazil-Mayor, abandoning the libel case into which he had been forced by Fullarton, left London for Trinidad. There was talk in the Council of keeping him out. It is not known whether he was allowed in; he disappears.

Castro, the curate, the Deputy Alguazil-Mayor: they were all Spaniards, and they had all been on the wrong side. It was so easy now to humiliate the Spaniards of Trinidad. They were divided; they had nothing to be loyal to; every man was on his own and had to make his own peace in his own way. Miranda ought to have noticed. But Miranda had developed the exile's compensating sense of temporariness; he couldn't see colonial Trinidad, with its Negroes and its Spanish contraband traders, as an extension of colonial Venezuela. Venezuela remained special: part Peru, part Europe.

He had sent a man to London to ask for four thousand troops. But London wasn't going to send four thousand troops, or four hundred; and it at last became clear that there was to be no British help of any kind for a third expedition. There was nothing more to wait for in Trinidad; and, even before his London emissary returned, Miranda prepared to go back to England.

But Governor Hislop's faith in Miranda and Miranda's cause remained high. Hislop longed to be free of Trinidad, with its 'many vexations', and he had begun to see Miranda's cause as his own opportunity. He had begun to think – in spite of Miranda's two defeats, the idle year, the London rebuffs – of giving up the

Trinidad governorship and offering his services as a soldier to Miranda.

For Hislop it had been an especially irritating year. Lieutenant Briarly had seized the ship that had brought the Chinese immigrants, and there had been a wrangle over many months to get it freed. And the Chinese themselves, of whom so much was expected, had turned out to have no horticultural skills at all. With their pigtails and parasols, they were idle and luxury-loving, addicted to opium and gambling, and very expensive to maintain. There was a story that while one Chinese worked in the Botanical gardens another held a parasol over him. There was another unforeseen problem. The free women of colour wouldn't look at the Chinese, and the Chinese wouldn't look at Negro women. The lack of women had gradually driven the Chinese mad. They began to clamour to be sent back to Calcutta, and in the end, to everybody's relief, they were put on the very ship that had brought them and sent back.

And there was more trouble with Lieutenant Briarly. Briarly, defying Hislop's express orders, for which he publicly said he didn't care a damn, seized another ship. He was imprisoned for 'showing contempt', and this enraged him further. 'The stench and filth of the place,' he protested from the jail, 'is sufficient to destroy any constitution from the quantity of Negroes and others confined in so small a space.' The provost-marshal said that the jail was washed out every day, was 'as clean as a jail can be kept', and that Briarly had even had his choice of 'apartment'. (Port of Spain and its jails! Two months before this, Miranda had rescued a penniless Swedish prisoner who couldn't pay the jail fees and was living on bread and water.)

Briarly went wild after his release. A Spanish contraband trader, who was under Briarly's protection, complained that an Englishman had been informing against him. Briarly's men lured the informer aboard Briarly's hulk in the harbour. The man was kicked and beaten, threatened with a twelve-pound shot and tarred. Afterwards, as he complained to Governor Hislop, 'your petitioner had his hat thrown after him' and he was allowed to go ashore in his own boat. But then he had been chased through the Port of Spain streets, trapped in a house, beaten about the head and face with staves while a midshipman stood on guard outside 'with his head down'. Escaping, to the shouts of 'Thief!' (tarred, he looked like a Negro), he ran, a crowd gathering now, into somebody's yard and hid below a 'Negro bed' in one of the Negro houses at the back.

'Who is here?' the owner asked.

'Me.'

'Who are you?'

'Mr Leake.'

But, though bleeding badly from two head-wounds, he was surrendered, and Briarly's men would have killed him if the harbour-master hadn't intervened. It was the sort of naval high spirits Mr Marryat's son would write about in some of his novels.

Governor Hislop just wanted to get away. He declared himself in a letter to Miranda just before Miranda left for England. In his letter, 'private and confidential and entrusted solely to Genl Miranda's own consideration and reflection', Hislop said that he wanted to be relieved of his governorship. He wanted to join any expedition of Miranda's, but he couldn't accept any rank below major-general. 'My principal object is to be actively and creditably employed and naturally without prejudice to my private interests, which for the sake of others and not for myself I feel particularly bound not to be indifferent about.'

Miranda's reply was brief: he said that Hislop could count on him. Hislop took the promise seriously; and, in preparation for his new career, began to spend an hour or two every morning learning Spanish.

To the end people turned to Miranda. On the ship he received a note from a naval cadet, a supernumerary on the voyage, going to 'pass my examination for a lieutenant'. The young man had got a 'little inebriated it being my birthday', and he was going to be turned before the mast. He wanted General Miranda to intercede.

AT HOME, in London, there was Fullarton, whose letter of goodwill and whose address Miranda had preserved through all the adventures of the last twenty-seven months. Everything Fullarton had said about Trinidad and the Pictonians was true; but Fullarton's fight was his alone. There had been nothing to write to him about. And now, at the end of 1807, Fullarton himself was very ill and in trouble. His supporters had been scattered. McCallum the pamphleteer had produced another pamphlet, but McCallum was finding another cause and another patron: the Duke of Kent. Picton's fortunes were rising. The case against him was distintegrating; the result of the retrial could be foretold. Fullarton's own libel action was going badly. He had been delaying, he had been interfering with witnesses, and there was a possibility that he might be committed to prison for contempt. To Fullarton Miranda brought no messages of hope or goodwill. The messages, from Governor Hislop and others, were all for Picton, once the friend, then the enemy, and now apparently the friend again, of the Spanish-American revolution.

It was Picton now who supplied Miranda with documents about the earliest days of British rule in Trinidad, and the favourable intentions then of the British government towards the revolution. Miranda made some return. He spoke about Picton to Wellington, whom he met for the first time at the end of January 1808. In London Miranda was a figure. He was someone the powerful might, for various reasons, want to meet; and that was a kind of power. It was a power that both Fullarton and Governor Hislop understood and Picton had come to understand. It wasn't a power that Pedro Vargas had understood when he transferred his allegiance to First Commissioner Fullarton, prodigal in his appointments, emptying the Trinidad Treasury.

For four years Miranda had kept silent about Vargas. But now in London he dug up the letter he had received from Vargas in 1799, just after Vargas had arrived as a refugee. Vargas had written of his part in the conspiracy in New Granada, and of the arrest and torture of the conspirators. Torture and the Spanish Empire: it contradicted the evidence Vargas had given at the first trial. It was something for Picton. Expediency, revenge. But Vargas had been a real revolutionary once; his experience, and his words, had excited Miranda; and those tortures had been real.

Miranda abandoned Vargas. He abandoned Vargas's master, Fullarton. And Fullarton was now quite alone. One letter went to him. It was from the man who had written up the journal of Miranda's country tour in Trinidad and had come back to England with Miranda. The letter was probably abusive. Fullarton was staying in a London hotel. He returned the letter to Miranda with a short formal note ('Colonel Fullarton presents his compliments'). A few days later, on February 13th 1808, he died.

Miranda, writing in Spanish to Governor Hislop, who was keeping up his Spanish studies for his new career, gave the news in a postscript. '*Murió Fullarton! Casi sin llamar la atención pública*. Fullarton died! And the public scarcely noticed.' – 'My dear General,' the journal-writer wrote to Miranda, 'I heard of Fullarton's death a few minutes after I left you: – my letter must have made him feel . . . I fear Fullarton took something to hurry himself off.' It had been just five years since Fullarton had sailed into Port of Spain harbour as First Commissioner, and waited to land in 'regular form'. The jail was waiting: the chained Negroes, the woman Vallot had bought as a speculation, the *cachots brûlants*: his cause, his obsession. And after five years it had killed him. The British national character, the principles of justice and protection, the concept of duty, the idea of a role: the righter of wrongs, the persecutor, the persecuted, the contemptible, the forgotten: it is like the revenge cycle of an old saga, in which sympathy makes the full circle.

Two months later Picton was appointed major-general. Six

weeks later, on a Saturday in June 1808, his retrial came up at the court of King's Bench before Lord Ellenborough and a special jury. Once again Luisa Calderon and the alguazil – both now, after five years in England, speaking English and needing no interpreter – described the two acts of torment of seven years before; and once again ('Come nearer, and show them to the jury') Luisa showed the marks on her wrists. Miranda, mentioning no names, noted the findings of the jury: torture was permitted by the Spanish law of Trinidad. There remained certain formalities, which would last for years; but Picton was acquitted. The public drama of his case had come to an end two years before. The trial of the moment, for Miranda as well, was that of General Whitelocke, who had attempted to retake Buenos Aires. Colonel Rutherfurd, the former Trinidad Surveyor-General, went every day to the trial and reported back.

Picton, making use of the letter Miranda had given him, began to press for the arrest of Pedro Vargas. Luisa Calderon and the alguazil, without a master, no longer of interest, both now touched with fraudulence, in spite of those marked wrists, asked through their lawyer for passports to return to Trinidad. They disappear. Porto Rico, Vallot's assistant, who had held the rope, had already disappeared, dead perhaps or part of the submerged Negro population of London.

On 23 November 1808 Picton wrote to the Colonial Under-Secretary: 'With respect to the letters on the subject of the perjury of Pedro Vargas, I have to request that they may be considered as never having been written.' Pedro Vargas had died; and in the squalor of defeat, treachery and waste Picton's action was like the abashed graciousness of a man who, though difficulties lay ahead, especially with Lord Castlereagh, was on the rise.

Of the whole affair there remained only Fullarton's hopeless libel case. Mrs Fullarton took that over. It dragged on for many months. There were always more affidavits. 'I do not know when we shall have an end of it,' Lord Ellenborough said, arguing against yet another adjournment. 'I am ready to sit here and attend to it while my strength continues, until that strength be wholly exhausted.' Mrs Fullarton sank more deeply with every effort at self-assertion. All her dead husband's petty peculations in Ireland and Scotland were raked over, and her own alleged carriage-rides with Luisa Calderon, an exotic then, in Ayrshire. And so much that was important and true was forgotten and made irrelevant: those dinners for the oppressed in the renovated Port of Spain house (now in ruin again), those elevating courtesies, the looks of approval in the streets, the jail that had been pulled down, the torture that had been stopped, the Negro-burnings that would never happen again.

'One of the most beneficial purposes of justice is to prevent any farther irritation or injury,' Lord Ellenborough said at last. 'The very hearing is a source of farther irritation, which every honourable and feeling mind would wish to be avoided on such a subject.' He stopped the trial.

For everyone sympathy made the full circle. The journal-keeper who thought his letter had helped to kill Fullarton: he had joined Miranda's expedition in Trinidad with the rank of colonel (but he wasn't): four months after Fullarton's death he was destitute, in jail for debt, and writing begging letters.

Miranda, too, had had his disappointments. He had talked seriously with Wellington of an invasion of South America. Then Napoleon had made the Spanish King abdicate and French troops had invaded Spain. Spain had become an ally of England; a British invasion of South America was no longer possible; Wellington was to go with his 10,000 troops to Spain instead. He took Miranda out into the streets to tell him. Miranda protested loudly. Wellington walked ahead 'just a little, that we might not attract notice'. 'I think I have never had a more difficult business,' he said later.

Earlier in the year a great fire had destroyed the 'clothing, arms and ammunition' Miranda had left behind in Port of Spain. It had been like a sign, another cause for exaggerated protest and exaggerated financial claim. But Miranda was fifty-eight. Like Ralegh, he was the man of action who had always had bad luck and had always bungled action; and perhaps his protests now at inaction were like the aged Ralegh's in the Tower, formal but fate-provoking. The events in Spain, with their repercussions in South America, were to involve both Miranda and Picton: glory for Picton in the Peninsula, for Miranda the unexpected final action in Venezuela, defeat again, disgrace, betrayal, and imprisonment for what remained of his life.

10. The Inheritors

1809–1813

WITH SPAIN OCCUPIED and warred over, her Empire was on its own. Spain and England were now allies, and free communication between Caracas and Port of Spain was possible. It was what the English merchants in Port of Spain had longed for: Caracas needed many things which they could supply. One of the first things Caracas asked for was a printing press – Caracas had a university, but no newspaper. Governor Hislop got an old press from the island of Grenada and sent over the editor of the *Trinidad Weekly Courant* to set it up for the *Gaceta de Caracas*. In return Governor Hislop asked Caracas for lawyers. Picton had chased away all the Spanish lawyers, and ever since there had been no one in Trinidad to help with matters of Spanish law.

For Governor Hislop the laws of the colony had remained a problem. A merchant who was being prosecuted for fraud fled to England and maintained, right up to the House of Lords, that he couldn't be tried by an English court for an offence against the Spanish laws. He set a fashion. A French surgeon and planter called Lebis committed the cliché of abolitionist propaganda. One morning he whipped one of his Negroes to death 'before breakfast', and said he hadn't broken any law. He appeared to be right. The Trinidad Negro Code of 1789 hadn't been ratified by the Audiencia of Caracas; Picton's code of 1800 hadn't received the royal sanction. All that Governor Hislop and his judge could do was to fine Lebis 150 dollars for 'treating his slave unskilfully in his capacity of surgeon'.

Just a few months before, there had been an even bigger scandal. A free woman of colour called Betsy Diggins, well known even to people like Picton and the Baron de Montalembert for her brutality towards the few Negroes she owned, accused an Indian, a Carib from St Vincent, of stealing some salt-fish and flour. She got some Negroes, men and women, her own as well as the neighbours', to hunt the Indian down. She tied the Indian up in her yard and tortured him. For much of the night her free Negro neighbour 'heard screamings and melancholy groans'. In the morning people who went to Betsy's yard 'to buy bread' saw the mutilated Indian tied to a post and lying face down on the ground. Some of them told Betsy, 'the mongrel woman', that the Indian was a free man, not one of her own Negroes, and she would get into trouble. But two or three days later Betsy and her two Negroes, one a creole Negro, the other a new Ibo Negro, dragged the Indian down to a ravine and stoned him to death. Then Betsy herself cut up the body with a cutlass.

The report of the bread-buyers reached the district commandant and he came to investigate. Betsy's husband was crippled with rheumatism; he was dying; he knew nothing; Betsy said she didn't know where the Indian was; he was a free man, not her property, and she wasn't going to look for him. But they searched with the help of Betsy's terrified Negroes. In the ravine the stench was high; one of the peons vomited. The body, or 'a part of the fragments', was found covered by some leaves of the wild plantain; the crows had already 'demolished' much. The Indian's head was missing. One of Betsy's Negroes took the searchers to a sort of grave, but the skull they dug up there was a Negro's: another mystery, but one that wasn't worth pursuing now.

Betsy was arrested and lodged in the jail with the galley Negroes. A day later her husband died. And some days after that, when the jail burned down in the great Port of Spain fire, Betsy escaped and somehow made her way to London where, with the help of a lawyer in Red Lion Square, she claimed immunity from the English laws.

'My bed,' Governor Hislop wrote to Miranda, turning the idiom into careful Spanish, 'has not been one of flowers.' He was keeping up his studies of the language, spending one hour a morning on it in his derelict house. Spanish, he wrote, would soon replace German as the universal military language. In other letters he lamented the absence of 'a Spanish society, where might be found ladies of fine and beautiful manners'. The Trinidad soldiers were now in very ragged greatcoats, pantaloons and shoes, though new ones had been paid for. Hislop lamented the absence of the real world. It was a reminder to Miranda of his readiness to be called. But these letters were private. The people in London saw only a conscientious, harassed and sometimes hysterical official; his enemies in Trinidad saw only a weak administrator, a gentleman, anxious to be liked, and a little too fond of food and drink. 'In the last six years,' Hislop wrote in Spanish to Miranda, 'I have seen more of the infamy and turpitude of mankind than I have seen in the rest of my life.'

But Governor Hislop complained too soon. The real world and the great events for which he had been preparing were at hand. Revolution was at last coming to Venezuela. Spain had suddenly withered away; and Venezuela, cut off from Spain, was being shivered into all its divisions and subdivisions of race and caste. But it was not the revolution Governor Hislop or Miranda had expected. It was the loss of law. The pacific, deficient colonial society had become bloody. Spain was now seen to be more than its administrative failures. It was, however remotely, a code and a reference that the colonial society by itself was incapable of generating. Without such a reference obedience, the association of consent, was no longer possible.

The colonial society, that could refer only to race and money, whose stored wisdom was only about cacao, tobacco, sugar and the management of Negroes, was as deformed as Governor Hislop had sensed in Trinidad and Miranda in his early life in Caracas and during his recent adventure at Coro. It wasn't only that the wines, the manners and the graces, the books and the art and the ideas of a living culture came from outside. The simple society bred simple people.

For the colonial it would have been a difficult, self-destroying conclusion. Miranda's analysis, in spite of his experience, had always been political, and in the irrelevant slogans of his acquired culture. Pedro Vargas, introducing himself to Pitt in 1799, had written with pride that South Americans were among the simplest people in the world. Vargas missed the sophistication of the European thought that found romance in the deficiency. And a further example of this simplicity: even now, when the revolution had clearly ceased to be Miranda's, Miranda's new agent in Trinidad – he was the Spaniard who had given Picton information about the Luisa Calderon affair; he lived in the notoriously lazy countryside near the Indian mission of Arima – was still dealing in rhetoric. He wrote that Miranda was 'worshipped like an idol' and was to Venezuelans as the Messiah to the Jews.

For Hislop, though he didn't see it then, it was the beginning of the end of his relationship with Miranda, the end of his dream of Venezuelan romance. He was the governor of a British colony and he couldn't officially countenance the dismemberment of an ally's empire. He was also the governor of a colony that was full of Negroes and recalcitrant mulattoes; and, like Picton more than ten years before, Hislop grew nervous about the revolution in Venezuela, with its unexpected racial encouragements. Miranda had talked about Indians and Spaniards, the mingled culture of Incas and Conquistadores. He hadn't talked about Negroes and mulattoes. He hadn't suggested that one aspect of the revolution, even in the province of Barcelona, where there were few Negroes, would be that white and mulatto officers would walk about the streets 'arm in arm and singing in concert'.

The Spanish Empire was sinking in what had been the province of El Dorado; the British Empire had risen. But the British colony that was being established was remarkably like the Spanish province which was being destroyed from within.

IN VENEZUELA the Spanish laws were going. In Trinidad, twelve years after the British conquest, no one knew as yet what the laws were. People were making the best of both codes, the Spanish and the English, and often doing as they pleased. The island's legal system was in chaos; there were hundreds of unsettled disputes. For years Governor Hislop had been asking for help. Now at last, in London, Lord Castlereagh decided that what was needed in Trinidad was someone like a Chief Justice.

The idea had been put to Castlereagh by a man called George Smith, who had served for some time as a judge in the West Indies in Grenada. Smith had had an interview with Castlereagh; and then for a year he had negotiated with Castlereagh for the job. The office, Smith had said, 'would be laborious and unceasing, but that with me would be one of the strongest motives for seeking it'. He asked for £4,000 a year; he settled for £2,000, exclusive of fees (it was said by an enemy that he was Castlereagh's brother-in-law); and in May 1809 George Smith was sent out to set the Trinidad laws right.

But Smith, though proud of being a member of the English bar, with 'a regular professional education' (unlike the colonial riff-raff he said he knew who passed for lawyers in the West Indies), Smith didn't come out as an English-style Chief Justice. He came out as a Spanish-style Royal Audience, a one-man Audience; and, bizarrely, he came from London laden with Spanish titles, all granted under the Sign Manual of the King of England. Smith was a friend of Miranda's; he had borrowed Miranda's Spanish law-books and carefully, after many drafts, had written out his own commission, including his titles of address.

In Trinidad Smith took his titles seriously. He was a bachelor, irritable and somewhat deaf; he liked to be addressed as 'Highness and Most Powerful'. Some people thought he was mad; but the English immigrant who provocatively addressed a letter to 'Geo. Smith *Esquire*' got into trouble for 'sacrilege'. Smith had come out prepared to deal with this kind of colonial impertinence. His previous colonial experience in the nearby island of Grenada appeared to have unhinged him; and in Trinidad it soon became clear that Smith had a cause beyond his salary and fees and his Spanish titles. The cause wasn't abolition, though his friendship with the abolitionists in London and especially with Wilberforce's brother-in-law was one of the sources of his influence. Smith's cause was the chastisement of English colonial society. It was an English social resentment, an internal English matter. It had little to do with Negroes, who remained to him only an anonymous and inescapable nuisance.

Before he came out he had written to Castlereagh of 'the general want of moral principle' in 'the colonial character'. Trinidad confirmed his prejudice. 'You can form no idea of a colonial public unless you mix with them,' he reported. 'Generally colonies are peopled by the refuse of the Mother Country, but Trinidad is peopled by the refuse of the other colonies.' He lay about him; he was willing to take on everybody. 'I care not one pinch of snuff for the opinion of anyone here,' he wrote to London, asking for police powers and promising to do the job well. He spoke as directly in Trinidad. He promised 'to leave a sting behind him'; and he acted as he spoke. He roughed up some officials as soon as he arrived; the Attorney-General was soon objecting to being treated like a schoolboy. A local man who thought he would approach Smith privately about a legal matter found himself kicked down the steps by Smith's English servant.

'The history of the private transactions of this colony for the past ten years is dreadful,' Smith reported; and in less than four months he settled seven hundred outstanding cases, picking up something like 5,000 dollars in fees. He said he was retrieving much property from lawyers and merchants, 'who themselves never possessed of a shilling of property, are now rioting in the spoils of their deceased friends whose families and heirs they have plundered'. The 'cries of horror' from exposed frauds and debtors had become 'a source of general amusement and laughter'. The debtors were planters like Sablich. In 1807, just before the British slave trade was made illegal, Sablich had ordered a whole cargo of new Negroes from a Liverpool shipper. The Negroes were worth nearly £13,000; Sablich hadn't paid and, until Smith came, there was no means of making him pay.

Smith's assessment of the society was close to Governor Hislop's; and Governor Hislop was delighted. At the same time – he didn't like making enemies, and he was a gentleman – he was able to say that the law was out of his hands. In his delight Hislop was willing to overlook Smith's irritability. Mme Vence, the wife of a merchant, one of Smith's own neighbours, was giving evidence in a petty case of debt. She went on too long. Smith told her that if she didn't hold her tongue and go about her business he would have the alguazils take her down to the jail. She fainted as soon as she got home.

And there was Smith's sensitivity to noise. His hearing was defective, but he couldn't bear the barking of dogs at night or the chatter of his neighbours' Negroes. His servants – who were English – had orders, which they zestfully followed, to kill any dog that barked. One night they stoned both the terrier and the house of the man who lived next door to Mme Vence, and there was something like a fight. Another night a quarrel broke out among the Negroes in the Count du Castellet's yard across the road. The Negroes were all arrested by Smith's English servants, taken to the jail, whipped by the jailer, thirty-nine lashes each, the maximum, and returned to their owner the next morning. It was the Count's pride that none of his Negroes, who were generally regarded as 'valuable and orderly', had ever been whipped. He protested to Hislop, who referred him to Smith; Smith, in curious apology, invited the Count to breakfast.

Slightly more irrational was Smith's treatment of MacIntosh. MacIntosh made a living by hiring out his twelve or thirteen Negroes. They were not of the best character; and, perhaps because they had heard of Smith's anti-English bias, they complained of ill-treatment. They were hoping to be confiscated. They were taken into the jail; and Smith summoned MacIntosh. He said that MacIntosh wasn't a fit person to look after his Negroes or his money. He ordered MacIntosh to deposit certain securities and then, surprising everybody, he ordered all the Negroes to be flogged.

He had punished both slaves and slave-owners. It represented fairly his attitude to slavery. Seven years before, the issue of slavery had left Fullarton confused. He too had come out with a sense of mission. But Fullarton quickly recognized that slavery existed, was the very foundation of the society, and that the Negroes had therefore to be kept in order; in the end all he had been able to say, in effect, was that the Negroes shouldn't be flogged too hard. Smith's outrage was more comprehensive: detesting the slave society, he detested both slave-owners and slaves, colonial white and servile black.

Dealing in racial or communal generalizations, though, Smith needed some point of reference, some hero community. At first he chose the French and the Spaniards; but though he represented them as dreading 'the boisterous and overbearing character of the English colonists', they didn't provide a satisfying enough contrast. The free people of colour did: oppressed but not Negroes, owning Negroes, teased by their half-privileges, carrying their mixed blood like disease. Smith became their champion. In the end this was the only colonial battleground. This was what stalled and perverted every stated metropolitan principle, French, Spanish, English, of revolution, intellectual advance, law, social drive, justice and freedom: race, the taint of slavery: it helped to make the colonial society simple.

Those noisy Negroes, those crooked merchants and planters:

after some weeks it began to occur to Smith that Hislop, by his softness, was partly responsible. And Hislop began to have his doubts about Smith. His irritability, given its head, was becoming like mania.

A Methodist preacher, recently arrived, complained that he had been bawled down by Mr Harvey, a militia captain. 'Alguazils!' Smith called. 'Alguazils! Where are the alguazils? Señor! Go and bring Mr Harvey.' Harvey asked under what Spanish law he was being arrested. Smith said, 'The Riot Act.'

There were other complaints. Fullarton's Provost-Marshal in London found that the £200 or so in fees which he was used to splitting with his deputy in Trinidad had dried up. When the deputy, 'a weak and tremulous person', went to Smith to ask about the fees, Smith insulted him, said his job was a nonsense job under Spanish law, that there were no police duties for him to perform now, that the fees 'wouldn't purchase a dinner' for his principal; and if the deputy or his London principal made any more trouble they had both better watch out.

The plunderers of the widows and orphans had been discomfited, and Smith had reported 'general amusement and laughter'. But it also began to be noted now, after the laughter, that fortunes were disappearing. All property in dispute and all dead men's estates and moneys had been passing into the hands of an official called the depositario. Since Smith's arrival property worth £180,000 had so passed, and only £4,000 had been given back. The depositario was a young man called William Burnley. It is so, suddenly, teamed with Smith, that this man appears in the records. Who was Burnley? Was he someone Smith had known during his previous West Indian service in Grenada? All Smith said about him was that he was a Virginian and a gentleman. Smith dismissed all protests about the depositario as trivial and trouble-making. He said that moneys taken in by the depositario went to a receiver in London and were invested in government securities; estates in Trinidad were managed by the depositario.

'Managed': that was the key word. That was the word that frightened local men of property, some of whom had started as managers. And the local men of property were right. Whether Smith knew it or not, the young Virginian gentleman who was his depositario was laying the foundation of the largest and most enduring Trinidad fortune.

SMITH HAD promised to leave a sting behind him, and he was succeeding. The Picton–Fullarton affair had only just died away, and it must have seemed to local white people that in the person of Smith, their one-man Royal Audience, both Picton and Fullarton had returned to torment them: he combined the violence and autocracy of the one with the sense of mission and money of the other.

An opposition declared itself. It asked for Smith's recall and, as in Picton's time, it began to petition for a British constitution. During the lax years of Hislop's governorship few people had worried about the rule of law; the general uncertainty about the laws had suited many, especially people with debts. Now, with the Smith terror, laws seemed important; and now, as in Picton's time, a British constitution meant much more than the rule of law. It meant rule by local white people and freedom from London officials like Smith; it meant cancelling all debts. And now it also meant disenfranchising the free people of colour. There was a reasonable excuse: Venezuela was in turmoil, and the trouble might spill over: in Trinidad, among the French people of colour, there were still embittered and disrespectful republican elements waiting for the day of glory.

Smith saw only the racial issue, the threat to the people of colour, his hero community, neither white nor Negro, and he prepared to do battle on their behalf. The *Courant*, ignoring Smith's orders, printed the petition for the British constitution, and supporting letters. Smith had the editor arrested at his printery, and imprisoned him for three months. Governor Hislop objected; he said that Smith was interfering with the freedom of the press. Smith said that it was nonsense to talk of freedom of the press in a slave colony.

And so the quarrel between Smith, the Royal Audience, and Hislop, the Governor, at last became open. They were not really quarrelling about the freedom of the press. They were quarrelling about the free people of colour. Hislop was a gentleman, anxious in spite of everything to be liked by his fellows in a colony where he had lived for seven years. But in any racial situation – and especially now, against the news of revolution and racial incitement in Venezuela – his side was chosen for him. He accepted the petition for the British constitution and, in spite of Smith's objections, sent it to London.

Smith wrote to London himself. A British constitution, he said, rested on 'a general liberty'. It became 'an absolute caricature' in a colony where four-fifths of the population were slaves. Trial by jury was absurd 'when the jurors know every case beforehand, when planters act as the judges and soldiers as the chancellor. There is on the contrary a simplicity in the Spanish code which gives it a decided preference for a country not abounding in intellectual means'. – 'When I look at these conflicts of interest, of passion, of prejudice in which in its turn every class of the community is in arms against the other, and when I compare the political wisdom of the Mother Country with the narrow bigoted policy which is uppermost in the brain of an ill-educated colonist I raise my voice to the utmost pitch against the establishment of an internal legislature.' A defence of illiberalism in the liberal cause: the racial issue set every principle on its head.

As to the petition itself, more than half of the people who had signed, Smith said, 'are unknown or are known not to be worth a dollar. This motley crew is composed of merchant's clerks, apprentice boys, printer's devils, and the offal of the community'. Such people, 'however respectable in their humble or menial state, are as improperly placed as regards the political part of this address as would be the village shopkeeper's shopman in one of a similar tendency presented by the freeholders of an English county to our Sovereign'. The cause of the free people of colour provided its social satisfactions: that internal English matter in which the proclaimed cause, like Luisa Calderon's torture, could sometimes be forgotten.

The letters and petitions to London kept the issue as an issue. In Port of Spain the battle became more personal. 'Your friendship I would esteem contamination,' one English immigrant wrote to Smith. 'When I prefix [the Honourable] to your name, remember, it is not that I address you as a Member of His Majesty's Council, a board which I respect. It is merely to distinguish you from a gentleman of the same name in Port of Spain, who would blush to be taken for you.' This was from a man called Lockhead, a Fellow of the Royal Society of Edinburgh; Smith had confiscated some of his Negroes.

Towards Negroes and their owners Smith continued to be intemperate, liking whenever possible to do violence to both together. The Chief of Police complained that the *petits marchands*, Negroes employed by their owners as hucksters, stayed on the street after eight at night and had continually to be moved on. 'Very well,' Smith said. 'Come to me on Monday evening next as soon as the gun fires.' Smith, on a horse, was ready at the appointed time; the Chief of Police was also mounted. They rode together for two or three blocks. 'There they are,' the Chief of Police said, reining back. 'Do you see that light, sir?' – 'Do you remain where you are, Major,' Smith said, 'and I will show you the way to disperse them.' He made straight for the pavement market at a full gallop. The Negroes bawled and scattered, abandoning their owners' goods. And that for the time being was the end of the huckster nuisance.

The free people of colour prepared their own petition to Governor Hislop: they wanted permission to address the Throne. The petition showed Smith's influence; it was the petition of a hero community, educated, submissive, correct. 'Penetrated with respect for the constituted authorities, friends of order and lovers of their country, they travel through the gloom of political humiliation with submission, patience and fortitude . . . It becomes their duty to employ such means as appear to them necessary (and at the same time consistent with the principles of order, respect and obedience towards the government, which they profess to act upon and from which they will never be found deviating) to awaken the reflection that there exists in this colony a numerous, opulent and useful class of free subjects who are entitled to *something*.'

Governor Hislop wasn't impressed. He asked the people of colour to speak more clearly. What were the 'vexatious regulations' they feared? They replied with even greater caution. 'As they have always considered that any specific claims or pretensions on their part would be highly unbecoming, they have never entertained or encouraged any discussion on the subject.' In fact, as everyone knew, what was frightening the people of colour was the rumour that when the British constitution came in free people of colour would be liable to be whipped like Negroes.

Hislop said he couldn't give permission for an address to the Throne. People would get the impression that the people of colour had something to be frightened about. The fear, he hinted, was all on the other side. The news from Venezuela was bad: 'Robespierrian terror' from the Juntas of the People, the European Spaniards especially suffering. And there was a local story that large numbers of French people of colour, republicans, were going to be brought into the island by Christmas. Seditious letters were being stuck up at night or dropped in the streets.

Then there was something like an incident. A French mulatto, 'in the public street and in the open day', threatened to kick and beat a Frenchman. The mulatto, a former aide-de-camp to a revolutionary general, had been banished to England seven years before but had come back under a false name. It was found that he had signed the petition of the people of colour. He was imprisoned; he escaped; the posters advertising rewards for his capture were torn down. After some imprisonments, banishings and a swift census of all free coloured males over twelve, the people of colour went silent.

In England Mr Marryat, balancing Smith's description of the English petitioners as offal, said that the West Indian coloureds were 'a vile and infamous race', incendiaries and desperadoes, without education or manners. Much damage had already been done 'from setting the doctrines of the Rights of Man afloat in the minds of these people. I can only compare the conduct of Mr Smith in stirring them up to that of a madman who scattered firebrands . . .'

It was the symmetry of all racial or religious argument. But nothing was done about a British constitution. It was a victory for Smith, his abolitionist friends in London and the free people of colour in Trinidad.

THERE REMAINED the internal English fight, between Smith and Governor Hislop, between Smith (he said he was 'an unperverted Englishman') and the English, between Smith and the colonial society. He claimed, and his victory appeared to prove, close connections with Lord Castlereagh, now Foreign Secretary, Lord Camden, Lord President of the Council, and the family of Lord Liverpool, who was to be the next Prime Minister. He continued to slap down the colonials, high and low.

Sablich, who owed £13,000 on his Negroes, was declared bankrupt. His sugars were seized and a levy placed on his estate; the depositario claimed all Sablich's debts. Sablich protested in the *Courant*. He was imprisoned for three days and threatened with a whipping, Negro's punishment. A Frenchwoman complained late one night that she had just been beaten by her husband and feared for her life. 'Go and take the fellow,' Smith said to his alguazils, 'and lodge him in jail.' The 'fellow' was an interpreter. He stayed in the 'nauseous filth' of the jail for six months, among the galley

Negroes. Then he was brought up to Smith's house, told to pay 1,000 dollars, or get off the island, or go back to jail. He went back to jail. 'The *circumstances* of Adrien,' Smith explained, 'render the attempt to punish him by fine nugatory.' It was what never ceased to irritate Smith, these ill-educated, penniless adventurers who, because of the Negroes, had forgotten their place. Even the free people of colour found that there were limits. A free coloured man who challenged another to a duel was straightaway sent off to jail for two months.

Smith's powers as a Spanish-style Royal Audience were very full. There was no way of telling where they became separate from the English-style powers of Governor Hislop. But there were now people who could give advice. They were the Venezuelan lawyers who, now that Spain and England were at peace, had been asked over to Trinidad to help with matters of Spanish law. These men at least could define the powers of a Royal Audience. And the Venezuelans were game; they zestfully took sides. Smith hired two Venezuelans and paid them 2,000 dollars out of his own pocket; Hislop hired one, and paid him 3,300 dollars. They were all distinguished lawyers in Caracas, but their concern now was with more than the Spanish law. They had fallen out over the revolution. They had begun to hate one another; and they prepared now to fight out their Venezuelan hatred through their English patrons.

The cleverest, and most expensive, of the lawyers, the man on Hislop's side, was Andrés Level de Goda. He was one of the first Venezuelans to come to Trinidad after the Spanish–English peace; and it was while he was in Trinidad that Level, able for the first time to compare, had begun to have doubts about Venezuelan independence, a cause he had supported since his student days. Level began to feel that Venezuelans weren't intellectually or socially equipped for independence, and that, without Spain and the Spanish Empire, Venezuela would fall apart. Level's attitude to Venezuela was like Smith's attitude to Trinidad; and, indeed, Level had at first offered his services to Smith. But he had been

Venezuelan and extravagant; he had said that Smith, as a Royal Audience, was everything and Hislop nothing. He had also perhaps asked for too much money. Smith dismissed him and he went to Hislop. Hislop paid – though the figure of 3,300 dollars suggests some bargaining – and Level immediately set about containing Smith and the lawyers Smith had hired. Smith's lawyers, Level said, were frauds, and they were making a mockery of the Spanish law by encouraging Smith, 'half-mad, very deaf and neither speaking Spanish nor understanding it', to believe that he could be a Royal Audience by himself.

Level de Goda was thirty-three. He remembered when Trinidad was part of the Spanish Empire; from his father's estates just across the Gulf of Paria they could hear the Port of Spain sunset gun. Level didn't mind practising Spanish law in a Spanish island that had become a British colony. He said it was an honour to serve a friendly country; and the money, he remembered even forty years later, was very good. English legal fees were beyond anything a Venezuelan knew; he was able to ride to and from Government House in his own calash. Level thought his success made Venezuelans jealous. The admission, and Level's position in Trinidad, give a scale to Venezuela (the editor of the *Courant* going over to set up a second-hand press for the main Caracas newspaper) and the revolution.

Level had his doubts about Venezuelan independence. But he had not yet openly reneged. He went over to Venezuela to address the Supreme Junta of the new creole government in May 1810. He made a rhetorical speech about independence and freedom and was cheered. But he was frightened of the new hatreds he had seen, 'that jealousy which devours us and is not like the jealousy of other lands and perhaps belongs only to these latitudes . . . satisfied only when it sees the bones of the enemy.' There were doctors and lawyers and musicians in Venezuela, Level said. But they were individuals; they didn't add up to a self-supporting society. He saw independence as a long and bloody chaos; he came back to Trinidad a proclaimed 'Goth', the South American word of abuse for a European Spaniard.

Level de Goda, *godismo*: it was an obvious play of words. And from Trinidad Level encouraged every pro-Spanish movement on the Main. There were requests from Venezuela for the expulsion of Level, 'this unnatural being unworthy of the name of an American'. And Level had his bitterest Venezuelan enemies in Trinidad itself. They were the lawyers on Smith's side; they were passionate republicans. They said that Level was no longer a lawyer, that he had been expelled from the college of advocates in Caracas for a swindle over some Negroes. Level said that *they* were fortune-seekers, as jealous of his own success among the English in Trinidad 'as grocers of the grocer next door'. The men Level abused in this way were Pedro Gual and Miguel Peña, Bolívar's future associates, ministers, negotiators. And one of them, Miguel Peña, was on Smith's personal payroll. Again, it gives a scale.

But if Smith and Hislop were the protectors of these warring Venezuelans, they were also their pawns. As when, for example, the lawyers appeared to decide that the Trinidad constitutional tangle would become clearer and more amenable to Spanish legal argument if Hislop, from being an English governor, could become something like a Spanish viceroy, against Smith's Royal Audience. Hislop found himself exchanging Spanish-style salutations and letters with Smith – 'God keep your honour many years', 'thus ordered the President and his brother judges', 'let this be put together with the other papers on this matter' – until in the end the letters became purely Spanish.

It was too much for Hislop. He had been governor for too long. He had lived through too many strains. He began to beg London to be replaced. 'In the opinion of professional men with whom I have consulted and above all from my own feelings', he wrote, he needed a change, a few months in England; and it would be nice if he could get back in May, 'when the season will be mild and best suited to a constitution which for fifteen years has had to contend with this climate'.

But a replacement wasn't immediately available. And the English immigrants didn't like the idea of being left alone with Smith. They insisted that Hislop should stay and fight it out like a Spanish viceroy, with the help of Level de Goda.

Hislop's position had been redefined. Now Level de Goda dressed up the Port of Spain cabildo, which for most of its two hundred and twenty years had been dormant or in the bush or, since the capitulation, a body of officials under a British governor. In Spanish America the cabildo had usually been a type of local executive council, ensuring the rule of the powerful. Level de Goda claimed much more for the Port of Spain cabildo. He claimed the cabildo's antique Castilian privileges. He declared it an independent tribune shielding the people from the sovereign.

It was the legalism by which some of the provinces of Venezuela had declared their independence. It was the legalism by which Hislop and the cabildo now questioned Smith's acts as Royal Audience. The cabildo said that the three-day imprisonment of Sablich in the common jail 'among Negroes' was illegal. Sablich was a man of standing and property and ought to have been handled more respectfully. Hislop published the resolution; and the same day, in token of their new dignity as protectors of the people, the chief magistrates of the cabildo began to wear red ribbons, the lesser officials white ribbons.

Some months before, opposing a British constitution, Smith had suggested that the cabildo might be raised again to its old status. But the twenty-five-page petition he now began to write to the King of England was full of hate for the cabildo. It was violating all the laws of Spain and the Indies; the ribbons were a sign of scorn, a 'usurpation of the prerogatives of the Crown'. Hislop ought to be punished, the cabildo dismissed, its members fined.

The cabildo and Level de Goda were not awed. They attacked Smith where he threatened most. They refused to recognize Smith's depositario and named their own. They had the Spanish laws on their side; it turned out that this appointment was the cabildo's privilege.

It was a defeat. Like Hislop, Smith thought he needed a rest. He thought he would spend Christmas with friends in Grenada; he asked Hislop for permission to leave. Level said it was out of the question. Hislop, as viceroy, couldn't give a Royal Audience permission to leave his post; the King alone could do so. The cabildo's depositario also protested; he wanted a statement of all 'judicial deposits' before the Royal Audience left the colony. The cabildo itself claimed the right to address the King directly on the subject of Smith. Smith said he was going to write to London for permission to burn the cabildo hall to the ground. But he didn't write and he didn't go away for Christmas.

Level de Goda, the prize-winning law-student of the University of Caracas, whose services Smith had turned down, had won. He had been too quick and many-sided for Miguel Peña and Smith's other lawyers. Smith began to feel that Venezuelan hatred for Level which Miguel Peña and the revolutionaries on the Main felt. For them Level de Goda, clever and awkward, 'our never-to-be-forgotten advocate', once a friend, had been 'converted into a fury turned loose from hell to disturb us'. They put a price on his head; they wanted him expelled. Hislop paid no attention; he thought Level should be given land in Trinidad for his services and to make up for his estates in Venezuela that had been confiscated.

The local intrigue had taken up only part of Level's time. He had been more active planning a counter-revolution in Cumaná, and had gone over at least once to the Main. But he was watched in Trinidad by Miguel Peña and others. The plot was denounced; two of the conspirators in Cumaná were arrested. It was this, and other Venezuelan events, rather than the legal battle with Smith, that Level wrote about in his bitter, exaggerated memoirs forty years later.

One of the great dramas of the Venezuelan revolution was

preparing. And for Level, as for Peña and the other Venezuelans, the most important event in Trinidad in the latter half of that year, 1810, was the arrival in Port of Spain harbour of HMS *Sapphire* from England.

THERE WAS A young Venezuelan 'Deputy' on board. He had gone to England to get recognition and support for an independent Venezuela. All he had got was a private promise from Wellington's brother that England would not be hostile, and a British warship to bring him back. Hislop did not get on with the Deputy. The young man, short, sharp-featured, with a tincture of African or Indian blood, spoke too openly of his admiration for Napoleon.

It was the old revolutionary tactic, playing off one great power against another. But it worried Hislop, and he wrote to London, sending on the most recent news from Venezuela: the European Spaniards expelled from New Barcelona, anti-British feeling growing there because of Hislop's own equivocal attitude (he heard the British, himself included, described as 'deceitful politicians'), the people of colour beginning to make trouble, French muskets and sabres arriving, a United States ship unloading arms at La Guaira. It seemed like the beginning of a French takeover.

The Deputy had a request. Like Miranda four and a half years before, the Deputy was interested in Manuel Gual, the revolutionary who had died in Trinidad in 1800, and was now regarded as one of the martyrs of the Venezuelan revolution. Gual's death by poison during Picton's governorship had remained something of a Trinidad mystery. Miranda had got a copy of Gual's death certificate. The Deputy now wanted to take away Gual's bones from the St Joseph cemetery. Hislop refused. 'For the English,' Level de Goda wrote, like a man more experienced than most Venezuelans in English matters, 'this digging about among corpses and human bones is a very serious business.' But Level – the whole story is his – said he told Hislop to give permission. It was all a piece of Venezuelan fancifulness anyway: Level had it from the

Spanish curate of St Joseph, who had made out the death certificate for Miranda, that Gual wasn't buried where people thought. Gual had died impenitent and his corpse had been thrown into the Caroni swamp. What the Deputy dug up and took aboard the *Sapphire*, Level said, were the bones of a very small and much-loved horse that had belonged to an English doctor. It is a Venezuelan story, reopening a mystery. It is also Level's Venezuelan mockery, forty years later, of the revolution, one of its martyrs and the Deputy.

Unknown to Hislop, there was something else aboard the *Sapphire*: the baggage of Miranda, recalled by the young Deputy from the books, the children and the housekeeper in Grafton Street to a revolution which belonged to no one and was already beyond anyone's management. Miranda had committed himself to men half his age. He was now sixty, the age at which Antonio de Berrio, coming out to the Indies to retire, had committed himself to El Dorado and those 'men of the Indies'.

Miranda was coming out in another British warship. Level de Goda says that a British frigate signalled one day from the Dragon's Mouth, the Deputy signalled back from the Port of Spain pier and shortly afterwards left in the *Sapphire*. The detail is fanciful; but Miranda was bypassing Trinidad, where he had been succoured for a year, and Governor Hislop, who had dreamed of a noble liberation and of fine Spanish ladies. The young Deputy was Bonapartist, at least in talk; and Miranda was getting ready to land in the uniform of a French Revolutionary general of nearly twenty years before. It was like a turning back on the years in London, a weak, self-wounding gesture of revenge and opportunism. So that at the end, after a life of preparation, Miranda was unexpectedly South American and operatic.

The summons home was not, after all, a moment of fulfilment. The Venezuelans made Miranda wait. All the failure of the next twenty months could have been foretold: the local resentments, the colonial cutting-down-to-size; the high doctrine of borrowed constitutions disappearing in the simple factions of race, colour, region, the imperfectly constituted society decaying into minute egoisms; Miranda's own attempt at the leadership of the unacknowledged people of colour, the effort of a sinking man; the defeat of the revolution by a Spanish government army which was truly of the people, who, fearing terror, spread terror. And then Miranda's appalling discovery, at the end of his long political life, which was like Level de Goda's at the beginning of his, that the society was wrong, the cause was wrong, that the good words didn't fit. An appalling discovery – those agents of his who had given up the cause and suffered – but it must also have been like reconciliation, because Miranda had lived out this truth in his own life. Defeated but still free to act, he began to think of Spain in a new way. He began to think of partnership. Then he was betrayed.

In Port of Spain now, towards the end of November 1810, that drama was beginning. There, in the harbour, was the *Sapphire*. It would be at La Guaira on that day of Miranda's betrayal, waiting; it would have taken Miranda to safety if he hadn't decided to spend a last night on shore. There now, in Port of Spain, were two of the men who would betray Miranda after his defeat: two rebels who, to buy their own freedom, would wake Miranda at three in the morning and walk him to the dungeon of the Castle of San Carlos. One of these men was Miguel Peña, Smith's lawyer. The other was the twenty-seven-year-old Deputy. Hislop thought him Bonapartist, but didn't send his name to London. It was Bolívar.

WITH OR WITHOUT HIS bones, of horse or martyr, Bolívar sailed away in the *Sapphire* to his rendezvous with Miranda, leaving Andrés Level de Goda and Miguel Peña and their English seconds to fight out the revolution in Port of Spain and to play at the Spanish Empire. For all of them the comedy was nearly over.

Level, proud of the price on his head, was plotting a second counter-revolution in Cumaná. He was watched by Peña and shadowed by a clumsy, impoverished Trinidad Spaniard. People were going to be killed this time; but in the multi-national city it was a piece of private theatre. The Spaniards – and in Trinidad that meant Spanish-Americans or Spanish mulattoes – were heroes or villains only to themselves. In Port of Spain the Spaniards had for long been a depressed element. The French were richer, the English livelier; and with the revolution in Venezuela the Spaniards had begun to define themselves as an alien, ill-organized people of words, uniforms, plots and blood. But they were dangerous only to themselves.

The editor of the *Courant* was part-owner of the press of the *Gaceta de Caracas*. As a journalist who felt he had suffered in Trinidad, like his fellows in England, for the freedom of the press, he wrote of 'the emigration of the Goddess from the continent of Europe to the Empire of Spain in the Indies – by which millions of our fellow-creatures will be relieved from an oppressive government, and taken under her shield to enjoy the rights allotted them by Nature'. But these very principles, and his anxiety as a businessman, showed the Trinidad editor the distance between the Venezuelans and himself. Even Governor Hislop, once a romantic about Venezuela, discovered the pro-consul in himself. The Venezuelans were giving the French too much encouragement; a sufficient deterrent, Hislop thought, would be 'a naval force accompanied by a decided tone of language'.

Miguel Peña and his friends had picked up some of Bolívar's Bonapartist, anti-British talk; they had seen how such talk could draw blood. The conversation turned one day to the war news from Europe. Masséna, after the victories of the summer, had been stalled outside Wellington's prepared lines at Torres Vedras in Portugal. One of Peña's friends said in Spanish, 'The English are swine. Their soldiers are cowardly and contemptible. They don't dare come out to face the French. Britain will soon be conquered. Sooner or later Bonaparte will be emperor of all the world.'

Such talk from a Venezuelan was more than Hislop could bear. In his dispatch to London he sent the Spanish words, without a translation. But Peña and his associates couldn't be touched. They were under Smith's protection. Peña, as Smith's lawyer, might even be said to be a government official.

Smith's authority had been challenged, but his power continued. His Virginian depositario continued to manage disputed estates, 'to buy in cheap and sell dear'. Acting like a man who sensed that time was short, he had even begun to seize the property of people who were temporarily absent. Smith punished protest. Protest was what he expected; it proved, and extended, his chastising mission; and the more he chastised the more it seemed his labours would never be done.

There was Sanderson, for instance, an English barrister who claimed to have some knowledge of Spanish law. Sanderson was one of the leaders of the English immigrants; he was just the sort of man Smith liked putting down. Sanderson talked of laws and rights and a British constitution, but all this supported a simple plan for slavery. Wilberforce's brother-in-law, who was Smith's friend, had written an abolitionist pamphlet called *The Crisis of the Sugar Colonies*; Sanderson had replied with *Emancipation in Disguise, or the True Crisis of the Colonies*. As an example of creeping Negro privilege in Trinidad Sanderson told of the white boy whose evidence in a murder trial Smith had rejected. The white boy 'couldn't communicate to his Honour an *idea of God*'; but in another case Smith 'had taken, with great exactness, the testimony of an African child; who was younger than the said white boy; by whose examination it appeared he not only had no *idea of God* but that he had no knowledge of any religion whatever'.

Smith, investigating, discovered that Sanderson had taken fees from both sides in a lawsuit. Sanderson was suspended. The cabildo supported Sanderson; Level de Goda advised him. Founding himself on Spanish law, Sanderson challenged Smith's authority as a Royal Audience in a letter to the *Courant*. 'I set the authority he has usurped at defiance and express my contempt of him as an unjust and dishonourable man.' Smith issued a warrant for the sequestration of Sanderson's property and 'the committal of his person to the common jail'. Level de Goda said that Sanderson, as a lawyer, couldn't be sent to the common jail 'with Negroes and malefactors'. Sanderson, as a gentleman, should take poison first. It was Venezuelan advice; Sanderson preferred to make a noisy objection.

He didn't go to jail. Instead, he was marched out of the city by the new Deputy Alguazil-Mayor and led up to the hill fort that Hislop had built six years before. He spent the night in a bare room; and the next day, 'through a torrent of rain to the great danger of his life under the sufferings of a liver complaint', he was marched down again, five miles in all, to Smith's court.

Smith had the court cleared and the doors closed. He was casually dressed in a white jacket and pantaloons and wasn't sitting on the bench. He asked Sanderson to take the oath. Sanderson wanted to know in what court he was, who the parties were, and the witnesses. Smith didn't reply. He ordered Sanderson to be taken back to the fort, 'under the same conditions of privation', as Sanderson wrote later that day to Hislop, 'as hereinbefore stated. All three journeys of five miles each have been performed under the midday heat, alternated with showers. Yet no means of conveyance were provided so that the said John Sanderson must have climbed the mountain on foot at the risk of life if he had not been allowed to use the horse of a friend.'

It was felt after this that Smith had gone completely mad and had to be handled as a 'runaway' (a local word: a runaway Negro was considered unnatural and dangerous). The matter was urgent. Hislop had at last been granted his leave and there were people who felt that without Hislop's protection 'it would be preferable to be banished' and leave 'the naked land' to Smith.

But Level had an idea. He had already asserted the ancient Castilian dignity of the cabildo. Now he thought that Smith's commission itself, though granted by the King of England, might under Spanish law be rejected by the cabildo, acting as protectors of the people. Hislop agreed, and events in Trinidad were manipulated into a further and more confused Venezuelan mimicry, in which the Venezuelan lawyers reversed their real-life roles. Peña, the revolutionary, was supporting the autocratic power of Smith. Level, the anti-revolutionary, began secretly to prepare the legal case for a provincial rebellion. It was fantasy and nonsense. But everyone, Venezuelan lawyers and British officials, now as principals, now as seconds, played solemnly.

Level wished, as before, to attack swiftly and on many fronts. He had seen that Smith didn't know much about the Spanish laws, and he wished first of all to strip Smith of his legal advisors. Miguel Peña and two of his friends were accused of sedition and forgery and at once, without a hearing, were ordered to leave the island.

Smith asked for explanations. Hislop gave none and refused to see Smith. Miguel Peña wrote a long letter of protest to Hislop. He had come to Trinidad by invitation; he had given up a distinguished post in Caracas. His conscience was clear; he wanted proofs of the charges made against him. An unknown person could be ordered about in this way, an adventurer, a boy, a launch-captain, a drunk, an idler; 'but not a Spanish-American gentleman'. 'In my country an English gentleman would not be treated with such disdain.' It didn't help; abuse of Level didn't help; the expulsion order stood.

Then Hislop ordered the release of Sanderson from his fort-prison. Three days later, while Smith was still objecting to Sanderson's release, the big blow fell. The cabildo laid a resolution before Hislop. Smith's powers, the resolution said, were contradictory and against the Spanish law and Smith ought to be suspended. Level had prepared the ten-point legal case for suspension some weeks before. Smith, stripped now of his lawyers, looked up his Spanish law-books and said that his commission could be challenged only if it was likely to cause 'notorious scandal or irreparable evil'. Level added those words – in Spanish – to the resolution of the cabildo. Smith suspended Level de Goda from practising as an advocate. He threatened to pursue Hislop 'through every court . . . in our common country'.

But he recognized the coup. He asked for a pass to go to England. Hislop said they had been through that before. Only the King could give a Royal Audience permission to leave his post, and then only after Smith had submitted to the usual residencia or investigation of his official conduct.

All that was open to Smith now, as to every deposed imperial official on the Main, was flight. The young Virginian who was Smith's depositario arranged it. One afternoon they rode north through the hills to the Prospect Estate. Next morning at five the two men, disguised as sailors, went aboard a brig and sailed to Grenada. There Smith, before transferring to a ship bound for England, made out a power of attorney to the depositario. The depositario returned to Port of Spain, where already in the Council it had been 'moved, seconded and resolved that the said George Smith had vacated his seat on the board, as well as all offices he held in the colony'. The coup was complete.

IN TRINIDAD it had been a mimic rebellion. Across the Gulf, in Venezuela, the rebellion was real. The day Miguel Peña was expelled from Port of Spain the pro-Spanish counter-insurrection Level and others had been plotting broke out in Cumaná. It didn't last long. The castle that had been seized was recaptured; more refugees came to Trinidad; and there were requests from Cumaná for the handing-over of 'our antagonists the European Spaniards . . . monsters of ingratitude'. It was the South American style now, the Venezuelan see-saw.

Miguel Peña, so negligible as 'a Spanish-American gentleman' in Port of Spain, was soon active in Caracas, an associate of Miranda's and Bolívar's. It was Miguel Peña who, with some contemptuous words about England, presented the motion for independence to the Venezuelan Congress. Loose paragraphs of high-flown thoughts, Level de Goda said, 'simplicities, hyperboles, exaggerations and poetic flights'. A summary of the declaration was printed in three languages in Caracas by the new English firm of Gallagher and Lamb (Gallagher was the editor of the *Trinidad Weekly Courant*); and a copy was sent to the Trinidad government. Everybody was to be free, but everybody had to be Roman Catholic. The importation of Negroes was forbidden, but those immigrants who already had Negroes could bring them in.

The chaos of thought, the chaos of deed: days later the mass arrests and executions of European Spaniards began. There was much grief among the English merchants in Port of Spain. Many of the people executed owed them money. The Spanish Empire had been broken, and its restrictive trade laws were no longer important; but the English dream of Port of Spain as the emporium for South America began to die.

In was the beginning of a year of blood in Venezuela, of communal terror and counter-terror. A colonial order was collapsing; everyone was insecure; and everyone – Indians, European Spaniards, mulattoes, priests, the marquises of cacao and tobacco – looked to defend himself against the potential enemy.

Governor Hislop, who had dreamt of service with Miranda and a noble war of liberation, was spared that year. Someone had been sent temporarily to relieve him, and at last, in April 1811, after nearly eight years in Trinidad, Hislop was free to leave. He got to England at the end of June. A summer in England was what he had been looking forward to for years, but he landed to trouble. Hislop's own little insurrection – his deposing of Smith, his rejection of the King's authority – had made Lord Liverpool, the Colonial Secretary, very angry.

Smith was in England, and so was Sanderson; both men were getting ready to continue their quarrel in the English courts. And now in Port of Spain it was Level de Goda, so recently victorious, so recently riding to and from Government House in his own calash, who was in limbo, a peripheral Venezuelan, without a country or a job. His patrons and his enemies had been suddenly scattered, as if by his legal skill; and he was alone. It was the fate of the exile who had merged his own cause in the causes of others. Level's interpretation of his situation was more fantastic. He saw, for instance, that Smith didn't return; he thought this was so because Lord Castlereagh in London 'had grown ashamed'.

Fantasy: from a Spanish imperial government that had almost ceased to exist Level began to claim some reward for his services to the British government of Trinidad. The reward came. Level was made governor and treasurer of the Venezuelan provinces of Cumaná, Barcelona and Margarita. All these provinces were in rebel hands. Level went to Puerto Rico. There was nothing for him to do there. He went on to Spain, 'in search of useful knowledge', but really to see whether he couldn't get a more realistic job with the Spanish government.

He found the government hanging on to Cadiz, overcrowded, under French bombardment, the rest of the country occupied by the French army. Spain itself had become only an idea; but it excited Level to be close for the first time to the great world and great events, to be in a country that could support classical allusion, a country that could be said to be like Greece at the time of the invasion by Xerxes, to be in the presence of the army that had made the names of Austerlitz, Jena and Marengo famous. As a Spanish-American, Level was privileged; he had access to all sides, French, Spanish, English. For the whole of that year, 1812, he remained in Spain.

In the Venezuela of Miranda's fantasy there were few Negroes. But now, manoeuvring through the factions of Venezuela, Miranda appeared more and more as a leader of coloured revolt. He alarmed many. Coin was scarce; people distrusted the new paper money. In March there was an earthquake in Caracas, and to some Venezuelans it was a sign of God's disapproval of the revolution. But events had already begun to turn against Miranda. A Spanish government force of just over two hundred men, led by a naval officer, had landed three months before; people of all colours were rallying to this force; and this wild army of the people, worked on by fear and the prospect of loot, was beginning to have its successes.

Spain itself was being liberated. Wellington was on the offensive. In April Picton, at the head of his division, stormed the castle at Badajoz and submitted the liberated Spanish inhabitants to a night of terror. It was the most famous sacking of the war. It was also Picton's most famous battle, 'an example of science and bravery', Lord Liverpool said a few days later in the House of Commons, 'which have been surpassed by no other officer'. The glory had come at last. Picton was fifty-three. His career as a fighting soldier had begun just two years before.

Level de Goda went to see Picton not long after Badajoz. They had met in Trinidad ten years before. Level may have wanted to talk to Picton about a job; but Level's story is that Picton sent for him after the great battle to find out how things were going on the Picton estates in Trinidad.

In London Sanderson's fight with Smith had reached the court of King's Bench. Lord Ellenborough was there, and some of the lawyers who had appeared in the Picton trials and the subsequent libel cases; they were getting to know the affairs of Trinidad well. Sanderson said he had been deprived of his livelihood and character; he wanted some compensation. Smith, wishing only to be obstructive, asked for a postponement; he said he wanted Level de Goda and Miguel Peña and other Caracas lawyers to be examined. The court offered to send someone to examine Spanish lawyers in Cadiz. Smith said it wouldn't do. 'We very well know,' the Attorney-General said, 'that the province of Venezuela and the city of Caracas are in a state of insurrection, and you may as well send us to the moon.' Lord Ellenborough became impatient. But Smith got his postponement.

Two months later the insurrection in Venezuela was over. Miranda, defeated, handed over to the enemy by Bolivar and Miguel Peña, was a prisoner in La Guaira. Day by day the republican prisoners came into the jail, some to be tortured, some to be tied up and beaten, some to be burnt, some to have their ears cut off. And Trinidad received more Venezuelan refugees.

The Spanish Empire appeared to have been re-established in Venezuela, and Level de Goda got ready to return home. It was time. The romance of the great world and great events had begun to fade. Level was in Madrid when the French, retreating before Wellington's advance, re-entered the city in the autumn. Level, not anxious, he said, to witness Wellington's 'reaction', had got out of Madrid at once and had raced day and night to Seville, not even stopping for food.

At the end of the year Level left Spain for Puerto Rico. When he got there he found that the situation in Venezuela had changed again. The Venezuelan see-saw: the Spanish naval officer who appeared to have re-imposed the authority of Spain had only established a personal tyranny, terror for the sake of terror. There were calls for rescue and revenge. And there had been a successful republican reinvasion of the eastern plains, from Port of Spain, by ninety-four men with five muskets between them, a barrel of powder and no cannon. It was the smaller, South American scale.

IT WAS the pattern now: small endeavour, great consequences. The republican leader was Santiago Mariño. He had estates in Guiria in Venezuela and in Trinidad; for a time Picton had confiscated his Trinidad estates. Santiago's widowed sister, who among other things ran a shop in Port of Spain, also helped. All the Spaniards in Port of Spain were in on the scheme. They talked and quarrelled about it, occasionally with threats of shooting, in the Spanish retail shops and grog-shops.

The men for the first two canoes assembled in Mr Marcos's shop. There was a scene on the wharf when one of the Venezuelan organizers challenged all the European Spaniards present to a duel with pistols. The Venezuelan said the invaders were going to cut off the head of every European Spaniard in Venezuela. He told a sympathetic American that the invasion had to come from Trinidad, because the Venezuelans themselves were 'imbeciles and cowards'. And, indeed, most of the people in the canoes were French people of colour. Some were wearing the red jackets of the Loyal Militia. There was one British man of colour, 'who used to beat the big drum' in Captain Parke's company. There were also some free Negroes, among them a man called Joe-Joe who had a Sea Fencible sabre and said, inconsequentially, that 'if he had his will he would cut every Englishman's head off'.

Negroes rowed the canoes down to Santiago's estate on the islet of Chacachacare. There, before the nine-hour crossing to Guiria, Santiago killed a white bullock and shared the meat out to his soldiers. A white man called Jim killed a goat. At six, when it was dark, they sailed in a schooner and a canoe. Most of the men were armed with a cutlass and nothing else. All of them had been paid ten dollars. It was said that the money came from a refugee Venezuelan marquis in Port of Spain; he had promised Santiago 5,000 dollars for every town he captured.

Martial law was declared the next day in Port of Spain, and a militia court of inquiry set up. But more canoes left Port of Spain openly at eight that evening. The leader strode about the wharf with a sword. The recruiting and arms-gathering continued. Susini, a Corsican, boasted to his friends in the square that he 'was about to purchase some of the King's arms from which he would make a good speculation by selling them to the republicans'. Susini bought thirty old muskets without bayonets, at five dollars apiece, from Harry the German.

Harry the German was the alguazil at Government House. Harry had his friends in the German corps. Susini sent three of his Negroes to Harry's yard in Duke Street to collect the muskets. Later Susini looked in at Santiago's sister's shop to ask whether anybody wanted thirty muskets. When the matter was inquired into a few days later Susini said he hadn't bought any muskets; he had just had a glass of grog with Harry the German. But Harry said Susini was the man the muskets had gone to. And Harry, defending himself, said that only two of the muskets were any good. He had 'bought them to mend others'; some of them didn't even have ramrods.

The advance given to a recruit was four dollars. The remaining six dollars were to be handed over in the canoes. Some coloured men had taken the four dollars without intending to go. They didn't fool Pantaleon. Pantaleon was a private in the Sea Fencibles. He had a pistol and, before the third set of canoes left Port of Spain, Pantaleon went round the mulatto yards frightening people. It was the canoes, or the four dollars back. Francisco and his brother gave the four dollars back, and Scilly, the bass-drummer in the Loyal Militia.

It was a moonlight night. Christian Ulsen, a German bombardier in the Royal Artillery, was strolling through the town. He went past the Spanish church and walked down the Rue des Trois Chandelles to the sea. Seven or eight men were sitting on the shore. One of them beckoned to him. Ulsen went up. A young man in a dark jacket, 'dressed like a gentleman', spoke to him. The man pointed to a canoe on the beach. There were a number of people in the canoe. The man said he would give Ulsen four dollars if Ulsen got into the canoe. Then he would give him eight more.

The money was good. Hard cash was the scarcest thing in Trinidad, but Ulsen wasn't sure; he wanted a little time to think it over. Ulsen had some mulatto friends; he went to their yard. They said they had all taken the four dollars; the man in the dark jacket was organizing recruits for the Venezuelan invasion; he was the man who two days before had challenged all the European Spaniards on the wharf. Ulsen went back to the barracks and talked to Blackett, 'the artilleryman who writes in the Brigade Office'. Blackett said Ulsen should tell the governor. Ulsen didn't go to Venezuela. He was lucky; Santiago Mariño didn't allow any of the people who went over to come back.

Don Francisco Rocatalada lived near the Spanish church. He

heard the commotion in the empty lot next to his house and went to his friend Ardila, the escribano, and said, 'Come and see what they are making of this martial law.'

Twenty men were talking together in the moonlight. Pantaleon, the private in the Sea Fencibles, seemed to be in command. He had his pistol. He was saying, and the others were arguing about it, that the ten dollars he had given them had to be earned. But he got them into the canoes at last.

'Let us go and earn the money,' he said. As the canoes moved off he fired his pistol in the air.

'OF VERY contemptible origin,' the acting governor reported a few days later to London, describing the invasion, 'and confined to a few vagabonds.' He had the facts. The militia court was inquiring into events even before they were completed. It was like journalism. Witnesses were seized as they rowed back from Venezuela. And the unlikely story that came out was one of instant victory: the landing at Santiago's Guiria estates at three in the morning, the half-hour march to the town, the 'nine cutlass chops' for the resisting contador or treasurer of Guiria (but he lived), the capture of the town.

It was in the militia court in Port of Spain, days after the event, that Santiago Mariño's first dispatches, exclamatory but laconic, 'written in the style of Bonaparte', were made public, in literal translations.

'Robbins! I am at Guiria with universal applause.'

'Paul! On the 13th at three in the morning we entered Guiria, on the 14th Punta de Piedra and on the 15th Yrapo with general rejoicing. To the point: the other towns invite us, but we want 100 Frenchmen more and some arms. Our hopes are on thee, that thou wilt drain every channel to send us them. Quickly, quickly, quickly, and thou shalt be in the end rewarded. Mariño. 16th January, 1st Year of Columbian Independence.'

'Vaneschi! Come and serve us as an officer in my troops, which are marching on Cumaná. And bring Courman.'

'Valdez! If thou hast a wish that we should be in Cumaná within 15 days come with 100 French and some arms.'

'Lordat! Already we have established Independence in this town. It is indispensably necessary you should send us some people. Dispatch! Dispatch!'

So that at last, after the humiliations and the banishments, the French people of colour, nervous, aggressive, cruel, had proved themselves. They had been set adrift by the French Revolution, which had promised so much. Now, after twenty years, their republican hour had come, though in a cause not their own. Most were in time to be killed; no Venezuelan victory was lasting. The reinvasion was an episode in the Venezuelan war, as was the arrival in Port of Spain some months later of an aggrieved emissary from the authorities in Caracas, requesting the mediation of the British governor.

The man from Caracas complained that the republicans were encouraging French-style ideas of equality among Negroes, mulattoes and others, and even encouraging British-owned Negroes to run away from Trinidad. The republicans, looking now for respectability and anxious to treat on equal terms with the British government in Trinidad, rejected the charge. They were not encouraging Negroes to run away from Trinidad; all Negroes who were caught would be kept at the disposal of their lawful proprietors.

The Venezuelan confusion was now complete. The imperfectly made society had disintegrated; it was too simple for lasting causes. The only cause was the self and survival: the tragedy of the simple, contained in the Port of Spain scene of fourteen years before, when Manuel de España, not yet twenty-one, was converted from his loyalty to his mother, his religion and the Empire by the promise of a general's uniform and the command of a frigate. 'After forty-one years,' Level de Goda wrote in 1851, 'this Venezuelan revolution has not ended.'

FROM THIS revolution, and from all action, Miranda was now released by his betrayal. He had been taken from Venezuela to the prison in Puerto Rico. It was there that Level de Goda met him in 1813. They were no longer enemies; they thought alike now about Spain and Venezuela. Level saw Miranda as 'a walking library' and was enchanted with his talk. Miranda, though still anxious for newspapers, had reduced the world once more to ideas; he was at peace. Level was awed by the physical presence of the old man. He studied details in order to remember them: Miranda squeezing half a lemon into an enormous cup of tea, making it into a 'lemonade', nibbling at the lemon hull while drinking his tea, so that both tea and lemon were finished at the same time.

Prison was perhaps the setting that Miranda, like Ralegh, subconsciously required. It dramatized inaction, failure and the condition of exile. He thought about London and the house in Grafton Street; he wanted money to be sent somehow to Sarah and the children. For Venezuela and South America he saw only chaos and foreign domination now. Not foreign rule, he told Level de Goda: the inhabitants would have the freedom, and the obligation, to 'keep the estate productive'. When he heard that he was going to be removed from the Indies and sent to Europe, to a prison in Cadiz, he said, 'Thank God,' and embraced the Captain-General of Puerto Rico who had brought the news.

For two and a half years, until his death in 1816, Miranda stayed in the prison at Cadiz. There was war in Venezuela: the revolution defeated again. There was war in Europe: Lieutenant-General Sir Thomas Picton dying gloriously at Waterloo at the age of fifty-six: the Quatre Bras wound concealed for two days, the anger at Wellington's order to withdraw, death coming a moment after his own order to his 5th division: 'Charge! Hurrah! Hurrah!' Miranda, in his prison, fussed to the end about his 'papers'.

IN TRINIDAD there was order; the British Empire was settling in. All the recent factions had been scattered; they had all lost; London had asserted itself. Smith was judged right in his war with the cabildo; he was to be reinstated, but he didn't go back to Trinidad; and then he was judged wrong. The cabildo, assuming Castilian privileges, challenging the Sovereign, was judged not only wrong but presumptuous and contemptible. The new governor, who was only twenty-eight, but of good family, reported that the members of the cabildo were ignorant of the laws they were supposed to administer; they paid little attention to their duty; their Treasury was 'in the worst repute'. They were all dismissed. The only person handled with respect was the young Virginian gentleman, William Hardin Burnley, who had made a fortune as Smith's depositario. He now owned so much of the accessible area of the colony that he couldn't be ignored; he owned so much that he had to be responsible and on the side of authority.

Authority was represented by the young governor. He had all the powers of a British governor and a Spanish governor. To administer the Spanish law, he had been invested by London with all the powers of the court of Royal Audience in Caracas, so that he was at one and the same time Dean, Oidor, Fiscal, Escribano, Relator. He was also Intendant of the Royal Domain and corregidor of the cabildo. He had yet another inherited function. He was Royal Vice-Patron of the Holy Roman Catholic Church. The young governor took this duty seriously; it was a subject some years later of an English petition.

'On a complaint being made to him by a Spanish priest that two gentlemen had neglected to take off their hats while he was passing by with the Holy Oils, in order to administer them to a sick person, Sir Ralph Woodford ordered them, though persons of most respectable families, to be put in jail, to do public penance in the church and then to be sent off the island.'

On solemn occasions Sir Ralph arrived at Government House in a carriage drawn by four horses, with outriders and mounted aides-de-camp. He inspected a guard of honour; in the Council Room he and members of the Illustrious Cabildo put on their Spanish robes. Then, on foot, between soldiers presenting arms, Sir Ralph, with his wand of office as Perpetual Regidor of the Illustrious Cabildo, led the procession to the Spanish church. There Sir Ralph was met by the priests and taken to his special chair. At a fixed time the Host was elevated. Outside, the soldiers presented arms; and the battery on the mole fired a salute of twenty-one arms.

Sir Ralph was not a Roman Catholic; in England Catholic Emancipation was some years away. The title he had inherited and honoured, of Royal Vice-Patron of the Holy Roman Catholic Church, derived from that granted in 1508 by Pope Julius to Ferdinand and Isabella, sovereigns of Aragon and Castile, for expelling the Moors from Spain and planting the Cross in America.

In 1508 Mexico had not been discovered; no Spaniard had come slave-raiding to Trinidad; the pearl fisheries of Margarita had not been established. The Gulf of Paria was busy with Indian canoes; coconut, sugar-cane and mango had not replaced the mangrove and high woods of Trinidad. In the altered, depopulated land much of what had intervened had been forgotten; the records of real people and real action had been lost in the paper in Simancas. The search for El Dorado, just two hundred years old, the dream of rediscovering the New World, had become myth; it was like going back to the beginning of the world. The oldest Spanish families in Port of Spain told of an early conquistador, Josef de Oruña, who had founded a city, had been defeated by Indians, and had been succeeded by someone called Antonio de Barrero. Both names had been lost: Berrio's, and the family name, Oruña, of the wife he wished to honour.

On both sides of the Gulf the Spanish Empire, after three hundred years, had inheritors.

EPILOGUE

The Death of Jacquet

ONCE AGAIN, as after the search for El Dorado, Port of Spain dropped out of history. What follows for a hundred and fifty years are the annals of a remote municipality. Port of Spain was not to be the great British trading post for an independent South America. That revolution had gone wrong. At the same time the 18th-century British empire of the sugar islands in the west and the slave plantations was closing down. The Empire was shifting east, to the diseased, rich and waiting lands of Asia. It gave a new chance to men who might otherwise have considered their careers over; it was part of the English luck, the reward for having in so many ways outstripped the rest of the world.

A disgraced Spanish official was now usually finished; an English official could always get another chance. It was in Ceylon that Smith got another high post; but he committed suicide. It was in India that Hislop, when he was over fifty, found himself, won a baronetcy and made his fortune, as commander of the Deccan army. But trouble followed him. His massacre of the three hundred men of the garrison at Talner and his hanging of the Mahratta governor excited some criticism – he was not mentioned in the vote of thanks in the House of Commons – and the dispute about the Talner booty reached the Privy Council. Hislop lost the case. Wellington said his only satisfaction was that if the money had gone to Hislop 'it would have vanished into Mexican bonds or Columbian securities like the rest of Hislop's fortune'.

In the west the abolition of the slave trade in 1807 and the abolition of slavery in 1834 – London decisions, London victories – were stages in the running-down and dereliction of the sugar islands. Admiral Cochrane, having liberated a hundred and seven Negroes from a slave-ship, thought that they might, in return for clothes and food, work on his Trinidad estates as 'apprentices' for fourteen years; he also thought that the government might give him more land to occupy his expanded labour-force. But for other immigrants there were fewer opportunities. The fees of the Trinidad surveyor-general fell; his fees depended on the surveying of grants of land, and these grants depended on the continuing importation of Negroes. For the ambitious and gifted, for merchants with money to lend, for lawyers and journalists who saw themselves engaged in high causes, there was no longer a future in Trinidad. The island was going to be no more than what it was, an outpost, a backwater. As a British colony Trinidad was as much an error and a failure as it had been as part of the Spanish Empire, 'these provinces of El Dorado'. And again, separate from the life of the Empire elsewhere, the imperial cycle was speeded up: a special virtue and vigour swiftly followed by the special decay which they contained.

In the Spanish–French–African city of planters, launch-captains, soldiers, slaves, whores, keepers of grog-shops and retail shops selling salt, tobacco and dried meat for peons, the early English immigrants had been new and startling. They were too grand for the setting: they looked absurd, ignorant and gullible. They were distinguished not only by their wealth and commercial adventurousness (sometimes folly), their clothes, the ritual of their English-style meals and the other emblems of a finer domestic self-cherishing, but also by their intellectual liveliness. They dominated naturally. This liveliness – the threats of letters to London lawyers and newspapers, the affirmation of rights and freedoms – was a carry-over from the metropolis. In the slave society, where self-fulfilment came so easily, this liveliness began to be perverted and then to fade, and the English saw their pre-eminence, more simply, as a type of racial magic. The shifting of the Empire to the east, the emigration of the ambitious, was a further intellectual depletion. The English in Trinidad became like the French. The quality of controversy declined, and the stature of men. What was left was a colony.

In 1807 one of the objections from Trinidad to the abolition of the British slave trade was that it was unfair to the Africans, who would now not only be denied civilizing contacts but would also be transported in cruel conditions in foreign ships. The argument, with its remote reference to several ideals, is recognizably English. The objection in 1823 to the regulation forbidding the whipping of Negro women is different.* The regulation, it was said, was a means of ruining white families, who were already sufficiently hard-pressed. Negro women were notoriously insolent; the regulation would encourage them to provoke their owners; a story was told of a very old and devout French couple who, obscenely provoked at table one day, had reacted with the whip and had found themselves ruined by a fine. The objection comes from people who have accepted the values of the new society, who have ceased to assess themselves by the standards of the metropolis and now measure their eminence only by their distance, economic and racial, from their Negroes.

The eminence was accepted by both sides; the colony was shaped for the century. In the beginning, in the time of intellectual liveliness, people like Fullarton, Hislop and Smith, expecting more of themselves and the world, felt in their various ways that the colony was incomplete and wrong. With intellectual decay this dissatisfaction disappeared. Such officials would not come that way again. There would be no visiting writer like McCallum, coming to Port of Spain as to an extension of the metropolis.

In 1900 Port of Spain, off the main shipping routes of the Empire, would be more remote than it had been in 1800. The 19th-century writers who came, Trollope, Kingsley, Froude, came as tourists from a leading industrial country to an imperial outpost,

* *See* note, page 363.

heroically manned. Imperial history, honouring Picton, suppressing Fullarton, had already become selective and anachronistic. Trollope was worried about the labour shortage; Kingsley wrote about the vegetation and with tenderness about the people; Froude wrote anxiously about race and the Empire. None questioned the lesser life of the agricultural colony, which made nothing, imported everything, where it had begun to be felt that education was an irrelevance, something for the ambitious poor, that the rich, the white or the secure needed only to be able to read and count.

All three writers were concerned to 'keep the estate productive'. To keep the estate productive, contract labour – some Chinese, some Portuguese, but mainly Indians from the ancient, distressed Indo-Gangetic plain – replaced the Negroes on the estates. It was a new human dereliction, in the pattern of what had gone before. The Indians were people to whom authority had always been remote; they had little sense of history, were governed and protected by rituals which were like privacy; and in the Trinidad countryside they created a simple, rural India. They were an aspect of the colony. The colony became an imperial amalgam, the Empire in little.

It was romantic; it was undiscovered; it awaited tourists. The early 20th-century tourists from England didn't come for the sun or the beaches. They came to the Caribbean for the history, to be in the waters where the great naval battles of the 18th century had been won. Suddenly, after the First World War, these victories seemed far away. The tourists who came then were mainly from the United States. They came for the voodoo, the Negro dances and cynical Negro songs, the bands at carnival time: the underground Negro life the slave-owner had tried to suppress. The past was many-sided and ambiguous. Who did it belong to?

TODAY I AM a stranger in the city myself. Port of Spain is bigger, brighter, noisier and better-educated than it was when I was at school there, between 1939 and 1948. Then, in spite of the war and the United States base, it felt like a place at the rim of the world. Venezuela, of which the island had once formed part, was just across the Gulf and could be seen on some days. But Venezuela was a fact in a geography book. The Spanish language had died in Trinidad; there was no trace of the Spanish Empire. British Guiana was closer; and it seemed absurd when a Venezuelan newspaper ran a front-page headline: ENGLAND, GIVE US BACK TRINIDAD AND GUIANA OR WE WILL TAKE THEM BY FORCE.

Venezuela was being transformed by its oil wealth. (In 1851, just before he died, Level de Goda was still lamenting that the Spanish government hadn't emigrated from Cadiz to Venezuela during the French war. With those 'savants, rich men, millionaire merchants, great agriculturists, statesmen and first-class craftsmen . . . civilization would have penetrated everywhere in these forty-one years. Even fevers would have been banished; even snakes and tigers would have disappeared, even mosquitoes; and we would have had nothing but wisdom, wealth and well-being in the Garden of Eden.') But in Port of Spain Venezuela was still a faraway country of dictators, an army, sadism, overnight revolutions and refugees who, when they appeared in the Port of Spain streets, were mulatto and curiously ordinary.

Port of Spain was a place where things had happened and nothing showed. Only people remained, and their past had dropped out of all the history books. Picton was the name of a street; no one knew more. History was a fairy-tale about Columbus and a fairytale about the strange customs of the aboriginal Caribs and Arawaks; it was impossible now to set them in the landscape. History was the Trinidad five-cent stamp: Ralegh discovering the Pitch Lake. History was also a fairytale not so much about slavery as about its abolition, the good defeating the bad. It was the only way the tale could be told. Any other version would have ended in ambiguity and alarm. The slave was never real. Like the extinct aboriginal, he had to be reconstructed from his daily routine. So he remains, existing, like Vallot's jail (of which no plan survives), only in the imagination. In the records the slave is faceless, silent, with an identification rather than a name. He has no story.

THERE IS AN exception. Jacquet, the *commandeur* or headman of the Bel-Air sugar estate, has a story. Bel-Air was owned by Dominique Dert. Dert was one of the earliest French settlers; a street in central Port of Spain preserves his name and indicates the site of his estate. In January 1806, when Governor Hislop was collecting evidence about Negro-poisonings, Dert told the story of Jacquet. Dert was a man of some education. He lived close to his Negroes, but he spoke as a planter who had suffered. In twenty-two years he had lost a hundred and twenty-five Negroes, children and grown-ups, mostly from poison.

In September 1803 Mme Dert's chamber-slave gave birth to a boy. The father was probably Dert himself; the baby became the pet of the whole estate. The baby was almost a year old when he was convulsed one morning as he lay in his basket outside his mother's hut. His stomach swelled; he died grotesquely. Everyone was upset; everyone recognized poison. Eight of Dert's Negroes had died from poison that month; many more had been made seriously ill. In the general mourning for the baby Dert called his Negroes together, his whole *atelier*, and told them they should try to find out who the poisoner was.

All the Negroes went to the baby's funeral. Only Jacquet, the *commandeur*, didn't go. He was too distressed. He was sixty-six, very old for a Negro; the estate was his life and he had grown to love Dert and Dert's family.

The next day Dert was told by one of his household Negroes that he would have to find a new *commandeur*: Jacquet had gone mad. Dert had Jacquet taken to the estate hospital, the *cep*; and there for a week Jacquet wept and shrieked night and day and especially at night. Then he became calm. He asked for the estate Negroes to be assembled. He told Dert he wanted to talk to some of them; he gave names.

In Dert's presence, then, Jacquet walked among the Negroes, stopping to talk to the eight or ten he had named.

'Do you remember,' Jacquet said (the dialogue, French in the original, is Dert's), 'that once I made you eat some rice and meat and drink some rum? And you vomited up blood and were put in the hospital?'

The Negroes remembered.

'You see, monsieur,' Jacquet said to Dert, 'I didn't lie to you.' And Jacquet had another confession. 'I wanted to poison you and your whole family. You know that as *commandeur* it was I who had your water-jug filled every morning. Three times I thought of putting in enough arsenic. But something always held me back, a sort of fear.' But he would have carried out his plan in the end. 'I would have ruined you. All these Negroes of yours here would have been dead. All your family would have been dead.' But then he had poisoned the baby. He hadn't known that the grief would be so great, that he himself would grieve so much. The death of the baby was his 'misfortune'.

Dert was more astonished and hurt than angry. He said he thought he had always been a good master to Jacquet.

That was the reason: Jacquet in his old age had grown jealous.

'You were *commandeur*,' Dert said. 'You managed these Negroes. Why didn't you poison many more of them?'

It wasn't for want of trying, Jacquet said. He kept offering them things to eat, but they didn't always accept.

The Negroes said this was so. Jacquet had been too pressing, too clumsy; they had known for some time that the estate *commandeur* was the estate poisoner.

The Negroes wanted Jacquet thrown into the furnace of the sugar-factory. Dert said no; he didn't feel he could punish the old man.

Jacquet insisted. He said he deserved to die. But he didn't want to be burnt. 'Give me a rope, and I will hang myself.'

Dert became curious. He had a rope and bracket brought.

Jacquet tied one end of the rope to the bracket. He fitted the noose around his neck. Then his courage failed.

Some days later Dert mustered the *atelier* again and asked Jacquet about the poisoning of the baby. Jacquet said he had noticed that the baby – so petted – was left alone in his basket at a certain time. He filled a snuff-box with arsenic. He kept it in his trouser-pocket and waited for his chance. When the time came he had had to act very quickly; he had given the baby far too much arsenic. He had bought two lots of arsenic from a man in Port of Spain; he had even sold a little to his friends; he knew poisoners on other estates.

Dert asked for the rest of the arsenic. Jacquet said he had thrown it into the furnace after the baby had died.

A few days later Jacquet was found dead. He had been poisoned. It was never known whether he had poisoned himself.

September 1966–November 1968
Revised, January 1973

Postscript

This narrative was structured mainly from documents – originals, copies, printed – in the British Museum, the Public Record Office, London, and the London Library. Most of the translations are my own. Dialogue occurs as dialogue in the sources.

ONE: THE THIRD MARQUISATE

THE VENEZUELAN BOUNDARY ARBITRATION PAPERS IN THE BRITISH MUSEUM.

These are the Spanish records of the region. They begin in 1530 – with a licence to a minor, slave-trading official from Puerto Rico to settle Trinidad and evangelize the natives, 'who eat human flesh, as is public and notorious' – and end with the disappearance of the Spanish Empire. The records were recovered by the British Foreign Office from the Archive of the Indies in Seville and assembled in 1897, at the time of the British Guiana–Venezuela border dispute; it was a formidable piece of research. The dispute, now inherited by the independent state of Guyana, can be traced back to the unrealized claims of conquistadores looking for El Dorado. There are Foreign Office translations of selected documents. I have occasionally leaned on them, especially welcoming 'Judge of All Irregularities' for *juez del derrotamiento.* I have made use of Ralegh's translations of the captured dispatches about Vera's 'discovery' of El Dorado. Ralegh's words are also used for parts of Albujar's story.

The Voyage of Robert Dudley to the West Indies, 1594–95. Edited by G. F. Warner, Hakluyt Society, London, 1899.

English Privateering Voyages 1588–95. Edited by Kenneth R. Adams. Hakluyt Society, London, 1959. For Abraham Kendall's previous 'villainy' at 'Trinidatho'.

Hakluyt's Voyages, Vol. 7. Everyman Library.

Historia de la Nueva Andalucia. By Fray Antonio Caulin, Madrid, 1779. Caulin deals with Ralegh's 1595 raid by leaving it out.

The Discovery of Guiana. Edited by V. T. Harlow, London, 1928. Ralegh's *Discovery* and a selection of the Spanish documents in the Foreign Office translation.

Ralegh's Last Voyage. Edited by V. T. Harlow, London, 1932. An excellent selection of English and Spanish documents, including the translation from Fray Simón.

The Discovery of Guiana. Edited by Sir R. H. Schomburgk, Hakluyt Society, London, 1848. With Ralegh's 1617 journal in an appendix.

THE ORIGINAL FOR ROBINSON CRUSOE. *Page 26.*

There is another version of the St Helena story. 'After our arrival at Santa Helena, I, Edmund Barker, went on shore with foure or five Peguins (or men of Pegu) which we had taken, and our surgion; where in an house by the chapell I found an Englishman, one John Segar of Burie in Suffolke, who was left there eighteene moneths before by Abraham Kendall, who put in there with the Roiall Merchant, and left him there to refresh him on the island, being otherwise like to have perished on shipboard; and at our coming we found him as fresh in colour and in as good plight of body to our seeming as might be, but crazed in minde and halfe out of his wits, as afterward wee perceived; for whether he were put in fright of us, not knowing at first what we were, whether friends or foes, or of sudden joy when he understood we were his olde consorts and countrymen, he became idle-headed and for eight days space neither night nor day tooke any naturall rest, and so at length died for lacke of sleepe.' From *The Voyages of Sir James Lancaster* 1591–1603. Edited by Sir William Foster. Hakluyt Society. London, 1940. Edmund Barker was Lancaster's lieutenant on that voyage that began 'with three tall ships'.

RALEGH'S DEFEAT AT CUMANÁ. *Page 51.*

Francisco de Vides's account both of Ralegh's defeat at Cumaná in 1595 by Indian archers, and of Ralegh's subsequent behaviour, has, I feel, to be accepted. The details are concrete, not vainglorious, and correctly cruel; and they appear to be confirmed not only by the accuracy – according to Schomburgk, himself a Guiana explorer – of Ralegh's description of the effects of poisoned arrows, but also by its implication: 'no one can endure to cure, or to attend them'.

TWO: THE SPANISH CAPITULATION

Histoire de l'Île de la Trinidad sous le gouvernement espagnol. By M. P. Borde, Paris, 1876. For the 18th-century cabildo records; documents about the French immigration, the Spanish surrender; French memories of Spanish persecution (the traitor Chacon) and English-Irish bad faith (the parcel of Barry and Black Negroes).

History of Trinidad. By E. L. Joseph, Trinidad, 1839. A late English immigrant's view of English colonial manners; local memories of the *Alarm* affair and the surrender.

History of Trinidad. By L. M. Fraser, Trinidad, 1891.

History of the Peoples of Trinidad and Tobago. By Eric Williams, London, 1964. For the Arenal miracle.

The Black Jacobins. By C. L. R. James, New York, 1963. For French racial legislation in Santo Domingo; the 128 shades; the course of the Negro Revolution.

Voyage aux Îles de Trinidad, de Tabago, de la Marguerite, et en Vénézuela. By M. Dauxion-Lavaysse, Paris, 1812. The 'French traveller'. He and McCallum supply all the local anti-Picton gossip.

THREE: THE TORTURE OF LUISA CALDERON

THE TRINIDAD PAPERS IN THE PUBLIC RECORD OFFICE, LONDON.

The main research area. The papers include the few issues of the *Courant* that survive and a copy, as fresh as on the day it left Gallagher's printery, of Picton's 1800 slave code.

Documentos Relativos a la Revolución de Gual y España. Edited by H. García Chuecos, Caracas, 1949. The Venezuelan intelligence reports.

The Life of Miranda. By W. S. Robertson, Chapel Hill, 1929. Less a biography than a ledger; but not complete. I have used some of its translations.

Archivo del General Miranda. Caracas and Havana, 1929–1950.

Antapodosis (1851). By Andrés Level de Goda. *Boletín de la Academia Nacional de la Historia.* Caracas, 1933.

Bolívar. By Salvador de Madariaga, London, 1952.

Six Months in the West Indies. By Henry Nelson Coleridge, London, 1825. For the beauty of Spanish and French mulatto women in Port of Spain.

Memoir of Lieutenant-General Sir Thomas Picton. By H. B. Robinson, London, 1835.

An Address to the British Public on the Case of Brigadier-General Picton. By Lieutenant-Colonel Edward Alured Draper, London, 1806. The pro-Picton book that set off the libel actions.

Travels in Trinidad during the months of February, March and April, 1803. By Pierre F. McCallum, Liverpool, 1805.

A Statement, Letters and Documents, Respecting the Affairs of Trinidad. By Colonel Fullarton, London, 1804.

Howell's State Trials, Vol. 30, London, 1822. The complete Picton case; it includes Castro's copy of the Negro Francisco's trial for murder in 1791–2 under Spanish law.

The Loss of El Dorado began with my discovery some years ago of the Picton trial in the Panther paperback of the *Newgate Calendar*. 'Bullo', the French jailer and torturer, sounded interesting, a character from Dumas; so did 'Don Pedro Bargass'. But no book about the region could tell me more about them or about the case. Fraser was not comprehensible: Fullarton is a spiteful madman who suddenly turns up in a peaceful colony and begins to persecute Picton for an old, unimportant punishment of a delinquent mulatto girl. It is how history is rewritten: people don't lie, they elide. And this was a complicated story. Add imperial statistics, the facts and figures of economic growth or deterioration; add the revolutionary and imperial failure, the anachronistic assumptions about the agricultural colony; add the geographical sense, the sense of the national frontier: the past begins to be fragmented and to disappear, for English and French, and even for Venezuelans. Robertson's *Life of Miranda* says little about the Trinidad intrigue and almost nothing about Miranda's year in Port of Spain. Picton, Fullarton and other puzzling people are virtually edited out of those volumes of Miranda's papers that were published, with 'apparatus', in Caracas. In Dr García Chuecos's selection of the Venezuelan intelligence reports, however, Picton is for some time the central figure of British intrigue; that Port of Spain waterfront world of agents and double agents comes to life. So it did again – with much else besides – in those volumes of Miranda's papers that were published in Havana, without too much editorial arrangement or typographical care, for the bicentenary of Miranda's birth in 1950. The pieces began to fit together; people could be reassembled from their fragmented roles. 'Bargass' became Pedro Vargas; 'Bullo' rounded, beyond all expectation, into Vallot. The past was accessible; but it had to be put together again.

THE JOKES OF THE SLAVE SOCIETY. *Page 178.*

The two jokes I have given (one from McCallum, one from Fraser) have this in common: they are dialect jokes, they have a passive victim, they pretend to be compassionate. It is, curiously, with a variant of such a joke that Trinidad enters Spanish history; and the joke was made – twice – by Las Casas, Apostle of the Indies. In 1510 a Basque slave trader named Juan Bono went to Trinidad. The Indians welcomed him; he took away a few and sold them. He went back. The Indians didn't want him to stay this time. They ran down to the beach crying, 'Juan Bono, *malo!* Juan Bono, *malo!*' Juan Bono said he had mended his ways; he wasn't *malo* any more; he had come to live with the Indians of Trinidad. They let him stay. He made them build a big straw house; he made them all go inside; then he set the house on fire. As the Indians ran out they were seized and hustled down to the shore. It isn't a convincing story, but Las Casas said he met and spoke to Bono afterwards. Bono said he hadn't met kinder or more welcoming people in all the world. 'But why then, you wretched man,' Las Casas said, 'did you treat them so badly?' – 'I give you my word, Father, those were my destructions, you see . . .' The Apostle of the Indies makes the private Spanish joke, the cruel Indian joke. It is unavoidable: to be a victim is also to be absurd. In Trinidad it was apparently (Joseph, 1839) told as a joke against the near-illiterate Vallot that he tried too clumsily to bar the *cachots brûlants* corridor during Fullarton's visit. I have the impression that humour was important to the slave society. The absurdity of the slave, in the eyes of the free, must have helped to make the society tolerable. The more sophisticated humour of the Trinidad slave society can be found in the poems – steadily deteriorating in quality – that were contributed to local newspapers. The jokes became more racist after the abolition of the slave trade.

SOME PERSONAL FOOTNOTES.

The Welsh immigrant – he went out with Fullarton, lost his wife and money, was given no land and was threatened with thirty-nine lashes and Negro's punishment – got back to England somehow. Every few months – supported by both Picton and Fullarton – he wrote a phonetic, complaining letter to a British minister; once he wrote to 'Lord Cassel Ray'. There is no record of his getting any compensation. His name was David Davies.

The man who wrote up the journal of Miranda's Trinidad country tour was John Downie. In London he appeared to have brought Picton and Miranda together; he got some money from Picton. Miranda begged Downie to stop calling himself a colonel and to join the army. Downie did. He went to Spain; he was one of the last to embark at Corunna. Days after the event, he wrote to Miranda about the death of Sir John Moore.

Begorrat, though sacked from the government in 1813, remained prominent as a planter, complaining, right into the 1830s, of financial ruin and always ready to get up a petition.

Burnley, Smith's depositario, became very grand. He presided over a labour inquiry in 1841, after abolition. He was anxious to prove then that free labour was cheaper than slave labour. One point that came out at the inquiry was that dirt-eating among Negroes stopped after abolition.

THE WHIPPING OF NEGRO WOMEN. *Page 351.*

The correct English objection would have been that the law forbidding the whipping of Negro women was unfair to the women. It was what Mrs Carmichael said (*Domestic Manners and Social Condition of the White, Coloured and Negro Population of the West Indies*, London 1833); but she wrote after she and her husband had sold up their estates and Negroes and returned to England. 'The parents of those who took an interest in their children, complained very much of the order in council, which prevented their girls being punished by order of the master. Strange as it may seem, they did not like to trust themselves to punish their child; and that, too, from the fear that they might punish too severely . . . In the greater number of cases young female negroes are now exposed to ten times greater severity of corporal punishment than they were when the master was the judge.'

Mrs Carmichael's husband (referred to in her book as 'Mr C.') came to Trinidad as a lieutenant in one of the invading British regiments. Mrs Carmichael divided her Negroes into 'good Negroes' and 'bad niggers'. Good Negroes knew when they had done wrong and took their whippings like men. They had little patience with lesser punishments; they said that to be chained up in stocks was a form of rest to a Negro; they always abused and denounced the 'bad niggers' who made trouble for Mr C. Most of Mrs Carmichael's Negroes were good; they complained more than Mr C. of the harassments of the reforming laws that came from London. But the harassments continued; the Negroes were corrupted. In the end Mrs Carmichael and Mr C., feeling that there could be no more good Negroes, only bad and ungrateful ones, decided to have nothing more to do with them, sold them all (just before abolition diminished their value), and returned to England.

The Frenchman who bought a Negro was likely to be more matter-of-fact than Mrs Carmichael. A fair example is M. de Montlezun, a romantic, philosophically inclined traveller (*Souvenirs des Antilles*, Paris 1818) who came to Trinidad in 1815 and didn't like it. 'Slavery here exists now only in name. You buy a Negro; you are a Frenchman; he tells you he doesn't wish to serve a Frenchman; he is just as insolent with everybody else. He carries on to such an extent that you are compelled to sell him. Perhaps you whip him. He is off, to lay his charge; he shows a spot of blood on his arm or somewhere else; and you have to hand him over for 30 *moades*, a fixed price, which often isn't half of what you paid for him.'

In the matter of child-beating, however (quite separate from the overseer's whipping of women in the field, as Mrs Carmichael well knew), it is almost certain that Mrs Carmichael was reporting what she saw. The severe, judicial whipping of children continues to be one of the solemn dramas of Trinidad backyard life. A badly beaten child is said to be 'blessed'. This is from the French *blesser*, to wound; but the word is spoken as an English word and has the associations of church, sacrament, awe. A blessing is an occasion for stillness. The blesser is handled with care by his womenfolk; while the mood of stillness lasts he is a man apart, fragile, touched by an unnatural and even divine frenzy. For the blessed child there is special affection and a special food of love: butter in hot sugared milk. The mood of stillness becomes a mood of sweetness: it is known that after a blessing everyone is closer. The drama that has been enacted – the drama that Mrs Carmichael may have superintended both in its master-slave reality and its man-child mimicry – is, of course, the drama of the plantation whip, transmuted into a dream of community. In the Negro kingdoms of the night the role of the Grand Judge, who punished at night as the overseer punished by day, was important.

ENVOI: THE JAIL IN 1825.

'The jail is the best in the Antilles, and really is respectable. An honest tread-wheel has been wisely provided, and this grand invention has been found to produce the same salutary effects in Trinidad, which it has done wherever it has revolved its portly body.' Coleridge: *Six Months in the West Indies*. This was the third Port of Spain jail. (Vallot's was pulled down in 1803–4; its successor was destroyed in the great Port of Spain fire of 1808.) With its high, blank, ochre-washed walls, it still stands, filling a block in what is now an elegant part of central Port of Spain. Over the recessed gate there is the year of its completion, 1812; and, in large but elegant Georgian characters, cast in metal, PRO REGE ET LEGE: For King and Law.

[illegible]

[illegible]

Index

ALSO BY V. S. NAIPAUL

AMONG THE BELIEVERS

An Islamic Journey

In this account of his seven-month journey across the Asian continent, V. S. Naipaul explores the life, the culture, and the current state of four Islamic nations: Iran, where the hysteria and rage of revolution continues; Pakistan, tragically underdeveloped thirty-two years after its founding; Malaysia, governed by Muslims but economically dominated by the Chinese who constitute half of its population; Indonesia, confused about both its Muslim and its national roots. Naipaul depicts an Islamic world at odds with the modern world, fueled only by an implacable determination to believe.

Current Events/Middle Eastern Studies/0-394-71195-5

BEYOND BELIEF

Islamic Excursions Among the Converted Peoples

Fourteen years after the publication of his landmark travel narrative *Among the Believers*, Naipaul returned to the four non-Arab Islamic countries he had reported on so vividly. *Beyond Belief* is the result of his five-month journey through these lands, where descendants of Muslim converts live at odds with indigenous traditions, and dreams of Islamic purity clash with economic and political realities. In conversations with a vast number of people, Naipaul deliberately effaces himself to let the voices of his subjects come through. Yet the result is a collection of stories that has the author's unmistakable stamp.

Current Events/Middle Eastern Studies/0-375-70648-8

THE MIDDLE PASSAGE

A Carribean Journey

In 1960, the government of Trinidad invited Naipaul to revisit his native country and record his impressions. The result was this remarkably prescient portrait of Trinidad and four adjacent countries—Surinam, Martinique, Guyana, and Jamaica—five societies haunted by the legacies of slavery and colonialism. Weaving scenes from his journey with ghastly episodes from the region's colonial past, Naipaul shows how they continue to inform its language, politics, and values. The result is a work of novelistic vividness and dazzling perspicacity that displays Naipaul at the peak of his powers.

Travel/History/0-375-70834-0

BETWEEN FATHER AND SON

Family Letters

At seventeen, V. S. Naipaul wanted to "follow no other profession" but writing. Awarded a scholarship by the Trinidadian government, he set out to attend Oxford. Separated from his family and grappling with depression, financial strain, and loneliness, "Vido" bridged the distance by corresponding with his father. Here, for the first time, we have the opportunity to read these profoundly moving letters, which illuminate with unalloyed candor the relationship between a sacrificing father and his determined son. For though his father's literary aspirations would go unrealized, Naipaul's triumphant career ultimately vindicate his beloved mentor's legacy.

Autobiography/0-375-70726-3

AN AREA OF DARKNESS

A Discovery of India

A classic of modern travel writing, *An Area of Darkness* is Naipaul's profound reckoning with his ancestral homeland and an extraordinary chronicle of his first encounter with India. Traveling from the clamor of Bombay to the ethereal beauty of Kashmir to a sacred ice cave in the Himalayas, he encounters a dizzying cross section of humanity. The book abounds with his strikingly original responses to India's paralyzing caste system, its apparently serene acceptance of poverty, and the conflict between its desire for self-determination and its nostalgia for the British raj. The result may be the most elegant and passionate book ever written about the subcontinent.

Travel/Literature/0-375-70835-9

INDIA

A Wounded Civilization

In 1975, at the height of Indira Gandhi's Emergency, Naipaul returned to India, the country his ancestors had left one hundred years before. Out of that journey he produced this concise masterpiece of journalism and cultural analysis, a vibrant, defiantly unsentimental portrait of a society traumatized by repeated foreign invasions and immured in a mythic vision of its past. Drawing on novels, news reports, and political memoirs—but most of all on his conversations with ordinary Indians, from princes to engineers and feudal village autocrats—Naipaul captures India's manifold complexities.

Travel/History/1-4000-3075-7